Sources of
Western Society

**VOLUME 2: FROM THE AGE OF
EXPLORATION TO THE PRESENT**

Sources of
Western Society

VOLUME 2: FROM THE AGE OF EXPLORATION TO THE PRESENT

John Beeler
UNIVERSITY OF ALABAMA

Charles Clark
UNIVERSITY OF ALABAMA

SECOND EDITION

BEDFORD/ST. MARTIN'S   BOSTON ◆ NEW YORK

For Bedford/St. Martin's

Publisher for History: Mary V. Dougherty
Executive Editor: Traci Mueller Crowell
Director of Development for History: Jane Knetzger
Senior Editor: Heidi L. Hood
Developmental Editor: Shannon Hunt
Editorial Assistant: Jennifer Jovin
Production Supervisor: Andrew Ensor
Executive Marketing Manager: Jenna Bookin Barry
Text Design and Project Management: DeMasi Design and Publishing Services
Cover Design: Billy Boardman
Cover Art: Le Chandail Rouge (detail), 1911, by Felix Vallotton © Musée d'Art et d'Histoire, Geneva/akg-images
Composition: Jeff Miller Book Design
Printing and Binding: RR Donnelley & Sons

President: Joan E. Feinberg
Editorial Director: Denise B. Wydra
Director of Marketing: Karen R. Soeltz
Director of Production: Susan W. Brown
Assistant Director, Editorial Production: Elise S. Kaiser
Manager, Publishing Services: Emily Berleth

Manufactured in the United States of America.

5 4 3
f e d

For information, write: Bedford/St. Martin's, 75 Arlington Street, Boston, MA 02116 (617-399-4000)

ISBN-10: 0-312-64080-3
ISBN-13: 978-0-312-64080-4

Acknowledgments

S ources of Western Society is a compilation of primary sources created by those who shaped and experienced the development of the Western world — among them rulers and subjects alike, men and women, philosophers, revolutionaries, economists, and laborers, from ancient times to the present. With a parallel chapter structure and documents handpicked to complement the text, this reader is designed to accompany both *A History of Western Society*, tenth edition, and *Western Society: A Brief History*, second edition. *Sources of Western Society* aspires to animate the past for students, providing resonant accounts of everyday life and the people and events that changed the face of Western history.

While a good textbook offers a clear framework of major historical figures and movements, *Sources* evokes the experiences of historical times at the moments they were lived and creates a dynamic connection for students, bridging the events of the past with their own understandings of power and its abuses, of the ripple effects of human agency, and of the material conditions of life. For example, John Locke's *Second Treatise of Civil Government* is cited in the textbook for its crucial role in the development of citizens' rights. In *Sources*, Locke himself makes a convincing case for the need for individual empowerment, as well as the study of history: "For he that thinks absolute power purifies men's blood, and corrects the baseness of human nature, need read but the history of this, or any other age, to be convinced of the contrary."

With input from the textbook authors, as well as from current instructors of the Western civilization survey course, we have compiled these documents with one goal foremost in mind: to make history's most compelling voices accessible to students, from the most well-known thinkers of their times to the galvanized or introspective commoner. In Chapter 21, for example, Thomas Malthus presents his economic theories on population and sustainability, while a threatening letter from worker Ned Ludd and his followers in Yorkshire protests the replacement of human textile workers by machines. Reformer Robert Owen expresses his views on the value of education for working-class youth, and a magazine illustration depicts the plight of children in a French cotton factory. John Aikin and Friedrich Engels provide very different opinions of the Industrial Revolution's impact on Manchester, England.

We have stepped back from drawing conclusions and instead provide just enough background to facilitate students' own analyses of the sources at hand. Chapter-opening paragraphs briefly review the major events of the time and place the documents that follow within the framework of the corresponding textbook chapter. A concise headnote for each document provides context about the author and the circumstances surrounding the document's creation, while gloss notes supply information to aid comprehension of unfamiliar terms and references. Each document is followed by Reading and Discussion Questions that spur deep student analysis of the material, while chapter-concluding Comparative Questions encourage students to contemplate the harmony and discord among the sources within and among the chapters. The excerpts range widely in length to allow for a range of class assignments.

NEW TO THIS EDITION

The second edition of *Sources* offers new pedagogical tools and provides instructors with greater flexibility in the development of their syllabus. Now expanded to an average of six sources per chapter with over one-third new sources overall, this edition offers a greater variety of topics to explore. Each chapter now features two or three "Viewpoints" selections that allow students to compare and contrast differing accounts of one topic or event, while new visual documents — nineteen in all — challenge students to analyze the historical meaning of art and photographs. In addition, new pronunciation guides make the language of historical documents more accessible. This edition aims for a balance of voices from all social classes and from the perspective of non-Europeans and Europeans alike, such as letters from King Affonso of Congo about the effects of the Portuguese slave trade on his kingdom and Heinrich Hauser's description of being unemployed in Germany during the Great Depression. *Sources of Western Society* now includes excerpts from popular classic sources such as Anna Comnena's *Alexiad*, Voltaire's *A Treatise on Toleration*, the People's Charter of 1838, and Wilfred Owen's *Poems*. Fresh sources include not only speeches and essays but letters, interviews, pamphlets, and poetry.

ACKNOWLEDGMENTS

Thanks to the reviewers whose thoughtful comments helped shape the second edition: Gemma Albanese, Dawson College; Melinda N. Brown,

Hinds Community College, Rankin Campus; David Byrne, Santa Monica College; Shane Caldwell, Zionsville Community High School; Joanna Carraway, Rockhurst University; Marie Therese Champagne, University of West Florida; Andrew Donson, University of Massachusetts Amherst; Robert C. Feinberg, Community College of Rhode Island; Melissa Korycinski, SUNY Onondaga Community College; Lara Kriegel, Florida International University; Andrew E. Larsen, Marquette University and University of Wisconsin-Milwaukee; Carole Levin, University of Nebraska-Lincoln; Nancy McLoughlin, University of California, Irvine; Laura M. Nelson, West Virginia University; Sherri Raney, Oklahoma Baptist University; and Jason L. Ward, Lee University. For their availability and insight, many thanks to the *History of Western Society* authors John P. McKay, John Buckler, Clare Crowston, Merry Wiesner-Hanks, and Joe Perry. We have worked as closely and cooperatively with Shannon Hunt in preparing this edition as we did with Lynn Sternberger for the first. To both we owe a large debt of gratitude for their editorial skills and efficiency, their valuable input and feedback, and, certainly not least of all, their unfailing patience and good humor. Thanks also to Heidi Hood and Jennifer Jovin, who played smaller but nonetheless important roles in the preparation of this edition. Emily Berleth of Bedford/St. Martin's and Linda DeMasi of DeMasi Design and Publishing Services made production of this reader possible with remarkable finesse.

CONTENTS

17 Toward a New Worldview 1540–1789   273

18 The Expansion of Europe 1650–1800   295

ACKNOWLEDGMENTS

CHAPTER 15
15-4 King Nzinga Mbemba Affonso of Congo, "Letters on the Slave Trade." From *The African Past* by Basil Davidson (Longmans, 1964), pp. 191–193. Reissued by Africa World Press 1990 as *African Civilization Revisited: From Antiquity to Modern Times* by Basil Davidson.

CHAPTER 20
20-4 Napoleon Bonaparte, *The Napoleonic Code*. From *A Documentary Survey of Napoleonic France*, edited and translated by E. A. Arnold (University Press of America, 1993), pp. 151–164. Reprinted by permission of the publisher.

20-6 François Dominique Toussaint L'Ouverture, "A Black Revolutionary Leader in Haiti." From C. L. R. James, *The Black Jacobins*, 2d ed., edited by C. L. R. James (New York: Vintage Books, 1963), pp. 195–197. Reproduced with permission of Curtis Brown Group Ltd. London on behalf of the Estate of C. L. R. James. Copyright © C. L. R. James 1963.

CHAPTER 25
25-2 Jules Ferry, "Speech Before the French Chamber of Deputies, March 28, 1884." From *Discours et Opinions de Jules Ferry*, edited by Paul Robiquet (Paris: Armand Colin & Cie., 1897), vol. 5, pp. 199–201, 210–211, 215–218. Translation by Ruth Kleinman is reprinted from *The Shaping of the Modern World: Core Curriculum 2.2 Readings*, 4th ed. (Boston: Pearson Custom Publishing, 2007), pp. 260–263, by permission of the Brooklyn College Department of History.

CHAPTER 26
26-1 Chancellor Theobald von Bethmann-Hollweg, "Telegram to the German Ambassador at Vienna." From *Documents of German History* by Louis L. Snyder, pp. 310–311. Copyright © 1958 by Rutgers, the State University. Reprinted by permission of Rutgers University Press.

26-3 Vera Brittain, *Testament of Youth*. Extracts from Vera Brittain's *Testament of Youth: An Autobiographical Study of the Years 1900–1925* (NY: Macmillan, 1933), pp. 164–166, 378–379, are reproduced by permission of Mark Bostridge and Timothy Brittain-Catlin, literary executors for the Estate of Vera Brittain, 1970.

CHAPTER 27
27-1 Friedrich Nietzsche, *The Gay Science*: "God Is Dead, the Victim of Science." From "The Madman" in *The Portable Nietzsche* by Friedrich Nietzsche, edited and translated by Walter Kaufmann, pp. 454–455. Copyright 1954 by The Viking Press, renewed © 1982 by Viking Penguin Inc. Used by permission of Viking Penguin, a division of Penguin Group (USA) Inc.

27-2 Sigmund Freud, *The Interpretation of Dreams*. From *The Interpretation of Dreams* by Sigmund Freud, pp. 613–621, translated by James Strachey, published by Basic Books c/o Perseus Books Group and the Hogarth Press c/o The Random House Group Ltd. Translation copyright © 1955 by James Strachey. Reprinted by permission of the publishers. Electronic rights administered in the USA by Basic Books.

CHAPTER 28
28-7 Traian Popovici, *Mein Bekenntnis*: "The Ghettoization of the Jews." "Mein Bekenntnis" (My Declaration)" in *Antisemitism in the Modern World*, edited and translated by Richard Levy (Lexington, Mass.: D.C. Heath, 1991), pp. 243–244, is reprinted by permission of Richard S. Levy.

CHAPTER 29
29-1 George C. Marshall, "An American Plan to Rebuild a Shattered Europe." "The Address of Secretary Marshall at Harvard," *The New York Times*, Friday, June 6, 1947, is reprinted courtesy of the George C. Marshall Research Library, Lexington, VA: http://www.marshallfoundation.org.

29-2 Alexander Solzhenitsyn, *One Day in the Life of Ivan Denisovich*: "The Stalinist Gulag." From *One Day in the Life of Ivan Denisovich*, by Alexander Solzhenitsyn, pp. 17–25, translated by Ralph Parker, copyright © 1963 by E. P. Dutton and Victor Gollancz, Ltd. Copyright renewed © 1991 by Penguin USA and Victor Gollancz, Ltd. Used by permission of Dutton, a division of Penguin Group (USA) Inc. and Victor Gollancz, an imprint of The Orion Publishing Group, London.

29-4 Frantz Fanon, *The Wretched of the Earth*. From "Conclusion" in *The Wretched of the Earth* by Frantz Fanon, translated by Constance Farrington (Grove Press, 1963) pp. 311–316, copyright © 1963 by *Présence Africaine*. Used by permission of Grove/Atlantic, Inc.

29-5 Simone de Beauvoir, *The Second Sex*: "Existential Feminism." From *The Second Sex* by Simone de Beauvoir, translated by Constance Borde & Sheila Malovany-Chevallier, pp. 721–723, 735–736, 751. Translation copyright © 2009 by Constance Borde and Sheila Malovany-Chevallier. Introduction copyright © 2010 by Judith Thurman. Used by permission of Alfred A. Knopf, a division of Random House, Inc. and Jonathan Cape c/o The Random House Group Ltd. Electronic rights administered by Georges Borchardt, Inc. for Editions Gallimard. Originally published in French as *Le deuxieme sexe*. Copyright © 1949 by Editions Gallimard.

CHAPTER 30
30-1 Solidarity Union, "Twenty-One Demands: A Call for Workers' Rights and Freedoms in a Socialist State." From *The Passion of Poland* by Lawrence Weschler, pp. 206–208, copyright ©1982, 1984 by Lawrence Weschler. Used by permission of Pantheon Books, a division of Random House, Inc.

30-2 Mikhail Gorbachev, *Perestroika: New Thinking for Our Country and the World*. From *Perestroika: New Thinking for Our Country and the World* by Mikhail Gorbachev, p. 3, 4, 5, 7, 8, 10, 22, 23, 24. Copyright © 1987 by Mikhail Gorbachev. Reprinted by permission of HarperCollins Publishers. Electronic rights administered by The Gorbachev Foundation.

30-4 Alex Harvey, "Give My Compliments To The Chef." Written by Alex Harvey, Hugh McKenna and Alistair Cleminson. Copyright © 1975 (Renewed 2003) BUG MUSIC-TRIO MUSIC COMPANY (BMI) and ALLEY MUSIC CORP. (BMI). All Rights Reserved. Used by permission. Reprinted by permission of Alley Music Corporation and Hal Leonard Corporation.

30-5 Vaclav Havel, "New Year's Address to the Nation, January 1, 1990." From http://old.hrad.cz/president/Havel/speeches/index_uk.html. Reprinted by permission of DILIA Theatrical, Literary, Audiovisual Agency.

CHAPTER 31
31-1 Kofi Annan, "The Fall of Srebrenica: An Assessment." From the Report of the Secretary-General Pursuant to General Assembly Resolution 53/35: The Fall of Srebrenica, 15 November 1999, paragraphs 467–506, pp. 105, 108–111. Copyright © 1999 United Nations. Reprinted by permission.

31-2 Amartya Sen, "A World Not Neatly Divided." Reprinted from *The New York Times*, November 23, 2001, Copyright © 2001 The New York Times. All rights reserved. Used by permission and protected by the Copyright Laws of the United States. The printing, copying, redistribution, or retransmission of the Material without express written permission is prohibited.

31-3 Tariq Ramadan, *Western Muslims and the Future of Islam*. From "Introduction: In Practice" in *Western Muslims and the Future of Islam* by Tariq Ramadan, pp. 1–7, copyright © 2004 by Oxford University Press, Inc. By permission of Oxford University Press, Inc.

31-4 Francis Fukuyama, *The End of History and the Last Man*. From *The End of History and the Last Man* by Francis Fukuyama, pp. 211–212, 215–217. Copyright © 1992 by Francis Fukuyama. All rights reserved. Reprinted and edited with the permission of The Free Press, a Division of Simon & Schuster, Inc. and Hamish Hamilton c/o Penguin Books Ltd. Electronic rights administered by Simon & Schuster, Inc. and International Creative Management, Inc.

CHAPTER 15

European Exploration and Conquest

1450–1650

I n the mid-1400s, western Europe faced a rapidly expanding Muslim power in the east. The Ottoman Empire captured Constantinople in 1453 and over time came to rule, directly or indirectly, much of eastern Europe. In the west, the Portuguese began exploring the west coast of Africa, eventually rounding the tip of Africa and reaching India. After the voyages of Columbus, the Spaniards and the Portuguese began to explore and conquer the Americas. The establishment of colonial empires in the Americas led to a new era of worldwide trade in African slaves. Through trade, travel, and missionary work, Europeans came into increasing contact with peoples of whom they had previously had little or no knowledge. Sometimes this contact led Europeans to question their own society, particularly in light of the religious wars dividing Europe.

DOCUMENT 15-1

DUCAS

Historia Turcobyzantia: *The Fall of Constantinople to the Ottomans*

ca. 1465

On May 29, 1453, Constantinople, the city that had been "the second Rome" — the capital of the eastern half of the Roman Empire — and a center of Christian learning throughout the Middle Ages, fell to the Ottoman Turks. In the years that followed Constantinople's fall, the Ottomans continued to

From Ducas, *Historia Turcobyzantia, 1341–1462,* in Byzantium: Church, Society, *and Civilization Seen Through Contemporary Eyes,* ed. Deno John Geanokoplos (Chicago: University of Chicago Press, 1984), p. 389.

advance into central Europe, seizing control of the Balkan Peninsula and even besieging Vienna, once in the sixteenth century and again in the seventeenth century. The author of this account was a descendant of the Ducas dynasty of Byzantine emperors who had ruled in the eleventh century.

And the entire City [its inhabitants and wealth] was to be seen in the tents of the [Turkish] camp, the city deserted, lying lifeless, naked, soundless, without either form or beauty. O City, City, head of all cities! O City, City, center of the four corners of the world! O City, City, pride of the Romans, civilizer of the barbarians! O City, second paradise planted toward the west, possessing all kinds of vegetation, laden with spiritual fruits! Where is your beauty, O paradise, where the beneficent strength of the charms of your spirit, soul, and body? Where are the bodies of the Apostles of my Lord, which were implanted long ago in the always-green paradise, having in their midst the purple cloak, the lance, the sponge, the reed, which, when we kissed them, made us believe that we were seeing him who was raised on the Cross? Where are the relics of the saints, those of the martyrs? Where the remains of Constantine the Great and the other emperors? Roads, courtyards, crossroads, fields, and vineyard enclosures, all teem with the relics of saints, with the bodies of nobles, of the chaste, and of male and female ascetics.[1] Oh what a loss! "The dead bodies of thy servants, O Lord, have they given to be meat unto the fowls of the heaven, the flesh of thy saints unto the beasts of the earth round about New Sion and there was none to bury them." [Psalm 78:2–3]

O temple [Hagia Sophia[2]]! O earthly heaven! O heavenly altar! O sacred and divine places! O magnificence of the churches! O holy books and words of God! O ancient and modern laws! O tablets inscribed by the finger of God! O Scriptures spoken by his mouth! O divine discourses of angels who bore flesh! O doctrines of men filled with the Holy Spirit! O teachings of semi-divine heroes! O commonwealth! O citizens! O army, formerly beyond number, now removed from sight like a ship sunk into the sea! O houses and palaces of every type! O sacred walls! Today I invoke you all, and as if incarnate beings I mourn with you, having Jeremiah[3] as [choral] leader of this lamentable tragedy!

---

[1] **ascetics:** Those who deny themselves material possessions and comforts.

[2] **Hagia Sophia:** At one time the largest Christian church in the world, it was built on the orders of Emperor Justinian in the sixth century. After the fall of Constantinople, it was converted to a mosque.

[3] **Jeremiah:** "Brokenhearted prophet" of the Hebrew Bible, who predicted the collapse of Assyria and the destruction of Jerusalem.

READING AND DISCUSSION QUESTIONS

1. This account was written more than ten years after the fall of Constantinople. How does this affect its value as an eyewitness account?

2. What does the reference to Psalm 78 at the end of the first paragraph tell you about both the siege and the author of this account?

3. How does Ducas describe the destruction of Constantinople, both physical and spiritual?

4. What does Ducas's account reveal about the place of Constantinople in the Christian world?

DOCUMENT 15-2

HERNANDO CORTÉS

Two Letters to Charles V: On the Conquest of the Aztecs

1521

In a number of letters to his sovereign, the Holy Roman emperor Charles V, who was also king of Spain, Hernando Cortés (1485–1547) described his conquest of the Aztec Empire of Mexico. While Cortés was surprised, even impressed by the advanced culture he encountered, his conquests were not without considerable violence. In one incident, one of his men ordered the massacre of thousands of unarmed members of the Aztec nobility who had assembled peaceably. Under examination, Cortés claimed that this act was done to instill fear and prevent future treachery. Some contemporaries speculated that Cortés embellished his accounts in order to retain the favor of the king.

[SECOND LETTER]

This great city of Tenochtitlan is built on the salt lake. . . . It has four approaches by means of artificial causeways. . . . The city is as large as Seville or Cordoba. Its streets . . . are very broad and straight, some of these, and all the others, are one half land, and the other half water on

From *Letters of Cortés*, trans. Francis A. MacNutt (New York: 1908), 1:256–257, 2:244.

which they go about in canoes. . . . There are bridges, very large, strong, and well constructed, so that, over many, ten horsemen can ride abreast. . . . The city has many squares where markets are held. . . . There is one square, twice as large as that of Salamanca, all surrounded by arcades, where there are daily more than sixty thousand souls, buying and selling . . . in the service and manners of its people, their fashion of living was almost the same as in Spain, with just as much harmony and order; and considering that these people were barbarous, so cut off from the knowledge of God and other civilized peoples, it is admirable to see to what they attained in every respect.

[Fifth Letter]

It happened . . . that a Spaniard saw an Indian . . . eating a piece of flesh taken from the body of an Indian who had been killed. . . . I had the culprit burned, explaining that the cause was his having killed that Indian and eaten him which was prohibited by Your Majesty, and by me in Your Royal name. I further made the chief understand that all the people . . . must abstain from this custom. . . . I came . . . to protect their lives as well as their property, and to teach them that they were to adore but one God . . . that they must turn from their idols, and the rites they had practiced until then, for these were lies and deceptions which the devil . . . had invented. . . . I, likewise, had come to teach them that Your Majesty, by the will of Divine Providence, rules the universe, and that they also must submit themselves to the imperial yoke, and do all that we who are Your Majesty's ministers here might order them.

READING AND DISCUSSION QUESTIONS

1. Although Cortés describes the people of Tenochtitlán as "barbarous" and laments that they are "cut off from the knowledge of God and other civilized peoples," what positive qualities does he attribute to the city and its people?

2. Why do you think Cortés chooses to describe an act of cannibalism? What does his commentary on this incident reveal about his conception of his mission?

3. What different images of Mexico was Cortés trying to impress upon Charles?

VIEWPOINTS
The Slave Trade in Africa

DOCUMENT 15-3

ALVISE DA CA' DA MOSTO

Description of Capo Bianco and the Islands Nearest to It: Fifteenth-Century Slave Trade in West Africa

1455–1456

Alvise da Ca' da Mosto (ca. 1428–1483) was an Italian trader and explorer. After his father was banished from Venice, Ca' da Mosto took up service with Prince Henry of Portugal, who was promoting exploration of the West African coast. In 1455, he traveled to the Canary and Madeira Islands and sailed past Cape Verde to the Gambia River. During another voyage in 1456, Ca' da Mosto discovered islands off Cape Verde and sailed sixty miles up the Gambia River. In the excerpt that follows, Ca' da Mosto describes the African Muslims who serve as middlemen in the Atlantic slave trade.

You should also know that behind this Cauo Bianco[4] on the land, is a place called Hoden,[5] which is about six days inland by camel. This place is not walled, but is frequented by Arabs, and is a market where the caravans arrive from Tanbutu [Timbuktu], and from other places in the land of the Blacks, on their way to our nearer Barbary. The food of the peoples of this place is dates, and barley, of which there is sufficient, for they grow in some of these places, but not abundantly. They drink the milk of camels

---

From Alvise da Ca' da Mosto, "Description of Capo Bianco and the Islands Nearest to It," in *European Reconnaissance: Selected Documents*, ed. J. H. Parry (New York: Walker, 1968), pp. 59–61.

[4] **Cauo Bianco**: West African port.

[5] **Hoden**: Wadan, an important desert market about 350 miles east of Arguim. Later, in 1487, when the Portuguese sought to penetrate the interior, they attempted to establish a trading factory at Wadan that acted as a feeder to Arguim, tapping the northbound caravan traffic and diverting some of it to the west coast.

and other animals, for they have no wine. They also have cows and goats, but not many, for the land is dry. Their oxen and cows, compared with ours, are small.

They are Muhammadans, and very hostile to Christians. They never remain settled, but are always wandering over these deserts. These are the men who go to the land of the Blacks, and also to our nearer Barbary. They are very numerous, and have many camels on which they carry brass and silver from Barbary and other things to Tanbutu and to the land of the Blacks. Thence they carry away gold and pepper, which they bring hither. They are brown complexioned, and wear white cloaks edged with a red stripe: their women also dress thus, without shifts. On their heads the men wear turbans in the Moorish fashion, and they always go barefooted. In these sandy districts there are many lions, leopards, and ostriches, the eggs of which I have often eaten and found good.

You should know that the said Lord Infante of Portugal [the crown prince, Henry the Navigator] has leased this island of Argin to Christians [for ten years], so that no one can enter the bay to trade with the Arabs save those who hold the license. These have dwellings on the island and factories where they buy and sell with the said Arabs who come to the coast to trade for merchandise of various kinds, such as woollen cloths, cotton, silver, and "alchezeli," that is, cloaks, carpets, and similar articles and above all, corn, for they are always short of food. They give in exchange slaves whom the Arabs bring from the land of the Blacks, and gold tiber [gold dust]. The Lord Infante therefore caused a castle to be built on the island to protect this trade for ever. For this reason, Portuguese caravels are coming and going all the year to this island.

These Arabs also have many Berber horses, which they trade, and take to the land of the Blacks, exchanging them with the rulers for slaves. Ten or fifteen slaves are given for one of these horses, according to their quality. The Arabs likewise take articles of Moorish silk, made in Granata and in Tunis of Barbary, silver, and other goods, obtaining in exchange any number of these slaves, and some gold. These slaves are brought to the market and town of Hoden; there they are divided: some go to the mountains of Barcha, and thence to Sicily, [others to the said town of Tunis and to all the coasts of Barbary], and others again are taken to this place, Argin, and sold to the Portuguese leaseholders. As a result every year the Portuguese carry away from Argin a thousand slaves. Note that before this traffic was organized, the Portuguese caravels, sometimes four, sometimes more, were wont to come armed to the Golfo d'Argin, and descending on the land by night, would assail the fisher villages, and so ravage the land. Thus they took of these Arabs both men and women, and carried them to Portugal for sale: behaving in a like manner along all the rest of the coast, which stretches from Cauo Bianco to the Rio di Senega and even beyond.

READING AND DISCUSSION QUESTIONS

1. Why do you think Ca' da Mosto wrote this account?
2. Describe the principal patterns of commerce in northern Africa.
3. Describe the groups that were involved in the various facets of the slave trade.
4. In what ways did the Portuguese change slavery and the slave trade?

DOCUMENT 15-4

KING NZINGA MBEMBA AFFONSO OF CONGO
Letters on the Slave Trade
1526

In 1491, the Portuguese were allowed to send merchants and missionaries into the West African kingdom of Congo. The king of Congo converted to Christianity, and the trading relationship between Portugal and Congo created many lucrative opportunities for merchants from both countries. In 1526, however, King Affonso of Congo noted the negative impact that the slave trade was having on his kingdom. The following selection contains two letters from Affonso to the king of Portugal, written in July and October 1526.

[FIRST LETTER]

Sir, Your Highness should know how our Kingdom is being lost in so many ways that it is convenient to provide for the necessary remedy, since this is caused by the excessive freedom given by your agents and officials to the

---

From Basil Davidson, *The African Past: Chronicles from Antiquity to Modern Times* (Boston: Little, Brown and Company, 1964), pp. 191–193; reissued by Africa World Press in 1990 as *African Civilization Revisited: From Antiquity to Modern Times*.

men and merchants who are allowed to come to this Kingdom to set up shops with goods and many things which have been prohibited by us, and which they spread throughout our Kingdoms and Domains in such an abundance that many of our vassals, whom we had in obedience, do not comply because they have the things in greater abundance than we ourselves; and it was with these things that we had them content and subjected under our vassalage and jurisdiction, so it is doing a great harm not only to the service of God, but the security and peace of our Kingdoms and State as well.

And we cannot reckon how great the damage is, since the mentioned merchants are taking every day our natives, sons of the land and the sons of our noblemen and vassals and our relatives, because the thieves and men of bad conscience grab them wishing to have the things and wares of this Kingdom which they are ambitious of; they grab them and get them to be sold; and so great, Sir, is the corruption and licentiousness that our country is being completely depopulated, and Your Highness should not agree with this nor accept it as in your service. And to avoid it we need from those [your] Kingdoms no more than some priests and a few people to teach in schools, and no other goods except wine and flour for the holy sacrament. That is why we beg of Your Highness to help and assist us in this matter, commanding your factors that they should not send here either merchants or wares, because it is *our will that in these Kingdoms there should not be any trade of slaves nor outlet for them.* . . .

[SECOND LETTER]

Moreover, Sir, in our Kingdoms there is another great inconvenience which is of little service to God, and this is that many of our people, keenly desirous as they are of the wares and things of your Kingdoms, which are brought here by your people, and in order to satisfy their voracious appetite, seize many of our people, freed and exempt men, and very often it happens that they kidnap even noblemen and the sons of noblemen, and our relatives, and take them to be sold to the white men who are in our Kingdoms; and for this purpose they have concealed them; and others are brought during the night so that they might not be recognized.

And as soon as they are taken by the white men they are immediately ironed and branded with fire, and when they are carried to be embarked, if they are caught by our guards' men the whites allege that they have bought them but they cannot say from whom, so that it is our duty to do justice and to restore to the freemen their freedom, but it cannot be done if your subjects feel offended, as they claim to be.

MISSIONARIES IN JAPAN   241

And to avoid such a great evil we passed a law so that any white man living in our Kingdoms and wanting to purchase goods in any way should first inform three of our noblemen and officials of our court whom we rely upon in this matter, and these are Dom Pedro Manipanza and Dom Manuel Manissaba, our chief usher, and Gonçalo Pires our chief freighter, who should investigate if the mentioned goods are captives or free men, and if cleared by them there will be no further doubt nor embargo for them to be taken and embarked. But if the white men do not comply with it they will lose the aforementioned goods. And if we do them this favor and concession it is for the part Your Highness has in it, since we know that it is in your service too that these goods are taken from our Kingdom, otherwise we should not consent to this.

READING AND DISCUSSION QUESTIONS

1. How is the slave trade affecting Congo economically, politically, and socially?

2. Who profits from the slave trade?

3. What does King Affonso propose to do about the slave trade in the first letter? In the second letter? Why do you think he changes his plan?

SAINT FRANCIS XAVIER

Missionaries in Japan

1552

The Society of Jesus (see Document 14-6) was founded in part to stop the spread of Protestant ideas and teach Catholic ideas in Europe. One of its

From Henry James Coleridge, ed., *The Life and Letters of St. Francis Xavier*, 3d ed. (London: Burns & Oates, 1876), 2:331–348.

other purposes was to spread Christianity around the world. Francis Xavier (1506–1552) was one of the first members of the Society of Jesus, and also one of the first Jesuits to travel across Asia as a missionary. His letters recount the activities of the missionaries as well as his observations of the peoples they encountered.

But to return to what we did in Japan. In the first place, we landed, as I told you, at Cagoxima,[6] Paul's[7] native place, where by his constant instructions he converted all his family to Jesus Christ, and where, but for the opposition of the bonzes,[8] he would easily have converted the whole town also. The bonzes persuaded the King, whose authority extends over a good part of the country, that, if he were to sanction the introduction of the divine law into his dominions, the result would infallibly be the ruin, not only of his entire kingdom, but also of the worship of the gods and of the institutions of his ancestors; and that he ought for the future to forbid any one becoming a Christian, on pain of death.

After the lapse of a year, seeing this prince openly opposed to the progress of the Gospel, we bade farewell to our [converts] at Cagoxima, and to Paul, in whose care we left them, and went on thence to a town in the kingdom of Amanguchi.[9] . . . I myself went on to . . . the capital of the kingdom, an immense city containing more than ten thousand houses. Here we preached the Gospel to the people in the public streets, to the princes and nobles in their own residences. Many heard us eagerly, others with reluctance. We did not always escape unhurt, having many insults offered us by the boys and the crowds in the streets. The King of the country summoned us to his presence, and, having asked the reason of our coming, invited us of his own accord to explain the law of God to him; he listened to us with deep attention for a whole hour while we spoke to him of religion. . . .

The king was made favorable to us by the letters and presents sent by the Bishop and the Governors from India and Malacca, and we obtained from him without difficulty the publication of edicts declaring his approval of the promulgation of the divine law in the cities of his dominions, and permitting such of his subjects as pleased to embrace it. When he had

---

[6] **Cagoxima**: Region in southwestern Japan.
[7] **Paul's**: A Japanese convert to Christianity.
[8] **bonzes**: Buddhist monks.
[9] **Amanguchi**: Yamaguchi, in southwestern Japan.

done us this favor he also assigned a monastery to us for a residence. Here by means of daily sermons and disputes with the bonzes, the sorcerers, and other such men, we converted to the religion of Jesus Christ a great number of persons, several of whom were nobles. Amongst them we found some able to inform us, and we made it our business to gain acquaintance with the various sects and opinions of Japan, and so know how to refute them by arguments and proofs prepared for the purpose.

READING AND DISCUSSION QUESTIONS

1. What is the Jesuits' goal in Japan?
2. How do the Japanese respond to the missionaries' preaching of Christianity?
3. Why is the king important to the Jesuits?

DOCUMENT 15-6

MICHEL DE MONTAIGNE
Of Cannibals
1580

Michel de Montaigne (duh mahn-TAYN) (1533–1592), a French lawyer and government official, wrote about his personal experiences and travels in his Essays *of 1580. By reflecting on his personal experiences, Montaigne critiqued European assumptions of philosophy, religion, government, and society during an age of religious warfare at home and expanding contact with the world. The essay "Of Cannibals" was written during the French Wars of Religion (1562–1598), decades of intermittent warfare between the French Calvinists (known as Huguenots) and Catholic factions. Even though he was Catholic, Montaigne did not take sides during the wars. In the essay, Montaigne recounts what he has heard about the peoples of the Americas.*

From *Essays of Montaigne*, trans. Charles Cotton, ed. William Carew Hazlitt (London: Reeves and Turner, 1902), I:237–252.

When King Pyrrhus[10] invaded Italy, having viewed and considered the order of the army the Romans sent out to meet him; "I know not," said he, "what kind of barbarians" (for so the Greeks called all other nations) "these may be; but the disposition of this army that I see has nothing of barbarism in it." . . . By which it appears how cautious men ought to be of taking things upon trust from vulgar opinion, and that we are to judge by the eye of reason, and not from common report.

I long had a man in my house that lived ten or twelve years in the New World, discovered in these latter days, and in that part of it where Ville-gaignon landed, which he called Antarctic France.[11] This discovery of so vast a country seems to be of very great consideration. I cannot be sure, that hereafter there may not be another, so many wiser men than we having been deceived in this. I am afraid our eyes are bigger than our bellies, and that we have more curiosity than capacity; for we grasp at all, but catch nothing but wind. . . .

This man that I had was a plain ignorant fellow, and therefore the more likely to tell truth: for your better-bred sort of men are much more curious in their observation; . . . they never represent things to you simply as they are, but rather as they appeared to them, or as they would have them appear to you. . . . I would have every one write what he knows, and as much as he knows, but no more; and that not in this only but in all other subjects. . . .

Now, to return to my subject, I find that there is nothing barbarous and savage in this nation, by anything that I can gather, excepting, that every one gives the title of barbarism to everything that is not in use in his own country. As, indeed, we have no other level of truth and reason than the example and idea of the opinions and customs of the place wherein we live: there is always the perfect religion, there the perfect government, there the most exact and accomplished usage of all things. . . .

These nations then seem to me to be so far barbarous, as having received but very little form and fashion from art and human invention, and consequently to be not much remote from their original simplicity. The laws of nature, however, govern them still, not as yet much [corrupted]

---

[10] **Pyrrhus**: Greek king of Sicily (319–272 B.C.E.) who attempted to prevent Roman armies from advancing into southern Italy.

[11] **and in that part . . . Antarctic France**: Nicolas Durand de Villegaignon (1510–1571) was an officer in the French navy who in 1555 captured the region surrounding what is now Rio de Janeiro, Brazil, from the Portuguese. In addition to creating new trading opportunities, his goal was to build a refuge for the French Calvinists to escape religious persecution in France. Portugal retook the colony in 1567.

with any mixture of ours: but 'tis in such purity, that I am sometimes troubled we were not sooner acquainted with these people, and that they were not discovered in those better times, when there were men much more able to judge of them than we are. . . . To my apprehension, what we now see in those nations, does not only surpass all the pictures with which the poets have adorned the golden age, and all their inventions in feigning a happy state of man, but, moreover, the fancy and even the wish and desire of philosophy itself; so native and so pure a simplicity, as we by experience see to be in them, could never enter into their imagination, nor could they ever believe that human society could have been maintained with so little artifice and human patchwork. I should tell Plato[12] that it is a nation wherein there is no manner of traffic, no knowledge of letters, no science of numbers, no name of magistrate or political superiority; no use of service, riches or poverty, no contracts, no successions, no dividends, no properties, no employments, but those of leisure, no respect of kindred, but common, no clothing, no agriculture, no metal, no use of corn or wine; the very words that signify lying, treachery, dissimulation, avarice, envy, detraction, pardon, never heard of. How much would he find his imaginary Republic short of his perfection? . . .

As to the rest, they live in a country very pleasant and temperate, so that, as my witnesses inform me, 'tis rare to hear of a sick person, and they moreover assure me, that they never saw any of the natives, either paralytic, bleary-eyed, toothless, or crooked with age. The situation of their country is along the sea-shore. . . . They have great store of fish and flesh that have no resemblance to those of ours: which they eat without any other cookery, than plain boiling, roasting, and broiling. The first that rode a horse thither, though in several other voyages he had contracted an acquaintance and familiarity with them, put them into so terrible a fright, with his centaur[13] appearance, that they killed him with their arrows before they could come to discover who he was. Their buildings are very long, and of capacity to hold two or three hundred people. . . . They have wood so hard, that they cut with it, and make their swords of it, and their grills of it to broil their meat. Their beds are of cotton, hung swinging from the roof, like our seamen's hammocks, every man his own, for the wives lie apart from their husbands. They rise with the sun, and so soon as they are up, eat for all day, for they have no more meals but that; they do not then drink, . . . but drink very often all day after, and sometimes to a rousing

---

[12] **Plato:** Greek philosopher (427–347 B.C.E.) and author of *The Republic*, who wrote about an ideal city in which people were ruled by philosophers (see Document 3-5).
[13] **centaur:** Half-human, half-horse creature from Greek mythology.

pitch. . . . The whole day is spent in dancing. Their young men go a-hunting after wild beasts with bows and arrows; one part of their women are employed in preparing their drink the while, which is their chief employment. One of their old men, in the morning before they fall to eating, preaches to the whole family, walking from the one end of the house to the other, and several times repeating the same sentence, till he has finished the round, for their houses are at least a hundred yards long. Valor towards their enemies and love towards their wives, are the two heads of his discourse. . . . They believe in the immortality of the soul, and that those who have merited well of the gods are lodged in that part of heaven where the sun rises, and the accursed in the west. . . .

They have continual war with the nations that live further within the mainland, beyond their mountains, to which they go naked, and without other arms than their bows and wooden swords, fashioned at one end like the head of our javelins. The obstinacy of their battles is wonderful, and they never end without great effusion of blood: for as to running away, they know not what it is. Every one for a trophy brings home the head of an enemy he has killed, which he fixes over the door of his house. After having a long time treated their prisoners very well, and given them all the regales they can think of, he to whom the prisoner belongs, invites a great assembly of his friends. They being come, he ties a rope to one of the arms of the prisoner, of which, at a distance, out of his reach, he holds the one end himself, and gives to the friend he loves best the other arm to hold after the same manner; which being done, they two, in the presence of all the assembly, dispatch him with their swords. After that, they roast him, eat him amongst them, and send some chops to their absent friends. They do not do this, as some think, for nourishment, . . . but as a representation of an extreme revenge; as will appear by this: that having observed the Portuguese, who were in league with their enemies, to inflict another sort of death upon any of them they took prisoners, which was . . . to shoot at [them] till [they were] stuck full of arrows, and then to hang them, they thought those people of the other world . . . did not exercise this sort of revenge without a meaning, and that it must needs be more painful than theirs, they began to leave their old way, and to follow this. I am not sorry that we should here take notice of the barbarous horror of so cruel an action, but that, seeing so clearly into their faults, we should be so blind to our own. I conceive there is more barbarity in eating a man alive, than when he is dead; in tearing a body limb from limb by racks and torments, that is yet in perfect sense; in roasting it by degrees; in causing it to be bitten and worried by dogs and swine (as we have not only read, but lately seen, not amongst inveterate and mortal enemies, but among neighbors and fellow-citizens, and, which is worse, under color of piety and religion), than to roast and eat him after he is dead. . . .

We may then call these people barbarous, in respect to the rules of reason: but not in respect to ourselves, who in all sorts of barbarity exceed them. Their wars are throughout noble and generous, and carry as much excuse and fair pretence, as that human malady is capable of; having with them no other foundation than the sole jealousy of valor. Their disputes are not for the conquest of new lands, for these they already possess are so fruitful by nature, as to supply them without labor or concern, with all things necessary, in such abundance that they have no need to enlarge their borders. And they are, moreover, happy in this, that they only covet so much as their natural necessities require: all beyond that is superfluous to them. . . . If their neighbors pass over the mountains to assault them, and obtain a victory, all the victors gain by it is glory only, and the advantage of having proved themselves the better in valor and virtue: for they never meddle with the goods of the conquered, but presently return into their own country, where they have no want of anything necessary, nor of this greatest of all goods, to know happily how to enjoy their condition and to be content. And those in turn do the same; they demand of their prisoners no other ransom, than acknowledgment that they are overcome. . . . There is not a man amongst them who had not rather be killed and eaten, than so much as to open his mouth to entreat he may not. They use them with all liberality and freedom, to the end their lives may be so much the dearer to them; but frequently entertain them with menaces of their approaching death, of the torments they are to suffer, of the preparations making in order to it, of the mangling of their limbs, and of the feast that is to be made, where their carcass is to be the only dish. All which they do, to no other end, but only to extort some gentle or submissive word from them, or to frighten them so as to make them run away, to obtain this advantage that they were terrified, and that their constancy was shaken; and indeed, if rightly taken, it is in this point only that a true victory consists. . . .

But to return to my story: these prisoners are so far from discovering the least weakness, for all the terrors that can be represented to them, that, on the contrary, during the two or three months they are kept, they always appear with a cheerful countenance; importune their masters to make haste to bring them to the test, defy, rail at them, and reproach them with cowardice, and the number of battles they have lost against those of their country. I have a song made by one of these prisoners, wherein he bids them "come all, and dine upon him, and welcome, for they shall withal eat their own fathers and grandfathers, whose flesh has served to feed and nourish him. These muscles," says he, "this flesh and these veins, are your own: poor silly souls as you are, you little think that the substance of your ancestors' limbs is here yet; notice what you eat, and you will find in it the taste of your own flesh:" in which song there is to be observed an invention that nothing relishes of the barbarian. Those that paint these people dying after this manner, represent the prisoner spitting in the faces of his executioners and making wry mouths at them. And 'tis most certain, that to the very last gasp, they never cease to brave and defy them both in word and gesture. In plain truth, these men are very savage in comparison of us; of necessity, they must either be absolutely so or else we are savages; for there is a vast difference betwixt their manners and ours.

READING AND DISCUSSION QUESTIONS

1. Why does Montaigne write that the words of a "plain ignorant fellow" are more reliable than the words of someone who has been educated? Why does he think it important that reason should be the guide to understanding?

2. How does Montaigne use the word *barbarian* in this essay? To him, what makes someone a barbarian, and why?

3. On what points does Montaigne compare and contrast this society with Portuguese society? In what ways does he find the Portuguese inferior to cannibals? Why?

COMPARATIVE QUESTIONS

1. Compare and contrast the fall of Constantinople as portrayed by Ducas and Cortés's capture of Tenochtitlán, taking into consideration the different perspective of each account.

2. Compare and contrast the two documents on the African slave trade. What tactics do the Portuguese use to operate the slave trade?

3. Based on your reading of these documents, which distinctions among peoples seem most important for Europeans of the fifteenth and sixteenth centuries? Do the Jesuits and Montaigne show similar or different attitudes to non-Europeans?

CHAPTER 16

Absolutism and Constitutionalism in Europe

ca. 1589–1725

S ixteenth- and seventeenth-century Europe witnessed a prolonged struggle between monarchs seeking to consolidate and extend their power, and social groups and institutions opposing those efforts. Many factors — political, social, and economic — influenced the course of this struggle, and the outcome varied from country to country. France's kings managed to suppress some of the opposition to royal power and thus are termed "absolutist" monarchs, although even the greatest of them, Louis XIV, lacked the power and authority to exert his unchallenged will over all of his subjects, in particular the great nobles. Eastern European rulers in Prussia, Austria, and Russia also augmented their power and authority, although there were significant differences from state to state, and none matched Louis XIV's achievement. Still, all experienced greater success in expanding royal authority than did their counterparts in the Netherlands and England. Two English kings, Charles I and James II, lost their thrones as a consequence of political revolutions, and the former was also tried and executed for crimes against his subjects.

DOCUMENT 16-1

HENRY IV

Edict of Nantes: *Limited Toleration*
for the Huguenots

1598

Prince Henry of Navarre (1553–1610) was a Huguenot, or Protestant, in an overwhelmingly Roman Catholic country. He ascended to the French throne as Henry IV in 1589 in the midst of the French Wars of Religion. A pragmatist, Henry realized that the country's Catholic majority would never accept a Protestant as their legitimate ruler, so he converted to Catholicism. However, in order to protect the Huguenots against religiously motivated attacks, as well as to establish peace among the people he was determined to rule, he issued the Edict of Nantes. In so doing, Henry legally sanctioned a degree of religious tolerance in a Europe previously characterized by the formula "one king, one people, one faith."

Among the infinite benefits which it has pleased God to heap upon us, the most signal and precious is his granting us the strength and ability to withstand the fearful disorders and troubles which prevailed on our advent in this kingdom. The realm was so torn by innumerable factions and sects that the most legitimate of all the parties[1] was fewest in numbers. God has given us strength to stand out against this storm; we have finally surmounted the waves and made our port of safety, — peace for our state. For which his be the glory all in all, and ours a free recognition of his grace in making use of our instrumentality in the good work. . . . We implore and await from the Divine Goodness the same protection and favor which he has ever granted to this kingdom from the beginning. . . .

From King Henry of Navarre, "Edict of Nantes," in *Readings in European History*, ed. James Harvey Robinson, 2 vols. (Boston: Ginn, 1906), 2:183–185.

[1] **the most legitimate of all the parties**: Faction supporting Valois King Henry III (r. 1574–1589) during the French Wars of Religion (1561–1598). Henry's subsequent reference to "one party or the other" refers to the three factions, two of them Catholic, one of them Protestant, that struggled for control of the French throne.

We have, by this perpetual and irrevocable edict, established and proclaimed and do establish and proclaim:

I. First, that the recollection of everything done by one party or the other between March, 1585, and our accession to the crown, and during all the preceding period of troubles, remain obliterated and forgotten, as if no such things had ever happened. . . .

III. We ordain that the Catholic Apostolic and Roman religion shall be restored and reestablished in all places and localities of this our kingdom and countries subject to our sway, where the exercise of the same has been interrupted, in order that it may be peaceably and freely exercised, without any trouble or hindrance; forbidding very expressly all persons, of whatsoever estate, quality, or condition, from troubling, molesting, or disturbing ecclesiastics in the celebration of divine service, in the enjoyment or collection of tithes, fruits, or revenues of their benefices, and all other rights and dues belonging to them; and that all those who during the troubles have taken possession of churches, houses, goods, or revenues, belonging to the said ecclesiastics, shall surrender to them entire possession and peaceable enjoyment of such rights, liberties, and sureties as they had before they were deprived of them. . . .

VI. And in order to leave no occasion for troubles or differences between our subjects, we have permitted, and herewith permit, those of the said religion called Reformed [Protestant] to live and abide in all the cities and places of this our kingdom and countries of our sway, without being annoyed, molested, or compelled to do anything in the matter of religion contrary to their consciences, . . . upon conditions that they comport themselves in other respects according to that which is contained in this our present edict.

VII. It is permitted to all lords, gentlemen, and other persons making profession of the said religion called Reformed, holding the right of high justice [or a certain feudal tenure], to exercise the said religion in their houses. . . .

IX. We also permit those of the said religion to make and continue the exercise of the same in all villages and places of our dominion where it was established by them and publicly enjoyed several and divers times in the year 1597, up to the end of the month of August, notwithstanding all decrees and judgments to the contrary. . . .

XIII. We very expressly forbid to all those of the said religion its exercise, either in respect to ministry, regulation, discipline, or the public instruction of children, or otherwise, in this our kingdom and lands of our dominion, otherwise than in the places permitted and granted by the present edict.

XIV. It is forbidden as well to perform any function of the said religion on our court or retinue, or in our lands and territories beyond the mountains, or in our city of Paris, or within five leagues of the said city. . . .

XVIII. We also forbid all our subjects, of whatever quality and condition, from carrying off by force or persuasion, against the will of their parents, the children of the said religion, in order to cause them to be baptized or confirmed in the Catholic Apostolic and Roman Church; and the same is forbidden to those of the said religion called Reformed, upon penalty of being punished with special severity. . . .

XXI. Books concerning the said religion called Reformed may not be printed and publicly sold, except in cities and places where the public exercise of the said religion is permitted.

XXII. We ordain that there shall be no difference or distinction made in respect to the said religion, in receiving pupils to be instructed in universities, colleges, and schools; or in receiving the sick and poor into hospitals, retreats and public charities.

XXIII. Those of the said religion called Reformed shall be obliged to respect the laws of the Catholic Apostolic and Roman Church, recognized in this our kingdom, for the consummation of marriages contracted, or to be contracted, as regards to the degrees of consanguinity and kinship.

READING AND DISCUSSION QUESTIONS

1. Why was Henry so intent on "obliterating" memory of "everything done by one party or the other" in the years immediately prior to his coronation as king of France?

2. Is the Edict of Nantes consistent with Henry's aim of increasing the monarchy's and the state's power? Why or why not?

3. Why might Henry's son, Louis XIII, have regarded the Huguenots as "a state within a state"?

4. Based on the details of the edict regarding ceremonies, property, liter-
    ature, and education, what sorts of practices defined a religion before
    and during Henry's reign? What, if any practices did he consider irre-
    ligious, or purely civil?

DOCUMENT 16-2

JACQUES-BÉNIGNE BOSSUET
Politics Drawn from the Very Words of Holy Scripture
1679

*French cleric Jacques-Bénigne Bossuet's (1627–1704) sermons earned him
the favor of Louis XIV. He preached to the court regularly from 1660 to 1669
and was especially renowned for his funeral orations. In 1670 he was appointed tutor to Louis's eldest son, and thus had the weighty task of instructing the heir to the throne on the duties of a king. The work from which the
following excerpts are taken was composed in 1679 for the Dauphin's
guidance.*

All power is of God. The ruler, [states] St. Paul, "is the minister of God to
thee for good. But if thou do that which is evil, be afraid; for he beareth not
the sword in vain: for he is the minister of God, a revenger to execute
wrath upon him that doeth evil." Rulers then act as the ministers of God
and as his lieutenants on earth. It is through them that God exercises his
empire. . . . Consequently, as we have seen, the royal throne is not the
throne of a man, but the throne of God himself. The Lord "hath chosen
Solomon my son to sit upon the throne of the kingdom of the Lord over
Israel." And again, "Solomon sat on the throne of the Lord."

Moreover, that no one may assume that the Israelites were peculiar in
having kings over them who were established by God, note what is said in
Ecclesiasticus: "God has given to every people its ruler, and Israel is manifestly reserved to him." He therefore governs all peoples and gives them

From James Harvey Robinson, ed. *Readings in European History*, 2 vols. (Boston:
Ginn, 1906), 2:273–77

their kings, although he governed Israel in a more intimate and obvious manner.

It appears from all this that the person of the king is sacred, and that to attack him in any way is sacrilege. God has the kings anointed by his prophets with the holy unction in like manner as he has bishops and altars anointed. But even without the external application in thus being anointed, they are by their very office the representatives of the divine majesty deputed by Providence for the execution of his purposes. Accordingly God calls Cyrus his anointed. "Thus saith the Lord to his anointed, to Cyrus, whose right hand I have holden, to subdue nations before him." . . . Kings should be guarded as holy things, and whosoever neglects to protect them is worthy of death. . . .

There is something religious in the respect accorded to a prince. The service of God and the respect for kings are bound together. St. Peter unites these two duties when he says, "Fear God. Honor the king." . . .

But kings, although their power comes from on high, as has been said, should not regard themselves as masters of that power to use it at their pleasure . . . they must employ it with fear and self-restraint, as a thing coming from God and of which God will demand an account. "Hear, O kings, and take heed, understand, judges of the earth, lend your ears, ye who hold the peoples under your sway, and delight to see the multitude that surround you. It is God who gives you the power. Your strength comes from the Most High, who will question your works and penetrate the depths of your thoughts, for, being ministers of his kingdom, ye have not given righteous judgments nor have ye walked according to his will. He will straightway appear to you in a terrible manner, for to those who command is the heaviest punishment reserved. The humble and the weak shall receive mercy, but the mighty shall be mightily tormented. For God fears not the power of any one, because he made both great and small and he has care for both." . . .

Kings should tremble then as they use the power God has granted them; and let them think how horrible is the sacrilege if they use for evil a power which comes from God. We behold kings seated upon the throne of the Lord, bearing in their hand the sword which God himself has given them. What profanation, what arrogance, for the unjust king to sit on God's throne to render decrees contrary to his laws and to use the sword which God has put in his hand for deeds of violence and to slay his children! . . .

The royal power is absolute. With the aim of making this truth hateful and insufferable, many writers have tried to confound absolute government with arbitrary government. But no two things could be more unlike, as we shall show when we come to speak of justice.

The prince need render account of his acts to no one. "I counsel thee to keep the king's commandment, and that in regard of the oath of God. Be not hasty to go out of his sight: stand not on an evil thing for he doeth whatsoever pleaseth him. Where the word of a king is, there is power: and who may say unto him, what doest thou? Whoso keepeth the command-ment shall feel no evil thing." Without this absolute authority the king could neither do good nor repress evil. It is necessary that his power be such that no one can hope to escape him, and, finally, the only protection of individuals against the public authority should be their innocence.

This conforms with the teaching of St. Paul: "Wilt thou then not be afraid of the power? Do that which is good."

I do not call majesty that pomp which surrounds kings or that exterior magnificence which dazzles the vulgar. That is but the reflection of maj-esty and not majesty itself. Majesty is the image of the grandeur of God in the prince.

God is infinite, God is all. The prince, as prince, is not regarded as a private person: he is a public personage, all the state is in him; the will of all the people is included in his. As all perfection and all strength are united in God, so all the power of individuals is united in the person of the prince. What grandeur that a single man should embody so much!

The power of God makes itself felt in a moment from one extremity of the earth to another. Royal power works at the same time throughout all the realm. It holds all the realm in position, as God holds the earth. Should God withdraw his hand, the earth would fall to pieces; should the king's authority cease in the realm, all would be in confusion.

Look at the prince in his cabinet. Thence go out the orders which cause the magistrates and the captains, the citizens and the soldiers, the provinces and the armies on land and on sea, to work in concert. He is the image of God, who, seated on his throne high in the heavens, makes all nature move. . . .

Finally, let us put together the things so great and so august which we have said about royal authority. Behold an immense people united in a single person; behold this holy power, paternal and absolute; behold the secret cause which governs the whole body of the state, contained in a single head: you see the image of God in the king, and you have the idea of royal majesty. God is holiness itself, goodness itself, and power itself. In these things lies the majesty of God. In the image of these things lies the majesty of the prince.

So great is this majesty that it cannot reside in the prince as in its source; it is borrowed from God, who gives it to him for the good of the people, for whom it is good to be checked by a superior force. Something of divinity itself is attached to princes and inspires fear in the people. The king should not forget this. "I have said," — it is God who speaks, — "I have said, Ye are gods; and all of you are children of the Most High. But ye shall die like men, and fall like one of the princes." "I have said, Ye are gods"; that is to say, you have in your authority, and you bear on your forehead, a divine imprint. "You are the children of the Most High"; it is he who has established your power for the good of mankind. But, O gods of flesh and blood, gods of clay and dust, "ye shall die like men, and fall like princes." Grandeur separates men for a little time, but a common fall makes them all equal at the end.

O kings, exercise your power then boldly, for it is divine and salutary for human kind, but exercise it with humility. You are endowed with it from without. At bottom it leaves you feeble, it leaves you mortal, it leaves you sinners, and charges you before God with a very heavy account.

READING AND DISCUSSION QUESTIONS

1. If, as Bossuet argued, kings were "the representatives of the divine majesty deputed by Providence for the execution of his purposes," then what need was there for clergymen like him?

2. Bossuet admits that "many writers have tried to confound absolute government with arbitrary government." How does he distinguish between the two, if, as he also claims, the "prince need render account of his acts to no one"?

3. Does Bossuet admit to *any* constraints on royal power?

4. According to Bossuet, the "only protection of individuals against the public authority should be their innocence." What sort of protection would that have been against "absolute" royal power?

DOCUMENT 16-3

JEAN-BAPTISTE COLBERT
Memoir on Finances
1670

Jean-Baptiste Colbert (1619–1683) came from a wealthy family of merchants. He first rose to prominence in the service of Cardinal Jules Mazarin, Louis XIV's political mentor and advisor. Following Mazarin's death in 1661, Louis assumed personal control of France's government, and Colbert served him as both minister of finance and minister of marine and colonies until his death in 1683. He was a staunch proponent of mercantilism, in which the state regulates economic activities in order to increase its wealth. Virtually all of his policies had this aim in view. The memorandum that follows was written for Louis's consideration.

There is only a given quantity of money which circulates in Europe and this quantity is increased from time to time by what comes in from the West Indies.[2] It is certain and clear that if there are only 150,000,000 livres which circulate publicly in France, one cannot increase it by 20,000,000, 30,000,000, and 50,000,000 without at the same time taking the same quantity from neighboring states, a fact which explains the double elevation which has been seen to go on so notably in the past few years: the one augmenting the power and greatness of your Majesty, the other lowering that of your enemies and those envious of you. . . .

I beg your Majesty to permit me to say that it appears to me that since you have taken charge of the administration of finances, you have undertaken a war of money [*une guerre d'argent*] against all the states of Europe. You have already conquered Spain, Italy, Germany, England, and some others in which you have caused great misery and want, and by despoiling them you have enriched yourself, whereby you have gained the means to do all the great things which you have done and still continue to do every

---

From Colbert, "Memoir on Finances" (1670), reprinted in *Pageant of Europe Sources and Selections from the Renaissance to the Present Day*, ed. Raymond Phineas Stearns (New York: Harcourt, Brace and Co., 1947), pp. 250–251.

[2] **what comes in from the West Indies**: Colbert is referring to shipments of silver from the Spanish empire in the Americas.

day. Only Holland is left, and it fights with great resources . . . Your Majesty has formed companies which, like armies, attack them everywhere. In the North, the company has already a capital of a million livres and 20 vessels; in Guinea, there are 6 French vessels which have begun their trading; in the West, your Majesty has excluded them from all the islands under your authority, and the company which you have formed already furnishes the entire kingdom with sugar, tobacco, and other merchandise which is sold in northern Italy and other foreign countries. In the Orient, your Majesty has 20 vessels employed . . . Those trading in the Levant have a capital of 12,000,000 livres and 12 vessels.[3] Your manufactures, your canal for navigation between the seas,[4] and all the other new establishments which your Majesty makes are so many reserve corps that your Majesty creates to do their duty in this war, in which your Majesty can see clearly that he is winning every year some great advantage.

READING AND DISCUSSION QUESTIONS

1. Why does Colbert equate trading companies like the French West and East India Companies to "armies" that attacked France's enemies, the Netherlands in particular?

2. Why couldn't France increase the amount of money in circulation "without at the same time taking the same quantity from neighboring states"?

3. What does the tone of Colbert's memorandum suggest about his relationship with Louis XIV and about the king's personality?

---

[3] **those trading in the Levant**: State-funded entities established by the Crown to carry on trade across various parts of the globe. "The Levant" refers to the Ottoman Empire and its possessions in the Near East.
[4] **your canal . . . between the seas**: Canal linking the Mediterranean Sea near Narbonne to the Garonne estuary on the Atlantic was under construction at this time. It opened in 1681.

DOCUMENT 16-4

PETER THE GREAT

Edicts and Decrees: Imposing Western Styles on the Russians

1699–1723

Peter the Great's reign (1682–1725) marked Russia's emergence as a major European power. Russia defeated Sweden in the grueling Great Northern War (1700–1721) and acquired a "window on Europe" at the head of the Gulf of Finland, where Peter built a new capital, St. Petersburg. In order to defeat the Swedes, who had routed his ill-trained army at Narva in 1700, Peter had reformed and modernized his military along western European lines. His enthusiasm for western technology and tactics extended also to other realms, including education, dress, and economic programs, as can be seen from the following excerpts.

DECREE ON THE NEW CALENDAR, 1699

It is known to His Majesty that not only many European Christian lands, but also Slavic nations which are in total accord with our Eastern Orthodox Church . . . agree to count their years from the eighth day after the birth of Christ, that is from the first day of January, and not from the creation of the world,[5] because of the many difficulties and discrepancies of this reckoning. It is now the year 1699 from the birth of Christ, and from the first of January will begin both the new year 1700 and a new century; and so His Majesty has ordered, as a good and useful measure, that from now on time will be reckoned in government offices and dates be noted on documents and property deeds, starting from the first of January 1700. And

---

From Marthe Blinoff, *Life and Thought in Old Russia* (University Park: Pennsylvania State University Press, 1961), pp. 49–50; Eugene Schuyler, *Peter the Great*, vol. 2 (New York: Charles Scribner's Sons, 1884), pp. 176–177; L. Jay Oliva, *Peter the Great* (Englewood Cliffs, NJ: Prentice-Hall, 1970), p. 50; George Vernadsky et al., *A Source Book for Russian History from Early Times to 1917*, vol. 2 (New Haven and London: Yale University Press, 1972), pp. 347, 329, 357.

[5] **agree to count their years . . . world**: Before January 1, 1700, the Russian calendar started from the date of the creation of the world, which was reckoned at 5508 B.C.E. The year began on September 1.

to celebrate this good undertaking and the new century . . . in the sovereign city of Moscow . . . let the reputable citizens arrange decorations of pine, fir, and juniper trees and boughs along the busiest main streets and by the houses of eminent church and lay persons of rank. . . . Poorer persons should place at least one shrub or bough on their gates or on their house. . . . Also . . . as a sign of rejoicing, wishes for the new year and century will be exchanged, and the following will be organized: when fireworks are lit and guns fired on the great Red Square, let the boyars [nobles], the Lords of the Palace, of the Chamber, and the Council, and the eminent personages of Court, Army, and Merchant ranks, each in his own grounds, fire three times from small guns, if they have any, or from muskets and other small arms, and shoot some rockets into the air.

DECREE ON THE INVITATION OF FOREIGNERS, 1702

Since our accession to the throne all our efforts and intentions have tended to govern this realm in such a way that all of our subjects should, through our care for the general good, become more and more prosperous. For this end we have always tried to maintain internal order, to defend the state against invasion, and in every possible way to improve and to extend trade. With this purpose we have been compelled to make some necessary and salutary changes in the administration, in order that our subjects might more easily gain a knowledge of matters of which they were before ignorant, and become more skillful in their commercial relations.

We have therefore given orders, made dispositions, and founded institutions indispensable for increasing our trade with foreigners, and shall do the same in the future. Nevertheless we fear that matters are not in such a good condition as we desire, and that our subjects cannot in perfect quietness enjoy the fruits of our labors, and we have therefore considered still other means to protect our frontier from the invasion of the enemy, and to preserve the rights and privileges of our State, and the general peace of all Christians. . . .

To attain these worthy aims, we have endeavored to improve our military forces, which are the protection of our State, so that our troops may consist of well-drilled men, maintained in perfect order and discipline. In order to obtain greater improvement in this respect, and to encourage foreigners, who are able to assist us in this way, as well as artisans profitable to the State, to come in numbers to our country, we have issued this manifesto, and have ordered printed copies of it to be sent throughout Europe. . . . And as in our residence of Moscow, the free exercise of religion of all other sects, although not agreeing with our church, is already allowed, so shall this be hereby confirmed anew in such manner that we, by the power granted to us by the Almighty, shall exercise no compulsion over the consciences of men, and shall gladly allow every Christian to care for his own salvation at his own risk.

An Instruction to Russian Students Abroad Studying Navigation, 1714

1. Learn how to draw plans and charts and how to use the compass and other naval indicators.
2. Learn how to navigate a vessel in battle as well as in a simple maneuver, and learn how to use all appropriate tools and instruments; namely, sails, ropes, and oars, and the like matters, on row boats and other vessels.
3. Discover . . . how to put ships to sea during a naval battle. . . . Obtain from foreign naval officers written statements, bearing their signatures and seals, of how adequately you are prepared for naval duties.
4. If, upon his return, anyone wishes to receive from the Tsar greater favors, he should learn, in addition to the above enumerated instructions, how to construct those vessels [aboard] which he would like to demonstrate his skills.
5. Upon his return to Moscow, every foreign-trained Russian should bring with him at his own expense, for which he will later be reimbursed, at least two experienced masters of naval science. They [the returnees] will be assigned soldiers, one soldier per returnee, to teach them what they have learned abroad. . . .

Decree on Western Dress, 1701

Western ["German"] dress shall be worn by all the boyars, okol'nichie,[6] members of our councils and of our court . . . gentry of Moscow, secretaries . . . provincial gentry, boiarskie,[7] gosti,[8] government officials, strel'tsy,[9] members of the guilds purveying for our household, citizens of Moscow of all ranks, and residents of provincial cities . . . excepting the clergy (priests, deacons, and church attendants) and peasant tillers of the soil. The upper dress shall be of French or Saxon cut, and the lower dress — [including] waistcoat, trousers, boots, shoes, and hats — shall be of the German type.

---

[6] **boyars, okol'nichie**: Nobles of the highest and second-highest rank, respectively.
[7] **boiarskie**: Sons of boyars.
[8] **gosti**: Merchants who often served the tsar in some capacity.
[9] **strel'tsy**: Members of the imperial guard stationed in Moscow.

They shall also ride German saddles. [Likewise] the womenfolk of all ranks, including the priests', deacons', and church attendants' wives, the wives of the dragoons, the soldiers, and the strel'tsy and their children, shall wear Western ["German"] dresses, hats, jackets, and underwear — undervests and petticoats — and shoes. From now on no one [of the above-mentioned] is to wear Russian dress or Circassian coats,[10] sheepskin coats, or Russian peasant coats, trousers, boots, and shoes. It is also forbidden to ride Russian saddles, and the craftsmen shall not manufacture them or sell them at the marketplaces.

Decree on Shaving, 1705

A decree to be published in Moscow and in all the provincial cities: Hence-forth, in accordance with this, His Majesty's decree, all court attendants . . . provincial service men, government officials of all ranks, military men, all the gosti, members of the wholesale merchants' guild, and members of the guilds purveying for our household must shave their beards and moustaches. But, if it happens that some of them do not wish to shave their beards and moustaches, let a yearly tax be collected from such persons. . . . Special badges shall be issued to them from the Administrator of Land Affairs [of Public Order] . . . which they must wear. . . . As for the peasants, let a toll of two half-copecks[11] per beard be collected at the town gates each time they enter or leave a town; and do not let the peasants pass the town gates, into or out of town, without paying this toll.

Decree on Promotion to Officer's Rank, 1714

Since there are many who promote to officer rank their relatives and friends — young men who do not know the fundamentals of soldiering, not having served in the lower ranks — and since even those who serve [in the ranks] do so for a few weeks or months only, as a formality; there-fore . . . let a decree be promulgated that henceforth there shall be no pro-motion [to officer rank] of men of noble extraction or of any others who have not first served as privates in the Guards. This decree does not apply to soldiers of lowly origin who, after long service in the ranks, have received their commissions through honest service or to those who are promoted on

---

[10] **Circassian coats**: Traditional outer garments worn by the people of Circassia, a Russian territory between the Caspian and Black Seas. The style was evidently adopted by the nobility.

[11] **half-copecks**: One-twentieth of a ruble, the basic unit of Russian money.

the basis of merit, now or in the future; it applies exclusively to those who have remained in the ranks for a short time, only as a formality, as described above.

STATUTE FOR THE COLLEGE OF MANUFACTURES, 1723

His Imperial Majesty is diligently striving to establish and develop in the Russian Empire such manufacturing plants and factories as are found in other states, for the general welfare and prosperity of his subjects. He [therefore] most graciously charges the College of Manufactures[12] to exert itself in devising the means to introduce, with the least expense, and to spread in the Russian Empire these and other ingenious arts, and especially those for which materials can be found within the empire; [the College of Manufactures] must also consider the privileges that should be granted to those who might wish to found manufacturing plants and factories.

His Imperial Majesty gives permission to everyone, without distinction of rank or condition, to open factories wherever he may find suitable. . . .

Factory owners must be closely supervised, in order that they have at their plants good and experienced [foreign] master craftsmen, who are able to train Russians in such a way that these, in turn, may themselves become masters, so that their produce may bring glory to the Russian manufactures. . . .

By the former decrees of His Majesty commercial people were forbidden to buy villages [i.e., to own serfs], the reason being that they were not engaged in any other activity beneficial for the state save commerce; but since it is now clear to all that many of them have started to found manufacturing establishments and build plants, both in companies and individually, which tend to increase the welfare of the state . . . therefore permission is granted both to the gentry and to men of commerce to acquire villages for these factories without hindrance. . . .

In order to stimulate voluntary immigration of various craftsmen from other countries into the Russian Empire, and to encourage them to establish factories and manufacturing plants freely and at their own expense, the College of Manufactures must send appropriate announcements to the Russian envoys accredited at foreign courts. The envoys should then, in an appropriate way, bring these announcements to the attention of men of various professions, urge them to come to settle in Russia, and help them to move.

---

[12] **College of Manufactures**: One of several administrative boards created by Peter in 1717, modeled on Swedish practice.

READING AND DISCUSSION QUESTIONS

1. Why do you think Peter decreed that the nobles, merchants, and townspeople wear German, rather than French, clothes, seeing that the French kings and their palaces were objects of emulation throughout Europe?

2. What does Peter's decree encouraging foreign soldiers and artisans to emigrate to Russia and his Statute for the College of Manufactures suggest about the state of its military forces and economy as of the early 1700s?

3. Why didn't Russia have a navy prior to 1700?

4. What, according to Peter, was wrong with the system of promotion in the Russian army, and how did he intend to redress it? What does his decree on promotion suggest about the power and benefits granted to the Russian nobility?

VIEWPOINTS

The Commonwealth and the State of Nature

DOCUMENT 16-5

THOMAS HOBBES

Leviathan

1651

Thomas Hobbes (1588–1679), the son of a Church of England clergyman, was educated at Oxford University and spent the years between 1608 and 1637 chiefly as a tutor to aristocratic families. Rising religious and political tensions in England drove Hobbes to flee to Paris in 1640, and there he

From Thomas Hobbes, *Leviathan, or the Matter, Form, and Power of a Commonwealth, Ecclesiastical and Civil* (London: George Routledge and Sons, 1886), pp. 64–66, 82, 84–85.

remained until the publication of Leviathan, *which aroused so much anger among English royalists that he was forced to seek protection from Cromwell's republican government.* Leviathan *originally referred to a biblical sea monster, but Hobbes used it as a synonym for the commonwealth; the frontispiece to his book depicts a gargantuan human figure made up of smaller people (members of the commonwealth) with the head of a monarch.* Leviathan *itself is based on the premise that without a sovereign authority invested with absolute power, human society is in a state of perpetual violence. Faced with such a prospect, he argued, individuals voluntarily relinquish their personal rights and liberties in return for protection.*

Nature hath made men so equal, in the faculties of body and mind, as that though there be found one man sometimes manifestly stronger in body, or of quicker mind than another; yet when all is reckoned together, the difference between man and man is not so considerable, as that one man can thereupon claim to himself any benefit, to which another may not pretend, as well as he. For as to the strength of body, the weakest has strength enough to kill the strongest, either by secret machination or by confederacy with others that are in the same danger with himself. . . .

From this equality of ability, ariseth equality of hope in the attaining of our ends. And therefore if any two men desire the same thing, which nevertheless they cannot both enjoy, they become enemies, and in the way to their end, . . . endeavor to destroy, or subdue one another. . . .

So that in the nature of man, we find three principal causes of quarrel. First, competition; secondly, diffidence; thirdly, glory.

The first maketh men invade for gain; the second, for safety; and the third, reputation. The first use violence to make themselves masters of other men's persons, wives, children, and cattle; the second, to defend them; the third, for trifles, as a word, a smile, a different opinion, and any other sign of undervalue, either direct in their persons, or by reflection in their kindred, their friends, their nation, their profession, or their name.

Hereby it is manifest, that during the time men live without a common power to keep them all in awe, they are in that condition which is called war; and such a war, as is of every man, against every man. . . .

[*On the "the state of nature":*]
Whatsoever therefore is consequent to a time of war, where every man is enemy to every man; the same is consequent to the time wherein men live without other security, than what their own strength and their own inven-

tion shall furnish them withall. In such condition, there is no place for industry, because the fruit thereof is uncertain, and consequently no culture of the earth; no navigation, nor use of the commodities that may be imported by sea; no commodious building; no instruments of moving and removing such things as require much force; no knowledge of the face of the earth; no account of time; no arts; no letters; no society; and, which is worst of all, continual fear, and danger of violent death; and the life of man, solitary, poor, nasty, brutish, and short. . . .

The passions that incline men to peace, are fear of death; desire of such things as are necessary to commodious living; and a hope by their industry to obtain them. And reason suggesteth convenient articles of peace, upon which men may be drawn to agreement. . . .

And because the condition of man, as hath been declared in the precedent chapter, is a condition of war of everyone against everyone; in which case everyone is governed by his own reason, and there is nothing he can make use of, that may not be a help unto him, in preserving his life against his enemies; It followeth that, in such a condition, every man has a right to every thing, even to one another's body. And therefore, as long as this natural right of every man to everything endureth, there can be no security to any man, how strong or wise soever he be, of living out the time, which Nature ordinarily alloweth men to live. . . .

If there be no power erected, or not great enough for our security, every man will and may lawfully rely on his own strength and art, for caution against all other men. . . .

The only way to erect such a common power, as may be able to defend them from the invasion of foreigners, and the injuries of one another, and thereby to secure them in such sort as that by their own industry and by the fruits of the earth they may nourish themselves and live contentedly, is to confer all their power and strength upon one man, or upon one assembly of men, that may reduce all their wills, by plurality of voices, unto one will: which is as much as to say, to appoint one man, or assembly of men, to bear their person; and every one to own and acknowledge himself to be author of whatsoever he that so beareth their person shall act, or cause to be acted, in those things which concern the common peace and safety; and therein to submit their wills, every one to his will, and their judgments to his judgment. This is more than consent, or concord; it is a real unity of them all in one and the same person, made by covenant of every man with every man, in such manner as if every man should say to every man: "I authorize and give up my right of governing myself to this man, or to this assembly of men, on this condition, that thou give up thy right to him, and authorize all his actions in like manner." This done, the multitude so united in one person is called a "commonwealth," in Latin, *civitas*. This is the generation of that great "leviathan," or rather, to speak more reverently, of that "mortal god," to which we owe under the "immortal God," our peace and defense. For by this authority, given him by every particular man in the commonwealth, he hath the use of so much power and strength conferred on him that by terror thereof, he is enabled to perform the wills of them all, to peace at home, and mutual aid against their enemies abroad. And in him consisteth the essence of the commonwealth; which, to define it, is "one person, of whose acts a great multitude, by mutual covenants one with another, have made themselves every one the author, to the end he may use the strength and means of them all as he shall think expedient, for their peace and common defense."

And he that carryeth this person is called "sovereign," and said to have "sovereign power"; and every one besides, his "subject." . . .

They that have already instituted a commonwealth, being thereby bound by covenant to own the actions and judgments of one, cannot lawfully make a new covenant, amongst themselves, to be obedient to any other, in anything whatsoever, without his permission. And therefore, they that are subjects to a monarch cannot without his leave cast off monarchy, and return to the confusion of a disunited multitude; nor transfer their person from him that beareth it to another man, other assembly of men . . . [he] that already is their sovereign shall do and judge fit to be done: so that any one man dissenting, all the rest should break their covenant made to that man, which is injustice: and they have also every man given the sovereignty to him that beareth their person; and therefore if they depose him, they take from him that which is his own, and so again it is injustice. . . . And whereas some men have pretended for their disobedience to their sovereign, a new covenant, made not with men but with God; this also is unjust: for there is no covenant with God but by mediation of somebody that representeth God's person; which none doth but God's lieutenant, who hath the sovereignty under God. But this pretence of covenant with God is so evident a lie, even in the pretenders' own consciences, that it is not only an act of an unjust, but also of a vile and unmanly disposition. . . .

Consequently none of [the sovereign's] subjects, by any pretence of forfeiture, can be freed from his subjection.

READING AND DISCUSSION QUESTIONS

1. How does Hobbes characterize human existence without the peace and order afforded by a ruler vested with absolute authority?

2. What is Hobbes's view of religious or divine justifications for absolute power?

3. Having placed themselves under the sovereign power of a ruler, what freedom of action do individuals have to govern their own affairs?

4. What options, according to Hobbes, do a sovereign's subjects have in the event that he abuses his power?

DOCUMENT 16-6

JOHN LOCKE

Second Treatise of Civil Government:
Vindication for the Glorious Revolution

1690

John Locke (1632–1704) was, along with Thomas Hobbes, one of the two greatest English political theorists of the seventeenth century. Unlike Hobbes, however, who provided a justification for monarchical absolutism, Locke's Second Treatise of Government, published anonymously in 1690, argued that government is an agreement between governors and the governed. The people submit to governmental authority in return for protection of their life, liberty, and property, and the governors' fundamental task is to provide those essential protections. According to Locke, a government that failed to do so or became tyrannical lost its claim to legitimacy, and could therefore be cast off by the governed.

87. Man being born, as has been proved, with a title to perfect freedom and an uncontrolled enjoyment of all the rights and privileges of the law of Nature, equally with any other man, or number of men in the world,

---

From John Locke, *Two Treatises on Civil Government* (London: George Routledge and Sons, 1887), pp. 234–38.

hath by nature a power not only to preserve his property — that is, his life, liberty and estate against the injuries and attempts of other men; but to judge of and punish the breaches of that law in others, as he is persuaded the offense deserves, even with death itself, in crimes where the heinousness of the fact, in his opinion, requires it. But because no political society can be, nor subsist, without having in itself the power to preserve the property, and in order thereunto punish the offenses of all those of that society, there, and there only is political society where every one of the members hath quitted this natural power, resigned it up into the hands of the community in all cases that exclude him not from appealing for protection to the law established by it. And thus all private judgment of every particular member being excluded, the community comes to be umpire, and by understanding indifferent rules and men authorized by the community for their execution, decides all the differences that may happen between any members of that society concerning any matter of right, and punishes those offenses which any member hath committed against the society with such penalties as the law has established; whereby it is easy to discern, who are, and are not, in political society together. Those who are united into one body, and have a common established law and judicature to appeal to, with authority to decide controversies between them and punish offenders, are in civil society one with another; but those who have no such common appeal, I mean on earth, are still in the state of Nature, each being where there is no other, judge for himself and executioner; which is, as I have before showed it, the perfect state of Nature.

88. And thus the commonwealth comes by a power to set down what punishment shall belong to the several transgressions they think worthy of it, committed amongst the members of that society (which is the power of making laws) as well as it has the power to punish any injury done unto any of its members by any one that is not of it (which is the power of war and peace); and all this for the preservation of the property of all the members of that society, as far as is possible. But though every man entered into society has quitted his power to punish offenses against the law of Nature in prosecution of his own private judgment, yet with the judgment of offenses which he has given up to the legislative, in all cases where he can appeal to the magistrate, he has given up a right to the commonwealth to employ his force, for the execution of the judgments of the commonwealth whenever he shall be called to it, which, indeed, are his own judgments, they being made by himself or his representative. And herein we have the original of the legislative and executive power of civil society, which is to judge by standing laws how far offenses are to be punished

when committed within the commonwealth; and also by occasional judgments founded on the present circumstances of the fact, how far injuries from without are to be vindicated; and in both these to employ all the force of all the members when there shall be need.

89. Wherever, therefore, any number of men so unite into one society as to quit every one his executive power of the law of Nature, and to resign it to the public, there and there only is a political or civil society. And this is done wherever any number of men, in the state of nature, enter into society to make one people one body politic under one supreme government; or else when any one joins himself to, and incorporates with any government already made. For hereby he authorizes the society, or which is all one, the legislative thereof, to make laws for him as the public good of the society shall require; to the execution whereof his own assistance (as to his own decrees) is due. And this puts men out of a state of Nature into that of a commonwealth, by setting up a judge on earth with authority to determine all the controversies and redress the injuries that may happen to any member of the commonwealth; which judge is the legislative or magistrates appointed by it. And wherever there are any number of men, however associated, that have no such decisive power to appeal to, there they are still in the state of Nature.

90. And hence it is evident that absolute monarchy, which by some men is counted for the only government in the world, is indeed inconsistent with civil society, and so can be no form of civil government at all. For the end of civil society being to avoid and remedy those inconveniencies of the state of nature which necessarily follow from every man's being judge in his own case by setting up a known authority to which every one of that society may appeal upon any injury received, or controversy that may arise, and which every one of the society ought to obey. Wherever any persons are who have not such an authority to appeal to, and decide any difference between them there, those persons are still in the state of Nature. And so is every absolute prince in respect of those who are under his dominion.

91. For he being supposed to have all, both legislative and executive, power in himself alone, there is no judge to be found, no appeal lies open to any one, who may fairly and indifferently, and with authority decide, and from whence relief and redress may be expected of any injury or inconveniency that may be suffered from him, or by his order. So that such a man, however entitled, Czar, or Grand Signior, or how you please, is as much in the state of Nature, with all under his dominion, as he is with the rest of mankind. For wherever any two men are, who have no standing

rule and common judge to appeal to on earth, for the determination of controversies of right betwixt them, there they are still in the state of Nature, and under all the inconveniencies of it, with only this woeful difference to the subject, or rather slave of an absolute prince. That whereas, in the ordinary state of nature, he has a liberty to judge of his right, and according to the best of his power to maintain it; but whenever his property is invaded by the will and order of his monarch, he has not only no appeal, as those in society ought to have, but as if he were degraded from the common state of rational creatures, is denied a liberty to judge of, or to defend his right, and so is exposed to all the misery and inconveniencies that a man can fear from one, who being in the unrestrained state of Nature, is yet corrupted with flattery and armed with power.

92. For he that thinks absolute power purifies men's bloods, and corrects the baseness of human nature, need read but the history of this, or any other age, to be convinced of the contrary.

READING AND DISCUSSION QUESTIONS

1. What, according to Locke, distinguishes "political, or civil society" from "a state of nature"?

2. What, in Locke's opinion, led to the creation of "political, or civil society"?

3. Why does he argue that "absolute monarchy, which by some men is counted the only government in the world, is indeed inconsistent with civil society, and so can be no form of civil government at all"?

4. Why do you think Locke published this work anonymously, rather than publicly claiming credit for what is now generally regarded as one of the classics of Western political theory?

COMPARATIVE QUESTIONS

1. What would Hobbes say of Bossuet's justification for absolute royal authority? What would Bossuet say of Hobbes's?

2. How does Hobbes's "social contract" theory differ from Locke's? How do Hobbes and Locke use "the state of nature" to further their arguments?

3. Compare and contrast how Locke and Hobbes view the scope of sovereign power and authority.

4. What do Henry IV's and Peter the Great's edicts tell you about their attitudes toward monarchy and their role in the lives of their subjects?

5. How would Bossuet, Hobbes, and Locke each respond to Peter the Great's edicts?

CHAPTER 17

Toward a New Worldview

1540–1789

Learning in the medieval period focused on studying ancient texts such as the Bible and Aristotle's writings and then using that knowledge to draw conclusions about the world. The Polish astronomer Nicolaus Copernicus (1473–1543) was one of the first thinkers to dispute effectively archaic ideas about astronomy, spurring a centuries-long challenge to the system of scientific and mathematical thinking that had shaped the Western world since antiquity. By the eighteenth century, the spirit of this "scientific revolution" had spread to human affairs. Philosophers and scientists of the European "Enlightenment," particularly in France, began to question forms of social and political organization. Some thinkers rejected the legitimacy of absolutism and divine right. In the climate of the age, especially beginning in the eighteenth century, even absolutist monarchs made efforts to incorporate new political ideas, though with varying degrees of enthusiasm and success.

DOCUMENT 17-1

NICOLAUS COPERNICUS

On the Revolutions of the Heavenly Spheres

1542

For over a thousand years Europeans widely believed that the earth was the center of the universe, based on the work of the Greek philosopher Aristotle, and his follower, Ptolemy. This view aligned with Scripture and the Christian belief that humans were the center of creation. Copernicus theorized

From Nicolaus Copernicus, *De Revolutionibus Orbium Celestium*, trans. A. M. Duncan (Newton Abbot, Devonshire: David and Charles, 1976), pp. 36, 37, 40–41, 43–44, 45–46.

that a sun-centered system made for easier, more precise calculations of planetary and stellar movements, both important accurate calendars, oceanic navigations, and, not least of all, horoscopes. Fearful of how the Catholic Church might react to his theory, Copernicus only published his work in 1542, shortly before his death.

THAT THE UNIVERSE IS SPHERICAL.

First we must remark that the universe is globe-shaped, either because that is the most perfect shape of all, needing no joint, an integral whole; or because that it is the most capacious of shapes, which is most fitting because it is to contain and preserve all things; or because the most finished parts of the universe, I mean the Sun, Moon, and stars, are observed to have that shape, or because everything tends to take on this shape, which is evident in drops of water and other liquid bodies, when they take on their natural shape. There should therefore be no doubt that this shape is assigned to the heavenly bodies.

THAT THE EARTH IS ALSO SPHERICAL.

The Earth is also globe-shaped, because every part of it tends towards its center. Although it is not immediately apparent that it is a perfect sphere, because the mountains project so far and the valleys are so deep, they produce very little variation in the complete roundness of the Earth. That is evident from the fact that as one moves northward from any point that pole [the North Pole] of the diurnal [daily] rotation rises little by little, while the other pole on the contrary sinks to the same extent, and several stars round the North Pole seem not to set, while some in the South no longer rise . . .

WHETHER THE EARTH HAS A CIRCULAR MOTION, AND CONCERNING THE LOCATION OF THE EARTH.

As it has now been shown that the Earth also has the shape of a globe, I believe we must consider whether its motion too follows its shape, and what place it holds in the universe, without which it is impossible to find a reliable explanation of celestial phenomena. Among the authorities it is generally agreed that the Earth is at rest in the middle of the universe, and they regard it as inconceivable and even ridiculous to hold the opposite opinion. However, if we consider it more closely the question will be seen to be still unsettled, and so decidedly not to be despised. For every apparent change in respect of position is due to motion of the object observed, or of the observer, or indeed to an unequal change of both. (Between objects which move equally in the same direction no motion is perceived,

I mean between that which is observed and the observer.) Now the Earth is the point from which the rotation of the heavens is observed, and brought into our view. If therefore some motion is imputed to the Earth, the same motion will appear in all that is external to the Earth, but in the opposite direction, as if it were passing by. The first example of this is the diurnal rotation. This seems to whirl round the whole universe, except the Earth and the things on it. But if you grant that the heaven has no part in this motion, but that the Earth revolves from west to east, as far as the apparent rising and setting of the Sun, Moon, and stars is concerned, if you consider the point seriously, you will find that this is the way of it. And as the heaven is that which contains and cloaks all things, where everything has its place, it is not at once apparent why motion is attributed to that which is contained rather than to the container, to that which is located rather than that which locates it. . . . If this assumption is made there follows another and no lesser problem about the position of the Earth, although almost everyone admits and believes the Earth to be the center of the universe. For if one argues that the Earth does not occupy the center or middle of the universe, not claiming that its distance is great enough to be comparable with the sphere of the fixed stars, but that it is appreciable and significant compared with the orbits of the Sun and other stars,[1] and believing that on this account their motion seems to be variable, as if they were regular with respect to [i.e., revolved around] some center other than the center of the Earth, he would perhaps be able to put forward a not unreasonable account of the apparently variable motion. For the fact that the wandering stars are observed to be sometimes nearer to the Earth and sometimes further away from it necessarily shows that the center of the Earth is not the center of their orbits. It is also undecided whether the Earth veers toward them and away from them or they towards and away from the Earth. It would also not be surprising if in addition to this daily revolution another motion should be supposed for the Earth. Indeed that the Earth revolves, wanders with several motions, and is one of the stars [i.e., planets] is said to have been the opinion of Philolaus the Pythagorean,[2] no mean mathematician. . . .

---

[1] **not claiming . . . other stars:** Copernicus is arguing here that the diameter of the earth's orbit is insignificant compared to the distance of the earth from the "fixed stars," which he, like his contemporaries, believed to be embedded in an invisible crystalline sphere, but is comparable to that of the "wandering stars," i.e., the visible planets.

[2] **Philolaus the Pythagorean:** Greek mathematician and philosopher (ca. 470–385 B.C.E.).

REFUTATION OF THE ARGUMENTS QUOTED, AND THEIR INSUFFICIENCY.[3]

From this and similar arguments, then, they say that the Earth is at rest in the middle of the universe, and that such is undoubtedly the state of affairs. Yet if anyone should hold the opinion that the Earth revolves, he will surely assert that its motion is natural, not violent. What is natural produces contrary effects to what is violent. For objects to which force or impulse is applied must necessarily be destroyed and cannot long subsist; but objects which exist naturally are in their proper state, and continue in their perfect form. There is therefore no need for Ptolemy to fear the scattering of the Earth and of all terrestrial objects in a revolution brought about through the workings of nature, which is far different from artifice, or what can be achieved by human abilities. Further, why is not the same question raised even more strongly about the universe, the motion of which must be much swifter in proportion as the heaven is greater than the Earth? Of has heaven become so immense, because it is drawn outwards from the middle by a motion of ineffable strength [i.e., centrifugal force], that it would collapse if it were not at rest? Certainly if this reasoning were to be accepted, the magnitude of the heaven will rise to infinity. For in proportion is it is thrown higher by the impulse of the motion, so the motion will be swifter, on account of the continual increase in the circumference which it must traverse in the space of twenty-four hours; and on the other hand as the motion increased, so would the immensity of the heaven. So the velocity would increase the magnitude, and the magnitude the velocity, to infinity. But according to that axiom in physics, that what is infinite cannot be traversed, nor moved by any means, the heaven will necessarily be at rest. But they say that outside the heaven there is no body, no place, no empty space, in fact nothing whatsoever, and therefore there is nothing to which the heaven can go out. In that case it is remarkable indeed if something can be restrained by nothing. But if the heaven is infinite, and finite only in its hollow interior, perhaps it will be more clearly proved that there is nothing outside the heaven, since every single thing will be within, whatever amount of space it occupies, but the heaven will remain immovable. For the strongest argument by which they try to establish that the universe is finite, is its motion. Therefore let us leave the question whether the universe is finite or infinite for the natural philoso-

---

[3] **the arguments quoted . . . insufficiency**: Arguments by ancient authorities, maintaining that "the Earth was at rest in the middle of the universe as if it was the center."

phers[4] to argue. What we do know for certain is that the Earth is limited by its poles and bounded by a globular surface. . . .

Surely Aristotle's division of simple motion into three types, away from the middle, towards the middle, and round the middle, will be regarded merely as an intellectual division; just as we distinguish between a line, a point, and a surface, although one cannot exist without the other, and none of them without a body. A further point is that immobility is considered a more noble and divine state than that of change and instability, which is for that reason more appropriate to the Earth than to the universe. I also add that it would seem rather absurd to ascribe motion to that which contains and locates, and not rather to that which is contained and located, that is the Earth. Lastly, since it is evident that the wandering stars are sometimes nearer, sometimes further from the Earth, this will also be an example of motion of a single body which is both round the middle, by which they mean the center, away from the middle, and towards it. Motion round the midpoint must therefore be accepted more generally, and as satisfactory, provided that each motion is motion about its own midpoint. You will see then that from all these arguments the mobility of the Earth is more probable than its immobility, especially in the daily revolution, as that is particularly fitting for the Earth.

READING AND DISCUSSION QUESTIONS

1. What justification does Copernicus offer for his opening premise that the universe is spherical? What is his justification for the premise that the earth too is spherical?

2. Why does Copernicus accuse Ptolemy of logical inconsistency?

3. On what grounds does Copernicus argue that the heavens (universe) are of finite extent? Does his logic on this score convince you? Why or why not?

4. What is Copernicus's argument that the earth, like the other planets, is in motion? Why did scientists before him accept the idea that the Earth was stationary?

---

[4] **natural philosophers**: Scientists.

DOCUMENT 17-2

FRANCIS BACON

On Superstition and the Virtue of Science

1620

Trained as a lawyer, Sir Francis Bacon (1561–1626) served in the court of the English king James I (r. 1603–1625) and conducted numerous experiments designed to illuminate the natural world. Bacon argued for a new method of observation and reasoning based on drawing conclusions from specific examples rather than on theory or, worse, on superstition. Most of the scientists (known in their day as natural philosophers) of the seventeenth century were religious men as well, and Bacon was no exception.

There is no soundness in our notions, whether logical or physical. Substance, quality, action, passion, essence itself are not sound notions; much less are heavy, light, dense, rare, moist, dry, generation, corruption, attraction, repulsion, element, matter, form, and the like; but all are fantastical and ill-defined. . . .

The discoveries which have hitherto been made in the sciences are such as lie close to vulgar notions, scarcely beneath the surface. In order to penetrate into the inner and further recesses of nature, it is necessary that both notions and axioms [be] derived from things by a more sure and guarded way, and that a method of intellectual operation be introduced altogether better and more certain. . . .

There are and can be only two ways of searching into and discovering truth. The one flies from the senses and particulars to the most general axioms, and from these principles, the truth of which it takes for settled and immovable, proceeds to judgment and the discovery of middle axioms. And this way is now in fashion. The other derives axioms from the senses and particulars, rising by a gradual and unbroken ascent, so that it arrives at the most general axioms last of all. This is the true way, but as yet untried. . . .

From Francis Bacon, "Aphorisms Concerning the Interpretation of Nature and the Kingdom of Man," in *The Works of Francis Bacon: Popular Edition, Based Upon the Complete Edition of Spedding, Ellis, and Heath*, vol. 1 (New York: Hurd and Houghton, 1877), pp. 70–71, 124–26.

It is not to be forgotten that in every age natural philosophy has had a troublesome adversary and hard to deal with — namely, superstition and the blind and immoderate zeal of religion. For we see among the Greeks that those who first proposed to man's uninitiated ears the natural causes for thunder and for storms were thereupon found guilty of impiety. Nor was much more forbearance shown by some of the ancient fathers of the Christian Church to those who, on most convincing grounds (such as no one in his senses would now think of contradicting), maintained that the earth was round and, of consequence, asserted the existence of the antipodes.[5]

Moreover, as things now are, to discourse of nature is made harder and more perilous by the summaries and systems of the schoolmen; who, having reduced theology into regular order as well as they were able, and fashioned it into the shape of an art, ended in incorporating the contentious and thorny philosophy of Aristotle, more than was fit, with the body of religion. . . .

Lastly . . . some are weakly afraid lest a deeper search into nature should transgress the permitted limits of sobermindedness; wrongfully wresting and transferring what is said in Holy Writ [the Christian Bible] against those who pry into sacred mysteries to the hidden things of nature, which are barred by no prohibition. Others, with more subtlety, surmise and reflect that if secondary causes are unknown everything can be more readily referred to the divine hand and rod, — a point in which they think religion greatly concerned; which is, in fact, nothing else but to seek to gratify God with a lie. Others fear from past example that movements and changes in philosophy will end in assaults on religion; and others again appear apprehensive that in the investigation of nature something may be found to subvert, or at least shake, the authority of religion, especially with the unlearned. But these two last fears seem to me to savor utterly of carnal wisdom; as if men in the recesses and secret thoughts of their hearts doubted and distrusted the strength of religion, and the empire of faith over the senses, and therefore feared that the investigation of truth in nature might be dangerous to them. But if the matter be truly considered,

---

[5] **maintained that the earth was round . . . antipodes**: Bacon refers to an ancient debate relating to the shape of the earth; if the earth was round, some Greek theorists argued, then there would be lands (or ocean) on the side of the world directly opposite the one they inhabited. The debate was largely mooted by the fifteenth-century voyages of European explorers, culminating in the 1492 discovery of the New World. The theorists were proven correct.

natural philosophy is, after the word of God, at once the surest medicine against superstition and the most approved nourishment for faith; and therefore she is rightly given to religion as her most faithful handmaid, since the one displays the will of God, the other his power.

READING AND DISCUSSION QUESTIONS

1. If, as Bacon argues, that moving from specific observations to general truths "by a gradual and unbroken ascent" is the "true way, but as yet untried," what reasons might he have for thinking it is a better way?

2. What reasons would Bacon have for referring to settled arguments instead of ongoing ones in order to make his points?

3. What does Bacon's relationship to religion suggest about the larger relationship between science and faith in the seventeenth century?

VIEWPOINTS

Monarchical Power and Responsibility

DOCUMENT 17-3

FREDERICK THE GREAT
Essay on the Forms of Government
ca. 1740

Frederick II of Prussia (r. 1740–1786) is renowned chiefly for his military genius, but his life and policies reflected his interest in Enlightenment thought. He was a patron of the arts and learning, modernized Prussia's bureaucracy and educational system in accordance with Enlightenment

From *The Foundations of Germany*, trans. J. Ellis Barker (New York: E. P. Dutton, 1916), pp. 22–23.

principles, abolished torture and corporal punishment, and favored religious tolerance. He also corresponded with French philosophe Jean d'Alembert and had a long, if at times stormy, friendship with Voltaire.

Princes, sovereigns, and king have not been given supreme authority in order to live in luxurious self-indulgence and debauchery. They have not been elevated by their fellow-men to enable them to strut about and to insult with their pride the simple-mannered, the poor, and the suffering. They have not been placed at the head of the State to keep around themselves a crowd of idle loafers whose uselessness drives them towards vice. The bad administration which may be found in monarchies springs from many different causes, but their principal cause lies in the character of the sovereign. A ruler addicted to women will become a tool of his mistresses and favorites, and these will abuse their power and commit wrongs of every kind, will protect vice, sell offices, and perpetrate every infamy. . . .

The sovereign is the representative of his State. He and his people form a single body. Ruler and ruled can be happy only if they are firmly united. The sovereign stands to his people in the same relation in which the head stands to the body. He must use his eyes and his brain for the whole community, and act on its behalf to the common advantage. If we wish to elevate monarchical above republican government, the duty of sovereigns is clear. They must be active, hard-working, upright and honest, and concentrate all their strength upon filling their office worthily. That is my idea of the duties of sovereigns.

A sovereign must possess an exact and detailed knowledge of the strong and of the weak points of his country. He must be thoroughly acquainted with its resources, the character of the people, and the national commerce. . . .

Rulers should always remind themselves that they are men like the least of their subjects. The sovereign is the foremost judge, general, financier, and minister of his country, not merely for the sake of his prestige. Therefore, he should perform with care the duties connected with these offices. He is merely the principal servant of the State. Hence, he must act with honesty, wisdom, and complete disinterestedness in such a way that he can render an account of his stewardship to the citizens at any moment. Consequently, he is guilty if he wastes the money of the people, the taxes which they have paid, in luxury, pomp, and debauchery. He who should improve the morals of the people, be the guardian of the law, and improve their education should not pervert them by his bad example.

READING AND DISCUSSION QUESTIONS

1. In what ways do you think Enlightenment principles informed Frederick's views on the duties of rulers?

2. Historians have used the term "Enlightened Absolutists" to describe some eighteenth-century European rulers, Frederick the Great among them. Are the principles enunciated by Frederick compatible with "absolutism"? Why or why not?

DOCUMENT 17-4

CHARLES DE SECONDAT, BARON DE MONTESQUIEU

From The Spirit of Laws: On the Separation of Governmental Powers

1748

The writings of Frenchman Charles de Secondat (1689–1755), better known as Baron Montesquieu (mahn-tuhs-KYOO), were composed as the spirit of the Enlightenment swept over Europe in the early eighteenth century. Montesquieu's political writings, excerpted here, were concerned with the makeup of the state and the effect of a government on the choices available to those it ruled. Rather than turn to ancient writers for evidence — Aristotle had produced a similar work, the Politics *— Montesquieu culled his examples from contemporary European experience. His work was highly influential and was heavily quoted by the American revolutionaries twenty years after his death.*

In every government there are three sorts of power: the legislative; the executive in respect to things dependent on the law of nations; and the executive in regard to matters that depend on the civil law.

By virtue of the first, the prince or magistrate enacts temporary or perpetual laws, and amends or abrogates those that have been already

From Baron de Montesquieu, *The Spirit of Laws*, trans. T. Nugent (New York: Hafner, 1949), pp. 151–152.

enacted. By the second, he makes peace or war, sends or receives embassies, establishes the public security, and provides against invasions. By the third, he punishes criminals, or determines the disputes that arise between individuals. The latter we shall call the judiciary power, and the other simply the executive power of the state.

The political liberty of the subject is a tranquillity of mind arising from the opinion each person has of his safety. In order to have this liberty, it is requisite the government be so constituted as one man need not be afraid of another.

When the legislative and executive powers are united in the same person, or in the same body of magistrates, there can be no liberty; because apprehensions may arise, lest the same monarch or senate should enact tyrannical laws, to execute them in a tyrannical manner.

Again, there is no liberty, if the judiciary power be not separated from the legislative and executive. Were it joined with the legislative, the life and liberty of the subject would be exposed to arbitrary control; for the judge would be then the legislator. Were it joined to the executive power, the judge might behave with violence and oppression.

There would be an end of everything, were the same man or the same body, whether of the nobles or of the people, to exercise those three powers, that of enacting laws, that of executing the public resolutions, and of trying the causes of individuals.

Most kingdoms in Europe enjoy a moderate government because the prince who is invested with the two first powers leaves the third to his subjects. In Turkey, where these three powers are united in the Sultan's person, the subjects groan under the most dreadful oppression.

In the republics of Italy, where these three powers are united, there is less liberty than in our monarchies. Hence their government is obliged to have recourse to as violent methods for its support as even that of the Turks; witness the state inquisitors, and the lion's mouth into which every informer may at all hours throw his written accusations.

What a situation must the poor subject be in, under those republics! The same body of magistrates are possessed, as executors of the laws, of the whole power they have given themselves in quality of legislators. They may plunder the state by their general determinations; and as they have likewise the judiciary power in their hands, every private citizen may be ruined by their particular decisions.

The whole power is here united in one body; and though there is no external pomp that indicates a despotic sway, yet the people feel the effects of it every moment.

Hence it is that many of the princes of Europe, whose aim has been levelled at arbitrary power, have constantly set out with uniting in their own persons, all the branches of magistracy, and all the great offices of state.

READING AND DISCUSSION QUESTIONS

1. What attitude toward representative government — as opposed to monarchy — does Montesquieu display in this excerpt? Hint: the "Italian republics" are the ones with no powerful central monarch.

2. How does Montesquieu's definition of liberty (see the third paragraph) differ from ours today? Does his understanding reflect his status as a nobleman?

3. What reasons might a French author have for discussing political organization and not citing France in his examples?

DOCUMENT 17-5

JEAN-JACQUES ROUSSEAU

The Social Contract: *On Popular Sovereignty and the General Will*

1762

Jean-Jacques Rousseau (1712–1778) was born in Swiss Geneva — not France — and came from the common, not the aristocratic, class. He left Geneva at the age of sixteen; after spending years living on charity and the income from odd jobs, he traveled to Paris seeking to make a name for himself. Rousseau's poverty and origins, combined with his prickly personality,

From Jean-Jacques Rousseau, *The Social Contract*, in *Translations and Reprints from the Original Sources of European History* (Philadelphia: University of Pennsylvania Press, 1898), 5/1:14–16.

made him something of an outsider in Enlightenment social circles. His 1762 work on political theory, The Social Contract, *was part of an extended argument in the seventeenth and eighteenth centuries over who, if anyone, had the right to change the form of government, and from where the government derived its power.*

Since no man has any natural authority over his fellowmen, and since force is not the source of right, conventions remain as the basis of all lawful authority among men. [Book I, Chapter 4].

Now, as men cannot create any new forces, but only combine and direct those that exist, they have no other means of self-preservation than to form by aggregation a sum of forces which may overcome the resistance, to put them in action by a single motive power, and to make them work in concert.

This sum of forces can be produced only by the combination of many; but the strength and freedom of each man being the chief instruments of his preservation, how can he pledge them without injuring himself, and without neglecting the cares which he owes to himself? This difficulty, applied to my subject, may be expressed in these terms.

"To find a form of association which may defend and protect with the whole force of the community the person and property of every associate, and by means of which each, coalescing with all, may nevertheless obey only himself, and remain as free as before." Such is the fundamental problem of which the social contract furnishes the solution. . . .

If then we set aside what is not of the essence of the social contract, we shall find that it is reducible to the following terms: "Each of us puts in common his person and his whole power under the supreme direction of the general will, and in return we receive every member as an indivisible part of the whole." [Book I, Chapter 6].

But the body politic or sovereign, deriving its existence only from the contract, can never bind itself, even to others, in anything that derogates from the original act, such as alienation of some portion of itself, or submission to another sovereign. To violate the act by which it exists would be to annihilate itself, and what is nothing produces nothing. [Book I, Chapter 7].

It follows from what precedes, that the general will is always right and always tends to the public advantage; but it does not follow that the resolutions of the people have always the same rectitude. Men always desire their own good, but do not always discern it; the people are never corrupted, though often deceived, and it is only then that they seem to will what is evil. [Book II, Chapter 3].

The public force, then, requires a suitable agent to concentrate it and put it in action according to the directions of the general will, to serve as a means of communication between the state and the sovereign, to effect in some manner in the public person what the union of soul and body effects in a man. This is, in the State, the function of government, improperly confounded with the sovereign of which it is only the minister.

What, then, is the government? An intermediate body established between the subjects and the sovereign for their mutual correspondence, charged with the execution of the laws and with the maintenance of liberty both civil and political. [Book III, Chapter 1].

It is not sufficient that the assembled people should have once fixed the constitution of the state by giving their sanction to a body of laws; it is not sufficient that they should have established a perpetual government, or that they should have once for all provided for the election of magistrates. Besides the extraordinary assemblies which unforeseen events may require, it is necessary that there should be fixed and periodical ones which nothing can abolish or prorogue; so that, on the appointed day, the people are rightfully convoked by the law, without needing for that purpose any formal summons. [Book III, Chapter 13].

So soon as the people are lawfully assembled as a sovereign body, the whole jurisdiction of the government ceases, the executive power is suspended, and the person of the meanest citizen is as sacred and inviolable as that of the first magistrate, because where the represented are, there is no longer any representative. [Book III, Chapter 14].

These assemblies, which have as their object the maintenance of the social treaty, ought always to be opened with two propositions, which no one should be able to suppress, and which should pass separately by vote. The first: "Whether it pleases the sovereign to maintain the present form of government." The second: "Whether it pleases the people to leave the administration to those at present entrusted with it."

I presuppose here what I believe I have proved, viz., that there is in the State no fundamental law which cannot be revoked, not even this social compact; for if all the citizens assembled in order to break the compact by a solemn agreement, no one can doubt that it could be quite legitimately broken. [Book III, Chapter 18].

READING AND DISCUSSION QUESTIONS

1. What might Rousseau mean when he says "force is not the source of right"?

2. From where does Rousseau see a government deriving its legitimacy, and on what basis?

3. How does Rousseau's concept of the "general will" relate to the concept of majority rule in a representative government?

4. In what way might the concept of dissolving an unrepresentative government be a dangerous one, particularly in a world of hereditary monarchs?

DOCUMENT 17-6

MARIE JEAN ANTOINE NICOLAS CARITAT,
MARQUIS DE CONDORCET

Outlines of an Historical View of the Progress of the Human Mind

1793–1794

Marie Jean Antoine Nicolas de Caritat, Marquis de Condorcet (CON-dohr-SAY; 1743–1794) was a key figure of the later Enlightenment; his views on the equality of the sexes and of races placed him far in advance of most contemporaries. Perhaps more than any other philosophe, *too, his thought reflected an unswerving faith in human progress. Those qualities are readily evident in the following excerpts, drawn from his posthumously published* Outlines of an Historical View of the Progress of the Human Mind. *Condorcet himself was a victim of the French Revolution. He was denounced as a traitor and went into hiding after criticizing the revolutionary regime's proposed constitution, but was eventually captured and died in prison.*

From Marie Jean Antoine Nicolas Caritat, Marquis de Condorcet, *Outlines of an Historical View of the Progress of the Human Mind* (Baltimore: G. Fryer, 1802), pp. 164–167, 169–171, 223–226, 234, 241–242.

A class of men [the *philosophes*] speedily made their appearance in Europe, whose object was less to discover and investigate truth, than to disseminate it; who, pursuing prejudice through all the haunts and asylums in which the clergy, the schools, governments, and privileged corporations had placed and protected it, made it their glory rather to eradicate popular errors, than add to the stores of human knowledge; thus aiding indirectly the progress of mankind, but in a way neither less arduous, nor less beneficial.

In England, Collins and Bolingbroke,[6] and in France, Bayle, Fontenelle, Montesquieu,[7] and the respective disciples of these celebrated men, combated on the side of truth with all the weapons that learning, wit and genius were able to furnish; assuming every shape, employing every tone, from the sublime and pathetic to pleasantry and satire, from the most labored investigation to an interesting romance or a fugitive essay; accommodating truth to those eyes that were too weak to bear its effulgence;[8] artfully caressing prejudice, the more easily to strangle it; never aiming a direct blow at errors, never attacking more than one at a time, nor even that one in all its fortresses; sometimes soothing the enemies of reason, by pretending to require in religion but a partial toleration, in politics but a limited freedom; siding with despotism, when their hostilities were directed against the priesthood, and with priests when their object was to unmask the despot; sapping the principle of both these pests of human happiness, striking at the root of both these baneful trees, while apparently wishing for the reform only of glaring abuses and seemingly confining themselves to lopping off the exuberant branches; sometimes representing to the partisans of liberty, that superstition, which covers despotism as with a coat of mail, is the first victim which ought to be sacrificed, the first chain that ought to be broken; and sometimes denouncing it to tyrants as the true enemy of their power, and alarming them with recitals of its hypocritical

---

[6] **Collins and Bolingbroke**: Anthony Collins (1676–1729), philosopher and free-thinker, and Henry St. John, 1st Viscount Bolingbroke (1678–1751), politician and political theorist.

[7] **Bayle, Fontenelle, Montesquieu**: Pierre Bayle (1647–1706), skeptical philosopher, author of the *Historical and Critical Dictionary*, a foundational Enlightenment text; Bernard de Fontenelle (1657–1757), secretary to the French Academy of Sciences and author of many texts, most notably *The Plurality of Worlds*, which championed the astronomical and mathematical discoveries of Galileo, Kepler, and Newton; Charles-Louis de Secondat, baron de La Brède et de Montesquieu (1689–1755), author of *The Persian Letters* and *The Spirit of the Laws* (see Document 17-4).

[8] **effulgence**: Radiance; brilliance.

conspiracies and its sanguinary vengeance. These writers, meanwhile, were uniform in their vindication of freedom of thinking and freedom of writing, as privileges upon which depended the salvation of mankind. They declaimed, without cessation or weariness, against the crimes both of fanatics and tyrants, exposing every feature of severity, of cruelty, of oppression, whether in religion, in administration, in manners, or in laws; commanding kings, soldiers, magistrates, and priests, in the name of truth and of nature, to respect the blood of mankind; calling upon them, with energy, to answer for the lives still profusely sacrificed in the field of battle or by the infliction of punishments, or else to correct this inhuman policy, this murderous insensibility; and lastly, in every place, and upon every occasion, rallying the friends of mankind with the cry of *reason, toleration, and humanity.*

Such was this new philosophy. Accordingly to those numerous classes that exist by prejudice, that live upon error, and that, but for the credulity of the people, would be powerless and extinct, it became a common object of detestation. It was every where received and every where persecuted, having kings, priests, nobles, and magistrates among the number of its friends as well as of its enemies. Its leaders, however, had almost always the art to elude the pursuits of vengeance, while they exposed themselves to hatred; and to screen themselves from persecution, while at the same time they sufficiently discovered [i.e., revealed] themselves not to lose the laurels of their glory.

It frequently happened that a government rewarded them with one hand, and with the other paid their enemies for calumniating[9] them, proscribed[10] them, yet was proud that fortune had honored its dominions with their birth; punished their opinions, and at the same time would have been ashamed not to be supposed a convert thereto.

These opinions were shortly embraced by every enlightened mind. By some they were openly avowed, by others concealed under an hypocrisy more or less apparent, according to the timidity or firmness of their characters, and accordingly as they were influenced by the contending interests of their profession or their vanity. At length the pride of ranging on the side of erudition became predominant, and sentiments were professed with the slightest caution, which, in the ages that preceded, had been concealed by the most profound dissimulation. . . .

---

[9] **calumniating**: Slandering.

[10] **proscribed**: Publicly ostracized or denounced.

The art of printing had been applied to so many subjects, books had so rapidly increased, they were so admirably adapted to every taste, every degree of information, and every situation of life, they afforded so easy and frequently so delightful an instruction, they had opened so many doors to, truth, which it was impossible ever to close again, that there was no longer a class or profession of mankind from whom the light of knowledge could be absolutely be excluded. Accordingly, though there still remained a multitude of individuals condemned to a forced or voluntary ignorance, yet was the barrier between the enlightened and unenlightened portioned [sic] of mankind nearly effaced, and an insensible gradation occupied the space which separates the two extremes of genius and stupidity.

Thus there prevailed a general knowledge of the natural rights of man; the opinion even that these rights are inalienable and imprescriptible; a decided partiality for freedom of thinking and writing; for the enfranchise-ment of industry and commerce; for the melioration of the condition of the people; for the repeal of penal statutes against religious nonconform-ists; for the abolition of torture and barbarous punishments; the desire of a milder system of criminal legislation; of a jurisprudence that should give to innocence a complete security: of a civil code more simple, as well as more conformable to reason and justice; indifference as to systems of reli-gion, considered at length as the offspring of superstition, or ranked in the number of political inventions; hatred of hypocrisy and fanaticism; con-tempt for prejudices; and lastly, a zeal for the propagation of truth. These principles, passing by degrees from the writings of philosophers into every class of society whose instruction was not confined to the catechism and the scriptures, became the common creed, the symbol and type of all men who were not idiots on the one hand, or, on the other, assertors of the policy of Machiavellism. In some countries these sentiments formed so nearly the general opinion, that the mass even of the people seemed ready to obey their dictates and act from their impulse.

The love of mankind, that is to say, that active compassion which interests itself in all the afflictions of the human race, and regards with horror whatever, in public institutions, in the acts of government, or the pursuits of individuals, adds to the inevitable misfortunes of nature, was the necessary result of these principles. It breathed in every work, it pre-vailed in every conversation, and its benign effects were already visible even in the laws and administration of countries subject to despotism.

The philosophers of different nations embracing, in their meditations, the entire interests of man, without distinction of country, of color, or of sect, formed, notwithstanding the difference of their speculative opinions, a firm and united phalanx against every description of error, every species of tyranny. Animated by the sentiment of universal philanthropy, they declaimed equally against injustice, whether existing in a foreign country or exercised by their own country against a foreign nation. They impeached in Europe the avidity which stained the shores of America, Africa, and Asia with cruelty and crimes. The philosophers of France and England gloried in assuming the appellation [sic], and fulfilling the duties, of *friends* to those very negroes whom their ignorant oppressors disdained to rank in the class of men. The French writers bestowed the tribute of their praise on the toleration granted in Russia and Sweden,[11] while Beccaria[12] refuted in Italy the barbarous maxims of Gallic jurisprudence. . . .

[*Having surveyed the progress achieved by the Enlightenment, Condorcet closed his work by speculating on the future of humankind:*]

It has never yet been supposed, that all the facts of nature, and all the means of acquiring precision in the computation and analysis of those facts, and all the connections of objects with each other, and all the possible combinations of ideas, can be exhausted by the human mind.

But, in proportion as facts are multiplied, man learns to class them, and reduce them to more general facts, at the same time that the instruments and methods for observing them, and registering them with exactness, acquire a new precision: . . . truths, the discovery of which was accompanied with the most laborious efforts, and which at first could not be comprehended but by men of the severest attention, will after a time be unfolded and proved in methods that are not above the efforts of an ordinary capacity. And thus should the methods that led to new combinations be exhausted, should their applications to questions, still unresolved, demand exertions greater than the time or the powers of the learned can bestow, more general methods, means more simple would soon come to their aid, and open a farther career to genius. . . .

---

[11] **the toleration granted in Russia and Sweden**: Religious toleration.

[12] **Beccaria**: Italian *philosophe* Cesare, Marquis of Beccaria-Bonesana (1738–1794), whose *An Essay on Crimes and Punishments* (1764) denounced torture and physical punishment, arguing that the purpose of punishments was "no other than to prevent the criminal from doing further injury to society, and to prevent others from committing the like offence. Such punishments, therefore, and such a mode of inflicting them, ought to be chosen, as will make the strongest and most lasting impressions on the minds of others, with the least torment to the body of the criminal."

By applying these general reflections to the different sciences, we might exhibit, respecting each, examples of this progressive improvement, which would remove all possibility of doubt as to the certainty of the further improvement that may be expected. We might indicate particularly in those which prejudice considers as nearest to being exhausted, the marks of an almost certain and early advance. We might illustrate the extent, the precision, the unity which must be added to the system comprehending all human knowledge, by a more general and philosophical application of the science of calculation to the individual branches of which that system is composed. We might show how favorable to our hopes a more universal instruction would prove, by which a greater number of individuals would acquire the elementary knowledge that might inspire them with a taste for a particular kind of study; and how much these hopes would be further heightened if this application to study were to be rendered still more extensive by a more general ease of circumstances. At present, in the most enlightened countries, scarcely do one in fifty of those whom nature has blessed with talents receive the necessary instruction for the development of them: how different would be the proportion in the case we are supposing? and of consequence how different the number of men destined to extend the horizon of the sciences?

We might show how much this equality of instruction, joined to the national equality we have supposed to take place, would accelerate those sciences, the advancement of which depends upon observations repeated in a greater number of instances, and extending over a larger portion of territory; how much benefit would be derived therefrom to mineralogy, botany, zoology, and the doctrine of meteors; in short, how infinite the difference between the feeble means hitherto enjoyed by these sciences, and which yet have led to useful and important truths, and the magnitude of those which man would then have it in his power to employ. . . .

And here we may observe, how much the abolition of the usages authorized by this prejudice, and of the laws which it has dictated, would tend to augment the happiness of families; to render common the virtues of domestic life, the fountain-head of all the others; to favor instruction, and, especially, to make it truly general, either because it would be extended to both sexes with greater equality, or because it cannot become general, even to men, without the concurrence of the mothers of families. . . .

All the causes which contribute to the improvement of the human species, all the means we have enumerated that insure its progress, must, from their very nature; exercise an influence always active, and acquire an extent for ever increasing. The proofs of this have been exhibited, and from their development in the work itself they will derive additional force: accordingly we may already conclude, that the perfectibility of man is indefinite. Meanwhile we have hitherto considered him as possessing only the same natural faculties, as endowed with the same organization. How much greater would be the certainty, how much wider the compass of our hopes, could we prove that these natural faculties themselves, that this very organization, are also susceptible of melioration? And this is the last question we shall examine.

The organic perfectibility or deterioration of the classes of the vegetable, or species of the animal kingdom, may be regarded as one of the general laws of nature.

This law extends itself to the human race; and it cannot be doubted that the progress of the sanative art, that the use of more wholesome food and more comfortable habitations, that a mode of life which shall develop the physical powers by exercise, without at the same time impairing them by excess; in fine, that the destruction of the two most active causes of deterioration, penury, and wretchedness on the one hand, and enormous wealth on the other, must necessarily tend to prolong the common duration of man's existence, and secure him a more constant health and a more robust constitution. It is manifest that the improvement of the practice of medicine, become more efficacious in consequence of the progress of reason and the social order, must in the end put a period to transmissible or contagious disorders, as well to those general maladies resulting from climate, aliments, and the nature of certain occupations. Nor would it be difficult to prove that this hope might be extended to almost every other malady, of which it is probable we shall hereafter discover the most remote causes. Would it even be absurd to suppose this quality of melioration in the human species as susceptible of an indefinite advancement; to suppose that a period must one day arrive when death will be nothing more than the effect either of extraordinary accidents, or of the slow and gradual decay of the vital powers; and that the duration of the middle space, of the interval between the birth of man and this decay, will itself have no assignable limit? Certainly man will not become immortal; but may not the distance between the moment in which he draws his first breath, and the common term when, in the course of nature, without malady or accident, he finds it impossible any longer to exist, be necessarily protracted?

READING AND DISCUSSION QUESTIONS

1. How does Condorcet characterize priests and despotic rulers? Why do you think he employs this characterization?

2. Why does Condorcet argue that gender inequality is "fatal even to the sex it favors"? Do you agree? Why or why not?

3. Surveying humankind's current condition, to what extent do you think that Condorcet's predictions, made more than two centuries ago, have been borne out?

COMPARATIVE QUESTIONS

1. Nicolaus Copernicus and Francis Bacon were separated by a lifetime (Copernicus died almost twenty years before Bacon was born). What similarities can you see between how they thought, and in what ways did they differ?

2. What differences do you see between Montesquieu's and Rousseau's theories about the nature of government and how it ought to interact with its citizens? Where do they seem to be in agreement?

3. Frederick the Great ruled a state in which "the legislative and executive powers [were] united in the same person." What would Montesquieu say to such an arrangement? How do you think Frederick would reply to Montesquieu's charge that under those conditions "there can be no liberty"?

4. Did Frederick the Great have an "enlightened mind" according to the criteria used by Condorcet? Why or why not?

5. What would Frederick think of Bossuet's divine-right monarchical theory (Document 16-2) and why? How would Rousseau respond to Frederick's and Bossuet's views on the monarchy?

CHAPTER 18

The Expansion of Europe

1650–1800

I n the early modern era (ca. 1500–1800), the economic policy followed by most European states was mercantilism, which, like the guild system, was protectionist and exclusionary. Mercantilism encouraged overseas colonization, of which the benefit was twofold: furnishing commodities that could not be produced in the parent country, and providing consumer markets for manufactured goods from the parent country. During the 1700s, mercantilism helped fuel a prolonged imperial conflict between France and Great Britain. The two rivals fought over North America, the Caribbean sugar islands, control of the Atlantic slave trade, and trade with India. The eventual outcome was the establishment of British rule over most of North America and much of India, as well as the involuntary transportation of millions of Africans to the Americas. By the latter half of the century, however, men like Adam Smith were criticizing the tenets of mercantilism, and opposition to the slave trade on humanitarian grounds began to emerge.

DOCUMENT 18-1

ARTHUR YOUNG

Political Essays Concerning the Present State of the British Empire

1772

Mercantilism remained the economic orthodoxy in Europe throughout the eighteenth century, and Arthur Young (1741–1820) was a representative of contemporary economic thought. He was a prolific author on numerous subjects, especially agriculture, and was a fervent advocate of the improvements

From Arthur Young, "Of Their Soil and Productions," in *Political Essays Concerning the State of the British Empire* (London: W. Strahan and T. Cadell, 1772), pp. 10–14.

described in the text here as the "agricultural revolution." At the same time, however, he firmly adhered to the belief that overseas colonies were essential to Britain's standing as a European power, and maintained that geography and other natural factors shaped national characteristics and destiny.

OF THEIR SOIL AND PRODUCTIONS.

In many cases the very being of a people depends on the productions of their soil. Those of the British isles are chiefly corn,[1] cattle, lead, tin, &c. such as tend to the maintenance of a numerous people, and yield them plenty of employment. Universal experience proves that such products are to be esteemed infinitely beyond diamonds, gold, and silver: Mines of such rich commodities are only found in the torrid zone;[2] that is, in the territories of people unable to defend them. But were they to be found amidst the most courageous people, there is great reason to believe they would change the characteristic of the nation; this has been nearly the case with Spain since she possessed herself of the Indies. But less valuable, although more necessary productions, conduce to industry and labor, employ greater numbers of people, and keep such people more virtuous. . . .

A most sensible modern author expresses himself in this subject with great justness: — "The soil of Switzerland, in general, is, perhaps, that very sort of soil, which a sober, sensible, industrious nation ought to wish for. It pours not forth its vegetable productions spontaneously; but there is a force of nature in it sufficient to produce great return, its virtue and diligence are the cultivators. The sagacious Machiavel[li] seems to think that a rich soil tends to lessen the industry of people that inhabit it; and if a nation like that of the Switzers [Swiss] is contented with the portion of land it enjoys, and meditates no future acquisitions of territory, then a tract of a earth which yields its productions with *some difficulty* will, in the long run, make its inhabitants a wealthy, happy, and powerful community. A rich soil easy to be cultivated, naturally inclines the inhabitants to indolence and remissness: and hence it is that travellers of the best sense have remarked that the cause of there being so many savage nations in America, is the fertility of the earth, and the vast supplies of animal food without care or trouble." . . . The country of the Grisons,[3] who have *almost no soil at all*, is well peopled and they live at their ease, whereas Lombardy, the

---

[1] **corn**: Generic term in Britain for grains.

[2] **torrid zone**: Areas around the Equator; the tropics.

[3] **Grisons**: Inhabitants of the easternmost of the Swiss cantons, or independent states.

finest in the world, has nothing but poverty and beggary over the whole. . . . Nature, with a small variation of more or less, has been almost equally bountiful to all her *industrious* children in all places. I lay some stress on the word industrious, because it is evident that the richest soils in themselves, if the cultivator is indolent and unattentive, do not always produce the largest and best crops. In this sense let us compare England and Sweden with Italy and Louisiana, and we shall soon find that the scale preponderates in favor of art and labor.

The soil of the British isles . . . will, in point of fertility, bear no comparison with the greatest part of Europe: But this deficiency is (as here proved) no inconsiderable excellency: The soil of Spain is so rich, that its husbandmen raise the brightest and firmest wheat in Christendom, and yet have no idea of destroying weeds, and scratch the ground instead of plowing it: But compare the English and Spanish husbandry — What a contrast! The Spaniards have scarce ever a sufficiency of bread.

The soil of these kingdoms is, upon the whole, what would be considered in all the southern parts of Europe as very indifferent. England and Ireland contain vast tracts of what her own inhabitants reckon bad; and Scotland vastly more. The medium of the three is such a soil as requires most unremitting diligence to render fertile in any considerable degree: We ought not therefore to conclude that it is more peculiar to the production of corn than that of our neighbors. . . .

I have insisted thus much on corn, as it is by far the most important product of all others. It is that which maintains the most people, and renders such people the most independent. But besides corn, the British isles are extremely happy in the mines with which they abound. Those of iron might be considerable, if necessity obliged the working [of] them; the importance of this commodity needs no enlarging on. Those of copper, lead, and tin are of great consequence, and the latter a monopoly;[4] but none of them are perhaps of equal value with those of coal; for by means of such vast plenty of this kind of fuel, the less quantity of wood is necessary, and of course the more land is applied to the production of corn: This is an advantage not equally boasted by any country in Europe; and in France the want of it is so heavily felt, that severe laws are made against decreasing the quantity of land covered with wood, which is necessarily a bar to the raising of plenty of corn. Wood is the worst crop a soil can support, for it is not only useless in the point of feeding people — but at the same time employs scarce any; grass employs but few, but then it feeds

---

[4] **the latter a monopoly**: Virtually all of Europe's tin came from British mines.

many. What a prodigious beneficial production therefore is coal! which yields an opportunity of converting such vast tracks of woods into arable lands.

It may not be amiss to observe likewise in this place, that mines of such bulky and little comparatively valuable commodities, as I have just mentioned, are by no means open to the objections so rationally formed against those of precious stones, gold and silver. The former yield no such compendious method of becoming rich, but employ a numerous body of hardy, daring and valuable men, to dig up their products; many more in the carriage and manufacturing, and when the whole process is completed, the return of profit is far from being so great, as to spread such a spirit of indolence as universally attends the superior produce of more valuable mines.

The soils and productions of the detached parts of the British dominions are as various as the climates in which they are situated; but the value of them can only be estimated with a view to their usefulness in a commercial light; for the European islands producing every thing necessary for the life of man, the colonies were planted for superfluous commodities, which must be procured by trade of other nations, if not produced at home: The American dominions will in this light be found of infinite consequence. The West India islands produce sugar, rum, coffee, and a long train of most valuable *et ceteras*. The southern continental settlements, rice, indigo, cotton, silk, vines, hemp, and flax, &c. The middle ones, tobacco and iron mines and both the last a vast variety of prodigiously valuable timbers of all kinds. Further north, I say nothing of the soil, but the sea is filled with an inexhaustible treasure in the cod fish. If we take a view of the whole earth's productions, we shall find none of consequence beyond these mentioned but spices and tea, both of which there is the greatest reason to believe might be produced in some of the above named American dominions.

It is not necessary to examine here into the diversity of opinions relative to particular parts of these American dominions, which are most proper for the best productions; all accounts agree that they are to be produced in vast quantities in them, however they may vary in other respects.

It may be asserted, without the imputation of a paradox, that the detached parts of the British dominions are of infinitely greater advantage to the principal than those of Spain; but at the same time it must be confessed, that the inferiority of the latter is owing to the possession of their mines; were it not for these, their American dominions most undoubtedly might, under *proper regulations*, be of equal, at least, if not superior benefit.

I lay some stress on the *regulations*, as the contrast between the climate of Old and New Spain is not so strong as between the British isles and some of the British colonies, from whence it results, that greater precautions and more political management are necessary with the former than with the latter. Nor are the settlements of the French, Portuguese, or Dutch to be compared with the British ones, in point of soil and products.

READING AND DISCUSSION QUESTIONS

1. What sorts of prejudices regarding other countries and peoples does Young reveal? Why do you think he held such views?

2. Why does Young regard coal mines as more valuable than those producing iron, tin, copper, precious metals, and gemstones?

3. Why does Young regard the American colonies as being "of infinite consequence" to Great Britain?

DOCUMENT 18-2

The Guild System in Germany

1704–1719

Guilds were closed, regulated craft organizations that originated in medieval towns. Many crafts, such as metalsmithing, textile production, and baking, were guild monopolies throughout much of medieval and early modern Europe. To attain full guild membership one typically had to spend several years in training, first as an apprentice and then as a journeyman. With few exceptions, women were barred from guild membership; yet, as these pictures reveal, they played active roles in preindustrial production. Many historians therefore refer to the "family" or "domestic" economy as the prevalent form of economic organization prior to the rise of the factory system.

The first image depicts bakers at work; the male in the background is kneading dough, the woman in the center is adding water to the dough, and

From Franciscus Philippus Florinus, *Oeconomus prudens et legalis, oder Allgemeiner Klug- und Rechts-verständiger Haus-Vatter* (Nuremberg, Frankfurt, and Leipzig: Christoph Riegel, 1704–1719), pp. 528, 1191.

the woman on the left is hauling a basket containing baked loaves. The oven is visible to the left, and loaves line the shelves behind. The second image shows basket makers, where again, both sexes are depicted at work at similar tasks. The woman in the background to the left appears to be churning butter.

READING AND DISCUSSION QUESTIONS

1. What do these illustrations suggest about the sexual division of labor in preindustrial households?

2. Judging by these pictures, what sorts of limitations might be inherent in the guild system of production?

> DOCUMENT 18-3

ADAM SMITH

The Wealth of Nations

1776

Adam Smith (1723–1790) is widely regarded as the father of modern economics. His most famous work, An Inquiry into the Nature and Causes of the Wealth of Nations *(1776), from which the following excerpts are drawn, was a sustained critique of mercantilism. Smith was not the first economist to advocate free trade, but he was certainly the most famous and persuasive. At the time* The Wealth of Nations *appeared, government policies throughout Europe were still firmly mercantilistic, but over the following decades his arguments gained more adherents, especially in Britain, and his theories formed the basis for classical liberal economics.*

BOOK I, CHAPTER 1. *OF THE DIVISION OF LABOR*

The greatest improvement in the productive powers of labor, and the greater part of the skill, dexterity, and judgment with which it is anywhere directed, or applied, seem to have been the effects of the division of labor. . . .

To take an example, . . . the trade of the pin-maker; a workman not educated to this business, . . . nor acquainted with the use of the machinery employed in it . . . , could scarce, perhaps, with his utmost industry, make one pin in a day, and certainly could not make twenty. But in the way in which this business is now carried on, not only the whole work is a

From Adam Smith, *An Inquiry into the Nature and Causes of the Wealth of Nations*, vol. 1, ed. James E. Thorold Rodgers (Oxford: Clarendon Press, 1869), pp. 5–7, 9, 12, 14–15, 30–31, 57–59, 62–65, 125, 128, 136.

peculiar trade, but it is divided into a number of branches, of which the greater part are likewise peculiar trades. One man draws out the wire, another straights it, a third cuts it, a fourth points it, a fifth grinds it at the top for receiving, the head; to make the head requires two or three distinct operations; to put it on is a peculiar business, to whiten the pins is another; it is even a trade by itself to put them into the paper [container in which they are sold]; and the important business of making a pin is, in this manner, divided into about eighteen distinct operations, which, in some manufactories, are all performed by distinct hands, though in others the same man will sometimes perform two or three of them. I have seen a small manufactory of this kind where ten men only were employed, and where some of them consequently performed two or three distinct operations. But though they were very poor, and therefore but indifferently accommodated with the necessary machinery, they could, when they exerted themselves, make among them about twelve pounds of pins in a day. There are in a pound upwards of four thousand pins of a middling size. Those ten persons, therefore, could make among them upwards of forty-eight thousand pins in a day. Each person, therefore, making a tenth part of forty-eight thousand pins, might be considered as making four thousand eight hundred pins in a day. But if they had all wrought separately and independently, and without any of them having been educated to this peculiar business, they certainly could not each of them have made twenty, perhaps not one pin in a day; that is, certainly, not the two hundred and fortieth, perhaps not the four thousand eight hundredth part of what they are at present capable of performing, in consequence of a proper division and combination of their different operations. . . .

The division of labor, so far as it can be introduced, occasions, in every art, a proportionable increase of the productive powers of labor. The separation of different trades and employments from one another seems to have taken place in consequence of this advantage. This separation, too, is generally called furthest in those countries which enjoy the highest degree of industry and improvement; what is the work of one man in a rude state of society being generally that of several in an improved one. . . .

This great increase of the quantity of work which, in consequence of the division of labor, the same number of people are capable of performing, is owing to three different circumstances; first, to the increase of dexterity in every particular workman; secondly, to the saving of the time which is commonly lost in passing from one species of work to another; and lastly, to the invention of a great number of machines which facilitate and abridge labor, and enable one man to do the work of many. . . .

It is the great multiplication of the productions of all the different arts, in consequence of the division of labor, which occasions, in a well-governed society, that universal opulence which extends itself to the lowest ranks of the people. Every workman has a great quantity of his own work to dispose of beyond what he himself has occasion for; and every other workman being exactly in the same situation, he is enabled to exchange a great quantity of his own goods for a great quantity, or, what comes to the same thing, for the price of a great quantity of theirs. He supplies them abundantly with what they have occasion for, and they accommodate him as amply with what he has occasion for, and a general plenty diffuses itself through all the different ranks of the society. . . .

Book I, Chapter 2. *Of the Principle Which Gives Occasion to the Division of Labor*

This division of labor, from which so many advantages are derived, is not originally the effect of any human wisdom, which foresees and intends that universal opulence to which it gives occasion. It is the necessary, though very slow and gradual consequence of a certain propensity in human nature which has in view no such extensive utility; the propensity to truck, barter, and exchange one thing for another. . . .

Man has almost constant occasion for the help of his brethren, and it is in vain for him to expect it from their benevolence only. He will be more likely to prevail if he can interest their self-love in his favor, and show them that it is for their own advantage to do for him what he requires of them. Whoever offers to another a bargain of any kind, proposes to do this. Give me that which I want, and you shall have this which you want, is the meaning of every such offer; and it is in this manner that we obtain from one another the far greater art of those good offices which we stand in need of. It is not from the benevolence of the butcher, the brewer, or the baker that we expect our dinner, but from their regard to their own interest. . . .

Book I, Chapter 5. *Of the Real and Nominal Price of Commodities, or Their Price in Labor, and Their Price in Money*

Every man is rich or poor according to the degree in which he can afford to enjoy the necessaries, conveniences, and amusements of human life. But after the division of labor has once thoroughly taken place, it is but a very small part of these with which a man's own labor can supply him. The far greater part of them he must derive from the labor of other people, and he must be rich or poor according to the quantity of that labor which he can command, or which he can afford to purchase. The value of any commodity, therefore, to the person who possesses it, and who means not to use or consume it himself, but to exchange it for other commodities, is equal to the quantity of labor which it enables him to purchase or command. Labor, therefore, is the real measure of the exchangeable value of all commodities.

The real price of everything, what everything really costs to the man who wants to acquire it, is the toil and trouble of acquiring it. What everything is really worth to the man who has acquired it, and who wants to dispose of it or exchange it for something else, is the toil and trouble which it can save to himself, and which it can impose upon other people. What is bought with money or with goods is purchased by labor as much as what we acquire by the toil of our own body. That money or those goods indeed save us this toil. . . .

BOOK I, CHAPTER 7. *OF THE NATURAL AND MARKET PRICE OF COMMODITIES*

There is in every society or neighborhood an ordinary or average rate both of wages and profit in every different employment of labor and stock. This rate is naturally regulated, as I shall show hereafter, partly by the general circumstances of the society, their riches or poverty, their advancing, stationary, or declining condition; and partly by the particular nature of each employment.

There is likewise in every society or neighborhood an ordinary or average rate of rent, which is regulated too, as I shall show hereafter, partly by the general circumstances of the society or neighborhood in which the land is situated, and partly by the natural or improved fertility of the land.

These ordinary or average rates may be called the natural rates of wages, profit, and rent, at the time and place in which they commonly prevail.

When the price of any commodity is neither more nor less than what is sufficient to pay the rent of the land, the wages of the labor, and the profits of the stock employed in raising, preparing, and bringing it to market, according to their natural rates, the commodity is then sold for what may be called its natural price. . . .

Though the price, therefore, which leaves him this profit is not always the lowest at which a dealer may sometimes sell his goods, it is the lowest at which he is likely to sell them for any considerable time; at least where there is perfect liberty, or where he may change his trade as often as he pleases.

The actual price at which any commodity is commonly sold is called its market price. It may either be above, or below, or exactly the same with its natural price. . . .

When the quantity of any commodity which is brought to market falls short of the effectual demand, all those who are willing to pay the whole value of the rent, wages, and profit, which must be paid in order to bring it thither, cannot be supplied with the quantity which they want. Rather than want it altogether, some of them will be willing to give more. . . .

When the quantity brought to market exceeds the effectual demand, it cannot be all sold to those who are willing to pay the whole value of the rent, wages, and profit, which must be paid in order to bring it thither. Some part must be sold to those who are willing to pay less, and the low price which they give for it must reduce the price of the whole. . . .

When the quantity brought to market is just sufficient to supply the effectual demand, and no more, the market price naturally comes to be either exactly, or as nearly as can be judged of, the same with the natural price. The whole quantity upon hand can be disposed of for this price, and cannot be disposed of for more. . . .

Such fluctuations affect both the value and the rate either of wages or of profit, according as the market happens to be either overstocked or understocked with commodities or with labor; with work done, or with work to be done. . . .

When by an increase in the effectual demand, the market price of some particular commodity happens to rise a good deal above the natural price, those who employ their stocks in supplying that market are generally careful to conceal this change. If it was commonly known, their great profit would tempt so many new rivals to employ their stocks in the same way that, the effectual demand being fully supplied, the market price would soon be reduced to the natural price, and perhaps for some time even below it. If the market is at a great distance from the residence of those who supply it, they may sometimes be able to keep the secret for several years together, and may so long enjoy their extraordinary profits without any new rivals. Secrets of this kind, however, it must be acknowledged, can seldom be long kept; and the extraordinary profit can last very little longer than they are kept. . . .

A monopoly granted either to an individual or to a trading company has the same effect as a secret in trade or manufactures. The monopolists, by keeping the market constantly understocked, by never fully supplying the effectual demand, sell their commodities much above the natural price, and raise their emoluments, whether they consist in wages or profit, greatly above their natural rate. . . .

The exclusive privileges of corporations, statutes of apprenticeship, and all those laws which restrain in particular employments the competition to a smaller number than might otherwise go into them, have the same tendency, though in a less degree. They are a sort of enlarged monopolies, and may frequently, for ages together, and in whole classes of employments, keep up the market price of particular commodities above the natural price, and maintain both the wages of the labor and the profits of the stock employed about them somewhat above their natural rate.

Such enhancements of the market price may last as long as the regulations of police which give occasion to them. . . .

BOOK I, CHAPTER 10. *OF WAGES AND PROFIT IN THE DIFFERENT EMPLOYMENTS OF LABOR AND STOCK*

First, the policy of Europe occasions a very important inequality in the whole of the advantages and disadvantages of the different employments of labor and stock, by restraining the competition in some employments to a smaller number than might otherwise be disposed to enter into them.

The exclusive privileges of corporations, or guilds, are the principal means it makes use of for this purpose. . . .

The property which every man has in his own labor, as it is the original foundation of all other property, so it is the most sacred and inviolable. The patrimony of a poor man lies in the strength and dexterity of his hands; and to hinder him from employing this strength and dexterity of his hands; and to hinder him from employing this strength and dexterity in what manner he thinks proper without injury to his neighbor is a plain violation of this most sacred property. It is a manifest encroachment upon the just liberty both of the workman and of those who might be disposed to employ him. . . .

The pretense that corporations are necessary for the better government of the trade is without any foundation. The real and effectual discipline which is exercised over a workman is not that of his corporation, but that of his customers. It is the fear of losing their employment which restrains his frauds and corrects his negligence. An exclusive corporation necessarily weakens the force of this discipline.

READING AND DISCUSSION QUESTIONS

1. On what grounds does Smith extol the division of labor? Can you think of any drawbacks that might result from such a form of labor organization?

2. What, according to Smith, motivates human activity? What are the consequences of this motive?

3. What, according to Smith, gives goods and services their value?

4. Explain what Smith means by "natural" and "market" prices. Why are the two often not the same?

5. What is Smith's attitude toward monopolies and why?

VIEWPOINTS

Trade and Empire in Africa and Asia

DOCUMENT 18-4

CAPTAIN WILLEM BOSMAN

On the Slave Trade in Guinea

ca. 1700

African American slavery was key to the economic development of not only the southern colonies of British North America but also the sugar industry in the West Indies and Brazil. Indeed, most of the slaves transported to the Americas during the period 1620–1850 went to those destinations (rather than to North America) due chiefly to the appalling mortality rate among slaves engaged in sugar production. As enslaved Africans died, more were imported to replenish the labor force. During the seventeenth century, the Dutch dominated the Atlantic slave trade. Captain Willem Bosman was sent to West Africa as a representative of the Dutch West India Company. He spent fourteen years there and published a detailed account of the trade in human beings.

Not a few in our country fondly imagine that parents here sell their children, men their wives, and one brother the other. But those who think so,

---

From Willem Bosman, "A New and Accurate Description . . ." (London: 1721), in *The Atlantic Slave Trade*, ed. David Northrup (Lexington, Mass.: D. C. Heath, 1994), pp. 72–73.

do deceive themselves; for this never happens on any other account but that of necessity, or some great crime; but most of the slaves that are offered to us, are prisoners of war, which are sold by the victors as their booty.

When these slaves come to Fida,[5] they are put in prison all together; and when we treat concerning buying them, they are all brought out together in a large plain; where, by our surgeons, whose province it is, they are thoroughly examined, even to the smallest member, and that naked both men and women, without the least distinction or modesty. . . .

The invalids and the maimed being thrown out, as I have told you, the remainder are numbered, and it is entered who delivered them. In the meanwhile, a burning iron, with the arms or name of the companies, lies in the fire, with which ours are marked on the breast. This is done that we may distinguish them from the slaves of the English, French, or others (which are also marked with their mark), and to prevent the Negroes [i.e., the traders] exchanging them for worse, at which they have a good hand. I doubt not but this trade seems very barbarous to you, but since it is followed by mere necessity, it must go on; but we yet take all possible care that they are not burned too hard, especially the women, who are more tender than the men.

We are seldom long detained in the buying of these slaves, because their price is established, the women being one fourth or fifth part cheaper than the men. The disputes which we generally have with the owners of these slaves are, that we will not give them such goods as they ask for them, especially the *boesies* [cowry shells] (as I have told you, the money of this country) of which they are very fond, though we generally make a division on this head, in order to make one part of the goods help off another; because those slaves which are paid for in *boesies*, cost the company one half more than those bought with other goods. . . .

When we have agreed with the owners of the slaves, they are returned to their prison; where, from that time forwards, they are kept at our charge, cost us two pence a day a slave; which serves to subsist them, like our criminals, on bread and water: so that to save charges, we send them on board our ships with the very first opportunity, before which their masters strip them of all they have on their backs; so that they come to us stark naked, as well women as men: in which condition they are obliged to continue, if the master of the ship is not so charitable (which he commonly is) as to bestow something on them to cover their nakedness.

---

[5] **Fida**: It is not clear to what place Bosman is referring; Fida is in Chad, hundreds of miles from the West African coast, where slaves were loaded onboard ships.

You would really wonder to see how these slaves live on board; for though their number sometimes amounts to six or seven hundred, yet by the careful management of our masters of ships, they are so [well] regulated, that it seems incredible. And in this particular our nation exceeds all other Europeans; for as the French, Portuguese, and English slave-ships are always foul and stinking; on the contrary, ours are for the most part clean and neat.

The slaves are fed three times a day with indifferent good victuals, and much better than they eat in their own country. Their lodging place is divided into two parts; one of which is appointed for the men, the other for the women, each sex being kept apart. Here they lie as close together as it is possible for them to be crowded.

READING AND DISCUSSION QUESTIONS

1. What does Bosman's matter-of-fact description of his activities as a slave trader suggest about contemporary European attitudes toward slavery?

2. What most shocks you in the description of slave trading in West Africa, and why is it shocking?

3. Which of the author's statements suggest that he might have been responding to criticism of the slave trade? From where (or whom) might that criticism have come?

DOCUMENT 18-5

ROBERT, FIRST BARON CLIVE
Speech in the House of Commons on India
1772

Robert Clive (1725–1774) was born into an English minor gentry family. Apprenticed as a "writer" (clerk) in the British East India Company, he arrived in India in 1744, in the midst of the War of the Austrian Succession.

From Speech given the House of Commons, March 30, 1772, from *The Parliamentary History of England from the Earliest Period to the Year 1803*, vol. 17 (London: T. C. Hansard, 1806–1820), pp. 354–357.

The conflict offered opportunities for bold and ambitious men like Clive,
and his bravery won him a commission in the company's army. In 1757 he
defeated an Indian army at the Battle of Plassey, and in 1765 received as a
gift from the Mughal emperor the province of Bengal, one of the richest and
most populous in India. Clive was thus responsible for transforming the East
India Company from a trading entity into a governmental one that directly
ruled Indian territory. Clive also reaped a fortune in the aftermath of Plassey
yet defended his wealth against those who denounced his greed.

Indostan [India] was always an absolute despotic government. The inhabitants, especially of Bengal, in inferior stations, are servile, mean [poor],
submissive, and humble. In superior stations, they are luxurious, effemi-
nate, tyrannical, treacherous, venal, cruel. The country of Bengal is called,
by way of distinction, the paradise of the earth. It not only abounds with
the necessaries of life to such a degree, as to furnish a great part of India
with its superfluity, but it abounds in very curious and valuable manufactures, sufficient not only for its own use, but for the use of the whole globe.
The silver of the west and the gold of the east have for many years been
pouring into that country, and goods only have been sent out in return.
This has added to the luxury and extravagance of Bengal.

From time immemorial it has been the custom of that country, for an
inferior never to come into the presence of a superior without a present.
It begins at the nabob,[6] and ends at the lowest man that has an inferior.
The nabob has told me, that the small presents he received amounted to
£300,000 a year; and I can believe him; because I know that I might have
received as much during my last government. The Company's servants
have ever been accustomed to receive presents. Even before we took part
in the country troubles, when our possessions were very confined and limited, the governor and others used to receive presents; and I will take upon
me to assert, that there has not been an officer commanding his Majesty's
fleet; nor an officer commanding his Majesty's army; not a governor, not
a member of council, not any other person, civil or military, in such a
station as to have connection with the country government, who has not
received presents. With regard to Bengal, there they flow in abundance
indeed. Let the House figure to itself a country consisting of 15 millions of
inhabitants, a revenue of four millions sterling, and a trade in proportion.
By progressive steps the Company have become sovereigns of that empire.

---

[6] **nabob:** More properly, nawab; a provincial ruler.

Can it be supposed that their servants will refrain from advantages so obviously resulting from their situation? The Company's servants, however, have not been the authors of those acts of violence and oppression, of which it is the fashion to accuse them. Such crimes are committed by the natives of the country acting as their agents and for the most part without their knowledge. . . . Let us for a moment consider the nature of the education of a young man who goes to India. The advantages arising from the Company's service are now very generally known; and the great object of every man is to get his son appointed a writer to Bengal; which is usually at the age of 16. His parents and relations represent to him how certain he is of making a fortune; that my lord such a one, and my lord such a one, acquired so much money in such a time; and Mr. such a one, and Mr. such a one, so much in such a time. Thus are their principles corrupted at their very setting out, and as they generally go a good many together, they inflame one another's expectations to such a degree, in the course of the voyage, that they fix upon a period for their return[7] before their arrival.

Let us now take a view of one of these writers arrived in Bengal, and not worth a groat.[8] As soon as he lands, a banyan,[9] worth perhaps £100,000. desires he may have the honor of serving this young gentleman, at 4s. 6d.[10] per month. The Company has provided chambers for him, but they are not good enough: the banyan finds better. The young man takes a walk about the town, he observes that other writers, arrived only a year before him, live in splendid apartments or have houses of their own, ride upon fine prancing Arabian horses, and in palanqueens[11] and chaises; that they keep seraglios,[12] make entertainments, and treat with champagne and claret. When he returns he tells the banyan what he has observed. The banyan assures him he may soon arrive at the same good fortune; he furnishes him with money; he is then at his mercy. The advantages of the banyan advance with the rank of his master, who in acquiring one fortune generally spends three. But this is not the worst of it: he is in a state of dependence under the banyan, who commits acts of violence and oppression, as his interest prompts him to, under the pretended sanction and

---

[7] **they fix upon a period for their return**: In other words, the date by which they expect to return to Britain, fortune in hand.

[8] **groat**: Four pence.

[9] **banyan**: Indian merchant or trader.

[10] **4s. 6d.**: Four shillings, six pence; a modest sum.

[11] **palanqueen**: More properly, *palanquin*: an enclosed litter, seating one, carried by four or six servants.

[12] **seraglio**: Harem.

authority of the Company's servant. Hence, Sir, arises the clamor against the English gentlemen in India. But look at them in a retired situation, when returned to England, when they are no longer nabobs and sovereigns of the east: see if there be any thing tyrannical in their disposition towards their inferiors: see if they are not good and humane masters: Are they not charitable? Are they not benevolent? Are they not generous? Are they not hospitable? If they are, thus far, not contemptible members of society, and if in all their dealings between man and man, their conduct is strictly honorable: if, in short, there has not yet been one character found amongst them sufficiently flagitious[13] for Mr. Foote[14] to exhibit on the theatre in the Haymarket, may we not conclude, that if they have erred, it has been because they were men, placed in situations subject to little or no control?

READING AND DISCUSSION QUESTIONS

1. What does Clive's description of Indian character suggest about his racial attitudes?
2. How does Clive justify out-and-out bribery and corruption in Indian government, and the East India Company's enrichment by that means?
3. How does Clive excuse the behavior of East India Company employees and exonerate them of "flagitious" actions?

COMPARATIVE QUESTIONS

1. What do you think Smith's attitude was toward guilds like those depicted in the illustrations, and why?
2. What do you think Smith's attitude toward the colonies extolled by Young and Clive was, and why?

---

[13] **flagitious**: Wicked, villainous.
[14] **Mr. Foote**: Playwright and theater impresario Samuel Foote (1721–1777), who in 1772 staged a play at Haymarket Theater titled *The Nabob*, a satire about the East India Company.

3. How would India, as described by Clive, conform to Young's views about the proper functions of colonies?

4. What points of similarity can you detect between Bosman's views of Africans and Clive's of Indians? What differences?

5. What do you think Condorcet (Document 17-6) would have to say about Clive's attitude toward Indians?

CHAPTER 19

The Changing Life of the People

1700–1800

While there are abundant sources about modern life, from letters and diaries to financial records and opinion polls (to mention only a few), other periods are markedly less recorded. For the social historian, the task of understanding how the "ordinary people" of early modern Europe lived — to say nothing of what they thought — is quite challenging. Most of the nonelite in the seventeenth and eighteenth centuries were illiterate and thus left no self-composed evidence of their existence. Historians studying the period have to rely on the limited writings left by common people or try to interpret their lives through the lens of the better-off classes. Nonetheless, we have considerable evidence about many aspects of everyday life, including attitudes about mortality, religious belief, children and education, and the state of medical knowledge.

DOCUMENT 19-1

EDMOND WILLIAMSON

Births and Deaths in an English Gentry Family

1709–1720

Little is known of Edmond Williamson. He lived in Bedfordshire, one of the "Home Counties" surrounding London. The mere fact that he was literate and kept a diary suggests that he was a man of means, as does his mention of the servants present at his wife's childbirths. Despite their brevity, his diary entries reveal that proximity of death was a central fact of life, even

---

From Edmond Williamson, "An Account of the Birth of My Children by My Second Wife (1709–1720)," in *The Past Speaks*, 2d ed., ed. Walter Arnstein (Lexington, Mass.: D. C. Heath, 1993), 2:33–34.

in the lives of the affluent. Three of Williamson's seven children died at birth or shortly afterward, and a fourth succumbed to smallpox before the age of three. Williamson's wife died as well, just a month after the birth of her last child.

1709

March 29. My wife fell into labor and a little after 9 in the morning was delivered of a son. Present: aunt Taylor, cousin White, sister Smith, cousin Clarkson, widow Hern, Mrs. Howe, midwife, Mr[s]. Wallis, nurse, Mrs. Holms, Eleanor Hobbs, servants.

April 4. He was baptised by Doctor Battle by the name of John. . . .

[April] 16. The child died about 1 o'clock in the morning.

1711

Sept. 17. My said wife was delivered of a son just before 4 in the morning. Present: Mrs. Thomas Molyneux's lady and maid, Mrs. Mann, midwife, Margaret Williamson, nurse, Susan Nuthall, servant.

Oct. 4. He was baptised by Mr. Trabeck by the name of Talbot after my grandmother's name. Sir John Talbot and John Pulteny esquire were gossips [godfathers], with my sister Smith godmother. . . .

1713

June 9. About 8 at night my said wife began her labor.

[June] 10. Half an hour after 1 in the morning was brought to bed of a son. Present: Mrs. Molyneux, Mrs. Bisset, Mrs. Mann, midwife, Nurse Williamson, Susan Nuthall and Betty Ginger, servants.

[June] 30. Baptised by Mr. Mompesson of Mansfield by the name of Edmond. . . .

1715

March 7. My said wife was brought to bed of a daughter 10 minutes before 6 in the morning. Present: Mrs. Molyneux, Mrs. Mann, midwife, Nurse Williamson, Mary Evans, Mary Cole and Mary Wheeler, servants.

[March] 29. Was baptised by Dr. Mandivel, chancellor of Lincoln, by the name of Christian.

1716

March 9. My wife was delivered of a daughter at 7 at night. Present: aunt Taylor, Mrs. Molyneux, Mrs. Oliver, Mrs. Mann, midwife, Mary Smith, nurse, Jane Kensey, and Mary Wheeler, servants.

[March] 31. Was baptised by Mr. Widmore, the reader of St. Margaret's, by the name of Elizanna. . . . Registered in St. Margaret's, Westminster, as all the rest were.

April 27. Died, was buried in the new chapel yard in the Broadway.

1718

Jan. 21. [Mrs. Williamson:] I was brought to bed of a son about 2 in the morning, Mrs. Mann, midwife, nurse Chatty, dry-nurse, present; Mrs. Taylor, Mrs. White and Mrs. Molyneux, Jane Beadle; servants: Mary Wells, Jane Griffith, Edmond Kinward. He was baptised by Mr. Widmore, reader of St. Margaret's, Westminster, by the name of Francis. . . .

1719

Feb. 21. [Mrs. Williamson:] I was brought to bed of a son between 6 and 7 in the evening, Mrs. Mann, midwife, nurse Chatty, dry-nurse; present: aunt Taylor, Mrs. Molyneux and Jane Beadle; servants: Rebecca Shippy, Betty Hall and Mathew Dowect.

March 7. He was baptised by Mr. Widmore, reader of St. Margaret's, Westminster, by the name of William. . . .

[Undated] Died and buried at Hadley.

1720

June. My wife brought to bed of a daughter, but the child did not live a minute.

July 21. My wife died and was buried at Isleworth.

Sept. 9. [Francis] died of the smallpox at Nurse Ward's.

READING AND DISCUSSION QUESTIONS

1. What does the Williamsons' account of the births of their children suggest about pregnancy in early eighteenth century England? What factors would account for this?

2. What does Williamson's record of the deaths of his children suggest about the incidence of infant mortality in early modern Europe?

3. Apart from labor, births, and deaths, what else did Williamson record, and what does this tell us?

4. In what ways did the ritual of childbirth in early-eighteenth-century England differ from that in modern developed countries? What could account for the differences?

DOCUMENT 19-2

JOHN LOCKE
Some Thoughts Concerning Education
1693

John Locke's (1632–1704) intellectual curiosity and influence ranged wide, from political theory to the nature of human consciousness, from economics to, in this piece, education. Originally composed as a series of letters to a friend who had sought Locke's advice concerning his son's education, "Some Thoughts" constitutes a companion piece to his "Essay Concerning Human Understanding" (1690), in which he argued that the mind at birth was a "blank slate" upon which ideas were imprinted, and that all knowledge was derived from sensory experience and reasoning. These concepts were at the core of Enlightenment beliefs in human rationality and progress.

The well educating of their children is so much the duty and concern of parents, and the welfare and prosperity of the nation so much depends on it, that I would have every one lay it seriously to heart; and after having well examined and distinguished what fancy, custom, or reason advises in the case, set his helping hand to promote every where that way of training up youth, with regard to their several conditions, which is the easiest, shortest, and likeliest to produce virtuous, useful, and able men in their distinct callings; tho' that most to be taken care of is the gentleman's calling. For if

From *English Philosophers of the Seventeenth and Eighteenth Centuries* (New York: P. F. Collier & Son, 1910), pp. 6–7, 9, 11, 28–29, 33–36, 39, 53–54, 111, 123, 136, 179, 184–85.

those of that rank are by their education once set right, they will quickly bring all the rest into order. . . .

A sound mind in a sound body, is a short, but full description of a happy state in this world. He that has these two, has little more to wish for; and he that wants either of them, will be but little the better for any thing else. Men's happiness or misery is most part of their own making. He, whose mind directs not wisely, will never take the right way; and he, whose body is crazy and feeble, will never be able to advance in it. I confess, there are some men's constitutions of body and mind so vigorous, and well framed by nature, that they need not much assistance from others; but by the strength of their natural genius, they are from their cradles carried towards what is excellent; and by the privilege of their happy constitutions, are able to do wonders. But examples of this kind are but few; and I think I may say, that of all the men we meet with, nine parts of ten are what they are, good or evil, useful or not, by their education. 'Tis that which makes the great difference in mankind. The little, or almost insensible impressions on our tender infancies, have very important and lasting consequences: and there 'tis, as in the fountains of some rivers, where a gentle application of the hand turns the flexible waters in channels, that make them take quite contrary courses; and by this direction given them at first in the source, they receive different tendencies, and arrive at last at very remote and distant places. . . .

I have said he here [as opposed to "she" or "they"], because the principal aim of my discourse is, how a young gentleman should be brought up from his infancy, which in all things will not so perfectly suit the education of daughters; though where the difference of sex requires different treatment, 'twill be no hard matter to distinguish. . . .

[*Locke provides extensive advice on healthy eating and drinking habits for children.*]

As the strength of the body lies chiefly in being able to endure hardships, so also does that of the mind. And the great principle and foundation of all virtue and worth is placed in this: that a man is able to deny himself his own desires, cross his own inclinations, and purely follow what reason directs as best, tho' the appetite lean the other way.

The great mistake I have observed in people's breeding their children, has been, that this has not been taken care enough of in its due season: that the mind has not been made obedient to discipline, and pliant to reason, when at first it was most tender, most easy to be bowed. Parents being wisely ordained by nature to love their children, are very apt, if reason watch not that natural affection very warily, are apt, I say, to let it run into fondness. They love their little ones and it is their duty; but they often, with them, cherish their faults too. . . .

It seems plain to me, that the principle of all virtue and excellency lies in a power of denying ourselves the satisfaction of our own desires, where reason does not authorize them. This power is to be got and improved by custom, made easy and familiar by an early practice. If therefore I might be heard, I would advise, that, contrary to the ordinary way, children should be used to submit their desires, and go without their longings, even from their very cradles. The first thing they should learn to know, should be, that they were not to have anything because it pleased them, but because it was thought fit for them. If things suitable to their wants were supplied to them, so that they were never suffered to have what they once cried for, they would learn to be content without it, would never, with bawling and peevishness, contend for mastery, nor be half so uneasy to themselves and others as they are, because from the first beginning they are not thus handled. If they were never suffered to obtain their desire by the impatience they expressed for it, they would no more cry for another thing, than they do for the moon. . . .

Those therefore that intend ever to govern their children, should begin it while they are very little, and look that they perfectly comply with the will of their parents. Would you have your son obedient to you when past a child; be sure then to establish the authority of a father as soon as he is capable of submission, and can understand in whose power he is. If you would have him stand in awe of you, imprint it in his infancy; and as he approaches more to a man, admit him nearer to your familiarity; so shall you have him your obedient subject (as is fit) while he is a child, and your affectionate friend when he is a man. For methinks they mightily misplace the treatment due to their children, who are indulgent and familiar when they are little, but severe to them, and keep them at a distance, when they are grown up: for liberty and indulgence can do no good to children; their want of judgment makes them stand in need of restraint and discipline; and on the contrary, imperiousness and severity is but an ill way of treating men, who have reason of their own to guide them; unless you have a mind to make your children, when grown up, weary of you, and secretly to say within themselves, When will you die, father? . . .

This being laid down in general, as the course that ought to be taken, 'tis fit we now come to consider the parts of the discipline to be used, a little more particularly. I have spoken so much of carrying a strict hand over children, that perhaps I shall be suspected of not considering enough, what is due to their tender age and constitutions. But that opinion will vanish, when you have heard me a little farther: for I am very apt to think, that great severity of punishment does but very little good, nay, great harm in education; and I believe it will be found that . . . those children who have been most chastised, seldom make the best men. All that I have hitherto contended for, is, that whatsoever rigor is necessary, it is more to be used, the younger children are; and having by a due application wrought its effect, it is to be relaxed, and changed into a milder sort of government. . . .

Beating them, and all other sorts of slavish and corporal punishments, are not the discipline fit to be used in the education of those we would have wise, good, and ingenuous men; and therefore very rarely to be applied, and that only in great occasions, and cases of extremity. On the other side, to flatter children by rewards of things that are pleasant to them, is as carefully to be avoided. He that will give to his son apples or sugar-plumbs, or what else of this kind he is most delighted with, to make him learn his book, does but authorize his love of pleasure, and cocker up that dangerous propensity, which he ought by all means to subdue and stifle in him. . . .

[Locke warns against the bad influence of servants upon children.]

Having named company, I am almost ready to throw away my pen, and trouble you no farther on this subject: for since that does more than all precepts, rules, and instructions, methinks 'tis almost wholly in vain to make a long discourse of other things, and to talk of that almost to no purpose. For you will be ready to say, what shall I do with my son? If I keep him always at home, he will be in danger to be my young master; and if I send him abroad, how is it possible to keep him from the contagion of rudeness and vice, which is every where so in fashion? In my house he will perhaps be more innocent, but more ignorant too of the world; wanting there change of company, and being used constantly to the same faces, he will, when he comes abroad, be a sheepish or conceited creature.

I confess both sides have their inconveniences. Being abroad, 'tis true, will make him bolder, and better able to bustle and shift among boys of his own age; and the emulation of school-fellows often puts life and industry into young lads. But still you can find a school, wherein it is possible for the master to look after the manners of his scholars, and can show as great effects of his care of forming their minds to virtue, and their carriage to good breeding, as of forming their tongues to the learned languages. . . .

Virtue is harder to be got than a knowledge of the world; and if lost in a young man, is seldom recovered. Sheepishness and ignorance of the world, the faults imputed to a private education, are neither the necessary consequences of being bred at home, nor if they were, are they incurable evils. Vice is the more stubborn, as well as the more dangerous evil of the two; and therefore in the first place to be fenced against. If that sheepish softness which often enervates those who are bred like fondlings [fools] at home, be carefully to be avoided, it is principally so for virtue's sake; for fear lest such a yielding temper should be too susceptible of vicious impressions, and expose the novice too easily to be corrupted. A young man before he leaves the shelter of his father's house, and the guard of a tutor, should be fortified with resolution, and made acquainted with men, to secure his virtues, lest he should be led into some ruinous course, or fatal precipice, before he is sufficiently acquainted with the dangers of conversation, and has steadiness enough not to yield to every temptation. Were it not for this, a young man's bashfulness and ignorance in the world, would not so much need an early care. Conversation would cure it in a great measure; or if that will not do it early enough, it is only a stronger reason for a good tutor at home. For if pains be to be taken to give him a manly air and assurance betimes, it is chiefly as a fence to his virtue when he goes into the world under his own conduct. . . .

[*Locke urges parents to choose tutors for their children discriminately, as children learn by example.*]

Curiosity in children . . . ought to be encouraged in them, not only as a good sign, but as the great instrument nature has provided to remove that ignorance they were born with; and which, without this busy inquisitiveness, will make them dull and useless creatures. . . .

That which every gentleman . . . desires for his son, besides the estate he leaves him, is contained . . . in these four things, virtue, wisdom, breeding, and learning. . . .

I place virtue as the first and most necessary of those endowments that belong to a man or a gentleman; as absolutely requisite to make him valued and beloved by others, acceptable or tolerable to himself. Without that, I think, he will be happy neither in this nor the other world.

You will wonder, perhaps, that I put learning last, especially if I tell you I think it the least part. This may seem strange in the mouth of a bookish man; and this making usually the chief, if not only bustle and stir about children, this being almost that alone which is thought on, when people talk of education, makes it the greater paradox. When I consider, what ado is made about a little Latin and Greek, how many years are spent in it, and what a noise and business it makes to no purpose, I can hardly forbear thinking that the parents of children still live in fear of the school-master's rod, which they look on as the only instrument of education; as a language or two to be its whole business. How else is it possible that a child should be chained to the oar seven, eight, or ten of the best years of his life, to get a language or two, which, I think, might be had at a great deal cheaper rate of pains and time, and be learned almost in playing? . . .

Reading and writing and learning I allow to be necessary, but yet not the chief business. I imagine you would think him a very foolish fellow, that should not value a virtuous or a wise man infinitely before a great scholar. . . .

To conclude this part . . . , his tutor should remember, that his business is not so much to teach him all that is knowable, as to raise in him a love and esteem of knowledge; and to put him in the right way of knowing and improving himself when he has a mind to it. . . .

Teach him to get a mastery over his inclinations, and submit his appetite to reason. This being obtained, and by constant practice settled into habit, the hardest part of the task is over. To bring a young man to this, I know nothing which so much contributes as the love of praise and commendation, which should therefore be instilled into him by all arts imaginable. Make his mind as sensible of credit and shame as may be; and when you have done that, you have put a principle into him, which will influence his actions when you are not by, to which the fear of a little smart of a rod is not comparable, and which will be the proper stock whereon afterwards to graft the true principles of morality and religion.

READING AND DISCUSSION QUESTIONS

1. Why does Locke advocate beginning a child's education at the earliest possible age?

2. What is Locke's opinion on the education of young women? What in the letter suggests his beliefs on sexual difference and gender roles?

3. What are Locke's views about the need for disciplining children and the nature of discipline to be used?

VIEWPOINTS

Organized Religion in the 1700s

DOCUMENT 19-3

JOHN WESLEY
The Ground Rules for Methodism
1749

John Wesley (1703–1791), the son of an Anglican clergyman, was himself trained to the ministry. He found little solace in the Anglicanism of his youth, however, and endured years of spiritual yearning until, in 1738, he had a religious awakening. His resulting theological message was quite simple: salvation was possible for all. The appeal of Wesley's message, coupled with his tireless preaching, often to huge crowds outdoors, quickly brought him a large following. These followers became known as "Methodists," after a Bible study group Wesley attended while at Oxford University.

THE NATURE, DESIGN, AND GENERAL RULES OF THE UNITED SOCIETIES

1. About ten years ago my brother [Charles Wesley] and I were desired to preach in many parts of London. We had no view therein but, so far as we were able (and we knew God could work by whomsoever it pleased Him) to convince those who would hear, what true Christianity was, and to persuade them to embrace it.

2. The points we chiefly insisted upon were four: First, that orthodoxy or right opinions is, at best, but a very slender part of religion, if it can be allowed to be any part of it at all; that neither does religion consist in negatives, in bare harmlessness of any kind, nor merely in externals in doing good or using the means of grace, in works of piety (so called) or of charity: that it is nothing short of or different from the mind that

From John Wesley, "A Plain Account of the People Called Methodists" (1749), in *The Past Speaks*, 2d ed., ed. Walter Arnstein (Lexington, Mass.: D. C. Heath, 1993), 2:87–89.

was in Christ, the image of God stamped upon the heart, inward righteousness attended with the peace of God and joy in the Holy Ghost.

Secondly, that the only way under heaven to this religion is to repent and believe the gospel, of (as the apostle words it) repentance toward God and faith in our Lord Jesus Christ.

Thirdly, that by this faith, he that worketh not, but believeth in Him that justifieth the ungodly, is justified freely by His grace, through the redemption which is in Jesus Christ.

And lastly, that being justified by faith we taste of the heaven to which we are going; we are holy and happy; we tread down sin and fear, and sit in heavenly places with Christ Jesus.

3. Many of those who heard this, began to cry out, that we brought strange things to their ears: that this was doctrine which they never heard before, or, at least, never regarded. They searched the scriptures, whether these things were so, and acknowledged the truth as it is in Jesus. Their hearts also were influenced as well as their understandings, and they determined to follow Jesus Christ and Him crucified.

4. Immediately [those who accepted this new way] were surrounded with difficulties. All the world rose up against them; neighbors, strangers, acquaintances, relations, friends began to cry out amain, "Be not righteous overmuch: why shouldst thou destroy thyself? Let not much religion make thee mad." . . .

DIRECTIONS GIVEN TO THE BAND SOCIETIES

You are supposed to have the faith that "overcometh the world." To you, therefore, it is not grievous:

  I. Carefully to abstain from doing evil; in particular:
1. Neither to buy nor sell anything at all on the Lord's day.
2. To taste no spiritous liquor, no dram of any kind, unless prescribed by a physician.
3. To be at a word [i.e., to be honest] both in buying and selling.
4. To pawn nothing, no, not to save life.
5. Not to mention the fault of any behind his back, and to stop those short that do.
6. To wear no needless ornaments, such as rings, earrings, necklaces, lace, ruffles.
7. To use no needless self-indulgence, such as taking snuff or tobacco, unless prescribed by a physician.

II. Zealously to maintain good works; in particular:

1. To give alms of such things as you possess, and that to the utter- most of your power.

2. To reprove all that sin in your sight, and that in love and meekness of wisdom.

3. To be patterns of diligence and frugality, of self-denial, and taking up the cross daily.

III. Constantly to attend on all the ordinances of God; in particular:

1. To be at church and at the Lord's table every week, and at every public meeting of the bands.

2. To attend the ministry of the word every morning unless distance, business or sickness prevent.

3. To use private prayer every day; and family prayer, if you are at the head of a family.

4. To read the scriptures, and meditate therein, at every vacant hour. And

5. To observe, as days of fasting or abstinence, all Fridays in the year.

READING AND DISCUSSION QUESTIONS

1. What, according to Wesley, is the *only* means of obtaining salvation? What is the true nature of religion?

2. Wesley admits that soon after Methodism's establishment, "the world rose up against them . . . to cry out amain, 'Be not righteous overmuch: why shouldst thou destroy thyself? Let not much religion make thee mad.'" Why do you think Methodists were so vehemently criticized?

3. Wesley maintains in his second paragraph, that "orthodoxy or right opinions is, at best, but a very slender part of religion . . . ; that neither does religion consist in negatives, in bare harmlessness of any kind, nor merely in externals in doing good or using the means of grace, in works of piety (so called) or of charity." Why, then, does he proceed to put forward his own "right opinions" through a set of rules that con- sist in large part of "negatives" (what Methodists should *not* do), and things that they should do, most of which could be described as "works of piety or of charity"?

4. Critics of Methodism have argued that it was a barely disguised tool of social control, promulgated by both traditional landed elites and the

growing British urban middle class as a means of keeping the rapidly expanding urban working class obedient and subdued despite appalling living and working conditions in early industrial cities. Why do you think this charge has been made? Is it persuasive? Why or why not?

DOCUMENT 19-4

VOLTAIRE

A Treatise on Toleration

1763

François-Marie Arouet (1694–1778), who used the pen name Voltaire, was arguably the greatest of the Enlightenment philosophes. An astonishingly prolific author, his output amounted to hundreds of books and pamphlets. In some respects he was unrepresentative of the general currents of Enlightenment thought, being skeptical of both human rationality and human progress. Like virtually all the philosophes, however, he was an unceasing critic of religious dogma and intolerance. The case of the Protestant merchant Jean Calas, who was tortured to death in 1763, prompted Voltaire to write A Treatise on Toleration, from which the following is extracted. Voltaire argued that Calas, accused of killing his son in order to prevent him from converting to Catholicism, was convicted solely on anti-Protestant sentiment.

CHAPTER XXI. UNIVERSAL TOLERATION

It does not require any great art or studied eloquence, to prove, that Christians should tolerate each other. I shall go further, and say, that we should regard all men as our brethren. What! a Turk my brother? a Chinese my brother? a Jew? a Siamese? my brother? Yes, without doubt; for are we not all children of the same father, and creatures of the same God?

But these people despise us and treat us as idolaters! It may be so; but I shall only tell them, they are to blame. It seems to me, I should stagger

---

From Voltaire, A Treatise on Toleration; The Ignorant Philosopher; and A Commentary on the Marquis of Becaria's [sic] Treatise on Crimes and Punishments, trans. David Williams (London: Fielding and Walker, 1779), pp. 118–123.

the haughty obstinacy of an Iman,[1] or a Talapoin,[2] if I spoke to them in the following manner:

This little globe, which is but a point, rolls in universal space, in the same manner as other globes, and we are lost in the immensity. Man, a being about five feet in height, is assuredly a thing of no great importance in the creation. One of those beings, called men, and who are hardly perceptible, says to some of his neighbors in Arabia or in the country of the Cafres:[3] "Attend to what I say, for the God of all these worlds has enlightened me. There are about nine hundred millions of little ants, such as we are, on this earth, but my ant-hill alone is [in] the care of God, all the rest have been hateful to him from [i.e., for] all eternity; we only shall be happy; all others will be eternally wretched."

They would stop me, and ask, who is this madman, who utters such folly? I should be obliged to answer each of them, It is you. I might then take occasion to meliorate their dispositions into something like humanity; but that I should find difficult.

I will now address myself to Christians; and venture to say to a Dominican,[4] who is an inquisitor, "My brother, you know, that every province of Italy has its jargon; that they do not speak at Venice and Bergamo as they do at Florence. The Academy de la Crusca[5] has fixed the general disposition and construction of the language; its dictionary is a rule from which no deviations are allowed; and the grammar of Buon mattei's[6] is an infallible guide, which must be followed. But do you think that the consul, president of the Academy, or in his absence, Buon mattei, could have the conscience, to order the tongues of all the Venetians and Bergamese to be cut out, who should persist in their provincial dialects?"

The inquisitor would answer me: "The cases are very different. The question here is the salvation of your soul; it is for your good, that the court of inquisition ordains, that you should be seized, on the deposition of a

---

[1] **Iman**: A Muslim religious leader.

[2] **Talapoin**: Buddhist priest or monk.

[3] **Cafres**: Kaffirs; South Africa.

[4] **Dominican**: The Dominicans were a Roman Catholic religious order who, as Voltaire suggests, conducted the Inquisition.

[5] **Academy de la Crusca**: Accademia della Crusca; an Italian learned society founded in 1582. Its members were chiefly linguists and philologists. In 1612 it sponsored publication of a dictionary of the Italian language.

[6] **Buon mattei**: Benedetto Buommattei (1581–1647), also rendered as Boum mattei and Buonmattei; Florentine lexicographer, author of *Della Lingua Toscana*.

single person, though he be infamous, and in the hands of justice; that you have no advocate[7] to plead for you; that the very name of your accuser should be unknown to you; that the inquisitor should promise you mercy, and afterwards condemn you; that he apply five different kinds of torture to you, and that afterwards you should be whipt [i.e., whipped] or sent to the galleys, or burnt [at the stake] as a spectacle in a religious ceremony.[8] Father Ivonet, [and] Doctor[s] Cuchalon, Zarchinus, Campegius, Royas, Telinus, Gomarus, Diabarus, and Gemelinus[9] lay down these things as laws, and this pious practice must not be disputed. "I would take the liberty to answer, "My brother, perhaps you are right; I am convinced of the good you wish to do me; but, without all this, is it not possible to be saved?"

It is true that these absurd horrors do not always deform the face of the earth; but they have been very frequent; and we might collect materials to compose a volume on these practices, much larger than the gospels which condemn them. It is not only cruel to persecute in this short life those who do not think as we do, but it is audacious to pronounce their eternal damnation. It seems to me, that it little becomes the atoms of a moment [i.e., such insignificant, ephemeral creatures], such as we are, thus to anticipate the decrees of the Creator. I am very far from opposing that opinion, "that out of [i.e., outside] the church there is no salvation." I respect it, as well as everything taught by the church: but, in truth, are we acquainted with all the ways of God, and the whole extent of his mercy? Is it not permitted that we should hope in him, as well as fear him? Is it not sufficient that we are faithful to the church? Is it necessary that every individual should usurp the power of the Deity, and decide, before him, the eternal lot of all mankind?

When we wear mourning for a king of Sweden, Denmark, England, or Prussia, do we say that we mourn for a reprobate who will burn eternally in hell? There are in Europe forty millions of inhabitants, who are not [members] of the Church of Rome; shall we say to each of them, "Sir, as you are to be infallibly damned, I would neither eat, deal, or converse with you."

Is it to be supposed, that an ambassador of France, presented to the Grand Seignior,[10] would say to himself, His highness will be burnt to all eternity, because he has submitted to circumcision? If he really thought

---

[7] **advocate**: Lawyer.
[8] Here Voltaire inserted a footnote instructing his readers to "See that excellent book, intitled [sic], *The Manual of the Inquisition*."
[9] **Father Ivonet, . . . Gemelinus**: Roman Catholic theologians.
[10] **Grand Seignior**: Grand Signeur; the Ottoman Sultan.

that the Grand Seignior was a mortal enemy to God, and the object of his vengeance, could he have spoken to him? Should he have been sent to him? With whom could we have dealings in trade? What duty of civil life could we ever fulfill, if we were in fact possessed with the idea, that we were conversing with persons eternally reprobated?

O ye followers of a merciful God! if you have cruel hearts. If, in adoring him, whose whole law consists in these words, "Love God and your neighbor," you have encumbered that pure and holy law with sophisms, and incomprehensible disputes! If you have lighted the fires of discord, sometimes for a new word, sometimes for a letter of the alphabet! If you have annexed eternal torments to the omission of some words, or some ceremonies, which other people cannot be [i.e., are not] acquainted with — I must say, while shedding tears for mankind: "Transport yourselves with me to that day, in which all men will be judged, and when God will render to every one according to his works.

"I see all the dead, of past and present ages, appearing in his presence. Are you very sure that our Creator and Father will say to the wise and virtuous Confucius, to the legislator Solon, to Pythagoras, Zaleucus, Socrates, Plato, the divine Antonini, the good Trajan, to Titus the delight of mankind, to Epictetus,[11] and to many others who have been the models of human nature: Go, monsters! Let your punishments be as eternal as my being! — and you, my well-beloved, Jean Châtel, Ravaillac, Damiens, Cartouche,[12] &c. who have died according to the forms which are enjoined, sit at my right hand and partake of my dominion, and of my felicity!"

---

[11] **Confucius, Solon, Pythagoras, Zaleucus, Socrates, Plato, the divine Antonini, Trajan, Titus, Epictetus**: Confucius (551–479 B.C.E.), Chinese philosopher; Solon (638–558 B.C.E.), Athenian statesman and lawgiver; Pythagoras (c. 570–495 B.C.E.), Greek philosopher, theologian, and mathematician; Zaleucus, (seventh century B.C.E.), Greek lawgiver; Socrates, (c. 469–399 B.C.E.), Greek philosopher; Plato (428–348 B.C.E.), Greek philosopher and mathematician; Antoninus Pius (r. 138–161), Roman emperor, and Marcus Aurelius Antoninus (r. 161–180), Roman emperor and Stoic philosopher; Trajan (r. 98–117), Roman emperor; Titus Pomponius Atticus (c. 112–c. 35 B.C.E.), Roman editor and man of letters; Epictetus (55–135), Greek Stoic philosopher.

[12] **Jean Châtel, Ravaillac, Damiens, Cartouche**: Jean Châtel (1575–1594), tortured and executed for attempting to assassinate Henry IV of France; François Ravaillac (1578–1610), tortured and drawn and quartered for assassinating Henry IV of France; Robert-François Damiens (1715–1757), tortured and drawn and quartered for attempting to assassinate Louis XV of France; Louis Dominique Bourguignon, known as Cartouche (1693–1721), French highwayman tortured to death.

You shrink with horror at these words; and after they have escaped me, I have nothing more to say to you.

CHAPTER XXII. PRAYER TO GOD

I no longer then look up to men; it is to thee, the God of all beings, of all worlds, and of all ages, I address myself — If weak creatures, lost in immensity and imperceptible to the rest of the universe, may dare to ask any thing of thee, who hast given [us] all things, and whose decrees are immutable and eternal! Deign to regard with pity the errors inseparable from our nature; let not these errors prove our calamities! Thou hast not given us hearts to hate, and hands to destroy each other; dispose us to mutual assistance, in supporting the burden of a painful and transitory life! Let the little differences in the garments which cover our frail bodies; in all our imperfect languages, in our ridiculous customs, our imperfect laws, our idle opinions, in our ranks and conditions, so unequal in our eyes, and so equal in thine: let all those little shades which distinguish the atoms called *men*, be no more signals of hatred and persecution! Let those who light tapers [i.e., candles] at noon-day, to glorify thee — bear with those who content themselves with the light of thy sun! Let not those who throw over their garments a white surplice, while they say it is the duty of men to love thee, hate those who say the same thing in a black woolen cloak! Let it be equal, to adore thee in a jargon formed from an ancient, or from a modern language! May those whose vestments are dipped in scarlet, or in purple who domineer over a small parcel of the small heap of the dirt and mud of this world; and those who possess a few round fragments of a certain metal, enjoy without pride, what they call grandeur and riches; and may others regard them without envy: for thou knowest, there is nothing in these things to inspire envy or pride!

May all men remember that they are brethren! May they regard in horror tyranny, the tyranny exercised over the mind, as they do rapine, which carries away by force the fruits of peaceable labor and industry! If the scourges of war be inevitable, let us not hate and destroy each other in the bosom of peace; let us employ the instant of our existence to praise, in a thousand different languages, from Siam to California, thy goodness which hath granted us that instant!

READING AND DISCUSSION QUESTIONS

1. How would you describe Voltaire's religious faith? What does he believe in?

2. What do his arguments suggest about his attitude toward theology and
    dogma?

3. How persuasive or unpersuasive do you find his arguments, and why?

DOCUMENT 19-5

MARY WORTLEY MONTAGU
On Smallpox Inoculations
ca. 1717

*Mary Wortley Montagu (1689–1762) was the daughter of an English aristo-
crat and married a member of the landed gentry. An unusually well-educated
woman, Montagu was the sole female contributor to Joseph Addison's renowned political journal* The Spectator. *She narrowly survived the often
fatal disease smallpox in 1715. In 1716, while accompanying her diplomat
husband in Constantinople, Montagu witnessed the common procedure of
smallpox inoculation. She subsequently had both of her children inoculated,
and, upon returning to England, championed the procedure despite strong
anti-"Oriental" sentiment against it. The following letter was written to a
close friend; its substance was made public in the 1720s.*

A propos of distempers, I am going to tell you a thing, that will make you
wish yourself here. The small-pox, so fatal, and so general amongst us, is
here entirely harmless, by the invention of engrafting, which is the term
they give it. There is a set of old women, who make it their business to
perform the operation, every autumn, in the month of September, when
the great heat is abated. People send to one another to know if any of their
family has a mind to have the small-pox; they make parties for this purpose, and when they are met (commonly fifteen or sixteen together) the
old woman comes with a nut-shell full of the matter of the best sort of
smallpox, and asks what vein you please to have opened. She immediately

From Lady Mary Wortley Montagu, *Letters of the Right Honourable Lady M — y
W — y M — e: Written During Her Travels in Europe, Asia and Africa . . .* , vol. 1 (Aix:
Anthony Henricy, 1796), pp. 167–169.

rips open that you offer to her, with a large needle (which gives you no more pain than a common scratch) and puts into the vein as much matter as can lie upon the head of her needle, and after that, binds up the little wound with a hollow bit of shell, and in this manner opens four or five veins. The Grecians have commonly the superstition of opening one in the middle of the forehead, one in each arm, and one on the breast, to mark the sign of the Cross; but this has a very ill effect, all these wounds leaving little scars, and is not done by those that are not superstitious, who choose to have them in the legs, or that part of the arm that is concealed. The children or young patients play together all the rest of the day, and are in perfect health to the eighth [day]. Then the fever begins to seize them, and they keep their beds two days, very seldom three. They have very rarely above twenty or thirty [pockmarks] in their faces, which never mark [i.e., leave scars] and in eight days time they are as well as before their illness. Where they are wounded [i.e., where pock marks appear], there remains running sores during the distemper, which I don't doubt is a great relief to it. Every year, thousands undergo this operation, and the French Ambassador says pleasantly, that they take the small-pox here by way of diversion, as they take the waters[13] in other countries. There is no example of any one that has died in it, and you may believe I am well satisfied of the safety of this experiment, since I intend to try it on my dear little son. I am patriot enough to take the pains to bring this useful invention into fashion in England, and I should not fail to write to some of our doctors very particularly about it, if I knew any one of them that I thought had virtue enough to destroy such a considerable branch of their revenue, for the good of mankind. But that distemper is too beneficial to them, not to expose to all their resentment, the hardy weight that should undertake to put an end to it. Perhaps if I live to return, I may, however, have courage to war with them. Upon this occasion, admire the heroism in the heart of

Your friend, etc. etc.

READING AND DISCUSSION QUESTIONS

1. What does Montagu's observation "I am patriot enough to take the pains to bring this useful invention into fashion in England" suggest about her sense of nationalism?

---

[13] **take the waters**: Upper-class men and women across Europe routinely visited spas with mineral waters or hot springs, like Bath in England, to "take the waters." Such trips combined medicinal and recreational motives.

2. What does her subsequent comment that "I should not fail to write to some of our doctors very particularly about it, if I knew any one of them that I thought had virtue enough to destroy such a considerable branch of their revenue, for the good of mankind," suggest about her attitude toward the medical profession?

3. What does Montagu's letter suggest about upper-class women's education and empowerment in early modern English society? Do you think she was representative of all women? Of all upper-class women? Why or why not?

4. What are some of the likely reasons English doctors dismissed the smallpox inoculation that was so successful abroad?

COMPARATIVE QUESTIONS

1. What can be gleaned from Williamson's and Wesley's accounts about the prevalence and nature of religious belief in eighteenth-century England?

2. What do Williamson's and Montagu's accounts suggest about the state and extent of medical knowledge in eighteenth-century Europe?

3. What can be gleaned from Williamson's, Locke's, and Montagu's accounts about attitudes toward children in the late seventeenth and eighteenth centuries?

4. On which aspects of religious belief might Voltaire and Wesley agree? On which would they disagree?

CHAPTER 20

The Revolution in Politics

1775–1815

By the late eighteenth century, the industrious yet often impoverished citizens who brought wealth to their nations began to voice their displeasure over the economic conditions and political structures in western Europe. In France, Louis XV (r. 1715–1774) had inherited Louis XIV's imperial ambitions, and spent much of the century unsuccessfully battling Britain for a world empire, finally bankrupting the state. In 1789, Louis XVI (r. 1774–1792) was unable to resolve the issues that confronted him, and gave in to noble pressure to summon the Estates General, the French representative body that had last met in 1614. However, the Estates General failed to meet its citizens' needs. The French Revolution (1789–1799) that followed had an enormous impact on the debate over rights, liberty, and equality that had long-term, global reverberations. While the Revolution itself was initially quite conservative, women and enslaved peoples seized the moment to articulate their conceptions of universal rights, conceptions that Napoleon Bonaparte challenged when he seized power in 1799.

DOCUMENT 20-1

COMMISSIONERS OF THE THIRD ESTATE

OF THE CARCASSONNE

Cahier de Doleances: *The Third Estate Speaks*

1789

Assuming the throne in 1774, Louis XVI inherited a bankrupt government that spent half its income just to pay the interest on the national debt. The

---

From Commissioners of Carcassonne, in *Readings in European History*, ed. James Harvey Robinson, 2 vols. (Boston: Ginn, 1904), 2:397–399.

Cahiers de Doleances (Notebooks of Grievances) *were an attempt to discover and catalog the issues the king would need to resolve at the meeting of the Estates General in order to get approval for new taxes. Long denied any formal avenue of complaint, the third estate — everyone not nobility or clergy — responded with a flood of complaints and suggestions that surprised Louis and his advisors. While phrased in respectful language, the* Cahiers *illuminate a society at odds with the absolutism of Louis XVI's predecessors.*

The third estate of the electoral district of Carcassonne,[1] desiring to give to a beloved monarch, and one so worthy of our affection, the most unmistakable proof of its love and respect, of its gratitude and fidelity, desiring to cooperate with the whole nation in repairing the successive misfortunes which have overwhelmed it, and with the hope of reviving once more its ancient glory, declares that the happiness of the nation must, in their opinion, depend upon that of its king, upon the stability of the monarchy, and upon the preservation of the orders which compose it and of the fundamental laws which govern it.

Considering, too, that a holy respect for religion, morality, civil liberty, and the rights of property, a speedy return to true principles, a careful selection and due measure in the matter of the taxes, a strict proportionality in their assessment, a persistent economy in government expenditures, and indispensable reforms in all branches of the administration, are the best and perhaps the only means of perpetuating the existence of the monarchy;

The third estate of the electoral district of Carcassonne very humbly petitions his Majesty to take into consideration these several matters, weigh them in his wisdom, and permit his people to enjoy, as soon as may be, fresh proofs of that benevolence which he has never ceased to exhibit toward them and which is dictated by his affection for them.

In view of the obligation imposed by his Majesty's command that the third estate of this district should confide to his paternal ear the causes of the ills which afflict them and the means by which they may be remedied or moderated, they believe that they are fulfilling the duties of faithful subjects and zealous citizens in submitting to the consideration of the nation, and to the sentiments of justice and affection which his Majesty entertains for his subjects, the following:

---

[1] **Carcassonne**: Town in southern France, near the Mediterranean coast.

1. Public worship should be confined to the Roman Catholic apostolic religion,[2] to the exclusion of all other forms of worship; its extension should be promoted and the most efficient measures taken to reestablish the discipline of the Church and increase its prestige.
2. Nevertheless the civil rights of those of the king's subjects who are not Catholics should be confirmed, and they should be admitted to positions and offices in the public administration, without however extending this privilege — which reason and humanity alike demand for them — to judicial or police functions or to those of public instruction.
3. The nation should consider some means of abolishing the annates[3] and all other dues paid to the holy see, to the prejudice and against the protests of the whole French people. . . .

[*The holding of multiple church positions should be prohibited, monasteries reduced in numbers, and holidays suppressed or decreased.*]

7. The rights which have just been restored to the nation should be consecrated as fundamental principles of the monarchy, and their perpetual and unalterable enjoyment should be assured by a solemn law, which should so define the rights both of the monarch and of the people that their violation shall hereafter be impossible.
8. Among these rights the following should be especially noted: the nation should hereafter be subject only to such laws and taxes as it shall itself freely ratify.
9. The meetings of the Estates General of the kingdom should be fixed for definite periods, and the subsidies judged necessary for the support of the state and the public service should be voted for no longer a period than to the close of the year in which the next meeting of the Estates General is to occur.
10. In order to assure to the third estate the influence to which it is entitled in view of the number of its members, the amount of its contributions to the public treasury, and the manifold interests which it

---

[2] **apostolic religion**: "Apostolic" meant that the leaders of the Roman Catholic Church claimed to have received their authority in succession from one of the original twelve apostles, specifically Peter. Of the Protestant churches, only the Church of England could claim apostolic succession.

[3] **annates**: Refers to the practice of claiming the first year's profits from a church district, or see, for the bishop who oversaw that district.

has to defend or promote in the national assemblies, its votes in the assembly should be taken and counted by head.

11. No order, corporation, or individual citizen may lay claim to any pecuniary exemptions. . . . All taxes should be assessed on the same system throughout the nation.

12. The due exacted from commoners holding fiefs[4] should be abolished, and also the general or particular regulations which exclude members of the third estate from certain positions, offices, and ranks which have hitherto been bestowed on nobles either for life or hereditarily. A law should be passed declaring members of the third estate qualified to fill all such offices for which they are judged to be personally fitted.

13. Since individual liberty is intimately associated with national liberty, his Majesty is hereby petitioned not to permit that it be hereafter interfered with by arbitrary orders for imprisonment. . . .

14. Freedom should be granted also to the press, which should however be subjected, by means of strict regulations, to the principles of religion, morality, and public decency. . . .

60. The third estate of the district of Carcassonne places its trust, for the rest, in the zeal, patriotism, honor, and probity of its deputies in the National Assembly in all matters which may accord with the beneficent views of his Majesty, the welfare of the kingdom, the union of the three estates, and the public peace.

READING AND DISCUSSION QUESTIONS

1. What implications would this document have for a system of government based on absolute royal authority?

2. What position do the commissioners take toward the relationship of government and religion?

3. What economic reforms does the *Cahier* propose, and how might those affect the social structure of France?

4. How do the suggested reforms take the rights of the individual into account?

---

[4] **fiefs**: Medieval gifts of land in return for military service. With the rise of professional armies, many fief holders were expected to make cash payments instead.

DOCUMENT 20-2

EDWARD RIGBY

On the Taking of the Bastille and Its Aftermath

1789

The Bastille was the French royal prison, a massive structure in the heart of Paris that served as a physical reminder of the monarchy's power. On the 14th of July, 1789, as the National Assembly debated at Versailles, the citizens of Paris seized arms and cannons from a retired soldier's home and forced their way into the Bastille. The fall of the Bastille became the symbolic turning point of the Revolution, still celebrated every year in France. Edward Rigby, an English physician, was traveling through France at the time and wrote this account.

July 14. A Canadian Frenchman, whom we found in the crowd and who spoke good English, was the first who intimated to us that it had been resolved to attack the Bastille. We smiled at the gentleman, and suggested the improbability of undisciplined citizens taking a citadel which had held out against the most experienced troops in Europe; little thinking it would be actually in the hands of the people before night. From the commencement of the struggle on Sunday evening there had been scarcely any time in which the firing of guns had not been heard in all quarters of the city, and, as this was principally produced by exercising the citizens in the use of the musket, in trying cannon, etc., it excited, except at first, but little alarm. Another sound equally incessant was produced by the ringing of bells to call together the inhabitants in different parts of the city. These joint sounds being constantly iterated, the additional noise produced by the attack on the Bastille was so little distinguished that I doubt not it had begun a considerable time, and even been completed, before it was known to many thousands of the inhabitants as well as to ourselves.

We ran to the end of the Rue St. Honore.[5] We here soon perceived an immense crowd proceeding towards the Palais Royal with acceleration of

---

From Edward Rigby, in *English Witnesses of the French Revolution*, ed. J. M. Thompson (Oxford: Basil Blackwell, 1938), pp. 55–60.

[5] **Rue St. Honore**: Street in central Paris, near the royal palace.

an extraordinary kind, but which sufficiently indicated a joyful event, and, as it approached we saw a flag, some large keys, and a paper elevated on a pole above the crowd, in which was inscribed "La Bastille est prise et les portes sont ouvertes." ["The Bastille is taken and the gates are open."] The intelligence of this extraordinary event thus communicated, produced an impression upon the crowd really indescribable. A sudden burst of the most frantic joy instantaneously took place; every possible mode in which the most rapturous feelings of joy could be expressed, were everywhere exhibited. Shouts and shrieks, leaping and embracing, laughter and tears, every sound and every gesture, including even what approached to nervous and hysterical affection, manifested, among the promiscuous crowd, such an instantaneous and unanimous emotion of extreme gladness as I should suppose was never before experienced by human beings. . . .

The crowd passed on to the Palais Royal, and in a few minutes another succeeded. Its approach was also announced by loud and triumphant acclamations, but, as it came nearer, we soon perceived a different character, as though bearing additional testimony to the fact reported by the first crowd, the impression by it on the people was of a very different kind. A deep and hollow murmur at once pervaded them, their countenances expressing amazement mingled with alarm. We could not at first explain these circumstances; but as we pressed more to the center of the crowd we suddenly partook of the general sensation, for we then, and not till then, perceived two bloody heads raised on pikes, which were said to be the heads of the Marquis de Launay, Governor of the Bastille, and of Monsieur Flesselles, Prevot des Marchands.[6] It was a chilling and a horrid sight! An idea of savageness and ferocity was impressed on the spectators, and instantly checked those emotions of joy which had before prevailed. Many others, as well as ourselves, shocked and disgusted at this scene, retired immediately from the streets. . . .

The night approached; the crowd without continued agitated. Reports of a meditated attack upon the city that night by a formidable army under the command of the Count d'Artois and the Marechal Broglie[7] were in circulation, and gained such credit as to induce the inhabitants to take

---

[6] **Prevot des Marchands**: Literally the "Provost of Merchants"; the holder of this title was effectively the mayor of Paris.

[7] **Count d'Artois . . . Marechal Broglie**: The Comte (Count) d'Artois was the brother of Louis XVI, and later ruled France as Charles X between 1824 and 1830. Marechal (marshal, a rank above general) Broglie was a distinguished French soldier who opposed the Revolution and commanded a foreign army trying to suppress it in 1792.

measures for opposing them. Trees were cut down and thrown across the principal approaches to the city; the streets were impaved, and the stones carried to the tops of houses which fronted the streets through which the troops might pass (for the fate of Pyrrhus[8] was not unknown to the French) and the windows in most parts of the city were illuminated. The night passed with various indications of alarm; guns were firing continually; the tocsin sounded unceasingly; groups of agitated citizens passed hastily along, and parties of the Milice Bourgeoise [citizens' militia] (for such was the name already assumed by those who had taken arms the day before) paraded the streets. . . .

I went (July 15) and was led by the sound of an approaching crowd towards the end of the Rue St. Honore, and there I witnessed a most affecting spectacle. The Bastille had been scarcely entered and the opposition subdued, when an eager search began to find out and liberate every unhappy captive immured within its walls. Two wretched victims of the detestable tyranny of the old Government had just been discovered and taken from some of the most obscure dungeons of this horrid castle, and were at this time conducted by the crowd to the Palais Royal. One of these was a little feeble old man, I could not learn his history; he exhibited an appearance of childishness and fatuity; he tottered as he walked, and his countenance exhibited little more than the smile of an idiot. . . . The other was a tall and rather robust old man; his countenance and whole figure interesting in the highest degree; he walked upright, with a firm and steady gait; his hands were folded and turned upwards, he looked but little at the crowd; the character of his face seemed a mixture of surprise and alarm, for he knew not whither they were leading him, he knew not what fate awaited him; his face was directed towards the sky, but his eyes were but little open. . . . He had a remarkably high forehead, which, with the crown of his head, was completely bald; but he had a very long beard, and on the back of his head the hair was unusually abundant. . . . His dress was an old greasy reddish tunic; the color and the form of the garb were probably some indication of what his rank had been; for we afterwards learned that he was a Count d'Auche, that he had been a major of cavalry, and a young man of some talent, and that the offense for which he had sustained this long imprisonment had been his having written a pamphlet against the

---

[8] **Pyrrhus:** Pyrrhus was the ancient king of Epirus who defeated the Romans in a series of battles in 280 and 279 B.C.E., losing so many men in the process that he had to give up his hopes of conquest. It is from Pyrrhus that we get the term "Pyrrhic victory."

Jesuits.[9] Every one who witnessed this scene probably felt as I did, an emotion which partook of horror and detestation of the Government which could so obdurately as well as unjustly expose human beings to such sufferings; and of pity for the miserable individuals before us. . . .

It had been reported that the King was to come to Paris on the Thursday (July 16), and great crowds filled the streets through which it was expected he would pass: but his coming did not take place till the Friday (July 17). We were very desirous of witnessing the spectacle of the monarch thus, I might almost say, led captive. The spectacle was very interesting, though not from the artificial circumstances which have usually given distinction to royal processions. The impression made on the spectator was not the effect of any adventitious splendor of costly robes or glittering ornaments — the appearance of the King was simple, if not humble; the man was no longer concealed in the dazzling radiance of the sovereign. . . . The streets were lined with the armed bourgeois, three deep — forming a line, as we were assured, of several miles extent. The procession began to pass the place where we were at a quarter past three. The first who appeared were the city officers and the police guards; some women followed them, carrying green branches of trees which were fancifully decorated; then more officers; then the Prevot des Marchands[10] and different members of the city magistracy. Many of the armed bourgeois followed on horseback; then some of the King's officers, some on horseback and some on foot; then followed the whole body of the Etats Generaux [Estates General] on foot, the noblesse, clergy, and Tiers-Etats [third estate], each in their peculiar dresses. That of the noblesse was very beautiful; they wore a peculiar kind of hat with large white feathers, and many of them were tall, elegant young men. The clergy, especially the bishops and some of the higher orders, were most superbly dressed; many of them in lawn dresses, with pink scarfs and massive crosses of gold hanging before them. The dress of the Tiers-Etats was very ordinary, even worse than that of the inferior order

---

[9] **the Jesuits**: A militant Catholic order, the Society of Jesus was founded in the wake of the Protestant Reformation and dedicated to the spread of Catholicism. In officially Catholic France, denouncing them would have been a political offense, though it is likely that Rigby and the crowd were mistaken about either the reason for the count's imprisonment or the fact that he was a prisoner in the Bastille at all. No political prisoners were liberated when the Bastille fell, only five common criminals and two madmen.

[10] **the Prevot des Marchands**: Possibly the successor of the man whose head was last seen on a pike.

of gownsmen at the English universities. More of the King's officers followed; then the King in a large plain coach with eight horses. After this more bourgeois; then another coach and eight horses with other officers of state; than an immense number of the bourgeois, there having been, it was said, two hundred thousand of them in arms. The countenance of the King was little marked with sensibility, and his general appearance by no means indicated alarm. He was accustomed to throw his head very much back on his shoulders, which, by obliging him to look upwards, gave a kind of stupid character to his countenance by increasing the apparent breadth of his face, by preventing that variation of expression which is produced by looking about. He received neither marks of applause nor insult from the populace, unless their silence could be construed into a negative sort of disrespect. Nor were any insults shown to the noblesse or clergy, except in the instance of the Archbishop of Paris, a very tall thin man. He was very much hissed, the popular clamor having been excited against him by a story circulated of his having encouraged the King to use strong measures against the people, and of his attempting to make an impression on the people by a superstitious exposure of a crucifix. He looked a good deal agitated, and whether he had a leaden eye or not I know not, but it certainly loved the ground. The warm and enthusiastic applause of the people was reserved for the Tiers-Etat. . . . "Vivent les Tiers-Etats! Vive la Liberte!" ["Long live the third estate! Long live liberty!"] were loudly iterated as they passed. . . .

On the Saturday (July 18) we visited more of the public places, but the most interesting object, and which attracted the greatest number of spectators, was the Bastille. We found two hundred workmen busily employed in the destruction of this castle of despotism. We saw the battlements tumble down amidst the applauding shouts of the people. I observed a number of artists taking drawings of what from this time was to have no existence but on paper. . . .

And this reminds me of our having a second time seen the other prisoner, the feeble old man. He was placed conspicuously at a window opposite the house where we saw the King pass, and at that time he was brought forward and made to wave his hat, having a three colored cockade[11] on it.

---

[11] **three colored cockade**: The tricolor knot of ribbons on the cockade-style hat — red, white, and blue — was the symbol of the Revolution, and therefore an insult to the king.

READING AND DISCUSSION QUESTIONS

1. Based on reading Rigby's account, what seemed to be the mood of the citizenry of Paris in July 1789? What was their attitude toward their former rulers?

2. How might a royalist have interpreted these same events? Where do the author's sympathies seem to lie and why might he feel as he does?

3. How much do these events seem to indicate a planned revolution, with specific goals, and how much do they indicate the third estate's relief at change without much thought for the future nature of French government?

VIEWPOINTS

The Legal Framework for a Revolutionary Government

DOCUMENT 20-3

NATIONAL ASSEMBLY OF FRANCE
Declaration of the Rights of Man and of the Citizen

1789

After the fall of the Bastille, rumors that the nobility were plotting to use foreign mercenaries to suppress the Revolution swept through the French countryside. In an effort to quell the "great fear," the National Assembly abolished feudalism and released the "Declaration of the Rights of Man," which laid out the basic principles upon which their government would be founded. While Enlightenment thinkers had used reason to critique social practices and customs but rarely produced actual reforms, the French revolutionaries applied the spirit of reason to practical politics. It is a measure of their success that their ideas about a citizen's relationship with their government no longer seem so radical.

From James Harvey Robinson, ed., *Readings in European History*, 2 vols. (Boston: Ginn, 1904), 2:409–411.

The representatives of the French people, organized as a National Assembly, believing that the ignorance, neglect, or contempt of the rights of man are the sole cause of public calamities and of the corruption of governments, have determined to set forth in a solemn declaration the natural, inalienable, and sacred rights of man, in order that this declaration, being constantly before all the members of the social body, shall remind them continually of their rights and duties; in order that the acts of the legislative power, as well as those of the executive power, may be compared at any moment with the objects and purposes of all political institutions and may thus be more respected; and, lastly, in order that the grievances of the citizens, based hereafter upon simple and incontestable principles, shall tend to the maintenance of the constitution and redound to the happiness of all. Therefore the National Assembly recognizes and proclaims, in the presence and under the auspices of the Supreme Being, the following rights of man and of the citizen:

ARTICLE 1. Men are born and remain free and equal in rights. Social distinctions may be founded only upon the general good.

2. The aim of all political association is the preservation of the natural and imprescriptible rights of man. These rights are liberty, property, security, and resistance to oppression.

3. The principle of all sovereignty resides essentially in the nation. No body nor individual may exercise any authority which does not proceed directly from the nation.

4. Liberty consists in the freedom to do everything which injures no one else; hence the exercise of the natural rights of each man has no limits except those which assure to the other members of the society the enjoyment of the same rights. These limits can only be determined by law.

5. Law can only prohibit such actions as are hurtful to society. Nothing may be prevented which is not forbidden by law, and no one may be forced to do anything not provided for by law.

6. Law is the expression of the general will. Every citizen has a right to participate personally, or through his representative, in its formation. It must be the same for all, whether it protects or punishes. All citizens, being equal in the eyes of the law, are equally eligible to all dignities and to all public positions and occupations, according to their abilities, and without distinction except that of their virtues and talents.

7. No person shall be accused, arrested, or imprisoned except in the cases and according to the forms prescribed by law. Any one soliciting, transmitting, executing, or causing to be executed, any arbitrary order,

shall be punished. But any citizen summoned or arrested in virtue of the law shall submit without delay, as resistance constitutes an offense.

8. The law shall provide for such punishments only as are strictly and obviously necessary, and no one shall suffer punishment except it be legally inflicted in virtue of a law passed and promulgated before the commission of the offense.

9. As all persons are held innocent until they shall have been declared guilty, if arrest shall be deemed indispensable, all harshness not essential to the securing of the prisoner's person shall be severely repressed by law.

10. No one shall be disquieted on account of his opinions, including his religious views, provided their manifestation does not disturb the public order established by law.

11. The free communication of ideas and opinions is one of the most precious of the rights of man. Every citizen may, accordingly, speak, write, and print with freedom, but shall be responsible for such abuses of this freedom as shall be defined by law.

12. The security of the rights of man and of the citizen requires public military forces. These forces are, therefore, established for the good of all and not for the personal advantage of those to whom they shall be intrusted.

13. A common contribution is essential for the maintenance of the public forces and for the cost of administration. This should be equitably distributed among all the citizens in proportion to their means.

14. All the citizens have a right to decide, either personally or by their representatives, as to the necessity of the public contribution; to grant this freely; to know to what uses it is put; and to fix the proportion, the mode of assessment and of collection and the duration of the taxes.

15. Society has the right to require of every public agent an account of his administration.

16. A society in which the observance of the law is not assured, nor the separation of powers defined, has no constitution at all.

17. Since property is an inviolable and sacred right, no one shall be deprived thereof except where public necessity, legally determined, shall clearly demand it, and then only on condition that the owner shall have been previously and equitably indemnified.

READING AND DISCUSSION QUESTIONS

1. Who, according to the authors of this document, make up the "nation"? What is the basis of the government they propose?

2. In what ways is this declaration revolutionary, and in what ways does it continue the status quo?

3. What sort of balance does the declaration attempt to strike between the rights and responsibilities of citizens?

DOCUMENT 20-4

NAPOLEON BONAPARTE

The Napoleonic Code

1804

Napoleon Bonaparte (1769–1821) first gained fame as a general in France's revolutionary army, but his military achievements proved less lasting than his civil ones. When he took power in 1799, Napoleon ordered a new law code written for France, incorporating many of the National Assembly's 1789 changes. Finished in 1804, the new civil code was easily read and understood by the average citizen. It reflected greater equality for men before the law, though women lost some of the rights they acquired during the Revolution. Everywhere Napoleon's armies conquered he imposed the code, and it still forms the basis of much European law to this day.

PRELIMINARY TITLE: OF THE PUBLICATION, EFFECT, AND APPLICATION OF THE LAWS IN GENERAL

1. The laws are executory throughout the whole French territory, by virtue of the promulgation thereof made by the First Consul. They shall be executed in every part of the Republic, from the moment at which their promulgation can have been known. The promulgation made by the First Consul shall be taken to be known in the department which shall be the seat of government, one day after the promulgation; and in each of the other departments, after the

---

From E. A. Arnold, ed. and trans., *A Documentary Survey of Napoleonic France* (Lanham, Md.: University Press of America, 1993), pp. 151–164, quoted in Laura Mason and Tracey Rizzo, eds., *The French Revolution: A Document Collection* (New York: Houghton Mifflin, 1999), pp. 340–347.

expiration of the same interval augmented by one day for every ten myriameters[12] (about twenty ancient leagues[13]) between the town in which the promulgation shall have been made, and the chief place of each department.

2. The law ordains for the future only; it has no retrospective operation.
3. The laws of police and public security bind all the inhabitants of the territory. Immovable property, although in the possession of foreigners, is governed by the French law. The laws relating to the condition and privileges of persons govern Frenchmen, although residing in a foreign country. . . .
6. Private agreements must not contravene the laws which concern public order and good morals.

Book I: Of Persons

Title I: Of the Enjoyment and Privation of Civil Rights
1. The exercise of civil rights is independent of the quality of citizen, which is only acquired and preserved conformably to the constitutional law. . . .
8. Every Frenchman shall enjoy civil rights.

Chapter VI: Of the Respective Rights and Duties of Married Persons
212. Married persons owe to each other fidelity, succor, assistance.
213. The husband owes protection to his wife, the wife obedience to her husband.
214. The wife is obliged to live with her husband, and to follow him to every place where he may judge it convenient to reside: the husband is obliged to receive her, and to furnish her with every necessity for the wants of life, according to his means and station.
215. The wife cannot plead in her own name, without the authority of her husband, even though she should be a public trader, or non-communicant, or separate in property.
216. The authority of the husband is not necessary when the wife is prosecuted in a criminal manner, or relating to police.

---

[12] **myriameters**: Ten thousand meters, or ten kilometers. One of the Revolution's accomplishments was to replace the many local systems of measurement in France with a unified, easy-to-use metric system.

[13] **leagues**: Roman leagues; about two kilometers. The Roman Empire's systems of measurement survived long after its political structure crumbled.

217. A wife, although noncommunicant or separate in property, cannot give, pledge, or acquire by free or chargeable title, without the concurrence of her husband in the act, or his consent in writing.

218. If the husband refuses to authorize his wife to plead in her own name, the judge may give her authority.

219. If the husband refuses to authorize his wife to pass an act, the wife may cause her husband to be cited directly before the court of the first instance, of the circle of their common domicil[e], which may give or refuse its authority, after the husband shall have been heard, or duly summoned before the chamber of council.

220. The wife, if she is a public trader, may, without the authority of her husband, bind herself for that which concerns her trade; and in the said case she binds also her husband, if there be a community between them. She is not reputed a public trader if she merely retails goods in her husband's trade, but only when she carries on a separate business.

221. When the husband is subjected to a condemnation, carrying with it an afflictive or infamous punishment, although it may have been pronounced merely for contumacy,[14] the wife, though of age, cannot, during the continuance of such punishment, plead in her own name or contract, until after authority given by the judge, who may in such case give his authority without hearing or summoning the husband. . . .

226. The wife may make a will without the authority of her husband.

Title VI: Of Divorce

Section II: Of the Provisional Measures to Which the Petition for Cause Determinate May Give Rise

267. The provisional management of the children shall rest with the husband, petitioner, or defendant, in the suit for divorce, unless it be otherwise ordered for the greater advantage of the children, on petition of either the mother, or the family, or the government commissioner.

271. Every obligation contracted by the husband at the expense of the community, every alienation made by him of immovable property dependent upon it, subsequent to the date of the order mentioned in article 238, shall be declared void, if proof be given, moreover,

---

[14] **contumacy**: Refusal to obey legal authority.

that it has been made or contracted in fraud of the rights of the wife.

Title IX: Of Paternal Power

375. A father who shall have cause of grievous dissatisfaction at the conduct of a child, shall have the following means of correction.
376. If the child has not commenced his sixteenth year, the father may cause him to be confined for a period which shall not exceed one month; and to this effect the president of the court of the circle shall be bound, on his petition, to deliver an order of arrest.
377. From the age of sixteen years commenced to the majority or emancipation, the father is only empowered to require the confinement of his child during six months at the most; he shall apply to the president of the aforesaid court, who, after having conferred thereon with the commissioner of government, shall deliver an order of arrest or refuse the same, and may in the first case abridge the time of confinement required by the father.
379. The father is always at liberty to abridge the duration of the confinement by him ordered or required. If the child after his liberation fall into new irregularities, his confinement may be ordered anew, according to the manner prescribed in the preceding articles.

BOOK III: MODES OF ACQUIRING PROPERTY

Title I: Of Successions

818. The husband may, without the concurrence of his wife, claim a distribution of objects movable or immovable fallen to her and which come into community; with respect to objects which do not come into community, the husband cannot claim the distribution thereof without the concurrence of his wife; he can only demand a provisional distribution in case he has a right to the enjoyment of her property. The co-heirs of the wife cannot claim final distribution without suing the husband and his wife.

Title II: Donations and Wills

905. A married woman cannot make donation during life without the assistance or the special consent of her husband, or without being thereto authorized by the law, conformably to what is prescribed by articles 217 and 219, under the title "Of Marriage." She shall not need either the consent of her husband, or the authorization of the law, in order to dispose by will.

Chapter IV: Of Donations During Life

**Section II: Of the Administration of the Community, and
of the Effect of the Acts of Either of the Married Parties
Relating to the Conjugal Union**

1421. The husband alone administers the property of the community. He may sell it, alienate and pledge it without the concurrence of his wife.

1424. Fines incurred by the husband for a crime not importing civil death, may be sued for out of the property of the community, saving the compensation due to the wife; such as are incurred by the wife cannot be put in execution except out of her bare property in her personal goods, so long as the community continues.

1427. The wife cannot bind herself nor engage the property of the community, even to free her husband from prison, or for the establishment of their children in case of her husband's absence, until she shall have been thereto authorized by the law.

1428. The husband has the management of all the personal property of the wife. He may prosecute alone all possessory actions and those relating to movables, which belong to his wife. He cannot alienate the personal immovables of his wife without her consent. He is responsible for all waste in the personal goods of his wife, occasioned by the neglect of conservatory acts.

READING AND DISCUSSION QUESTIONS

1. What groups in French society would benefit most from these laws?

2. What about these laws seems radical, and what seems rooted in tradition?

DOCUMENT 20-5

MARY WOLLSTONECRAFT

A Vindication of the Rights of Woman

1792

The French Constitution of 1791, drafted by the same National Assembly that passed the "Declaration of the Rights of Man," confined full citizenship to a limited number of property-holding men. While many Enlightenment ideals that underlay the Revolution had developed in salons overseen by upper-class women, prevailing thought held that women lacked the intellectual and emotional capacity to participate in politics. The English radical Mary Wollstonecraft disagreed. Her response was A Vindication of the Rights of Woman, *written to French diplomat Charles Talleyrand, who had recently advocated a very limited and domestic education for women.*

My own sex, I hope, will excuse me, if I treat them like rational creatures, instead of flattering their fascinating graces, and viewing them as if they were in a state of perpetual childhood, unable to stand alone. I earnestly wish to point out in what true dignity and human happiness consists — I wish to persuade women to endeavor to acquire strength, both of mind and body, and to convince them that the soft phrases, susceptibility of heart, delicacy of sentiment, and refinement of taste, are almost synonymous with epithets of weakness, and that those beings who are only the objects of pity will soon become objects of contempt.

Dismissing those soft pretty feminine phrases, which the men condescendingly use to soften our slavish dependence, and despising that weak elegancy of mind, exquisite sensibility, and sweet docility of manners, supposed to be the sexual characteristics of the weaker vessel, I wish to show that elegance is inferior to virtue, that the first object of laudable ambition is to obtain a character as a human being, regardless of the distinction of sex.

Youth is the season for love in both sexes; but in those days of thoughtless enjoyment provision should be made for the more important years of

From Mary Wollstonecraft, *A Vindication of the Rights of Woman* (1792), ed. Carol H. Poston (New York: W. W. Norton, 1975), pp. 9–10, 27, 31.

life, when reflection takes place of sensation. The woman who has only been taught to please will soon find that her charms are oblique sunbeams and that they cannot have much effect on her husband's heart when they are seen every day, when the summer is passed and gone. Will she then have sufficient native energy to look into herself for comfort, and cultivate her dormant faculties? or, is it not more rational to expect that she will try to please other men?

Why must the female mind be tainted by coquettish arts to gratify the sensualist and prevent love from subsiding into friendship, or compassionate tenderness, when there are not qualities on which friendship can be built? Let the honest heart show itself, and reason teach passion to submit to necessity; or, let the dignified pursuit of virtue and knowledge raise the mind above those emotions. . . .

If then women are not a swarm of ephemeron triflers, why should they be kept in ignorance under the specious name of innocence? . . . As to the argument respecting the subjection in which the sex has ever been held, it retorts on man. The many have always been enthralled by the few; and monsters, who scarcely have shown any discernment of human excellence, have tyrannized over thousands of their fellow-creatures. . . . China is not the only country where a living man has been made a God. Men have submitted to superior strength to enjoy with impunity the pleasure of the moment; women have only done the same, and therefore till it is proved that the courtier, who servilely resigns the birthright of a man, is not a moral agent, it cannot be demonstrated that woman is essentially inferior to man because she has always been subjugated.

READING AND DISCUSSION QUESTIONS

1. How might a man and a woman read this document differently? Is it addressed to men or women?

2. In what ways does Wollstonecraft accept that women are inferior? Does this weaken or strengthen her argument?

3. Based on Wollstonecraft's argument, what can you discern about a stereotypical woman of the time? How does she behave? How do men respond to her?

4. Of what is the title of Wollstonecraft's argument reminiscent? If this was not merely coincidence, what was the author's purpose?

DOCUMENT 20-6

FRANÇOIS DOMINIQUE TOUSSAINT L'OUVERTURE
A Black Revolutionary Leader in Haiti
1797

The French Revolution had an impact in the New World as well, as representatives of the oppressed slaves on the Caribbean sugar-growing islands seized the opportunity to make their voices heard. In 1792, after French colonial rulers arrested the leader of a Caribbean slave delegation in Paris, freed slave Toussaint Breda (who later changed his name to "L'Ouverture," as he had "opened" the way to liberty) emerged as the leader of a massive Haitian revolt. The revolutionaries faced not only the French plantation owners, but British and Spanish forces hoping to capture the lucrative island while the French were distracted.

The impolitic and incendiary discourse of Vaublanc[15] has not affected the blacks nearly so much as their certainty of the projects which the proprietors of San Domingo are planning: insidious declarations should not have any effect in the eyes of wise legislators who have decreed liberty for the nations. But the attempts on that liberty which the colonists propose are all the more to be feared because it is with the veil of patriotism that they cover their detestable plans. We know that they seek to impose some of them on you by illusory and specious promises, in order to see renewed in this colony its former scenes of horror. Already perfidious emissaries have stepped in among us to ferment the destructive leaven prepared by the hands of liberticides [i.e., murderers of liberty]. But they will not succeed. I swear it by all that liberty holds most sacred. My attachment to France, my knowledge of the blacks, make it my duty not to leave you ignorant either of the crimes which they meditate or the oath that we renew, to bury ourselves under the ruins of a country revived by liberty rather than suffer the return of slavery.

From François Dominique Toussaint L'Ouverture, Letter, in *The Black Jacobins*, 2d ed., ed. C. L. R. James (New York: Vintage Books, 1963), pp. 195–197.

[15] **Vaublanc**: The count of Vaublanc was a royalist and proponent of freeing the slaves and giving them citizenship, in opposition to L'Ouverture's more moderate views.

It is for you, Citizens Directors, to turn from over our heads the storm which the eternal enemies of our liberty are preparing in the shades of silence. It is for you to enlighten the legislature, it is for you to prevent the enemies of the present system from spreading themselves on our unfortunate shores to sully it with new crimes. Do not allow our brothers, our friends, to be sacrificed to men who wish to reign over the ruins of the human species. But no, your wisdom will enable you to avoid the dangerous snares which our common enemies hold out for you. . . .

I send you with this letter a declaration which will acquaint you with the unity that exists between the proprietors of San Domingo who are in France, those in the United States, and those who serve under the English banner. You will see there a resolution, unequivocal and carefully constructed, for the restoration of slavery; you will see there that their determination to succeed has led them to envelop themselves in the mantle of liberty in order to strike it more deadly blows. You will see that they are counting heavily on my complacency in lending myself to their perfidious views by my fear for my children. It is not astonishing that these men who sacrifice their country to their interests are unable to conceive how many sacrifices a true love of country can support in a better father than they, since I unhesitatingly base the happiness of my children on that of my country, which they and they alone wish to destroy.

I shall never hesitate between the safety of San Domingo and my personal happiness; but I have nothing to fear. It is to the solicitude of the French Government that I have confided my children. . . . I would tremble with horror if it was into the hands of the colonists that I had sent them as hostages; but even if it were so, let them know that in punishing them for the fidelity of their father, they would only add one degree more to their barbarism, without any hope of ever making me fail in my duty. . . . Blind as they are! They cannot see how this odious conduct on their part can become the signal of new disasters and irreparable misfortunes, and that far from making them regain what in their eyes liberty for all has made them lose, they expose themselves to a total ruin and the colony to its inevitable destruction. Do they think that men who have been able to enjoy the blessing of liberty will calmly see it snatched away? They supported their chains only so long as they did not know any condition of life more happy than that of slavery. But to-day when they have left it, if they had a thousand lives they would sacrifice them all rather than be forced into slavery again. But no, the same hand which has broken our chains will not enslave us anew. France will not revoke her principles, she will not withdraw from us the greatest of her benefits. She will protect us against all our enemies; she will not permit her sublime morality to be perverted, those principles which do her most honor to be destroyed, her most beautiful achievement to be degraded, and her Decree of 16 Pluviose[16] which so honors humanity to be revoked. But if, to re-establish slavery in San Domingo, this was done, then I declare to you it would be to attempt the impossible: we have known how to face dangers to obtain our liberty, we shall know how to brave death to maintain it.

This, Citizens Directors, is the morale of the people of San Domingo, those are the principles that they transmit to you by me.

My own you know. It is sufficient to renew, my hand in yours, the oath that I have made, to cease to live before gratitude dies in my heart, before I cease to be faithful to France and to my duty, before the god of liberty is profaned and sullied by the liberticides, before they can snatch from my hands that sword, those arms, which France confided to me for the defense of its rights and those of humanity, for the triumph of liberty and equality.

READING AND DISCUSSION QUESTIONS

1. Who is the intended audience of this document? What is L'Ouverture trying to convince them to do?

2. What reasons might persuade the French to reimpose slavery in Haiti, and what reasons might they have for defending its abolition?

3. In what way is L'Ouverture seeking to find common ground with the French? Why?

---

[16] **Decree of 16 Pluviose**: In 1793, French revolutionaries reorganized their calendar to remove the Christian elements; the event marking year one moved from the birth of Jesus to the adoption of the French constitution in 1792. The fifth month, roughly corresponding to April, known for its rains, became Pluviose, which loosely translates as "rainy." The specific decree to which L'Ouverture refers abolished slavery in French colonies in April 1794.

COMPARATIVE QUESTIONS

1. How did the attitude of the people of France seem to change between the creation of the *Cahier de Doleances* and the fall of the Bastille?

2. In what ways did the points expressed in the *Cahier de Doleances* find their way into the "Declaration of the Rights of Man"? Were any points left out of the declaration? If so, why do you suppose they were excluded?

3. Compare the Napoleonic Code with the "Declaration of the Rights of Man and Citizen." What ideas do they seem to have most in common? What does this say about the early stages of the French Revolution?

4. What similarities exist between the arguments of Mary Wollstonecraft and Toussaint L'Ouverture for their groups' inclusion in the new political order? What differences can you discern?

5. Based on the "Declaration of the Rights of Man," Mary Wollstonecraft's argument, and Toussaint L'Ouverture's letter, what were the limits of liberty and equality promised by the Revolution?

6. In what ways does Rousseau's *Social Contract* (Document 17-5) seem to have influenced the writing of the *Cahier* and the "Declaration of the Rights of Man"? How have the citizens of France departed from his thinking?

CHAPTER 21

The Revolution in Energy and Industry

ca. 1780–1850

T he term "Industrial Revolution" was coined almost 150 years ago to describe the technological, economic, and social transformations that took place first in Great Britain and then elsewhere in Europe and the United States. Between 1780 and 1850, traditional English society, in which the overwhelming majority of the population worked in agriculture, gave way to an industrial society wherein the majority lived in urban settings and worked in the manufacturing or service sectors. These changes gave rise to similarly momentous alterations in patterns of work, and working and living conditions worsened in the short term, owing chiefly to urban overcrowding, squalid housing, nonexistent sanitation, and air and water pollution. Despite these and other problems, including widespread reliance on child labor, industrialization led to a vast expansion in the economy, providing jobs and goods for a rapidly growing population. Historians still debate whether "revolution" is an apt description for changes that took place over several decades, but there is little doubt that the consequences of those changes were profound.

DOCUMENT 21-1

THOMAS MALTHUS

An Essay on the Principle of Population

1798

Thomas Malthus (1766–1834) was an Anglican clergyman by training but was deeply interested in demography, or the study of human population. His

From Thomas Malthus, *An Essay on the Principle of Population* (London: J. Johnson, 1798), pp. 18–38.

1798 book An Essay on the Principle of Population *is widely regarded as the foundational text on the subject, and his argument — that, unchecked by birth control, human populations increase faster than their food supplies — remains relevant today, as manufacturers, farmers, politicians, and scientists alike debate the earth's ability to sustain its population indefinitely.*

I said that population, when unchecked, increased in a geometrical ratio, and subsistence for man in an arithmetical ratio.

Let us examine whether this position be just. I think it will be allowed, that no state has hitherto existed (at least that we have any account of) where the manners were so pure and simple, and the means of subsistence so abundant, that no check whatever has existed to early marriages, among the lower classes, from a fear of not providing well for their families, or among the higher classes, from a fear of lowering their condition in life. Consequently in no state that we have yet known has the power of population been left to exert itself with perfect freedom.

Whether the law of marriage be instituted or not, the dictate of nature and virtue seems to be an early attachment to one woman. Supposing a liberty of changing in the case of an unfortunate choice, this liberty would not affect population till it arose to a height greatly vicious; and we are now supposing the existence of a society where vice is scarcely known. In a state therefore of great equality and virtue, where pure and simple manners prevailed, and where the means of subsistence were so abundant that no part of the society could have any fears about providing amply for a family, the power of population being left to exert itself unchecked, the increase of the human species would evidently be much greater than any increase that has been hitherto known.

In the United States of America, where the means of subsistence have been more ample, the manners of the people more pure, and consequently the checks to early marriages fewer, than in any of the modern states of Europe, the population has been found to double itself in twenty-five years. This ratio of increase, though short of the utmost power of population, yet as the result of actual experience, we will take as our rule, and say, that population, when unchecked, goes on doubling itself every twenty-five years or increases in a geometrical ratio.

Let us now take any spot of earth, this Island for instance, and see in what ratio the subsistence it affords can be supposed to increase. We will begin with it under its present state of cultivation. If I allow that by the best possible policy, by breaking up more land and by great encouragements to agriculture, the produce of this Island may be doubled in the first twenty-five years, I think it will be allowing as much as any person can well demand.

In the next twenty-five years, it is impossible to suppose that the produce could be quadrupled. It would be contrary to all our knowledge of the qualities of land. The very utmost that we can conceive, is, that the increase in the second twenty-five years might equal the present produce. Let us then take this for our rule, though certainly far beyond the truth, and allow that, by great exertion, the whole produce of the Island might be increased every twenty-five years, by a quantity of subsistence equal to what it at present produces. The most enthusiastic speculator cannot suppose a greater increase than this. In a few centuries it would make every acre of land in the Island like a garden.

Yet this ratio of increase is evidently arithmetical. It may be fairly said, therefore, that the means of subsistence increase in an arithmetical ratio.

Let us now bring the effects of these two ratios together. The population of the Island is computed to be about seven millions, and we will suppose the present produce equal to the support of such a number. In the first twenty-five years the population would be fourteen millions, and the food being also doubled, the means of subsistence would be equal to this increase. In the next twenty-five years the population would be twenty-eight millions, and the means of subsistence only equal to the support of twenty-one millions. In the next period, the population would be fifty-six millions, and the means of subsistence just sufficient for half that number. And at the conclusion of the first century the population would be one hundred and twelve millions and the means of subsistence only equal to the support of thirty-five millions, which would leave a population of seventy-seven millions totally unprovided for.

A great emigration necessarily implies unhappiness of some kind or other in the country that is deserted. For few persons will leave their families, connections, friends, and native land, to seek a settlement in untried foreign climes, without some strong subsisting causes of uneasiness where they are, or the hope of some great advantages in the place to which they are going. But to make the argument more general and less interrupted by the partial views of emigration, let us take the whole earth, instead of one spot, and suppose that the restraints to population were universally removed. If the subsistence for man that the earth affords was to be increased every twenty-five years by a quantity equal to what the whole world at present produces, this would allow the power of production in the earth to be absolutely unlimited, and its ratio of increase much greater than we can conceive that any possible exertions of mankind could make it.

Taking the population of the world at any number, a thousand millions, for instance, the human species would increase in the ratio of — 1, 2, 4, 8, 16, 32, 64, 128, 256, 512, etc. and subsistence as — 1, 2, 3, 4, 5, 6, 7, 8, 9, 10, etc. In two centuries and a quarter, the population would be to the means of subsistence as 512 to 10: in three centuries as 4096 to 13, and in two thousand years the difference would be almost incalculable, though the produce in that time would have increased to an immense extent.

No limits whatever are placed to the productions of the earth; they may increase for ever and be greater than any assignable quantity. Yet still the power of population being a power of a superior order, the increase of the human species can only be kept commensurate to the increase of the means of subsistence by the constant operation of the strong law of necessity acting as a check upon the greater power. The effects of this check remain now to be considered.

Among plants and animals the view of the subject is simple. They are all impelled by a powerful instinct to the increase of their species, and this instinct is interrupted by no reasoning or doubts about providing for their offspring. Wherever therefore there is liberty, the power of increase is exerted, and the superabundant effects are repressed afterwards by want of room and nourishment, which is common to animals and plants, and among animals by becoming the prey of others.

The effects of this check on man are more complicated. Impelled to the increase of his species by an equally powerful instinct, reason interrupts his career and asks him whether he may not bring beings into the world for whom he cannot provide the means of subsistence. In a state of equality, this would be the simple question. In the present state of society, other considerations occur. Will he not lower his rank in life? Will he not subject himself to greater difficulties than he at present feels? Will he not be obliged to labor harder? And if he has a large family, will his utmost exertions enable him to support them? May he not see his offspring in rags and misery, and clamoring for bread that he cannot give them? And may he not be reduced to the grating necessity of forfeiting his independence, and of being obliged to the sparing hand of charity for support?

These considerations are calculated to prevent, and certainly do prevent, a very great number in all civilized nations from pursuing the dictate of nature in an early attachment to one woman. And this restraint almost necessarily, though not absolutely so, produces vice. Yet in all societies, even those that are most vicious, the tendency to a virtuous attachment is so strong that there is a constant effort towards an increase of population. This constant effort as constantly tends to subject the lower classes of the society to distress and to prevent any great permanent amelioration of their condition.

The way in which these effects are produced seems to be this. We will suppose the means of subsistence in any country just equal to the easy support of its inhabitants. The constant effort towards population, which is found to act even in the most vicious societies, increases the number of people before the means of subsistence are increased. The food therefore which before supported seven millions must now be divided among seven millions and a half or eight millions. The poor consequently must live much worse, and many of them be reduced to severe distress. The number of laborers also being above the proportion of the work in the market, the price of labor must tend toward a decrease, while the price of provisions would at the same time tend to rise. The laborer therefore must work harder to earn the same as he did before. During this season of distress, the discouragements to marriage, and the difficulty of rearing a family are so great that population is at a stand. In the mean time the cheapness of labor, the plenty of laborers, and the necessity of an increased industry amongst them, encourage cultivators to employ more labor upon their land, to turn up fresh soil, and to manure and improve more completely what is already in tillage, till ultimately the means of subsistence become in the same proportion to the population as at the period from which we set out. The situation of the laborer being then again tolerably comfortable, the restraints to population are in some degree loosened, and the same retrograde and progressive movements with respect to happiness are repeated. . . .

Many reasons occur why this oscillation has been less obvious, and less decidedly confirmed by experience, than might naturally be expected. One principal reason is that the histories of mankind that we possess are histories only of the higher classes. We have but few accounts that can be depended upon of the manners and customs of that part of mankind where these retrograde and progressive movements chiefly take place. A satisfactory history of this kind, on one people, and of one period, would require the constant and minute attention of an observing mind during a long life. Some of the objects of inquiry would be, in what proportion to the number of adults was the number of marriages, to what extent vicious customs prevailed in consequence of the restraints upon matrimony, what was the comparative mortality among the children of the most distressed part of the community and those who lived rather more at their ease, what were the variations in the real price of labor, and what were the observable differences in the state of the lower classes of society with respect to ease and happiness, at different times during a certain period.

Such a history would tend greatly to elucidate the manner in which the constant check upon population acts and would probably prove the existence of the retrograde and progressive movements that have been mentioned, though the times of their vibrations must necessarily be rendered irregular from the operation of many interrupting causes, such as the introduction or failure of certain manufactures, a greater or less prevalent spirit of agricultural enterprise, years of plenty, or years of scarcity, wars and pestilence, poor laws, the invention of processes for shortening labor without the proportional extension of the market for the commodity, and, particularly, the difference between the nominal and real price of labor, a circumstance which has perhaps more than any other contributed to conceal this oscillation from common view. . . .

But the want of freedom in the market of labor, which occurs more or less in all communities, either from parish laws, or the more general cause of the facility of combination among the rich, and its difficulty among the poor, operates to prevent the price of labor from rising at the natural period, and keeps it down some time longer; perhaps till a year of scarcity, when the clamor is too loud and the necessity too apparent to be resisted. The true cause of the advance in the price of labor is thus concealed, and the rich affect to grant it as an act of compassion and favor to the poor, in consideration of a year of scarcity, and, when plenty returns, indulge themselves in the most unreasonable of all complaints, that the price does not again fall, when a little rejection would show them that it must have risen long before but from an unjust conspiracy of their own. But though the rich by unfair combinations contribute frequently to prolong a season of distress among the poor, yet no possible form of society could prevent the almost constant action of misery upon a great part of mankind, if in a state of inequality, and upon all, if all were equal.

The theory on which the truth of this position depends appears to me so extremely clear that I feel at a loss to conjecture what part of it can be denied. That population cannot increase without the means of subsistence is a proposition so evident that it needs no illustration. That population does invariably increase where there are the means of subsistence, the history of every people that have ever existed will abundantly prove. And that the superior power of population cannot be checked without producing misery or vice, the ample portion of these too bitter ingredients in the cup of human life and the continuance of the physical causes that seem to have produced them bear too convincing a testimony.

READING AND DISCUSSION QUESTIONS

1. How, according to Malthus, do wages and the availability of work influence population growth?

2. What do Malthus's arguments, especially those on the means of limiting human population growth voluntarily, suggest about views on gender relations? What does he mean in arguing that the considerations that lead men not to marry at an early age "almost necessarily, though not absolutely so, [produce] vice"?

VIEWPOINTS

The Industrialization of Manchester, England

DOCUMENT 21-2

JOHN AIKIN

Manchester Becomes a Thriving Industrial City

1795

John Aikin was trained as a physician but is better known today as a writer and editor of biography. In 1795, Aikin published A Description of the Country from Thirty to Forty Miles Round Manchester, *one of the most complete accounts of the center of Britain's cotton textile industry in its formative stages. As of 1773, Manchester was a market town of about 23,000 people but, blessed with ample water to drive mill wheels, it became a thriving manufacturing center. By 1801, when Britain conducted its first national census, Manchester's population topped 84,000.*

No exertions of the masters or workmen could have answered the demands of trade without the introduction of *spinning machines* [that spun cotton fibers into thread].

From John Aikin, "A Description of the Country from Thirty to Forty Miles Round Manchester," in *The Past Speaks*, 2d ed., ed. Walter Arnstein (Lexington, Mass.: D. C. Heath, 1993), 2:148–149.

These were first used by the country people on a confined scale,[1] twelve spindles being thought a great matter; while the awkward posture required to spin on them was discouraging to grown up people, who saw with surprise children from nine to twelve years of age manage them with dexterity, whereby plenty was brought into families formerly overburthened with children, and the poor weavers were delivered from the bondage in which they had lain from the insolence of spinners. . . .

The improvements kept increasing, till the capital engines for twist [i.e., the machinery that twisted cotton fibers into thread] were perfected, by which thousands of spindles are put in motion by a water wheel,[2] and managed mostly by children, without confusion and with less waste of cotton than by the former methods. But the carding [wherein cotton fibers were combed out straight and parallel] and slubbing [wherein carded fibers were drawn together and twisted into yarn] preparatory to twisting required a greater range of invention. The first attempts were in carding engines, which are very curious, and now brought to a great degree of perfection; and an engine has been contrived for converting the carded wool [cotton] to slubbing, by drawing it to about the thickness of candle-wick preparatory to throwing it into twist. . . .

These machines exhibit in their construction an aggregate of clock-maker's work and machinery most wonderful to behold. The cotton to be spun is introduced through three sets of rollers, so governed by the clock-work, that the set which first receives the cotton makes so many revolutions than the next in order, and these more than the last which feed the spindles, that it is drawn out considerably in passing through the rollers; being lastly received by spindles, which have every one on the bobbin a fly [an arm which revolves around the bobbin, adding additional twist to the thread] like that of a flax wheel. . . .

Upon these machines twist is made of any fineness [thickness] proper for warps [threads that run lengthwise on a loom]; but as it is drawn length way of the staple, it was not so proper for weft;[3] wherefore on the introduction of fine calicoes [coarse cotton cloth] and muslins [fine cotton cloth],

---

[1] **country people . . . scale**: Aikin refers to the cottage industry, in which individual families labored as a unit in their own homes to convert raw cotton into woven cloth.

[2] **water wheel**: Aikin is describing an early thread-spinning machine called a "water frame," owing to the water wheel that powered it. The water frame's invention is usually attributed to pioneer textile manufacturer Richard Arkwright.

[3] **as it is drawn . . . weft**: Aikin suggests that thread produced by water frames lacked the flexibility and strength to be used for the weft, the threads that cross from side to side on a loom at right angles to the warp.

mules[4] were invented, having a name expressive of their species, being a mixed machinery between jennies and the machines for twisting, and adapted to spin weft as fine as could be desired. . . .

These mules carry often to a hundred and fifty spindles, and can be set to draw weft to an exact fineness up to 150 hanks in the pound, of which muslin has been made, which for a while had a prompt sale; but the flimsiness of its fabric has brought the finer sorts into discredit, and a stagnation of trade damped the sale of the rest. . . .

The prodigious extension of the several branches of the Manchester manufactures has likewise greatly increased the business of several trades and manufactures connected with or dependent upon them. The making of paper at mills in the vicinity has been brought to great perfection, and now includes all kinds, from the strongest parceling paper to the finest writing sorts, and that on which banker's bills are printed. To the iron-mongers shops, which are greatly increased of late, are generally annexed smithies [blacksmiths], where many articles are made, even to nails. A considerable iron foundry is established in Salford, in which are cast most of the articles wanted in Manchester and its neighborhood, consisting chiefly of large cast wheels for the cotton machines; cylinders, boilers, and pipes for steam engines; cast ovens, and grates of all sizes. This work belongs to Batemen and Sharrard, gen[tle]men every way qualified for so great an undertaking. Mr. Sharrard is a very ingenious and able engineer, who has improved upon and brought the steam engine to great perfection. . . .

The tin-plate workers have found additional employment in furnishing many articles for spinning machines; as have also the braziers in casting wheels for the motion-work of the rollers used in them; and the clock-makers in cutting them. Harness-makers have been much employed in making bands for carding engines, and large wheels for the first operation of drawing out the cardings, whereby the consumption of strong curried leather has been much increased. . . .

Within the last twenty or thirty years the vast increase of foreign trade has caused many of the Manchester manufacturers to travel abroad, and agents or partners to be fixed for a considerable time on the continent, as well as foreigners to reside at Manchester. And the town has now in every respect assumed the style and manners of one of the commercial capitals of Europe.

---

[4] **mules:** Samuel Crompton's "spinning mule" (1772), so called because, like its namesake, which combined the virtues of the donkey (nimbleness, endurance) with those of a horse (strength), it combined the productive capacity of the water frame with the spinning jenny's ability to spin the finest thread.

READING AND DISCUSSION QUESTIONS

1. What is Aikin's reaction to the prevalence of child labor in the spin-
    ning mills he describes? What might this imply about English labor
    standards at the time?

2. Where was the demand that drove this "prodigious extension of the
    several branches of the Manchester manufactures" coming from, and
    why? Put another way, why were cotton textile producers and other
    manufacturers employing machinery to increase production, rather
    than relying on the traditional cottage industry?

3. Based on Aikin's account, what can be inferred about Britain's popula-
    tion and its purchasing power?

4. In addition to the water supply, what elements made Manchester an
    ideal location for manufacturing? What different businesses or work
    forces did manufacturers rely upon?

DOCUMENT 21-3

FRIEDRICH ENGELS

The Condition of the Working Class
in England in 1844

1844

Friedrich Engels (1820–1895) is best known today as Karl Marx's collabora-
tor and coauthor of The Communist Manifesto *(1848). He was also a social*
scientist in his own right, and The Condition of the Working Class in
England in 1844 *was a pioneering sociological study. His account of condi-*
tions in Manchester's working-class neighborhoods was based on extensive
firsthand experience acquired while overseeing his family's cotton textile
interests in the city.

Manchester lies at the foot of the southern slope of a range of hills, which
stretch hither from Oldham . . . and contains about four hundred thou-

From Friedrich Engels, *The Condition of the Working-Class in England in 1844*
(London: Swan Sonnenschein & Co., 1892), pp. 45, 48–53.

sand inhabitants, rather more than less. The town itself is peculiarly built, so that a person may live in it for years, and go in and out daily without coming into contact with a working-people's quarter or even with workers, that is, so long as he confines himself to his business or to pleasure walks. This arises chiefly from the fact, that by unconscious tacit agreement, as well as with outspoken conscious determination, the working-people's quarters are sharply separated from the sections of the city reserved for the middle-class. . . .

I may mention just here that the mills almost all adjoin the rivers or the different canals that ramify throughout the city, before I proceed at once to describe the laboring quarters. First of all, there is the old town of Manchester, which lies between the northern boundary of the commercial district and the Irk. Here the streets, even the better ones, are narrow and winding, as Todd Street, Long Millgate, Withy Grove, and Shude Hill, the houses dirty, old, and tumble-down, and the construction of the side streets utterly horrible. Going from the Old Church to Long Millgate, the stroller has at once a row of old-fashioned houses at the right, of which not one has kept its original level; these are remnants of the old premanufacturing Manchester, whose former inhabitants have removed with their descendants into better built districts, and have left the houses, which were not good enough for them, to a population strongly mixed with Irish blood. Here one is in an almost undisguised working-men's quarter, for even the shops and beer houses hardly take the trouble to exhibit a trifling degree of cleanliness. But all this is nothing in comparison with the courts and lanes which lie behind, to which access can be gained only through covered passages, in which no two human beings can pass at the same time. Of the irregular cramming together of dwellings in ways which defy all rational plan, of the tangle in which they are crowded literally one upon the other, it is impossible to convey an idea. And it is not the buildings surviving from the old times of Manchester which are to blame for this; the confusion has only recently reached its height when every scrap of space left by the old way of building has been filled up and patched over until not a foot of land is left to be further occupied.

The south bank of the Irk is here very steep and between fifteen and thirty feet high. On this declivitous hillside there are planted three rows of houses, of which the lowest rise directly out of the river, while the front walls of the highest stand on the crest of the hill in Long Millgate. Among them are mills on the river, in short, the method of construction is as crowded and disorderly here as in the lower part of Long Millgate. Right and left a multitude of covered passages lead from the main street into numerous courts, and he who turns in thither gets into a filth and disgusting grime, the equal of which is not to be found — especially in the courts which lead down to the Irk, and which contain unqualifiedly the most horrible dwellings which I have yet beheld. In one of these courts there stands directly at the entrance, at the end of the covered passage, a privy without a door, so dirty that the inhabitants can pass into and out of the court only by passing through foul pools of stagnant urine and excrement. This is the first court on the Irk above Ducie Bridge — in case any one should care to look into it. Below it on the river there are several tanneries which fill the whole neighborhood with the stench of animal putrefaction [i.e., rotting carcasses]. Below Ducie Bridge the only entrance to most of the houses is by means of narrow, dirty stairs and over heaps of refuse and filth. The first court below Ducie Bridge, known as Allen's Court, was in such a state at the time of the cholera[5] that the sanitary police ordered it evacuated, swept, and disinfected with chloride of lime. Dr. Kay[6] gives a terrible description of the state of this court at that time. Since then, it seems to have been partially torn away and rebuilt; at least looking down from Ducie Bridge, the passer-by sees several ruined walls and heaps of debris with some newer houses. The view from this bridge, mercifully concealed from mortals of small stature by a parapet as high as a man, is characteristic for the whole district. At the bottom flows, or rather stagnates, the Irk, a narrow, coal-black, foul-smelling stream, full of debris and refuse, which it deposits on the shallower right bank.

In dry weather, a long string of the most disgusting, blackish-green, slime pools are left standing on this bank, from the depths of which bubbles of miasmatic gas constantly arise and give forth a stench unendurable even on the bridge forty or fifty feet above the surface of the stream. But besides this, the stream itself is checked every few paces by high weirs, behind which slime and refuse accumulate and rot in thick masses. Above the bridge are tanneries, bone mills, and gasworks, from which all drains and refuse find their way into the Irk, which receives further the contents of all the neighboring sewers and privies. It may be easily imagined, therefore, what sort of residue the stream deposits. Below the bridge you look

---

[5] **at the time of the cholera**: Cholera, a disease caused by the contamination of water supplies with human excrement, first appeared in Britain in 1831.

[6] **Dr. Kay**: Dr. James Kay, later Sir James Kay-Shuttlesworth (1804–1877), author of *The Moral and Physical Condition of the Working-Class Employed in the Cotton Manufacture in Manchester* (1832).

upon the piles of debris, the refuse, filth, and offal from the courts on the steep left bank; here each house is packed close behind its neighbor and a piece of each is visible, all black, smoky, crumbling, ancient, with broken panes and window frames. The background is furnished by old barrack-like factory buildings. On the lower right bank stands a long row of houses and mills; the second house being a ruin without a roof, piled with debris; the third stands so low that the lowest floor is uninhabitable, and therefore without windows or doors. Here the background embraces the pauper burial-ground, the station of the Liverpool and Leeds railway, and, in the rear of this, the Workhouse, the "Poor-Law Bastille"[7] of Manchester, which, like a citadel, looks threateningly down from behind its high walls and parapets on the hilltop, upon the working-people's quarter below.

Above Ducie Bridge, the left bank grows more flat and the right bank steeper, but the condition of the dwellings on both banks grows worse rather than better. He who turns to the left here from the main street, Long Millgate, is lost; he wanders from one court to another, turns countless corners, passes nothing but narrow, filthy nooks and alleys, until after a few minutes he has lost all clue, and knows not whither to turn. Everywhere half or wholly ruined buildings, some of them actually uninhabited, which means a great deal here; rarely a wooden or stone floor to be seen in the houses, almost uniformly broken, ill-fitting windows and doors, and a state of filth! Everywhere heaps of debris, refuse, and offal; standing pools for gutters, and a stench which alone would make it impossible for a human being in any degree civilized to live in such a district. The newly-built extension of the Leeds railway, which crosses the Irk here, has swept away some of these courts and lanes, laying others completely open to view. Immediately under the railway bridge there stands a court, the filth and horrors of which surpass all the others by far, just because it was hitherto so shut off, so secluded that the way to it could not be found without a good deal of trouble. I should never have discovered it myself, without the breaks made by the railway, though I thought I knew this whole region thoroughly. Passing along a rough bank, among stakes and washing-lines, one penetrates into this chaos of small one-storied, one-roomed huts, in most of which there is no artificial floor; kitchen, living and sleeping-room all in one. In such a hole, scarcely five feet long by six broad, I found two beds —

---

[7] **Poor Law Bastille**: The Poor Law legislation passed in 1834 mandated that all able-bodied recipients of public charity forfeit any property they possessed and live and labor in workhouses.

and such bedsteads and beds! — which, with a staircase and chimney-place, exactly filled the room. In several others I found absolutely nothing, while the door stood open, and the inhabitants leaned against it. Everywhere before the doors refuse and offal; that any sort of pavement lay underneath could not be seen but only felt, here and there, with the feet. This whole collection of cattle-sheds for human beings was surrounded on two sides by houses and a factory, and on the third by the river, and besides the narrow stair up the bank, a narrow doorway alone led out into another almost equally ill-built, ill-kept labyrinth of dwellings. . . .

If we leave the Irk and penetrate once more on the opposite side from Long Millgate into the midst of the working-men's dwellings, we shall come into a somewhat newer quarter, which stretches from St. Michael's Church to Withy Grove and Shude Hill. Here there is somewhat better order. In place of the chaos of buildings, we find at least long straight lanes and alleys or courts, built according to a plan and usually square. But if, in the former case, every house was built according to caprice, here each lane and court is so built, without reference to the situation of the adjoining ones. . . .

Here, as in most of the working-men's quarters of Manchester, the pork-raisers rent the courts and build pig-pens in them. In almost every court one or even several such pens may be found, into which the inhabitants of the court throw all refuse and offal, whence the swine grow fat; and the atmosphere, confined on all four sides, is utterly corrupted by putrefying animal and vegetable substances. . . .

Such is the Old Town of Manchester, and on re-reading my description, I am forced to admit that instead of being exaggerated, it is far from black enough to convey a true impression of the filth, ruin, and uninhabitableness, the defiance of all considerations of cleanliness, ventilation, and health which characterize the construction of this single district, containing at least twenty to thirty thousand inhabitants. And such a district exists in the heart of the second city of England, the first manufacturing city of the world. If any one wishes to see in how little space a human being can move, how little air — and *such* air! — he can breathe, how little of civilization he may share and yet live, it is only necessary to travel hither. True, this is the *Old* Town, and the people of Manchester emphasize the fact whenever any one mentions to them the frightful condition of this Hell upon Earth; but what does that prove? Everything which here arouses horror and indignation is of recent origin, belongs to the *industrial epoch*.

READING AND DISCUSSION QUESTIONS

1. How was it possible, as Engels claimed, that middle-class residents of Manchester's suburbs could pass through the working-class districts closer to the city center on their way to and from work, "without coming into contact with a working-people's quarter or even with workers"? What does this claim suggest about economic segregation in the city?

2. "Of the irregular cramming together of dwellings in ways which defy all rational plan, of the tangle in which they are crowded literally one upon the other, it is impossible to convey an idea," Engels remarked of one district. Why might Manchester have developed in this way?

3. What might his remark about the Long Millgate district containing a "population strongly mixed with Irish blood" suggest about Engels's racial attitudes?

DOCUMENT 21-4

NED LUDD

Yorkshire Textile Workers Threaten a Factory Owner

ca. 1811–1812

In the early nineteenth century, the new mechanization of textile manufacturing endangered the livelihoods of the handworkers engaged in manual textile production. During the years 1811–1816, many English hosiery weavers found themselves replaced by stocking frames. Croppers, whose task was to finish woven cloth by cropping (shearing) it, were threatened by the introduction of the shearing frame. The workers retaliated by smashing the "detestable" machines that had claimed their jobs. They adopted the name "Luddites" after an apocryphal (probably) Edward "Ned" Ludd, lauded as

From G. D. H. Cole and A. W. Filson, eds., *British Working Class Documents: Selected Documents 1789–1875* (London: Macmillan, 1951), pp. 113–115.

the first to destroy a shearing frame. Hostile missives, like that which follows, were often sent to the owners of stocking or shearing frames, and made frequent reference to "King Ludd," a protector of the downtrodden.

Sir,

Information has just been given in, that you are a holder [owner] of those detestable Shearing Frames, and I was desired by my men to write to you, and give you fair warning to pull them down, and for that purpose I desire that you will understand I am now writing to you, you will take notice that if they are not taken down by the end of next week, I shall detach one of my lieutenants with at least 300 men to destroy them, and further more take notice that if you give us the trouble of coming thus far, we will increase your misfortunes by burning your buildings down to ashes. . . . We hope for assistance from the French Emperor[8] in shaking off the Yoke of the Rottenest, wickedest, and most Tyrannical Government that ever existed. . . . We will never lay down our arms till the House of Commons passes an act to put down all the machinery hurtfull [*sic*] to the Commonality and repeal that[9] to the Frame Breakers. . . .

Signed by the General of the Army of Redressers,
Ned Ludd, Clerk

READING AND DISCUSSION QUESTIONS

1. Why do you think the Luddites resorted to threats and violence rather than peacefully seeking redress through the political process?

2. Why, in a threat to an individual factory owner, do you think the anonymous author of this letter denounced Britain's government as "the Rottenest, wickedest, and most Tyrannical . . . that ever existed"?

3. Why might the Luddites have expected the French emperor Napoleon to be their savior?

---

[8] **assistance from the French Emperor**: Great Britain was engaged in a lengthy war against the French emperor, Napoleon Bonaparte.
[9] **repeal that**: In response to the wave of machine breaking, Parliament made such crimes capital offenses.

DOCUMENT 21-5

ROBERT OWEN

A New View of Society

1813

Robert Owen (1771–1858) first gained prominence as a successful textile manufacturer who treated his employees generously and beneficently. He later became a tireless promoter of educational reform, and was an early "utopian" socialist and trade union advocate, providing the inspiration for the founding of the Grand National Consolidated Trades Union in 1834. None of Owen's schemes for socialist communities succeeded, nor did the early trade unions, but his theories about educating children were very influential during his own lifetime and remain current today.

According to the last returns under the Population Act, the poor and working classes of Great Britain and Ireland have been found to exceed twelve millions of persons, or nearly three-fourths of the population of the British Islands.

The characters of these persons are now permitted to be very generally formed without proper guidance or direction, and, in many cases, under circumstances which *must* train them to the extreme of vice and misery; and of course render them the worst and most dangerous subjects in the empire; while the far greater part of the remainder of the community are educated upon the most mistaken principles of human nature, such, indeed, as cannot fail to produce a general conduct throughout society, totally unworthy of the character of rational beings.

The first thus unhappily situated are the poor and the uneducated profligate among the working classes, who are now trained to commit crimes, which they are afterwards *punished* for committing.

The second is the remaining mass of the population, who are now *instructed* to *believe*, or at least to acknowledge, that certain principles are *unerringly true*, and to *act* as though they were *grossly false*; thus filling the

From Robert Owen, *A New View of Society, or Essays on the Principle of the Formation of Human Character and the Application of the Principle to Practice* (London: Richard Taylor and Co., 1813), pp. 5–6, 9, 26–28, 35–36, 38–41, 49–51.

world with *folly* and *inconsistency*, and making society, throughout all its ramifications, a scene of insincerity.

This state of matters has continued for a long period, its evils have been and are continually increasing, until they now cry aloud for efficient corrective measures, or general disorder must ensue. . . .

Did these circumstances not exist to an extent almost incredible, could it be necessary *now* to contend for a principle regarding Man, which scarcely requires more than to be fairly stated to make it self-evident? This principle is, "THAT ANY CHARACTER, FROM THE BEST TO THE WORST, FROM THE MOST IGNORANT TO THE MOST EN-LIGHTENED, MAY BE GIVEN TO ANY COMMUNITY, EVEN TO THE WORLD AT LARGE, BY APPLYING CERTAIN MEANS WHICH ARE TO A GREAT EXTENT AT THE COMMAND AND UNDER THE CONTROL, OR EASILY MADE SO, OF THOSE WHO POSSESS THE GOVERNMENT OF NATIONS."

The principle as now stated is a broad one, and, if it should be found to be true, cannot fail to give a new character to legislative proceedings, and *such* a character as will be most favorable to the well-being of society. . . .

Children are without exception passive agents, or wonderfully con-trived compounds, which by due preparation and accurate attention, founded on a correct knowledge of the subject, may be formed collectively into any Human character. And although these original compounds like all the other works of the Great Directing Power of the Universe, possess endless varieties, yet they all partake of that plastic nature or quality, which, by perseverance under judicious management, may be ultimately molded into the very image of rational wishes and desires.

And in the next place, these principles cannot fail soon to create those feelings, which without force, or the production of any counteracting motive, will irresistibly lead those who possess them to make due allow-ance for the difference of sentiments and manners not only among their friends and countrymen, but also among the inhabitants of every region on the earth, even including their enemies. For, with this insight into the formation of character, where is there any conceivable foundation for pri-vate displeasure or public enmity? Say, if it be within the sphere of possi-bility that children can be trained to acquire *that* knowledge and *these* feelings? The child of eight years growth, who from infancy has been ratio-nally trained in these principles, will readily discover and trace from whence the opinions and habits of his associates have arisen, and why they possess them. And at the same age he will have acquired reasons suffi-ciently powerful to exhibit to him in strong colors the irrationality of being angry with an individual for possessing qualities which, as an unavoidable passive agent during the formation of those qualities, he had not the means of preventing. Such must be the impressions which these principles will make on the mind of every such child; and in lieu of generating anger or displeasure, they will produce commiseration and pity for those individuals, who possess either habits or sentiments which appear to him to be destructive of their own comfort, pleasure, or happiness, and will promote in him a desire to remove those causes of distress, that his own feelings of commiseration and pity may be also removed. And the pleasure which he cannot avoid experiencing by this mode of conduct, will likewise stimulate him to the most active endeavors to withdraw all those circumstances which surround any part of mankind with causes of misery, and to replace them with others which have a tendency to increase their happiness. He must then also strongly entertain the desire to "do good to *all* men," and even to "love his enemies."

In the year 1784 the late Mr. Dale[10] of Glasgow founded a spinning and weaving manufactory near the falls of the Clyde, in the county of Lanark in Scotland; and about that period cotton mills were first introduced into the northern part of the kingdom.

It was the power which could be obtained from the falls of water which induced Mr. Dale to erect his mills in this situation, for in other respects it was not well chosen: the country around was uncultivated; the inhabitants were poor, and few in number; and the roads in the neighborhood were so bad, that the falls of Clyde now so celebrated were then unknown to strangers.

It was therefore necessary to collect a new population to supply the infant establishment with laborers. This however was no light task; for all the regularly trained Scotch peasantry disdained the idea of working from early till late, day after day, within cotton mills. Two modes only to obtain these laborers occurred: the one, to procure children from the various public charities in the country; and the other, to induce families to settle around the works.

To accommodate the first, a large house was erected, which ultimately contained about five hundred children, who were procured chiefly from workhouses and charities in Edinburgh.

These children were to be fed, clothed, and educated; and these duties Mr. Dale performed with the benevolence which he was known to possess. . . .

The benevolent proprietor spared no expense which could give comfort to the poor children which it contained. The rooms provided for them

---

[10] **the late Mr. Dale**: Robert Owen's father-in-law.

were spacious, always clean, and well ventilated; the food was of the best quality, and most abundant; the clothes were neat and useful; a surgeon was kept in constant pay to direct how to prevent as well as cure disease; and the best instructors which the country afforded were appointed to teach such branches of education as were deemed likely to be useful to children in their situation; and kind, well disposed persons were appointed to superintend all their proceedings. Nothing, in short, at first sight seemed wanting to render it a most complete charity.

But to defray the expense of these well devised arrangements, and support the establishment generally, it was absolutely necessary that the children should be employed within the mills from six o'clock in the morning to seven in the evening summer and winter; and after these hours their education commenced. The directors of the public charities from mistaken economy, would not consent to send the children under their care to cotton mills, unless the children were received by the proprietors at the ages of six, seven, and eight. And Mr. Dale was under the necessity of accepting them at those ages, or stopping the manufactory which he had commenced.

It is not to be supposed that children so young could remain, with the interval of meals only, from six in the morning until seven in the evening, in constant employment on their feet within cotton mills, and afterwards acquire much proficiency in education. And so it proved; for the greater part of them became dwarfs in body and mind, and many of them deformed. Their labor through the day, and their education at night, became so irksome, that numbers of them continually ran away, and almost all looked forward with impatience and anxiety to the expiration of their apprenticeship of seven, eight, and nine years, which generally expired when they were from thirteen to fifteen years old. At this period of life, unaccustomed to provide for themselves, and unacquainted with the world, they usually went to Edinburgh or Glasgow, where boys and girls were soon assailed by the innumerable temptations which all large towns present; and many of them fell sacrifices to those temptations.

Thus were Mr. Dale's arrangements and kind solicitude for the comfort and happiness of these children rendered in their ultimate effect almost nugatory. They were sent to be employed, and without their labor he could not support them; but, while under his care, he did all that any individual circumstanced as he was could do for his fellow-creatures.

The error proceeded from the children being sent from the workhouses at an age far too young for employment; they ought to have been detained four years longer, and educated; and then all the evils which followed would have been prevented.

And if such be a true picture not overcharged of parish apprentices to our manufacturing system under the best and most humane regulations, in what colors must it be exhibited under the worst? . . .

[Once Owen himself was put in charge of the factory,] the system of receiving apprentices from public charities was abolished; permanent settlers with large families were encouraged, and comfortable houses were built for their accommodation.

The practice of employing children in the mills, of six, seven, and eight years of age, was discontinued, and their parents advised to allow them to acquire health and education until they were ten years old. (It may be remarked, that even this age is too early to keep them at constant employment in manufactories, from six in the morning to seven in the evening. Far better would it be for the children, their parents, and for society, that the first should not commence employment until they attain the age of twelve, when their education might be finished, and their bodies would be more competent to undergo the fatigue and exertions required of them. When parents can be trained to afford this additional time to their children without inconvenience, they will, of course, adopt the practice now recommended.)

The children were taught reading, writing, and arithmetic, during five years, that is, from five to ten, in the village school, without expense to their parents; and all the modern improvements in education have been adopted, or are in process of adoption: some facilities in teaching arithmetic have been also introduced, which were peculiar to this school, and found very advantageous. They may therefore be taught and well trained before they engage in any regular employment. Another important consideration is, that all their instruction is rendered a pleasure and delight to them; they are much more anxious for the hour of school time to arrive, than end: they therefore make a rapid progress; and it may be safely asserted, that if they shall not be trained to form such characters as may be the most wished and desired, not one particle of the fault will proceed from the children; but the cause will rest in the want of a true knowledge of human nature, in those who have the management of them and their parents.

READING AND DISCUSSION QUESTIONS

1. Why was Owen opposed to child labor?
2. What does Owen believe regarding human nature and behavior, especially as they pertain to the poor, criminal, or undereducated?
3. According to Owen, what purposes did education serve for the children of the working class?

The Child of the Factory
1842

Child labor was neither a novelty nor a product of the Industrial Revolution; children in traditional agricultural societies were (and are) put to work as soon as they were capable of contributing to the family economy. Yet the circumstances associated with industrialization, in particular the factory system of labor organization, focused public attention on the phenomenon as never before — first in Britain and then, as the illustration suggests, in continental Europe. The consequence, again beginning in Britain, was a humanitarian outcry leading to legislation limiting and eventually prohibiting child labor in factories. This illustration accompanied an article written about children in the cotton textile industry in France.

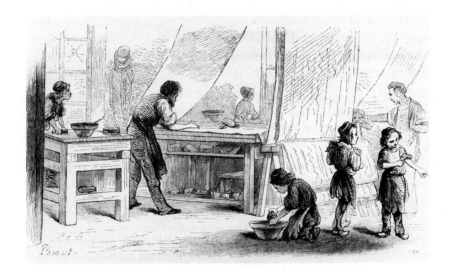

From *Les Français Peints par Eux-Mêmes: Encyclopédie Morale du Dix-Neuvième Siècle*, vol. 1 (Paris: L. Curmer, 1841), p. 257. Bibliothèque des Arts Decoratifs, Paris, France/Archives Charmet/The Bridgeman Art Library.

READING AND DISCUSSION QUESTIONS

1. On what grounds might contemporaries, including many members of the working class, have defended child labor?

2. Are all of the children depicted in the illustration actually working? If not, then why might they be in the factory?

COMPARATIVE QUESTIONS

1. What similarities do you see between Malthus's arguments and those of Adam Smith (Document 18-3) regarding the "wages of labor"? What differences?

2. What do Aikin and Engels choose to focus on in their descriptions of industrial Manchester? How do the people of Manchester figure into their descriptions, and how does that affect your opinion of their arguments?

3. How and why might Malthus have reacted to the conditions in Manchester described by Engels?

4. What do you think Malthus would say about Owen's views on human nature? Why? What do you think John Locke (Document 16-6) would say about them and why?

5. What do you think Robert Owen thought of the Luddites? Why?

6. Compare Owen's views on child labor with those of John Aikin. What might account for the differences between the two? How would they react to the depiction of the children in the French cotton factory?

CHAPTER 22

Ideologies and Upheavals

1815–1850

T he rapid social changes brought about by the Industrial Revolution in the early nineteenth century led to the rise of a number of competing ideologies, often proposed as responses to the appalling living and working conditions in early industrial cities. Protectionist legislation, favored by conservatives and mercantilists, aimed to keep the prices of food and other items artificially high while controlling their distribution. Liberals, by contrast, sought an end to government controls to stimulate business and encourage free trade. Communists offered yet another solution — the seizure of the means and ownership of production by the working class — while Chartists sought the enfranchisement of all adult males. For all the hardships wrought by industrialization, the population of England rose dramatically in nineteenth century. At the same time, the population of Ireland shrank from about eight million to scarcely six million during the 1840s as people fled the devastating conditions of the potato famine.

DOCUMENT 22-1

DAVID RICARDO

On Wages

1817

After Adam Smith, David Ricardo (1772–1823) is almost certainly the most famous classical liberal economist. A prolific writer on "political economy," Ricardo penned the 1817 treatise On the Principles of Political Economy and Taxation, *from which the following excerpt is drawn. Unlike Smith, who*

From *The Works of David Ricardo*, ed. J. R. McCulloch (London: John Murray, 1881), pp. 31, 50–58.

advocated the "liberal reward of labor" because "it increases the industry of the common people," Ricardo argued that laws of supply and demand should apply to wages as well as to products. Given a surplus of labor like that in nineteenth-century England, wages would inevitably sink. In the wake of Ricardo's highly influential writings, economics became widely known as "the dismal science."

Money, from its being a commodity obtained from a foreign country, from its being the general medium of exchange between all civilized countries, and from its being also distributed among those countries in proportions which are ever changing with every improvement in commerce and machinery, and with every increasing difficulty of obtaining food and necessaries for an increasing population, is subject to incessant variations. In stating the principles which regulate exchangeable value and price, we should carefully distinguish between those variations which belong to the commodity itself, and those which are occasioned by a variation in the medium in which value is estimated, or price expressed.

A rise in wages, from an alteration in the value of money, produces a general effect [i.e., inflation] on price, and for that reason it produces no real effect whatever on profits. On the contrary, a rise of wages, from the circumstance of the laborer being more liberally rewarded, or from a difficulty of procuring the necessaries on which wages are expended, does not, except in some instances, produce the effect of raising price, but has a great effect in lowering profits. In the one case, no greater proportion of the annual labor of the country is devoted to the support of the laborers; in the other case, a larger portion is so devoted.

Labor, like all other things which are purchased and sold, and which may be increased or diminished in quantity, has its natural and its market price. The natural price of labor is that price which is necessary to enable the laborers, one with another, to subsist and to perpetuate their race, without either increase or diminution.

The power of the laborer to support himself, and the family which may be necessary to keep up the number of laborers, does not depend on the quantity of money which he may receive for wages, but on the quantity of food, necessaries, and conveniences become essential to him from habit, which that money will purchase.[1] The natural price of labor, therefore,

---

[1] **The quantity of food . . . purchase**: The concept of "real wages" or "purchasing power." It is not the wage itself that matters, but what that wage can buy.

depends on the price of the food, necessaries, and conveniences required for the support of the laborer and his family. With a rise in the price of food and necessaries, the natural price of labor will rise; with the fall in their price, the natural price of labor will fall.

With the progress of society the natural price of labor has always a tendency to rise, because one of the principal commodities by which its natural price is regulated [food], has a tendency to become dearer, from the greater difficulty of producing it. As, however, the improvements in agriculture, the discovery of new markets, whence provisions may be imported, may for a time counteract the tendency to a rise in the price of necessaries, and may even occasion their natural price to fall, so will the same causes produce the correspondent effects on the natural price of labor.

The natural price of all commodities, excepting raw produce and labor, has a tendency to fall, in the progress of wealth and population; for though, on one hand, they are enhanced in real value, from the rise in the natural price of the raw material of which they are made, this is more than counterbalanced by the improvements in machinery, by the better division and distribution of labor, and by the increasing skill, both in science and art, of the producers.

The market price of labor is the price which is really paid for it, from the natural operation of the proportion of the supply to the demand; labor is dear when it is scarce, and cheap when it is plentiful. However much the market price of labor may deviate from its natural price, it has, like commodities, a tendency to conform to it.

It is when the market price of labor exceeds its natural price, that the condition of the laborer is flourishing and happy, that he has it in his power to command a greater proportion of the necessaries and enjoyments of life, and therefore to rear a healthy and numerous family.

When, however, by the encouragement which high wages give to the increase of population, the number of laborers is increased, wages again fall to their natural price, and indeed from a reaction sometimes fall below it.

When the market price of labor is below its natural price, the condition of the laborers is most wretched: then poverty deprives them of those comforts which custom renders absolute necessaries. It is only after their privations have reduced their number, or the demand for labor has increased, that the market price of labor will rise to its natural price, and that the laborer will have the moderate comforts which the natural rate of wages will afford.

Notwithstanding the tendency of wages to conform to their natural rate, their market rate may, in an improving society, for an indefinite period, be constantly above it; for no sooner may the impulse, which an increased capital gives to a new demand for labor, be obeyed, than another increase of capital may produce the same effect; and thus, if the increase of capital be gradual and constant, the demand for labor may give a continued stimulus to an increase of people. . . .

Thus, then, with every improvement of society, with every increase in its capital, the market wages of labor will rise; but the permanence of their rise will depend on the question, whether the natural price of labor has also risen; and this again will depend on the rise in the natural price of those necessaries on which the wages of labor are expended. . . .

As population increases, these necessaries will be constantly rising in price, because more labor will be necessary to produce them. If, then, the money wages of labor should fall, whilst every commodity on which the wages of labor were expended rose, the laborer would be doubly affected, and would be soon totally deprived of subsistence. Instead, therefore, of the money wages of labor falling, they would rise; but they would not rise sufficiently to enable the laborer to purchase as many comforts and necessaries as he did before the rise in the price of those commodities. . . .

These, then, are the laws by which wages are regulated, and by which the happiness of far the greatest part of every community is governed. Like all other contracts, wages should be left to the fair and free competition of the market, and should never be controlled by the interference of the legislature.

The clear and direct tendency of the poor laws[2] is in direct opposition to these obvious principles: it is not, as the legislature benevolently intended, to amend the condition of the poor, but to deteriorate the condition of both poor and rich; instead of making the poor rich, they are calculated to make the rich poor; and whilst the present laws are in force, it is quite in the natural order of things that the fund for the maintenance of the poor should progressively increase till it has absorbed all the net revenue of the country, or at least so much of it as the state shall leave to us, after satisfying its own never-failing demands for the public expenditure.

This pernicious tendency of these laws is no longer a mystery, since it has been fully developed by the able hand of Mr. Malthus;[3] and every friend to the poor must ardently wish for their abolition.

---

[2] **poor laws**: The English Poor Law (1601) enabled local authorities to levy taxes (the "poor rates") for the assistance and relief of the deserving poor. As such, they amounted to a rudimentary social safety net.

[3] **Mr. Malthus**: Thomas Malthus, whose *Essay on the Principle of Population* (see Document 21-1) was a major influence on Ricardo's thought.

READING AND DISCUSSION QUESTIONS

1. Explain the difference between "natural price" and "market price."

2. Given a free market (that is to say no minimum wage laws or other government interference) for labor and a surplus of laborers, what would, according to Ricardo, happen to wages?

3. Why do you think Ricardo argues that the Poor Law, which was intended "to amend the condition of the poor," conversely "deteriorate the condition of both poor and rich; instead of making the poor rich, they are calculated to make the rich poor"?

4. To what extent did the mechanization of manufacturing and the replacement of skilled handicraft workers by semiskilled "machine tenders" reinforce Ricardo's argument?

VIEWPOINTS

Conservatism and Liberalism

DOCUMENT 22-2

KLEMENS VON METTERNICH
Political Confession of Faith
1820

Prince Klemens von Metternich (1773–1859) was Austria's foreign secretary from 1809 until driven into exile during the revolution of 1848. As the key figure at the Congress of Vienna, he was widely credited as principal architect of the peace settlement that ended the Napoleonic wars and ushered in the "long peace" of the nineteenth century. As a member of the landed aristocracy and a staunch upholder of the established social hierarchy, Metternich was a fervent foe of liberalism and nationalism, both of which he regarded as revolutionary doctrines.

From Klemens von Metternich, *Memoirs of Prince Metternich, 1815–1829*, vol. 3, ed. Richard von Metternich (New York: Charles Scribner and Sons, 1881), pp. 456–458, 461–463, 469–471, 473–476.

THE SOURCE OF THE EVIL

Man's nature is immutable. The first needs of society are and remain the same, and the differences which they seem to offer find their explanation in the diversity of influences, acting on the different races by natural causes, such as the diversity of climate, barrenness or richness of soil, insular or continental position, &c. &c. These local differences no doubt produce effects which extend far beyond purely physical necessities; they create and determine particular needs in a more elevated sphere; finally, they determine the laws, and exercise an influence even on religions.

It is, on the other hand, with institutions as with everything else. Vague in their origin, they pass through periods of development and perfection, to arrive in time at their decadence; and, conforming to the laws of man's nature, they have, like him, their infancy, their youth, their age of strength and reason, and their age of decay.

Two elements alone remain in all their strength, and never cease to exercise their indestructible influence with equal power. These are the precepts of morality, religious as well as social, and the necessities created by locality. From the time that men attempt to swerve from these bases, to become rebels against these sovereign arbiters of their destinies, society suffers from a *malaise* which sooner or later will lead to a state of convulsion. The history of every country, in relating the consequences of such errors, contains many pages stained with blood, but we dare to say, without fear of contradiction, one seeks in vain for an epoch when an evil of this nature has extended its ravages over such a vast area as it has done at the present time. . . .

The progress of the human mind has been extremely rapid in the course of the last three centuries. This progress having been accelerated more rapidly than the growth of wisdom (the only counterpoise to passions and to error); a revolution prepared by the false systems, the fatal errors into which many of the most illustrious sovereigns of the last half of the eighteenth century fell, has at last broken out in a country advanced in knowledge [i.e., France], and enervated by pleasure, in a country inhabited by a people whom one can only regard as frivolous, from the facility with which they comprehend and the difficulty they experience in judging calmly. . . .

France had the misfortune to produce the greatest number of these men. It is in her midst that religion and all that she holds sacred, that morality and authority, and all connected with them, have been attacked with a steady and systematic animosity, and it is there that the weapon of ridicule has been used with the most ease and success.

Drag through the mud the name of God and the powers instituted by His divine decrees, and the revolution will be prepared! Speak of a social contract, and the revolution is accomplished! The revolution was already completed in the palaces of Kings, in the drawing-rooms and boudoirs of certain cities, while among the great mass of the people it was still only in a state of preparation. . . .

The scenes of horror which accompanied the first phases of the French Revolution prevented the rapid propagation of its subversive principles beyond the frontiers of France, and the wars of conquest which succeeded them gave to the public mind a direction little favorable to revolutionary principles. Thus the Jacobin propaganda failed entirely to realize criminal hopes.

Nevertheless the revolutionary seed had penetrated into every country and spread more or less. It was greatly developed under the *régime* of the military despotism of Bonaparte. His conquests displaced a number of laws, institutions, and customs; broke through bonds sacred among all nations, strong enough to resist time itself; which is more than can be said of certain benefits conferred by these innovators. From these perturbations it followed that the revolutionary spirit could in Germany, Italy, and later on in Spain, easily hide itself under the veil of patriotism. . . .

We are convinced that society can no longer be saved without strong and vigorous resolutions on the part of the Governments still free in their opinions and actions.

We are also convinced that this may yet be, if the Governments face the truth, if they free themselves from all illusion, if they join their ranks and take their stand on a line of correct, unambiguous, and frankly announced principles.

By this course the monarchs will fulfill the duties imposed upon them by Him who, by entrusting them with power, has charged them to watch over the maintenance of justice, and the rights of all, to avoid the paths of error, and tread firmly in the way of truth. Placed beyond the passions which agitate society, it is in days of trial chiefly that they are called upon to despoil realities of their false appearances, and to show themselves as they are, fathers invested with the authority belonging by right to the heads of families, to prove that, in days of mourning, they know how to be just, wise, and therefore strong, and that they will not abandon the people whom they ought to govern to be the sport of factions, to error and its consequences, which must involve the loss of society. The moment in which we are putting our thoughts on paper is one of these critical moments. The crisis is great; it will be decisive according to the part we take or do not take. . . .

Union between the monarchs is the basis of the policy which must now be followed to save society from total ruin. . . .

The first principle to be followed by the monarchs, united as they are by the coincidence of their desires and opinions, should be that of maintaining the stability of political institutions against the disorganized excitement which has taken possession of men's minds — the immutability of principles against the madness of their interpretation; and respect for laws actually in force against a desire for their destruction. . . .

Let [the Governments] in these troublous times be more than usually cautious in attempting real ameliorations, not imperatively claimed by the needs of the moment, to the end that good itself may not turn against them — which is the case whenever a Government measure seems to be inspired by fear.

Let them not confound concessions made to parties with the good they ought to do for their people, in modifying, according to their recognized needs, such branches of the administration as require it.

Let them give minute attention to the financial state of their kingdoms, so that their people may enjoy, by the reduction of public burdens, the real, not imaginary, benefits of a state of peace.

Let them be just, but strong; beneficent, but strict.

Let them maintain religious principles in all their purity, and not allow the faith to be attacked and morality interpreted according to the *social contract* or the visions of foolish sectarians.

Let them suppress Secret Societies, that gangrene of society.

In short, let the great monarchs strengthen their union, and prove to the world that if it exists, it is beneficent, and ensures the political peace of Europe: that it is powerful only for the maintenance of tranquility at a time when so many attacks are directed against it; that the principles which they profess are paternal and protective, menacing only the disturbers of public tranquility. . . .

To every great State determined to survive the storm there still remain many chances of salvation, and a strong union between the States on the principles we have announced will overcome the storm itself.

READING AND DISCUSSION QUESTIONS

1. Why would Metternich maintain that societies or civilizations "[conform] to the laws of man's nature, [and] have, like him, their infancy, their youth, their age of strength and reason, and their age of decay"?

2. What is Metternich's attitude toward organized religion?
3. Why does Metternich place such emphasis on monarchical power?

DOCUMENT 22-3

KARL MARX AND FRIEDRICH ENGELS
The Communist Manifesto
1848

Karl Marx (1818–1883) and Friedrich Engels (1820–1895) are credited as the founders of communism. In formulating their theories, Marx and Engels drew on the work of earlier economists, particularly Adam Smith and David Ricardo, and on Thomas Malthus's demographic theories, as well as their familiarity with living and working conditions in England's industrial centers. Their Communist Manifesto, first published in London as a pamphlet (written in German), opens with the proclamation that "the history of all hitherto existing society is the history of class struggles." The authors predicted the eventual triumph of the working class (proletariat) over the middle class (bourgeoisie) and the establishment of a classless society in which wealth would be equally distributed.

[PREAMBLE:]

A specter is haunting Europe — the specter of communism. All the powers of old Europe have entered into a holy alliance to exorcise this specter: Pope and Tsar, Metternich and Guizot,[4] French Radicals and German police-spies.

Where is the party in opposition that has not been decried as communistic by its opponents in power? Where is the opposition that has not hurled back the branding reproach of communism, against the more advanced opposition parties, as well as against its reactionary adversaries?

From Karl Marx and Friedrich Engels, *Selected Works*, vol. 1 (Moscow: Progress Publishers, 1969), pp. 2–12, 32, http://www.marxists.org/archive/marx/works/download/manifest.pdf.

[4] **Guizot**: François Pierre Guillaume Guizot (1787–1874), French politician and prime minister (1847–1848).

Two things result from this fact:

I. Communism is already acknowledged by all European powers to be itself a power.
II. It is high time that Communists should openly, in the face of the whole world, publish their views, their aims, their tendencies, and meet this nursery tale of the Specter of Communism with a manifesto of the party itself.

To this end, Communists of various nationalities have assembled in London and sketched the following manifesto, to be published in the English, French, German, Italian, Flemish, and Danish languages.

CHAPTER 1: BOURGEOIS AND PROLETARIANS

The history of all hitherto existing society is the history of class struggles.

Freeman and slave, patrician and plebeian, lord and serf, guild-master and journeyman, in a word, oppressor and oppressed, stood in constant opposition to one another, carried on an uninterrupted, now hidden, now open fight, a fight that each time ended, either in a revolutionary reconstitution of society at large, or in the common ruin of the contending classes.

In the earlier epochs of history, we find almost everywhere a complicated arrangement of society into various orders, a manifold gradation of social rank. In ancient Rome we have patricians, knights, plebeians, slaves; in the Middle Ages, feudal lords, vassals, guild-masters, journeymen, apprentices, serfs; in almost all of these classes, again, subordinate gradations.

The modern bourgeois society that has sprouted from the ruins of feudal society has not done away with class antagonisms. It has but established new classes, new conditions of oppression, new forms of struggle in place of the old ones.

Our epoch, the epoch of the bourgeoisie, possesses, however, this distinct feature: it has simplified class antagonisms. Society as a whole is more and more splitting up into two great hostile camps, into two great classes directly facing each other — Bourgeoisie and Proletariat.

From the serfs of the Middle Ages sprang the chartered burghers of the earliest towns. From these burgesses the first elements of the bourgeoisie were developed.

The discovery of America, the rounding of the Cape, opened up fresh ground for the rising bourgeoisie. . . .

The feudal system of industry, in which industrial production was monopolized by closed guilds, now no longer sufficed for the growing wants of the new markets. The manufacturing system took its place. The guild-masters were pushed on one side by the manufacturing middle class; division of labor between the different corporate guilds vanished in the face of division of labor in each single workshop.

Meantime the markets kept ever growing, the demand ever rising. Even manufacturer no longer sufficed. Thereupon, steam and machinery revolutionized industrial production. The place of manufacture was taken by the giant, Modern Industry; the place of the industrial middle class by industrial millionaires, the leaders of the whole industrial armies. . . . The modern bourgeoisie is itself the product of a long course of development, of a series of revolutions in the modes of production and of exchange.

Each step in the development of the bourgeoisie was accompanied by a corresponding political advance of that class. An oppressed class under the sway of the feudal nobility, an armed and self-governing association in the medieval commune: here independent urban republic (as in Italy and Germany); there taxable "third estate" of the monarchy (as in France); afterwards, in the period of manufacturing proper, serving either the semi-feudal or the absolute monarchy as a counterpoise against the nobility, and, in fact, cornerstone of the great monarchies in general, the bourgeoisie has at last, since the establishment of Modern Industry and of the world market, conquered for itself, in the modern representative State, exclusive political sway. The executive of the modern state is but a committee for managing the common affairs of the whole bourgeoisie.

The bourgeoisie, historically, has played a most revolutionary part.

The bourgeoisie, wherever it has got the upper hand, has put an end to all feudal, patriarchal, idyllic relations . . . [and] has substituted naked, shameless, direct, brutal exploitation.

The bourgeoisie has stripped of its halo every occupation hitherto honored and looked up to with reverent awe. It has converted the physician, the lawyer, the priest, the poet, the man of science, into its paid wage laborers.

The bourgeoisie has torn away from the family its sentimental veil, and has reduced the family relation to a mere money relation. . . .

The bourgeoisie cannot exist without constantly revolutionizing the instruments of production, and thereby the relations of production, and with them the whole relations of society. Conservation of the old modes of production in unaltered form, was, on the contrary, the first condition of existence for all earlier industrial classes. Constant revolutionizing of production, uninterrupted disturbance of all social conditions, everlasting uncertainty and agitation distinguish the bourgeois epoch from all earlier ones. . . .

The need of a constantly expanding market for its products chases the bourgeoisie over the entire surface of the globe. It must nestle everywhere, settle everywhere, establish connections everywhere.

The bourgeoisie has through its exploitation of the world market given a cosmopolitan character to production and consumption in every country. To the great chagrin of Reactionists, it has drawn from under the feet of industry the national ground on which it stood. All old-established national industries have been destroyed or are daily being destroyed. They are dislodged by new industries, whose introduction becomes a life and death question for all civilized nations, by industries that no longer work up indigenous raw material, but raw material drawn from the remotest zones; industries whose products are consumed, not only at home, but in every quarter of the globe. . . .

The bourgeoisie, by the rapid improvement of all instruments of production, by the immensely facilitated means of communication, draws all, even the most barbarian, nations into civilization. The cheap prices of commodities are the heavy artillery with which it batters down all Chinese walls, with which it forces the barbarians' intensely obstinate hatred of foreigners to capitulate. It compels all nations, on pain of extinction, to adopt the bourgeois mode of production; it compels them to introduce what it calls civilization into their midst, i.e., to become bourgeois themselves. In one word, it creates a world after its own image.

The bourgeoisie has subjected the country to the rule of the towns. It has created enormous cities, has greatly increased the urban population as compared with the rural, and has thus rescued a considerable part of the population from the idiocy of rural life. Just as it has made the country dependent on the towns, so it has made barbarian and semi-barbarian countries dependent on the civilized ones, nations of peasants on nations of bourgeois, the East on the West.

The bourgeoisie keeps more and more doing away with the scattered state of the population, of the means of production, and of property. . . .

We see then: the means of production and of exchange, on whose foundation the bourgeoisie built itself up, were generated in feudal society. At a certain stage in the development of these means of production and of exchange, the conditions under which feudal society produced and exchanged, the feudal organization of agriculture and manufacturing industry, in one word, the feudal relations of property became no longer compatible with the already developed productive forces; they became so many fetters. They had to be burst asunder; they were burst asunder.

Into their place stepped free competition, accompanied by a social and political constitution adapted in it, and the economic and political sway of the bourgeois class.

A similar movement is going on before our own eyes. . . . It is enough to mention the commercial crises that by their periodical return put the existence of the entire bourgeois society on its trial, each time more threateningly. In these crises, a great part not only of the existing products, but also of the previously created productive forces, are periodically destroyed. In these crises, there breaks out an epidemic that, in all earlier epochs, would have seemed an absurdity — the epidemic of over-production. Society suddenly finds itself put back into a state of momentary barbarism; it appears as if a famine, a universal war of devastation, had cut off the supply of every means of subsistence; industry and commerce seem to be destroyed; and why? Because there is too much civilization, too much means of subsistence, too much industry, too much commerce. The productive forces at the disposal of society no longer tend to further the development of the conditions of bourgeois property; on the contrary, they have become too powerful for these conditions, by which they are fettered, and so soon as they overcome these fetters, they bring disorder into the whole of bourgeois society, endanger the existence of bourgeois property. The conditions of bourgeois society are too narrow to comprise the wealth created by them. And how does the bourgeoisie get over these crises? On the one hand by enforced destruction of a mass of productive forces; on the other, by the conquest of new markets, and by the more thorough exploitation of the old ones. That is to say, by paving the way for more extensive and more destructive crises, and by diminishing the means whereby crises are prevented.

The weapons with which the bourgeoisie felled feudalism to the ground are now turned against the bourgeoisie itself.

But not only has the bourgeoisie forged the weapons that bring death to itself; it has also called into existence the men who are to wield those weapons — the modern working class — the proletarians.

In proportion as the bourgeoisie, i.e., capital, is developed, in the same proportion is the proletariat, the modern working class, developed — a class of laborers, who live only so long as they find work, and who find work only so long as their labor increases capital. These laborers, who must sell themselves piecemeal, are a commodity, like every other article of commerce, and are consequently exposed to all the vicissitudes of competition, to all the fluctuations of the market.

Owing to the extensive use of machinery, and to the division of labor, the work of the proletarians has lost all individual character, and, consequently, all charm for the workman. He becomes an appendage of the machine, and it is only the most simple, most monotonous, and most easily acquired knack, that is required of him. Hence, the cost of production of a workman is restricted, almost entirely, to the means of subsistence that he requires for maintenance, and for the propagation of his race. But the price of a commodity, and therefore also of labor, is equal to its cost of production. In proportion, therefore, as the repulsiveness of the work increases, the wage decreases. Nay more, in proportion as the use of machinery and division of labor increases, in the same proportion the burden of toil also increases, whether by prolongation of the working hours, by the increase of the work exacted in a given time or by increased speed of machinery, etc.

Modern Industry has converted the little workshop of the patriarchal master into the great factory of the industrial capitalist. Masses of laborers, crowded into the factory, are organized like soldiers. As privates of the industrial army they are placed under the command of a perfect hierarchy of officers and sergeants. Not only are they slaves of the bourgeois class, and of the bourgeois State; they are daily and hourly enslaved by the machine, by the overlooker, and, above all, by the individual bourgeois manufacturer himself. The more openly this despotism proclaims gain to be its end and aim, the more petty, the more hateful and the more embittering it is.

The less the skill and exertion of strength implied in manual labor, in other words, the more modern industry becomes developed, the more is the labor of men superseded by that of women. Differences of age and sex have no longer any distinctive social validity for the working class. All are instruments of labor, more or less expensive to use, according to their age and sex.

No sooner is the exploitation of the laborer by the manufacturer, so far, at an end, that he receives his wages in cash, than he is set upon by the other portions of the bourgeoisie, the landlord, the shopkeeper, the pawnbroker, etc.

The lower strata of the middle class — the small tradespeople, shopkeepers, and retired tradesmen generally, the handicraftsmen and peasants — all these sink gradually into the proletariat, partly because their diminutive capital does not suffice for the scale on which Modern Industry is carried on, and is swamped in the competition with the large capitalists, partly because their specialized skill is rendered worthless by new methods of production. Thus the proletariat is recruited from all classes of the population.

The proletariat goes through various stages of development. With its birth begins its struggle with the bourgeoisie. At first the contest is carried on by individual laborers, then by the workpeople of a factory, then by the operative of one trade, in one locality, against the individual bourgeois who directly exploits them. They direct their attacks not against the bourgeois conditions of production, but against the instruments of production themselves; they destroy imported wares that compete with their labor, they smash to pieces machinery, they set factories ablaze, they seek to restore by force the vanished status of the workman of the Middle Ages.

At this stage, the laborers still form an incoherent mass scattered over the whole country, and broken up by their mutual competition. If anywhere they unite to form more compact bodies, this is not yet the consequence of their own active union, but of the union of the bourgeoisie, which class, in order to attain its own political ends, is compelled to set the whole proletariat in motion, and is moreover yet, for a time, able to do so. At this stage, therefore, the proletarians do not fight their enemies, but the enemies of their enemies, the remnants of absolute monarchy, the landowners, the non-industrial bourgeois, the petty bourgeois. Thus, the whole historical movement is concentrated in the hands of the bourgeoisie; every victory so obtained is a victory for the bourgeoisie.

But with the development of industry, the proletariat not only increases in number; it becomes concentrated in greater masses, its strength grows, and it feels that strength more. The various interests and conditions of life within the ranks of the proletariat are more and more equalized, in proportion as machinery obliterates all distinctions of labor, and nearly everywhere reduces wages to the same low level. The growing competition among the bourgeois, and the resulting commercial crises, make the wages of the workers ever more fluctuating. The increasing improvement of machinery, ever more rapidly developing, makes their livelihood more and more precarious; the collisions between individual workmen and individual bourgeois take more and more the character of collisions between two classes. Thereupon, the workers begin to form combinations (Trades Unions) against the bourgeois; they club together in order to keep up the rate of wages; they found permanent associations in order to make provision beforehand for these occasional revolts. Here and there, the contest breaks out into riots.

Now and then the workers are victorious, but only for a time. The real fruit of their battles lies, not in the immediate result, but in the ever expanding union of the workers. This union is helped on by the improved means of communication that are created by modern industry, and that place the workers of different localities in contact with one another. It was just this contact that was needed to centralize the numerous local struggles, all of the same character, into one national struggle between classes. But every class struggle is a political struggle. And that union, to attain which the burghers of the Middle Ages, with their miserable highways, required centuries, the modern proletarian, thanks to railways, achieve in a few years.

This organization of the proletarians into a class, and, consequently into a political party, is continually being upset again by the competition between the workers themselves. But it ever rises up again, stronger, firmer, mightier. It compels legislative recognition of particular interests of the workers, by taking advantage of the divisions among the bourgeoisie itself. Thus, the ten-hours' bill in England was carried.

Altogether collisions between the classes of the old society further, in many ways, the course of development of the proletariat. The bourgeoisie finds itself involved in a constant battle. At first with the aristocracy; later on, with those portions of the bourgeoisie itself, whose interests have become antagonistic to the progress of industry; at all time with the bourgeoisie of foreign countries. In all these battles, it sees itself compelled to appeal to the proletariat, to ask for help, and thus, to drag it into the political arena. The bourgeoisie itself, therefore, supplies the proletariat with its own elements of political and general education, in other words, it furnishes the proletariat with weapons for fighting the bourgeoisie. . . .

Of all the classes that stand face to face with the bourgeoisie today, the proletariat alone is a really revolutionary class. The other classes decay and finally disappear in the face of Modern Industry; the proletariat is its special and essential product.

The lower middle class, the small manufacturer, the shopkeeper, the artisan, the peasant, all these fight against the bourgeoisie, to save from extinction their existence as fractions of the middle class. They are therefore not revolutionary, but conservative. Nay more, they are reactionary, for they try to roll back the wheel of history. If by chance, they are revolutionary, they are only so in view of their impending transfer into the proletariat; they thus defend not their present, but their future interests, they desert their own standpoint to place themselves at that of the proletariat.

The "dangerous class," [*lumpenproletariat*] the social scum, that passively rotting mass thrown off by the lowest layers of the old society, may, here and there, be swept into the movement by a proletarian revolution; its conditions of life, however, prepare it far more for the part of a bribed tool of reactionary intrigue.

In the condition of the proletariat, those of old society at large are already virtually swamped. . . .

All the preceding classes that got the upper hand sought to fortify their already acquired status by subjecting society at large to their conditions of appropriation. The proletarians cannot become masters of the productive forces of society, except by abolishing their own previous mode of appropriation, and thereby also every other previous mode of appropriation. They have nothing of their own to secure and to fortify; their mission is to destroy all previous securities for, and insurances of, individual property.

All previous historical movements were movements of minorities, or in the interest of minorities. The proletarian movement is the self-conscious, independent movement of the immense majority, in the interest of the immense majority. The proletariat, the lowest stratum of our present society, cannot stir, cannot raise itself up, without the whole superincumbent strata of official society being sprung into the air. Though not in substance, yet in form, the struggle of the proletariat with the bourgeoisie is at first a national struggle. The proletariat of each country must, of course, first of all settle matters with its own bourgeoisie.

In depicting the most general phases of the development of the proletariat, we traced the more or less veiled civil war, raging within existing society, up to the point where that war breaks out into open revolution, and where the violent overthrow of the bourgeoisie lays the foundation for the sway of the proletariat.

Hitherto, every form of society has been based, as we have already seen, on the antagonism of oppressing and oppressed classes. But in order to oppress a class, certain conditions must be assured to it under which it can, at least, continue its slavish existence. . . . The essential conditions for the existence and for the sway of the bourgeois class is the formation and augmentation of capital; the condition for capital is wage-labor. Wage-labor rests exclusively on competition between the laborers. The advance of industry, whose involuntary promoter is the bourgeoisie, replaces the isolation of the laborers, due to competition, by the revolutionary combination, due to association. The development of Modern Industry, therefore, cuts from under its feet the very foundation on which the bourgeoisie produces and appropriates products. What the bourgeoisie therefore produces, above all, are its own grave-diggers. Its fall and the victory of the proletariat are equally inevitable. . . .

CHAPTER 4: POSITION OF THE COMMUNISTS IN RELATION TO THE VARIOUS EXISTING OPPOSITION PARTIES

The Communists disdain to conceal their views and aims. They openly declare that their ends can be attained only by the forcible overthrow of all existing social conditions. Let the ruling classes tremble at a Communistic revolution. The proletarians have nothing to lose but their chains. They have a world to win.

WORKERS OF ALL COUNTRIES, UNITE!

READING AND DISCUSSION QUESTIONS

1. How do Marx and Engels describe the power relationship between the bourgeoisie and the proletariat, and how is it changing?

2. Why, in a manifesto exhorting the proletariat to rise up against their bourgeoisie oppressors, do you think Marx and Engels devote so much space to *praising* the latter? For example, "during its rule of scarcely one hundred years, [the bourgeoisie] has created more massive and more colossal productive forces than have all preceding generations together."

3. Why, according to Marx and Engels, is a working-class revolution against the capitalist middle class inevitable?

DOCUMENT 22-4

CASPAR DAVID FRIEDRICH

Monastery Graveyard in the Snow

ca. 1817–1819

Caspar David Friedrich (1774–1840) was arguably the greatest and certainly the most famous painter associated with the Romantic movement. He was especially renowned for his landscapes, which are often set in winter, featuring bare, gnarled tree limbs and ruined buildings. Such works vividly convey his personal, emotional response to the natural world. Romanticism was in many respects an anti-Enlightenment ideology. Whereas philosophes *like Condorcet (Document 17-6) extolled the ability of human rationality to control nature, Romantics emphasized the sublime power and grandeur of nature and in doing so contrasted it with mankind's insignificance. Unlike Voltaire (Document 19-4) they also celebrated the spiritual realm and, rather than stressing man's "rationality" as did Condorcet, John Locke (Document 16-6), and Robert Owen (Document 21-5), they championed the emotional. In doing so, they often consciously harked back to the medieval era, an era of faith.*

READING AND DISCUSSION QUESTIONS

1. What emotions does Friedrich's painting arouse? Why?
2. What does Friedrich's depiction of the graveyard and monastery ruins suggest about his attitude toward the past?

DOCUMENT 22-5

The People's Charter

1838

In 1832 a major reform of Britain's Parliament took place. Although working-class agitation was a significant factor in pressuring the government to act, the newly created uniform borough (town) voting franchise excluded almost the entire working class from the electorate. One response to this outcome was Chartism, an explicitly working-class political movement based on "The People's Charter," a list of demands embodied in a petition to Parliament. The charter was drawn up by six members of Parliament — Daniel O'Connell, John Arthur Roebuck, John Temple Leader, Charles Hindley, Thomas Perronet Thompson, and William Sharman Crawford — and six working-class radicals — Henry Hetherington, John Cleave, James Watson, Richard Moore, William Lovett, and Henry Vincent. Although overwhelmingly rejected when it was presented to Parliament in 1839, 1842, and 1848, five of the charter's six demands (annual Parliamentary elections being the exception) became law by 1918.

1. **A vote** for every man twenty-one years of age, of sound mind, and not undergoing punishment for crime.
2. **The ballot**[5] — To protect the elector in the exercise of his vote.
3. **No property qualification** for Members of Parliament[6] — thus enabling the constituencies to return the man of their choice, be he rich or poor.
4. **Payment of members**, thus enabling an honest tradesman, working man, or other person, to serve a constituency, when taken from his business to attend to the interests of the Country.

London Working Men's Association, "Six Points of the People's Charter," http://www
.chartists.net/The-six-points.htm, accessed May 19, 2010.

[5] **The ballot:** Secret ballot. At the time voting took place *viva voce*, out loud and in public, which many argued led to intimidation of voters.
[6] **No property qualification . . . Parliament:** At the time candidates for Parliament had to possess at least £300 in property. Since a skilled working man might earn £75 a year, the property qualification amounted to four years' wages.

5. **Equal constituencies** securing the same amount of representation for the same number of electors, instead of allowing small constituencies to swamp the votes of large ones.

6. **Annual Parliaments**, thus presenting the most effectual check to bribery and intimidation, since though a constituency might be bought once in seven years (even with the ballot), no purse could buy a constituency (under a system of universal suffrage) in each ensuing twelvemonth; and since members, when elected for a year only, would not be able to defy and betray their constituents as now.

READING AND DISCUSSION QUESTIONS

1. Given that roughly 80 percent of Great Britain's population was working class, what would have been the political consequences of the first point of the Charter's enactment?

2. The Charter calls for an end to property qualifications for members of Parliament and also for payment of MPs. What do these two demands suggest about the nature of Parliamentary representation in early- and mid-nineteenth-century Britain? Who was running the country?

DOCUMENT 22-6

WILLIAM STEUART TRENCH

Realities of Irish Life: *The Misery of the Potato Famine*

1847

As an Irish land agent, William Steuart Trench (1808–1872) was a firsthand witness to the ravages of the potato famine. A fungus, the potato blight, attacked the crop repeatedly during the years 1845–1848. The British government's limited efforts to provide help for the Irish were wholly inadequate. The Irish poor, whose diets consisted of little other than potatoes, were the

From William Steuart Trench, *Realities of Irish Life* (London: Longmans, Green, 1868), pp. 394–398.

victims of a Malthusian demographic disaster; between 1841 and 1851 Ire-
land's population fell between 20 and 25 percent. Estimates of the death toll
range from around 750,000 to double that figure. Hundreds of thousands of
the more fortunate Irish emigrated.

I did not see a child playing in the streets or on the roads; no children are
to be seen outside the doors but a few sick and dying children. . . . In the
districts which are now being depopulated by starvation, coffins are only
used for the more wealthy. The majority were taken to the grave without
any coffin, and buried in their rags: in some instances even the rags are
taken from the corpse to cover some still living body. . . .

I then proceeded to Cappagh, which is a coast-guard station, in the
midst of a starving population, which had been collected round mines
which are not now worked. . . . On the evening before, I had heard of a
boy living on the road to Cappagh, who had seen a dog tearing the head,
and neck, and ribs of a man. I wished to learn the truth of this from the boy
himself. He told me that the fact was so, and that his little brother had on
another occasion seen another dog tearing the head of a man. The younger
boy remarked that he had seen the remains of the head the day before in
an adjoining field. I asked him to lead me to the spot, which he did, and I
there found a part of the human head and under-jaw, gnawed, but marked
with blood. I placed it under ground. . . .

On arriving at Cappagh, in the first house I saw a dead child lying in
a corner of the house, and two children, pale as death, with their heads
hanging down upon their breasts sitting by a small fire. The father had
died on the road coming home from work. One of the children, a lad seventeen years of age, had been found, in the absence of his mother, who
was looking for food, lying dead, with his legs held out of the fire by the
little child which I then saw lying dead. Two other children had also died.
The mother and the two children still alive had lived on one dish of barley
for the last four days. On entering another house the doctor said, "Look
there, Sir, you can't tell whether they are boys or girls." Taking up a skel-
eton child, he said, "Here is the way it is with them all; their legs swing and
rock like the legs of a doll, they have the smell of mice."

READING AND DISCUSSION QUESTIONS

1. Why do you think the British government failed to take effectual
    action to alleviate the famine?

2. The blight, which affected potato harvests throughout northern Europe, did not produce a similar catastrophe in Britain. Why might Britain have been spared?

COMPARATIVE QUESTIONS

1. In what ways did Thomas Malthus's theories in his *Essay on the Principle of Population* (Document 21-1) affect Ricardo's views about the supply and demand of labor?

2. What would Metternich say regarding the views on human nature expressed by Condorcet (Document 17-6) and Robert Owen (Document 21-5), and why?

3. What do you think Marx and Engels derived from Ricardo's essay "On Wages" in formulating their theory of class struggle?

4. Why do you think Marx and Engels specifically named Metternich as one of communism's foes in the preamble to the *Communist Manifesto?* Was their emphasis warranted? What would Metternich think of his detractors, and why?

5. How do you think Marx and Engels regarded the Chartist movement, and why?

6. How might Metternich respond to the scene depicted in Friedrich's painting? What would Marx and Engels take from it? How about Voltaire (Document 19-4) and Locke (Document 16-6)?

7. Describe the connections between the conditions of the Irish potato famine detailed in Trench's account and the economic philosophy outlined by David Ricardo.

CHAPTER 23

Life in the Emerging Urban Society

1840–1900

I n the second half of the nineteenth century, Germany, France, and the United States followed Britain's lead as industrialized nations. All witnessed the growth of the middle and working classes — and experienced the deplorable sanitary conditions that accompanied rapid urbanization. By the 1860s, however, significant advances in public health and medical science had increased the life expectancy of the urban poor. Politically, the expansion of the electorate in Britain, Germany, and France meant that, by 1884, the working class was the largest voting bloc in all three nations, although throughout Europe, women of all classes still lacked the vote. In the intellectual realm, literary realists challenged the romanticism of the first half of the century, basing their work on observation instead of emotion and rejecting pastoral scenes for gritty depictions of urban working-class life, while the theory of evolution and its outgrowth, Social Darwinism, seemed to directly defy the religious revival cultivated during the Romantic movement. The following documents reflect the facts that Britain set the mold for urbanization and industrialization — modernity — and that British thinkers were at the forefront of public health, scientific, and pseudoscientific advances.

DOCUMENT 23-1

SIR EDWIN CHADWICK
Inquiry into the Sanitary Condition of the Poor
1842

Edwin Chadwick (1800–1880), a disciple of the radical philosopher Jeremy Bentham, spent his life in pursuit of social and sanitary reform. Bentham, Chadwick, and other radicals known as utilitarians shared many views with nineteenth-century liberals; both believed in human rationality and the concept of human progress, and both believed that poverty was chiefly the consequence of individual moral failings. They parted ways sharply, however, over the role of government. Liberals argued that it was an impediment to progress; utilitarians believed that government policy and intervention could speed the rate of progress.

After as careful an examination of the evidence collected as I have been enabled to make, I beg leave to recapitulate the chief conclusions which that evidence appears to me to establish.

First, as to the extent and operation of the evils which are the subject of this inquiry: —

That the various forms of epidemic, endemic, and other disease[1] caused, or aggravated, or propagated chiefly amongst the laboring classes by atmospheric impurities produced by decomposing animal and vegetable substances, by damp and filth, and close and overcrowded dwellings prevail amongst the population in every part of the kingdom, whether dwelling in separate houses, in rural villages, in small towns, in the larger towns — as they have been found to prevail in the lowest districts of the metropolis.

That such disease, wherever its attacks are frequent, is always found in connection with the physical circumstances above specified, and that

From Edwin Chadwick, *Report . . . from the Poor Law Commissioners on an Inquiry into the Sanitary Conditions of the Labouring Population of Great Britain* (London: W. Clowes and Sons, 1842), pp. 369–372.

[1] **epidemic, endemic, and other disease**: The laboring classes were plagued by cholera, typhus, typhoid fever, tuberculosis (known then as "consumption"), and numerous respiratory ailments primarily caused by air pollution and occupational hazards such as cotton dust ("Brown Lung").

where those circumstances are removed by drainage, proper cleansing, better ventilation, and other means of diminishing atmospheric impurity, the frequency and intensity of such disease is abated; and where the removal of the noxious agencies appears to be complete, such disease almost entirely disappears.

The high prosperity in respect to employment and wages, and various and abundant food, have afforded to the laboring classes no exemptions from attacks of epidemic disease, which have been as frequent and as fatal in periods of commercial and manufacturing prosperity as in any others.

That the formation of all habits of cleanliness is obstructed by defective supplies of water.

That the annual loss of life from filth and bad ventilation are greater than the loss from death or wounds in any wars in which the country has been engaged in modern times.

That of the 43,000 cases of widowhood, and 112,000 cases of destitute orphanage relieved from the poor's rates in England and Wales alone, it appears that the greatest proportion of deaths of the heads of families occurred from the above specified and other removable causes; that their ages were under 45 years; that is to say, 13 years below the natural probabilities of life as shown by the experience of the whole population of Sweden. . . .

That, measuring the loss of working ability amongst large classes by the instances of gain, even from incomplete arrangements for the removal of noxious influences from places of work or from abodes, that this loss cannot be less than eight or ten years.

That the ravages of epidemics and other diseases do not diminish but tend to increase the pressure of population.

That in the districts where the mortality is greatest the births are not only sufficient to replace the numbers removed by death, but to add to the population.

That the younger population, bred up under noxious physical agencies, is inferior in physical organization and general health to a population preserved from the presence of such agencies.

That the population so exposed is less susceptible of moral influences, and the effects of education are more transient than with a healthy population.

That these adverse circumstances tend to produce an adult population short-lived, improvident, reckless, and intemperate, and with habitual avidity for sensual gratifications.

That these habits lead to the abandonment of all the conveniences and decencies of life, and especially lead to the overcrowding of their homes, which is destructive to the morality as well as the health of large classes of both sexes.

That defective town cleansing fosters habits of the most abject degradation and tends to the demoralization of large numbers of human beings, who subsist by means of what they find amidst the noxious filth accumulated in neglected streets and bye-places.

That the expenses of local public works are in general unequally and unfairly assessed, oppressively and uneconomically collected, by separate collections, wastefully expended in separate and inefficient operations by unskilled and practically irresponsible officers.

That the existing law for the protection of the public health and the constitutional machinery for reclaiming its execution, such as the Courts Leet,[2] have fallen into desuetude, and are in the state indicated by the prevalence of the evils they were intended to prevent.

Secondly. As to the means by which the present sanitary condition of the laboring classes may be improved: —

The primary and most important measures, and at the same time the most practicable, and within the recognized province of public administration, are drainage, the removal of all refuse of habitations, streets, and roads, and the improvement of the supplies of water.

That the chief obstacles to the immediate removal of decomposing refuse of towns and habitations have been the expense and annoyance of the hand labor and cartage requisite for the purpose.

That this expense may be reduced to one-twentieth or to one-thirtieth, or rendered inconsiderable, by the use of water and self-acting means of removal by improved and cheaper sewers and drains. . . .

That appropriate scientific arrangements for public drainage would afford important facilities for private land-drainage, which is important for the health as well as sustenance of the laboring classes.

That the expense of public drainage, of supplies of water laid on in houses, and of means of improved cleansing would be a pecuniary [monetary] gain, by diminishing the existing charges attendant on sickness and premature mortality.

---

[2] **Courts Leet**: Law courts dating back to medieval times, when the administration of justice was overseen by individual noblemen. Many early industrial towns, Manchester among them, lacked comprehensive municipal governments until the 1830s and afterward, and thus such antiquated institutions like Courts Leet confronted situations which their creators had never envisioned and for which they were, as Chadwick suggests, wholly inadequate.

That for the protection of the laboring classes and of the ratepayers against inefficiency and waste in all new structural arrangements for the protection of the public health, and to ensure public confidence that the expenditure will be beneficial, securities should be taken that all new local public works are devised and conducted by responsible officers qualified by the possession of the science and skill of civil engineers. . . .

That for the prevention of the disease occasioned by defective ventilation and other causes of impurity in places of work and other places where large numbers are assembled, and for the general promotion of the means necessary to prevent disease, that it would be good economy to appoint a district medical officer independent of private practice, and with the securities of special qualifications and responsibilities to initiate sanitary measures and reclaim the execution of the law.

That by the combinations of all these arrangements, it is probable that the full ensurable period of life indicated by the Swedish tables; that is, an increase of 13 years at least, may be extended to the whole of the laboring classes.

That the attainment of these and the other collateral advantages of reducing existing charges and expenditure are within the power of the legislature, and are dependent mainly on the securities taken for the application of practical science, skill, and economy in the direction of local public works.

And that the removal of noxious physical circumstances, and the promotion of civic, household, and personal cleanliness, are necessary to the improvement of the moral condition of the population; for that sound morality and refinement in manners and health are not long found coexistent with filthy habits amongst any class of the community.

READING AND DISCUSSION QUESTIONS

1. What, according to Chadwick, was the chief source of disease? Why does he say this?

2. What sorts of solutions does he offer to improve public health?

3. According to Chadwick, what is the relationship between sanitation and morality? Do you agree with his assessment? Why or why not?

VIEWPOINTS

Poverty and Prosperity in Urban Life

DOCUMENT 23-2

JACK LONDON
The People of the Abyss
1902

Although known chiefly for works of fiction like The Call of the Wild, *American author (and socialist) Jack London (1876–1916) also published nonfiction works.* The People of the Abyss *was based on his firsthand experience of living in the slums of London's East End for several months, where he pretended to be a stranded American sailor in order to observe the realities of working-class life.*

CHAPTER XLX: THE GHETTO

At one time the nations of Europe confined the undesirable Jews in city ghettos. But to-day the dominant economic class, by less arbitrary but none the less rigorous methods, has confined the undesirable yet necessary workers into ghettos of remarkable meanness and vastness. East London is such a ghetto, where the rich and the powerful do not dwell, and the traveler cometh not, and where two million workers swarm, procreate, and die.

It must not be supposed that all the workers of London are crowded into the East End, but the tide is setting strongly in that direction. The poor quarters of the city proper are constantly being destroyed, and the main stream of the unhoused is toward the east. In the last twelve years, one district, "London over the Border," as it is called, which lies well beyond Aldgate, Whitechapel, and Mile End,[3] has increased 260,000 or

From Jack London, *The People of the Abyss* (New York: Macmillan, 1903), pp. 210–218, 276–277, 314–317.

[3] **Aldgate, Whitechapel, and Mile End**: Districts east of the City of London, the financial and commercial heart of the metropolis.

over sixty percent. The churches in this district, by the way, can seat but one in every thirty-seven of the added population.

The City of Dreadful Monotony the East End is often called, especially by well-fed, optimistic sightseers, who look over the surface of things and are merely shocked by the intolerable sameness and meanness of it all. If the East End is worthy of no worse title than The City of Dreadful Monotony, and if working people are unworthy of variety and beauty and surprise, it would not be such a bad place in which to live. But the East End does merit a worse title. It should be called The City of Degradation.

While it is not a city of slums, as some people imagine, it may well be said to be one gigantic slum. From the standpoint of simple decency and clean manhood and womanhood, any mean street, of all its mean streets, is a slum. Where sights and sounds abound which neither you nor I would care to have our children see and hear is a place where no man's children should live, and see and hear. Where you and I would not care to have our wives pass their lives is a place where no other man's wife should have to pass her life. For here, in the East End, the obscenities and brute vulgarities of life are rampant. There is no privacy. The bad corrupts the good, and all fester together. Innocent childhood is sweet and beautiful; but in East London innocence is a fleeting thing, and you must catch them before they crawl out of the cradle, or you will find the very babes as unholily wise as you.

The application of the Golden Rule determines that East London is an unfit place in which to live. Where you would not have your own babe live, and develop, and gather to itself knowledge of life and the things of life, is not a fit place for the babes of other men to live. . . . Political economy and the survival of the fittest can go hang if they say otherwise. What is not good enough for you is not good enough for other men, and there's no more to be said.

There are 300,000 people in London, divided into families, that live in one-room tenements. Far, far more live in two and three rooms and are as badly crowded, regardless of sex, as those that live in one room. The law demands 400 cubic feet of space for each person. In army barracks each soldier is allowed 600 cubic feet. Professor Huxley,[4] at one time himself a medical officer in East London, always held that each person should have 800 cubic feet of space, and that it should be well ventilated with pure air.

---

[4]**Professor Huxley**: Thomas Henry Huxley (1825–1895), one of the most renowned scientists in Victorian Britain; an ardent champion of Darwin's theory of evolution. Huxley was the grandfather of author Aldous Huxley.

Yet in London there are 900,000 people living in less than the 400 cubic feet prescribed by the law.

Mr. Charles Booth,[5] who engaged in a systematic work of years in charting and classifying the toiling city population, estimates that there are 1,800,000 people in London who are *poor* and *very poor*. It is of interest to mark what he terms *poor*. By *poor* he means families which have a total weekly income of from $4.50 to $5.25. The *very poor* fall greatly below this standard.

The workers, as a class, are being more and more segregated by their economic masters; and this process, with its jamming and overcrowding, tends not so much toward immorality as unmorality. Here is an extract from a recent meeting of the London County Council, terse and bald, but with a wealth of horror to be read between the lines: —

> Mr. Bruce asked the Chairman of the Public Health Committee whether his attention had been called to a number of cases of serious overcrowding in the East End. In St. Georges-in-the-East a man and his wife and their family of eight occupied one small room. This family consisted of five daughters, aged twenty, seventeen, eight, four, and an infant, and three sons, aged fifteen, thirteen, and twelve. . . . He asked whether it was not the duty of the various local authorities to prevent such serious overcrowding.

But with 900,000 people actually living under illegal conditions, the authorities have their hands full. When the overcrowded folk are ejected they stray off into some other hole; and, as they move their belongings by night, on hand-barrows (one hand-barrow accommodating the entire household goods and the sleeping children), it is next to impossible to keep track of them. If the Public Health Act of 1891[6] were suddenly and completely enforced, 900,000 people would receive notice to clear out of their houses and go on to the streets, and 500,000 rooms would have to be built before they were all legally housed again.

---

[5] **Charles Booth**: Booth (1840–1916) was a pioneering sociologist, who directed a massive survey of London's inhabitants, published as *Life and Labour of the People in London* (1889–1897).

[6] **Public Health Act of 1891**: This legislation empowered local sanitary authorities to conduct regular inspections of dwellings in order to detect "nuisances," among which were "any premises in such a state as to be a nuisance or injurious or dangerous to health" and "any house or part of a house so overcrowded as to be injurious or dangerous to the health of the inmates, whether or not members of the same family."

The mean streets merely look mean from the outside, but inside the walls are to be found squalor, misery, and tragedy. While the following tragedy may be revolting to read, it must not be forgotten that the existence of it is far more revolting. In Devonshire Place, Lisson Grove, a short while back died an old woman of seventy-five years of age. At the inquest the coroner's officer stated that "all he found in the room was a lot of old rags covered with vermin. He had got himself smothered with the vermin. The room was in a shocking condition, and he had never seen anything like it. Everything was absolutely covered with vermin."

The doctor said: "He found deceased lying across the fender on her back. She had one garment and her stockings on. The body was quite alive with vermin, and all the clothes in the room were absolutely gray with insects. Deceased was very badly nourished and was very emaciated. She had extensive sores on her legs, and her stockings were adherent to those sores. The sores were the result of vermin."

A man present at the inquest wrote: "I had the evil fortune to see the body of the unfortunate woman as it lay in the mortuary; and even now the memory of that grewsome [sic] sight makes me shudder. There she lay in the mortuary shell, so starved and emaciated that she was a mere bundle of skin and bones. Her hair, which was matted with filth, was simply a nest of vermin. Over her bony chest leaped and rolled hundreds, thousands, myriads of vermin."

If it is not good for your mother and my mother so to die, then it is not good for this woman, whosoever's mother she might be, so to die.

Bishop Wilkinson, who has lived in Zululand, recently said, "No headman of an African village would allow such a promiscuous mixing of young men and women, boys and girls." He had reference to the children of the overcrowded folk, who at five have nothing to learn and much to unlearn which they will never unlearn.

It is notorious that here in the Ghetto the houses of the poor are greater profit earners than the mansions of the rich. Not only does the poor worker have to live like a beast, but he pays proportionately more for it than does the rich man for his spacious comfort. A class of house-sweaters has been made possible by the competition of the poor for houses. There are more people than there is room, and numbers are in the workhouse because they cannot find shelter elsewhere. Not only are houses let, but they are sublet, and sub-sublet down to the very rooms.

"A part of a room to let." This notice was posted a short while ago in a window not five minutes' walk from St. James's Hall. The Rev. Hugh Price Hughes is authority for the statement that beds are let on the three-relay system — that is, three tenants to a bed, each occupying it eight hours, so that it never grows cold; while the floor space underneath the bed is likewise let on the three-relay system. Health officers are not at all unused to finding such cases as the following: in one room having a cubic capacity of 1000 feet, three adult females in the bed, and two adult females under the bed; and in one room of 1650 cubic feet, one adult male and two children in the bed, and two adult females under the bed.

Here is a typical example of a room on the more respectable two-relay system. It is occupied in the daytime by a young woman employed all night in a hotel. At seven o'clock in the evening she vacates the room, and a bricklayer's laborer comes in. At seven in the morning he vacates, and goes to his work, at which time she returns from hers.

The Rev. W. N. Davies, rector of Spitalfields, took a census of some of the alleys in his parish. He says: — ". . . In one house with 8 rooms are 45 people in one room containing 9 persons, one 8, two 7, and another 6." . . .

In such conditions, the outlook for children is hopeless. They die like flies, and those that survive, survive because they possess excessive vitality and a capacity of adaptation to the degradation with which they are surrounded. They have no home life. In the dens and lairs in which they live they are exposed to all that is obscene and indecent. And as their minds are made rotten, so are their bodies made rotten by bad sanitation, overcrowding, and underfeeding. When a father and mother live with three or four children in a room where the children take turn about in sitting up to drive the rats away from the sleepers, when those children never have enough to eat and are preyed upon and made miserable and weak by swarming vermin, the sort of men and women the survivors will make can readily be imagined. . . .

Five men can produce bread for a thousand. One man can produce cotton cloth for 250 people, woolens for 300, and boots and shoes for 1000. Yet it has been shown throughout the pages of this book that English folk by the millions do not receive enough food, clothes, and boots. Then arises the third and inexorable question: *If Civilization has increased the producing power of the average man, why has it not bettered the lot of the average man?*

There can be one answer only — MISMANAGEMENT. Civilization has made possible all manner of creature comforts and heart's delights. In these the average Englishman does not participate. If he shall be forever unable to participate, then Civilization falls. There is no reason for the continued existence of an artifice so avowed a failure. But it is impossible that men should have reared this tremendous artifice in vain. It stuns the intellect. To acknowledge so crushing a defeat is to give the death-blow to striving and progress.

One other alternative, and one other only, presents itself. *Civilization must be compelled to better the lot of the average man.* This accepted, it becomes at once a question of business management. Things profitable must be continued; things unprofitable must be eliminated. Either the Empire is a profit to England or it is a loss. If it is a loss, it must be done away with. If it is a profit, it must be managed so that the average man comes in for a share of the profit.

If the struggle for commercial supremacy is profitable, continue it. If it is not, if it hurts the worker and makes his lot worse than the lot of a savage, then fling foreign markets and industrial empire overboard. For it is a patent fact that if 40,000,000 people, aided by Civilization, possess a greater individual producing power than the Inuit,[7] then those 40,000,000 people should enjoy more creature comforts and heart's delights than the Inuits enjoy. . . .

In short, society must be reorganized, and a capable management put at the head. That the present management is incapable, there can be no discussion. . . . Blood empire is greater than political empire, and the English of the New World and the Antipodes are strong and vigorous as ever. But the political empire under which they are nominally assembled is perishing. The political machine known as the British Empire is running down. In the hands of its management it is losing momentum every day.

It is inevitable that this management, which has grossly and criminally mismanaged, shall be swept away. Not only has it been wasteful and inefficient, but it has misappropriated the funds. Every worn-out, pasty-faced pauper, every blind man, every prison babe, every man, woman, and child whose belly is gnawing with hunger pangs, is hungry because the funds have been misappropriated by the management.

Nor can one member of this managing class plead not guilty before the judgment bar of Man. "The living in their houses, and in their graves the dead," are challenged by every babe that dies of innutrition, by every girl that flees the sweater's den to the nightly promenade of Piccadilly,[8] by every worked-out toiler that plunges into the canal. The food this managing class eats, the wine it drinks, the shows it makes, and the fine clothes it

---

[7] **Inuit**: Aboriginal peoples of the arctic regions of Russia, North America, and Greenland.

[8] **that flees the sweater's den . . . Piccadilly**: That leaves work in a sweatshop to engage in prostitution.

wears, are challenged by eight million mouths which have never had enough to fill them, and by twice eight million bodies which have never been sufficiently clothed and housed.

There can be no mistake. Civilization has increased man's producing power an hundred fold, and through mismanagement the men of Civilization live worse than the beasts, and have less to eat and wear and protect them from the elements than the savage Inuit in a frigid climate who lives to-day as he lived in the stone age ten thousand years ago.

READING AND DISCUSSION QUESTIONS

1. To what causes does Jack London attribute the widespread poverty and misery among metropolitan London's poor?
2. What solutions does he propose?

DOCUMENT 23-3

ISABELLA BEETON

Mrs. Beeton's Book of Household Management
1861

Isabella Beeton (1836–1865) was a British journalist whose earliest articles appeared in the English Woman's Domestic Magazine, *the first magazine targeted specifically at middle-class women.* Mrs. Beeton's Book of Household Management, *first published in 1861, contained more than 2,700 entries of recipes and practical instructions, from how to keep moths from attacking clothes to how to care for horses. A best seller that was continually reprinted, it was almost certainly the most widely consulted book on the subject in the decades following its appearance.*

Masters and Mistresses. — It has been said that good masters and mistresses make good servants, and this to a great extent is true. There are certainly

From Isabella Beeton, *Mrs. Beeton's Book of Household Management* (London: Ward, Lock and Co., 1888), pp. 1454, 1471, 1473, 1478–79, 1481–82.

some men and women in the wide field of servitude whom it would be impossible to train into good servants, but the conduct of both master and mistress is seldom without its effect upon these dependents. They are not mere machines, and no one has a right to consider them in that light. The sensible master and the kind mistress know, that if servants depend on them for their means of living, in their turn they are dependent on their servants for very many of the comforts of life; and that, with a proper amount of care in choosing servants, and treating them like reasonable beings, and making slight excuses for the shortcomings of human nature, they will, save in some exceptional case, be tolerably well served, and, in most instances, surround themselves with attached domestics. . . .

The Lady's-Maid. — The qualifications a lady's maid should possess are a thorough knowledge of hair dressing, dressmaking and repairing and restoring clothes. She should be able to pack well, and her taste, being often called into requisition in matters of dress, should be good. It is also essential that she be well spoken, quiet in manner and quick; that she should be clean and honest goes without saying. A lady's maid having so much more intercourse with her mistress than any other servant should not only possess, but learn, discretion from day to day. To know when to speak and when to be silent, and to be willing to bear with patience any little caprices of taste and temper with which she may have to contend.

Her first duty in the morning, after having performed her own toilet, is to prepare the bath and everything for dressing for her mistress, taking her an early cup of tea if she requires one. She then examines the clothes put off by her mistress the evening before, either to put them away, or to see that they are all in order to put on again. During the winter and in wet weather, the dresses should be carefully examined, and the mud removed. Dresses of tweed, and other woolen materials may be laid out on a table and brushed all over; but in general, even in woolen fabrics, the lightness of the tissues renders brushing unsuitable to dresses, and it is better to remove the dust from the folds by beating them lightly with a handker-chief or thin cloth. Silk dresses should never be brushed, but rubbed with a piece of merino, or other soft material, of a similar color, kept for the purpose. Summer dresses . . . simply require shaking; but if the muslin be tumbled, it must be ironed afterwards. If the dresses require slight repair, it should be done at once: "a stitch in time saves nine." . . .

A waiting-maid who wishes to make herself useful will study the fashion-books with attention, so as to be able to aid her mistress's judgment in dressing, according to the prevailing fashion, with such modifications as her style and figure require. She will also, if she has her mistress's interest at heart, employ her spare time in repairing and making up dresses which have served one purpose, to serve another also; or turning many things, unfitted for her mistress, to use for the younger branches of the family. The lady's-maid may thus render herself invaluable to her mistress, and increase her own happiness in so doing. The exigencies of fashion and luxury are such, that all ladies, except those of the very highest rank, will consider themselves fortunate in having about them a thoughtful person, capable of diverting their finery to a useful purpose. . . .

Duties of the Housemaid. — "Cleanliness is next to godliness," saith the proverb, and "order" is in the next degree; the housemaid, then, may be said to be the handmaiden to two of the most prominent virtues. Her duties are very numerous, and many of the comforts of the family depend on their performance; but they are simple and easy to a person naturally clean and orderly, and desirous of giving satisfaction. In all families, whatever the habits of the master and mistress, servants will find it advantageous to rise early; their daily work will thus become easy to them. If they rise late, there is a struggle to overtake it, which throws an air of haste and hurry over the whole establishment. Where the master's time is regulated by early business or professional engagements, this will, of course, regulate the hours of the servants; but even where that is not the case, servants will find great personal convenience in rising early and getting through their work in an orderly and methodical manner. The housemaid who studies her own ease will certainly be at her work by six o'clock in the summer, and, probably, half-past six or seven in the winter months, having spent a reasonable time in her own chamber in dressing. Earlier than this would, probably, be an unnecessary waste of coals and candle in winter.

The first duty of the housemaid in winter is to open the shutters of all the lower rooms in the house, and take up the hearthrugs of those rooms which she is going to "do" before breakfast. In some families, where there is only a cook and housemaid kept, and where the drawing-rooms are large, the cook has the care of the dining-room, and the housemaid that of the breakfast-room, library, and drawing-rooms. After the shutters are all opened, she sweeps the breakfast-room, sweeping the dust towards the fireplace, of course previously removing the fender. She should then lay a cloth (generally made of coarse wrappering) over the carpet in front of the stove, and on this should place her housemaid's box, containing blacklead brushes, leathers, emery-paper, cloth, black lead, and all utensils necessary for cleaning a grate, with the cinder-pail on the other side. She now sweeps up the ashes, and deposits them in her cinder-pail, which is a japanned tin pail, with a wire-sifter inside, and a closely-fitting top. In this pail the cinders are sifted, and reserved for use in the kitchen or under the copper, the ashes only being thrown away. The cinders disposed of, she proceeds to black-lead the grate, producing the black lead, the soft brush for laying it on, her blacking and polishing brushes, from the box which contains her tools. This housemaid's box should be kept well stocked. Having blackened, brushed, and polished every part, and made all clean and bright, she now proceeds to lay the fire. . . .

Bright grates require unceasing attention to keep them in perfect order. A day should never pass without the housemaid rubbing with a dry leather the polished parts of a grate, as also the fender and fire-irons. A careful and attentive housemaid should have no occasion ever to use emery-paper for any part but the bars, which, of course, become blackened by the fire. (Some mistresses, to save labor, have a double set of bars, one set bright for the summer, and another black set to use when fires are in requisition.) . . .

The several fires lighted, the housemaid proceeds with her dusting, and polishing the several pieces of furniture in the breakfast-parlor, leaving no corner unvisited. Before sweeping the carpet, it is a good practice to sprinkle it all over with tea-leaves, which not only lay all dust, but give a slightly fragrant smell to the room. It is now in order for the reception of the family; and where there is neither footman nor parlor-maid, she now proceeds to the dressing-room, and lights her mistress's fire, if she is in the habit of having one to dress by. Her mistress is called, hot water placed in the dressing-room for her use, her clothes — as far as they are under the house-maid's charge — put before the fire to air, hanging a fire-guard on the bars where there is one, while she proceeds to prepare the breakfast. . . .

Breakfast served, the housemaid proceeds to the bed-chambers, throws up the sashes, if not already done, pulls up the blinds, throwing back curtains at the same time, and opens the beds, by removing the clothes, placing them over a horse, or, failing that, over the backs of chairs. She now proceeds to empty the slops. In doing this, everything is emptied into the slop-pail, leaving a little scalding-hot water for a minute in such vessels as require it; adding a drop of turpentine to the water, when that is not sufficient to cleanse them. The basin is emptied, well rinsed with clean water, and carefully wiped; the ewers emptied and washed; finally, the water-jugs themselves emptied out and rinsed, and wiped dry. As soon as this is done, she should remove and empty the pails, taking care that they also are well washed, scalded, and wiped as soon as they are empty. Next follows bed-making, at which the cook or kitchen-maid, where one is kept, usually assists; but, before beginning, velvet chairs, or other things injured by dust, should be removed to another room. In bedmaking, the fancy of its occupant should be consulted; some like beds sloping from the top towards the feet, swelling slightly in the middle; others, perfectly flat: a good housemaid will accommodate each bed to the taste of the sleeper, taking care to shake, beat, and turn it well in the process. Some persons prefer sleeping on the mattress; in which case a feather bed is usually beneath, resting on a second mattress, and a straw paillasse at the bottom. In this case, the mattresses should change places daily; the feather bed placed on the mattress shaken, beaten, taken up, and opened several times, so as thoroughly to separate the feathers: if too large to be thus handled, the maid should shake and beat one end first, and then the other, smoothing it afterwards equally all over into the required shape, and place the mattress gently over it. Any feathers which escape in this process a tidy servant will put back through the seam of the tick; she will also be careful to sew up any stitch that gives way the moment it is discovered. The bedclothes are laid on, beginning with an under blanket and sheet, which are tucked under the mattress at the bottom. The bolster is then beaten and shaken, and put on, the top of the sheet rolled round it, and the sheet tucked in all round. The pillows and other bedclothes follow, and the counterpane over all, which should fall in graceful folds, and at equal distance from the ground all round. The curtains are drawn to the head and folded neatly across the bed, and the whole finished in a smooth and graceful manner. Where spring-mattresses are used, care should be taken that the top one is turned every day. The housemaid should now take up in a dustpan any pieces that may be on the carpet; she should dust the room, shut the door, and proceed to another room. When all the bedrooms are finished, she should dust the stairs, and polish the handrail of the banisters, and see that all ledges, window-sills, &c., are quite free from dust. It will be necessary for the housemaid to divide her work, so that she may not have too much to do on certain days, and not sufficient to fill up her time on other days. In the country, bedrooms should be swept and thoroughly cleaned once a week; and to be methodical and regular in her work, the housemaid should have certain days for doing certain rooms thoroughly. For instance, two bedrooms on Monday, two on Tuesday, the drawing-room on Wednesday, and so on, reserving a day for thoroughly cleaning the plate, bedroom candlesticks, &c. &c., which she will have to do where there is no parlormaid or footman kept. By this means the work will be divided, and there will be no unnecessary bustling and hurrying, as is the case where the work is done any time, without rule or regulation.

READING AND DISCUSSION QUESTIONS

1. What do Beeton's instructions about the management and duties of household servants tell us about how life in modern urban societies has altered over the past century and a half?

2. What does Beeton infer are some of the most typical problems that exist between masters and servants?

3. What does this excerpt tell us about class divisions, and about Beeton's attitudes toward the "lower orders," from which servants came?

4. What do the daily chores described here reveal about nineteenth-century attitudes toward work and the use of time?

5. Britain's aristocracy had been managing servants for centuries at the time this guide was published. To whom do you think Beeton was imparting her instructions, regardless of the grandeur of the households she describes?

DOCUMENT 23-4

CLARA ZETKIN

Women's Work and the Trade Unions

1887

German socialist and feminist Clara Zetkin (1857–1933) was an influential politician and women's suffragist from 1878 until her forced exile by the Nazi regime shortly before her death. A friend of many prominent German radicals including Wilhelm Liebknecht, one of the founders of the German Social Democratic (i.e., Socialist) Party, Zetkin was part of the first generation of modern European feminists. Like their British, French, and American counterparts, late-nineteenth-century German feminists — most of them, like Zetkin, from middle-class backgrounds — devoted the bulk of

From Clara Zetkin, "Women's Work and the Trade Unions" in *Clara Zetkin, Selected Writings*, ed. Philip S. Foner (New York: International Publishers, 1984), pp. 54–56.

their energies to obtaining the vote. Zetkin founded the German social dem-
ocratic women's movement and, for more than twenty-five years, edited the
Social Democratic Party's women's newspaper Die Gleichheit (Equality).

It is not just the women workers who suffer because of the miserable payment of their labor. The male workers, too, suffer because of it. As a consequence of their low wages, the women are transformed from mere competitors into unfair competitors who push down the wages of men. Cheap women's labor eliminates the work of men and if the men want to continue to earn their daily bread, they must put up with low wages. Thus women's work is not only a cheap form of labor, it also cheapens the work of men and for that reason it is doubly appreciated by the capitalist, who craves profits. The economic advantages of the industrial activity of proletarian women only aid the tiny minority of the sacrosanct guild of coupon clippers and extortionists of profit.

Given the fact that many thousands of female workers are active in industry, it is vital for the trade unions to incorporate them into their movement. In individual industries where female labor plays an important role, any movement advocating better wages, shorter working hours, etc., would be doomed from the start because of the attitude of those women workers who are not organized. Battles which began propitiously enough, ended up in failure because the employers were able to play off non-union female workers against those that are organized in unions. These non-union workers continued to work (or took up work) under any conditions, which transformed them from competitors in dirty work to scabs [nonunion strikebreakers].

Certainly one of the reasons for these poor wages for women is the circumstances that female workers are practically unorganized. They lack the strength which comes with unity. They lack the courage, the feeling of power, the spirit of resistance, and the ability to resist which is produced by the strength of an organization in which the individual fights for everybody and everybody fights for the individual. Furthermore, they lack the enlightenment and the training which an organization provides.

READING AND DISCUSSION QUESTIONS

1. Why, according to Zetkin, do women and men compete for jobs? What is the consequence of that competition? What is Zetkin's solution to such competition?

2. Why might Zetkin have advocated the peaceful organization of women into trade unions rather than striving for a communist revolution?

3. What do the author's arguments suggest about the nature and extent of working-class political power in late nineteenth-century Germany?

DOCUMENT 23-5

CHARLES DARWIN

The Descent of Man

1871

Charles Darwin (1809–1882) was the most prominent scientist in nineteenth-century Britain. His major works, On the Origin of Species by Means of Natural Selection *(1859) and* The Descent of Man *(1871) put forward the theory of natural selection, and argued that humans were closely related to the great apes, respectively. They are the foundational texts for modern evolutionary science, although they were immensely controversial on publication, and are still objects of heated contention.*

The main conclusion here arrived at, and now held by many naturalists who are well competent to form a sound judgment, is that man is descended from some less highly organized form. . . . He who is not content to look, like a savage, at the phenomena of nature as disconnected, cannot any longer believe that man is the work of a separate act of creation. He will be forced to admit that the close resemblance of the embryo of man to that, for instance, of a dog — the construction of his skull, limbs, and whole frame on the same plan with that of other mammals, independently of the uses to which the parts may be put — the occasional re-appearance of various structures, for instance of several muscles, which man does not normally possess, but which are common to the Quadrumana[9] — and a crowd of analogous facts — all point in the plainest manner to the

From Charles Darwin, *The Descent of Man and Selection in Relation to Sex* (New York: Appleton and Co., 1883), pp. 620–621, 623–624, 626–629, 633–634.
[9] **Quadrumana**: Term once used to describe primates with opposable digits (thumbs) on all four feet.

conclusion that man is the co-descendant with other mammals of a common progenitor.

We have seen that man incessantly presents individual differences in all parts of his body and in his mental faculties. These differences or variations seem to be induced by the same general causes, and to obey the same laws as with the lower animals. In both cases similar laws of inheritance prevail. Man tends to increase at a greater rate than his means of subsistence; consequently he is occasionally subjected to a severe struggle for existence, and natural selection will have effected whatever lies within its scope. A succession of strongly-marked variations of a similar nature is by no means requisite; slight fluctuating differences in the individual suffice for the work of natural selection; not that we have any reason to suppose that in the same species, all parts of the organization tend to vary to the same degree. . . .

By considering the embryological structure of man, — the homologies which he presents with the lower animals, — the rudiments which he retains, — and the reversions to which he is liable, we can partly recall in imagination the former condition of our early progenitors; and can approximately place them in their proper place in the zoological series. We thus learn that man is descended from a hairy, tailed quadruped, probably arboreal in its habits, and an inhabitant of the Old World. This creature, if its whole structure had been examined by a naturalist, would have been classed amongst the Quadrumana, as surely as the still more ancient progenitor of the Old and New World monkeys. The Quadrumana and all the higher mammals are probably derived from an ancient marsupial animal, and this through a long line of diversified forms, from some amphibian-like creature, and this again from some fish-like animal. In the dim obscurity of the past we can see that the early progenitor of all the Vertebrata must have been an aquatic animal, provided with branchiæ,[10] with the two sexes united in the same individual, and with the most important organs of the body (such as the brain and heart) imperfectly or not at all developed. This animal seems to have been more like the larvæ of the existing marine Ascidians[11] than any other known form.

The high standard of our intellectual powers and moral disposition is the greatest difficulty which presents itself, after we have been driven to this conclusion on the origin of man. But every one who admits the principle of evolution, must see that the mental powers of the higher animals,

---

[10] **branchiæ**: Gills.

[11] **Ascidians**: Genus of mollusks.

which are the same in kind with those of man, though so different in degree, are capable of advancement. . . .

The moral nature of man has reached its present standard, partly through the advancement of his reasoning powers and consequently of a just public opinion, but especially from his sympathies having been rendered more tender and widely diffused through the effects of habit, example, instruction, and reflection. It is not improbable that after long practice virtuous tendencies may be inherited. With the more civilized races, the conviction of the existence of an all-seeing Deity has had a potent influence on the advance of morality. Ultimately man does not accept the praise or blame of his fellows as his sole guide though few escape this influence, but his habitual convictions, controlled by reason, afford him the safest rule. His conscience then becomes the supreme judge and monitor. Nevertheless the first foundation or origin of the moral sense lies in the social instincts, including sympathy; and these instincts no doubt were primarily gained, as in the case of the lower animals, through natural selection.

The belief in God has often been advanced as not only the greatest but the most complete of all the distinctions between man and the lower animals. It is however impossible, as we have seen, to maintain that this belief is innate or instinctive in man. On the other hand a belief in all-pervading spiritual agencies seems to be universal, and apparently follows from a considerable advance in man's reason, and from a still greater advance in his faculties of imagination, curiosity, and wonder. I am aware that the assumed instinctive belief in God has been used by many persons as an argument for His existence. But this is a rash argument, as we should thus be compelled to believe in the existence of many cruel and malignant spirits, only a little more powerful than man; for the belief in them is far more general than in a beneficent Deity. The idea of a universal and beneficent Creator does not seem to arise in the mind of man, until he has been elevated by long-continued culture. . . .

I am aware that the conclusions arrived at in this work will be denounced by some as highly irreligious; but he who denounces them is bound to show why it is more irreligious to explain the origin of man as a distinct species by descent from some lower form, through the laws of variation and natural selection, than to explain the birth of the individual through the laws of ordinary reproduction. The birth both of the species and of the individual are equally parts of that grand sequence of events, which our minds refuse to accept as the result of blind chance. The understanding revolts at such a conclusion, whether or not we are able to believe that every slight variation of structure, — the union of each pair in marriage, — the dissemination of each seed, — and other such events, have all been ordained for some special purpose.

Sexual selection has been treated at great length in this work, for, as I have attempted to show, it has played an important part in the history of the organic world. I am aware that much remains doubtful, but I have endeavored to give a fair view of the whole case. In the lower divisions of the animal kingdom, sexual selection seems to have done nothing. . . . When, however, we come to the Arthropoda and Vertebrata,[12] even to the lowest classes in these two great Sub-Kingdoms, sexual selection has effected much. . . .

Sexual selection depends on the success of certain individuals over others of the same sex, in relation to the propagation of the species; while natural selection depends on the success of both sexes, at all ages, in relation to the general conditions of life. The sexual struggle is of two kinds; in the one it is between the individuals of the same sex, generally the males, in order to drive away or kill their rivals, the females remaining passive; while in the other, the struggle is likewise between the individuals of the same sex, in order to excite or charm those of the opposite sex, generally the females, which no longer remain passive, but select the more agreeable partners. . . .

The main conclusion arrived at in this work, namely that man is descended from some lowly organized form, will, I regret to think, be highly distasteful to many. But there can hardly be a doubt that we are descended from barbarians. The astonishment which I felt on first seeing a party of Fuegians[13] on a wild and broken shore will never be forgotten by me, for the reflection at once rushed into my mind — such were our ancestors. These men were absolutely naked and bedaubed with paint, their long hair was tangled, their mouths frothed with excitement, and their expression was wild, startled, and distrustful. They possessed hardly any arts, and like wild animals lived on what they could catch; they had no government, and were merciless to every one not of their own small tribe. He who has seen a savage in his native land will not feel much shame, if forced to acknowledge that the blood of some more humble creature flows in his veins. For my own part I would as soon be descended from that

---

[12] **Arthropoda and Vertebrata**: Insects and vertebrates (animals with internal skeletons).

[13] **Fuegians**: Inhabitants of Tierra del Fuego, at the tip of South America; Patagonians.

heroic little monkey, who braved his dreaded enemy in order to save the life of his keeper, or from that old baboon, who descending from the mountains, carried away in triumph his young comrade from a crowd of astonished dogs — as from a savage who delights to torture his enemies, offers up bloody sacrifices, practices infanticide without remorse, treats his wives like slaves, knows no decency, and is haunted by the grossest superstitions.

Man may be excused for feeling some pride at having risen, though not through his own exertions, to the very summit of the organic scale; and the fact of his having thus risen, instead of having been aboriginally placed there, may give him hope for a still higher destiny in the distant future. But we are not here concerned with hopes or fears, only with the truth as far as our reason permits us to discover it; and I have given the evidence to the best of my ability. We must, however, acknowledge, as it seems to me, that man with all his noble qualities, with sympathy which feels for the most debased, with benevolence which extends not only to other men but to the humblest living creature, with his god-like intellect which has penetrated into the movements and constitution of the solar system — with all these exalted powers — Man still bears in his bodily frame the indelible stamp of his lowly origin.

READING AND DISCUSSION QUESTIONS

1. On what grounds does Darwin base his argument "that man is descended from some less highly organized form"? Are they compelling? Why or why not?

2. Why does Darwin maintain that the "assumed instinctive belief in God [that] has been used by many persons as an argument for His existence," is "a rash argument"?

DOCUMENT 23-6

HERBERT SPENCER

Social Statics: *Survival of the Fittest Applied to Humankind*

1851

Like Darwin, Herbert Spencer (1820–1903) was an English intellectual, although his work concerned philosophy and social theory rather than science. Spencer was one of the earliest champions of what would later be called "Social Darwinism" — the idea that the very struggle for survival which characterized life in the natural world also applied to human societies. Indeed, Spencer coined the phrase "survival of the fittest," later adopted by Darwin (not the other way around!). The following excerpt comes from his first major work, Social Statics *(1851), which attracted relatively little attention on publication, but contains many of the ideas that would make Spencer one of the most well-known and influential British intellectuals during the 1870s and 1880s.*

In common with its other assumptions of secondary offices, the assumption by a government of the office of Reliever-general to the poor, is necessarily forbidden by the principle that a government cannot rightly do anything more than protect. In demanding from a citizen contributions for the mitigation of distress — contributions not needed for the due administration of men's rights — the state is, as we have seen, reversing its function, and diminishing that liberty to exercise the faculties which it was instituted to maintain. Possibly . . . some will assert that by satisfying the wants of the pauper, a government is in reality extending his liberty to exercise his faculties. . . . But this statement of the case implies a confounding of two widely different things. To enforce the fundamental law — to take care that every man has freedom to do all that he wills, provided he infringes not the equal freedom of any other man — this is the special purpose for which the civil power exists. Now insuring to each the right to pursue within the specified limits the objects of his desires without let or hindrance, is quite a separate thing from insuring him satisfaction. . . .

From Herbert Spencer, "Social Statics," in *Liberalism: Its Meaning and History*, ed. J. Salwyn Schapiro (New York: Van Nostrand Reinhold, 1958), pp. 136–137.

Pervading all nature we may see at work a stern discipline, which is a little cruel that it may be very kind. That state of universal warfare maintained throughout the lower creation, to the great perplexity of many worthy people, is at bottom the most merciful provision which the circumstances admit of. . . . The poverty of the incapable, the distresses that come upon the imprudent, the starvation of the idle, and those shoulderings aside of the weak by the strong, which leave so many "in shallows and in miseries," are the decrees of a large, farseeing benevolence. It seems hard that an unskillfulness which with all its efforts he cannot overcome, should entail hunger upon the artisan. It seems hard that a laborer incapacitated by sickness from competing with his stronger fellows, should have to bear the resulting privations. It seems hard that widows and orphans should be left to struggle for life or death. Nevertheless, when regarded not separately, but in connection with the interests of universal humanity, these harsh fatalities are seen to be full of the highest beneficence — the same beneficence which brings to early graves the children of diseased parents, and singles out the low-spirited, the intemperate, and the debilitated as the victims of an epidemic.

READING AND DISCUSSION QUESTIONS

1. What, according to Spencer, is the "fundamental law"? Do you agree with it? Why or why not? Where else have you seen this "fundamental law"?

2. On what grounds could Spencer argue that the death of "the children of diseased parents" was in the "interests of universal humanity" and "full of the highest beneficence" for mankind?

COMPARATIVE QUESTIONS

1. In what ways does Beeton's *Book of Household Management* reflect the new nineteenth-century awareness of sanitation's relationship to health, made explicit in Chadwick's report?

2. Contrast Beeton's depiction of a middle-class home with London's description of the housing of the working-class poor. What does this suggest about the distribution of wealth in industrial Britain?

3. How might Spencer respond to the condition of the British poor as described by Chadwick and Jack London? What might Chadwick and London say to Spencer?

4. What would Robert Owen (Document 21-5) propose as a solution to the problems described by London and Chadwick?

5. How would Locke (Document 19-2) and Metternich (Document 22-2) each respond to Darwin's contention that "the moral nature of man has reached its present standard, partly through the advancement of his reasoning powers and consequently of a just public opinion, but especially from his sympathies having been rendered more tender and widely diffused through the effects of habit, example, instruction, and reflection"?

6. Compare and contrast Darwin's and Spencer's views on civilization and human survival.

7. What do you think Darwin and Spencer would say in response to Zetkin's arguments about women and labor competition? Why?

CHAPTER 24

The Age of Nationalism

1850–1914

B efore 1848, nationalism was a revolutionary ideology, often concerned with rebelling against deeply rooted, outmoded governments. In the second half of the nineteenth century, leaders such as Germany's Otto von Bismarck used nationalist feeling to garner support for policies designed to build the power of the central government. Not all new governments fared well in the court of public opinion. The United States fought a bloody and bitter civil war between 1861 and 1865 over the power of the federal government to stop the expansion of slavery; France went from the Second Republic to the Second Empire, and then faced the secession of Paris from France in 1871. Toward the end of the century, the adoption of nationalism as the basis for personal identity led to horrifying violence against perceived outsiders, particularly Europe's Jewish population. The Dreyfus affair in France (1894–1906) spurred a Jewish movement — Zionism — to gain a nation for themselves and prevent future persecution.

VIEWPOINTS
The State and the People

DOCUMENT 24-1

ABRAHAM LINCOLN
The Gettysburg Address
1863

With the election of Abraham Lincoln to the U.S. presidency in 1860, eleven southern states left the Union to form the Confederate States of America —

Abraham Lincoln, "The Gettysburg Address," November 19, 1863.

in large part because of Lincoln's commitment to ending the expansion of slavery. The ensuing Civil War sped the centralizing process already under way in Europe, and federal power expanded dramatically. In his address President Lincoln dedicates the national cemetery for the soldiers killed at the Battle of Gettysburg, the largest battle ever waged in North America (fought July 1–3, 1862), and rallies a weary nation to continue the war.

Four score and seven years ago[1] our fathers brought forth on this continent, a new nation, conceived in Liberty, and dedicated to the proposition that all men are created equal.

Now we are engaged in a great civil war, testing whether that nation, or any nation so conceived and so dedicated, can long endure. We are met on a great battle-field of that war. We have come to dedicate a portion of that field, as a final resting place for those who here gave their lives that that nation might live. It is altogether fitting and proper that we should do this.

But, in a larger sense, we can not dedicate — we can not consecrate — we can not hallow — this ground. The brave men, living and dead, who struggled here, have consecrated it, far above our poor power to add or detract. The world will little note, nor long remember what we say here, but it can never forget what they did here. It is for us the living, rather, to be dedicated here to the unfinished work which they who fought here have thus far so nobly advanced. It is rather for us to be here dedicated to the great task remaining before us — that from these honored dead we take increased devotion to that cause for which they gave the last full measure of devotion — that we here highly resolve that these dead shall not have died in vain — that this nation, under God, shall have a new birth of freedom — and that government of the people, by the people, for the people, shall not perish from the earth.

READING AND DISCUSSION QUESTIONS

1. In what ways does Lincoln tie his policies to the past in this speech? In what ways does he look to the future?

2. What is the basis of Lincoln's argument for asserting federal power (abolishing slavery) and continuing the conflict with the Confederate forces?

---

[1] **four score and seven years ago**: A score is twenty, thus Lincoln means eighty-seven years ago: 1776.

DOCUMENT 24-2

OTTO VON BISMARCK

Speech Before the Reichstag: On the Law for Workers' Compensation

1884

*Otto von Bismarck, the chancellor of Germany from 1871 to 1890, com-
bined two ideas that were considered opposites in the first half of the century:
nationalism and conservatism. The nineteenth-century liberal focus on indi-
vidualism stripped the upper classes of their obligation to the lower, while
conservatives like Bismarck expected obedience in return for the protection
they gave. One of the places this struggle played out was in the protections
afforded to workers, which liberals saw as interfering with the property rights
of factory owners. Below, Bismarck lays out his vision of the proper relationship between the state and its citizens.*

Deputy von Vollmar has expressed his astonishment that . . . we are making new and different proposals. Gentlemen, that is not our fault. Yesterday Deputy Bamberger[2] compared the business of government with that
of a cobbler who measures shoes, which he thereupon examines as to
whether they are suitable for him or not and accordingly accepts or rejects
them. I am by no means dissatisfied with this humble comparison, by
which you place the united governments in the perspective of a shoe-
maker taking measurements for Herr Bamberger. The profession of government in the sense of Frederick the Great is to serve the people, and
may it be also as a cobbler; the opposite is to dominate the people. We
want to serve the people. But I make the demand on Herr Bamberger that
he act as my co-shoemaker in order to make sure that no member of the
public goes barefoot, and to create a suitable shoe for the people in this
crucial area.

From Jan Goldstein and John W. Boyer, eds., *University of Chicago, Readings in
Western Civilization*, vol. 8, *Nineteenth-Century Europe: Liberalism and Its Critics*,
trans. John W. Boyer (Chicago: University of Chicago Press, 1988), pp. 419–425.
[2] **Deputy Bamberger**: Ludwig Bamberger (1823–1899) was an economist and
founder of the German Liberal Party, one of Bismarck's sometimes reluctant allies.

Deputy von Vollmar[3] then proceeded to the connection that he imputes between our proposal and the Socialist Law.[4] It is not correct, as he conceives it, that we made the proposal in order to win more support for the Socialist Law. There is, indeed, a connection between the two, but it is quite different. At the time of the submission of the Socialist Law the government, and particularly His Majesty the Emperor and, if I am not in error, also the majority of the Reichstag, underwrote certain promissory notes for the future and gave assurances that as a corollary to this Socialist Law a serious effort for the betterment of the fate of the workers should go hand in hand. In my opinion that is the complement to the Socialist Law; if you have persistently decided not to improve the situation of the workers, then I understand that you reject the Socialist Law. For it is an injustice on the one hand to hinder the self-defense of a large class of our fellow citizens and on the other hand not to offer them aid for the redress of that which causes the dissatisfaction. That the Social Democratic leaders wish no advantage for this law, that I understand; dissatisfied workers are just what they need. Their mission is to lead, to rule, and the necessary prerequisite for that is numerous dissatisfied classes. They must naturally oppose any attempt of the government, however well intentioned it may be, to remedy this situation, if they do not wish to lose control over the masses they mislead. Therefore, I place no value on the objections that come from the leaders of the Social Democrats; I would place a very high value on the objections that come from the workers in general. Our workers, thank God, are not all Social Democrats and are not to such a degree unresponsive to the efforts of the confederated governments to help them, perhaps also not to the difficulties that these efforts meet in the parliamentary arena. . . . I in no way support an absolutist government. . . .

[The real question] is whether the state — by state I always mean the empire — whether the state has the right to abandon to chance the performance of a responsibility of the state, namely, to protect the worker from accidents and need when he is injured or becomes old, so that private companies form that charge premiums from the workers and the employers at whatever rates the market will bear. . . . As soon as the state concerns itself with these matters at all, however — and I believe that it is the state's duty to concern itself — it must strive for the least expensive form and must

---

[3] **Deputy von Vollmar**: Georg Heinrich von Vollmar (1850–1922) was a Socialist politician and thus one of Bismarck's opponents in this debate.
[4] **the Socialist Law**: Passed in 1878, it made illegal the meetings and publications of the German Social Democratic Party, though members could (and did) still run for office.

take no advantage from it, and above all not lose sight of the benefit for the poor and the needy. Otherwise one could indeed relinquish the fulfillment of certain state duties, such as among other things the care of the poor, in the widest sense of the word, as well as schools and national defense to private stock companies. . . . In the same way one can continue to believe that the whole of the state's responsibility must in the end be left to the voluntary formation of private stock companies. The whole problem is rooted in the question: does the state have the responsibility to care for its helpless fellow citizens, or does it not? I maintain that it does have this duty, and to be sure, not simply the Christian state, as I once permitted myself to allude to with the words "practical Christianity," but rather every state by its very nature. It would be madness for a corporate body or a collectivity to take charge of those objectives that the individual can accomplish; those goals that the community can fulfill with justice and profit should be relinquished to the community. There are objectives that only the state in its totality can fulfill. . . . Among the last mentioned objectives [of the state] belong national defense [and] the general system of transportation. . . . To these belong also the help of persons in distress and the prevention of such justified complaints as in fact provide excellent material for exploitation by the Social Democrats. That is the responsibility of the state from which the state will not be able to withdraw in the long run.

If one argues against my position that this is socialism, then I do not fear that at all. The question is, where do the justifiable limits of state socialism lie? Without such a boundary we could not manage our affairs. Each law for poor relief is socialism. . . .

There scarcely exists nowadays a word with which more abuse is committed than the word *free*. . . . According to my experience, everyone understands by *freedom* only the freedom for oneself and not for others, as well as the responsibility of others to refrain absolutely from any limitation of one's own freedom. In short, by *freedom* they actually mean *domination*; by *freedom of speech* they understand the domination of the speaker; by *freedom of the press* the predominant and preponderant influence of editorial offices and of newspapers. Indeed gentlemen, and I am not speaking here in confessional terms, in all confessions, by *freedom of the church* the domination of the priests is very frequently understood. . . . I have no desire to speak of human weakness, but rather of the human custom which establishes the importance of the individual person, the dominance of individual persons and their influence over the general public, precisely on the pretext that freedom demands it. That is indeed more strikingly realized in our own history than in any other. In the centuries of the decay of the German Empire, German freedom was always sharply accentuated.

What did this mean? The freedom of the princes from the emperor, and the power of the nobles over the serfs! They wanted for their part to be free; that means, *to be free* was for them and also for others identical with the concept *to dominate*. They did not feel themselves to be free unless they dominated. Therefore, whenever I read the word *free* before another adjective, I become very suspicious. . . . Deputy Bamberger expressed subsequently his regret concerning the "socialist fad." It is, however, a harsh expression when one characterizes as a "socialist fad" the careful decision of the allied governments in Germany, weighed for three years, which they again, for the third time, propose to you in the hope finally to obtain your approval. Perhaps the whole institution of the state is a socialist fad. If everyone could live on his own, perhaps everyone would be much more free, but also much less protected and guarded. If the Deputy calls the proposal a socialist whim, I reply simply that it is untrue, and my assertion is as justified as his. He uses further the expression that the old age and disability care "were chimerical plans." . . . There is nothing about our proposal that is chimerical. Our proposals are completely genuine; they are the result of an existing need. . . . The fulfillment of a state responsibility is never a chimera, and as such I recognize it as a legislative responsibility. It is in fact not a pleasant occupation to devote these public cobbler services to a customer like Deputy Bamberger, who treats us with scorn and ingratitude in the face of real exertions, and who characterizes as a "fad" and a "chimera" the proposal that was worked out in order to make it acceptable to you. I would like to suggest in general that we might be somewhat milder in the expressions with which we mutually characterize our efforts.

READING AND DISCUSSION QUESTIONS

1. What is Bismarck's conception of "freedom," and what role does he see for it in the German Empire over which he presides?

2. What, according to Bismarck, makes his proposals different from those of the socialists he opposes?

3. What areas does Bismarck trust to private for-profit activity, and in what areas does he imply that he finds it lacking? What reasons might he have for these beliefs?

DOCUMENT 24-3

JOHN LEIGHTON
Paris Under the Commune
1871

The triumph of the centralized nation-state that Bismarck and Lincoln proposed was not predestined, and there were periodic outbursts of resistance to it. One came in the spring of 1871, when the Parisian government ended the suspension of rent payments that had been declared when the war broke out. When the French National Guard was ordered to suppress the revolt that developed, they murdered their officers and joined it instead. For a few months, the Paris Commune promoted a decentralized, bottom-up approach to government, before being suppressed by the armed forces of the newly formed Third Republic. Here an Englishman, John Leighton, gives his (often hostile) impressions of the commune.

"Citizens," says the *Official Journal* this morning, "your Commune is constituted." Then follows decree upon decree. White posters are being stuck up everywhere. Why are they at the Hôtel de Ville, if not to publish decrees? The conscription is abolished. We shall see no more poor young fellows marching through the town with their numbers in their caps, and fired with that noble patriotism which is imbibed in the cabarets at so much a glass. We shall have no more soldiers, but to make up for that we shall all be National Guards. As to the landlords, their vexation is extreme; even the tenants do not seem so satisfied as they ought to be. Not to have to pay any rent is very delightful, certainly, but they scarcely dare believe in such good fortune. Thus when Orpheus, trying to rescue Eurydice from "the infernal regions," interrupts with "his harmonious strains" the tortures of eternal punishment, Prometheus did not doubtless show as much delight as he ought to have done, on discovering that the beak of the vulture was no longer gnawing at his vitals, "scarcely daring to believe in such good fortune." Orpheus is the Commune; Eurydice, Liberty; "the infernal regions," the Government of the 4th September; "the harmonious strains,"

From John Leighton, *Paris Under the Commune, or, The Seventy-three Days of the Second Siege* (London: Bradbury, Evans, and Co., 1871), pp. 79–82.

the decrees of the Commune; Prometheus, the tenant; and the vulture, the landlord![5]

In plain terms, however — forgive me for joking on such a subject — the decree which annuls the payment of the rents for the quarters ending October 1870, January 1871, and April 1871, does not appear to me at all extravagant, and really I do not see what there is to object to in the following lines which accompany it: —

> In consideration of the expenses of the war having been chiefly sustained by the industrial, commercial, and working portion of the population, it is but just that the proprietors of houses and land should also bear their part of the burthen. . . .

Let us talk it over together, Mr. Landlord. You have a house and I live in it. It is true that the chimneys smoke, and that you most energetically refuse to have them repaired. However, the house is yours, and you possess most decidedly the right of making a profit by it. Understand, once for all, that I never contest your right. As for me, I depend upon my wit, I do not possess much, but I have a tool — it may be either a pen, or a pencil, or a hammer — which enables me, in the ordinary course of things, to live and to pay with more or less regularity my quarter's rent. If I had not possessed this tool, you would have taken good care not to let me inhabit your house or any part or portion thereof, because you would have considered me in no position to pay you your rent. Now, during the war my tool has unquestionably rendered me but poor service. It has remained ignobly idle in the inkstand, in the folio, or on the bench. Not only have I been unable to use it, but I have also in some sort lost the knack of handling it; I must have some time to get myself into working order again. While I was working but little, and eating less, what were you doing? Oh! I do not mean to say that you were as flourishing as in the triumphant days of the Empire, but still I have not heard of any considerable number of landlords being found begging at the corners of the streets, and I do not fancy you made yourselves

---

[5] **Orpheus . . . the landlord**: In Greek mythology, Orpheus, who charmed the king and queen of the underworld with the music from his lyre, was allowed to bring his dead wife Eurydice back to earth as long as he did not look behind him. When he turned around too soon, Eurydice had to return to the underworld forever. Prometheus stole fire from the god Zeus and gave it to humans; as punishment, Zeus chained him to a rock, where every day a vulture came to eat his liver, and every day it grew back, so that he had to endure the torment over again.

conspicuous by your assiduous attendance at the Municipal Cantines. I have even heard that you or many of your brother-landlords took pretty good care not to be in Paris during the Prussian siege, and that you contented yourselves with forming the most ardent wishes, for the final triumph of French arms, from beneath the wide-spreading oaks of your châteaux in Touraine and Beauce, or from the safe haven of a Normandy fishing village; while we, accompanied it is true by your most fervent prayers, took our turn at mounting guard, on the fortifications during the bitter cold nights, or knee-deep in the mud of the trenches. However, I do not blame those who sought safety in flight; each person is free to do as he pleases; what I object to is your coming back and saying, "During seven or eight months you have done no work, you have been obliged to pawn your furniture to buy bread for your wife and children; I pity you from the bottom of my heart — be so kind as to hand me over my three quarters' rent." No, a thousand times no; such a demand is absurd, wicked, ridiculous; and I declare that if there is no possible compromise between the strict execution of the law and his decree of the Commune, I prefer, without the least hesitation, to abide by the latter; I prefer to see a little poverty replace for a time the long course of prosperity that has been enjoyed by this very small class of individuals, than to see the last articles of furniture of five hundred thousand suffering wretches, put up to auction and knocked down for one-twentieth part of their value. There must, however, be some way of conciliating the interests of both landlords and tenants. Would it be sufficient to accord delays to the latter, and force the former to wait a certain time for their money? I think not; if I were allowed three years to pay off my three quarters' rent, I should still be embarrassed. The tool of the artisan is not like the peasant's plot of ground, which is more productive after having lain fallow. During the last few sad months, when I had no work to do, I was obliged to draw upon the future, a future heavily mortgaged; when I shall perhaps scarcely be able to meet the expenses of each day, will there be any possibility of acquitting the debts of the past? You may sell my furniture if the law gives you the right to do so, but I shall not pay!

The only possible solution, believe me, is that in favor of the tenants, only it ought not to be applied in so wholesale a fashion. Inquiries should be instituted, and to those tenants from whom the war has taken away all possibility of payment an unconditional receipt should be delivered: to those who have suffered less, a proportionate reduction should be allowed; but those whom the invasion has not ruined or seriously impoverished — and the number is large, among provision merchants, café keepers, and private residents — let those pay directly. In this way the landlords will lose less than one may imagine, because it will be the lowest rents that will be forfeited. The decree of the Commune is based on a right principle, but too generally applied.

The new Government — for it is a Government — does not confine itself to decrees. It has to install itself in its new quarters and make arrangements.

In a few hours it has organized more than ten committees — the executive, the financial, the public-service, the educational, the military, the legal, and the committee of public safety. No end of committees and committeemen: it is to be hoped that the business will be promptly dispatched!

READING AND DISCUSSION QUESTIONS

1. Who, based on Leighton's discussion, makes up the nation? How does it affect your reading of this passage to know that Leighton spent much of his book mocking and denouncing the Paris Commune?

2. What is Leighton's complaint with this specific decree of the commune? Does he seem reasonable?

DOCUMENT 24-4

ÉMILE ZOLA
"J'Accuse" the French Army
1898

Alfred Dreyfus was a Jewish French artillery officer arrested and convicted in 1894 for selling military secrets to the Germans. His case revealed the ambiguity of nineteenth-century nationalists toward Jewish citizens as well as the pressure the state's needs placed on its courts. Dreyfus's innocence was well established by the time Émile Zola, a famous novelist, wrote this letter, but his opponents — the Anti-Dreyfusards — argued that it was better that an

From Émile Zola, "J'Accuse" in Armand Charpentier, *The Dreyfus Case*, trans. Lewis May (London: Geoffrey Bles, 1935), pp. 142–144.

innocent man be imprisoned than the government admit it had made a mistake and thereby undermine the nation. A sizable faction — the Dreyfusards — disagreed, and the argument split French politics for years.

Dreyfus knows several languages: a crime. No compromising papers were found in his possession: a crime. He sometimes visited his native country:[6] a crime. He is industrious and likes to find out about everything: a crime. He is calm: a crime. He is worried: a crime. . . .

I accuse Lieutenant-Colonel du Paty de Clam[7] of having been the diabolical, but I would fain believe the unwitting, artisan of the miscarriage of justice, and thereafter of having defended his unhallowed work for three years by the most clumsy and culpable machinations.

I accuse General Mercier[8] of having become, at all events through weakness, an accomplice in one of the greatest iniquities of the age.

I accuse General Billot[9] of having had in his hands sure proofs of the innocence of Dreyfus and of having hushed them up, of having incurred the guilt of crimes against humanity and justice, for political ends and to save the face of the General Staff.

I accuse General de Boisdeffre and General Gonse[10] of having been participators in the same crime, actuated, the one no doubt by clerical partisanship, the other, it may be, by that esprit de corps which would make the Army and the War Office the sacred Ark of the Covenant.

---

[6] **his native country**: Dreyfus was from Alsace (Alsatia in German), a French province at the time of his birth, but taken by Germany in 1871. For Dreyfus to visit his childhood home, he had to cross the new national border.

[7] **Lieutenant-Colonel du Paty de Clam**: Armand Mercier Paty de Clam was the French counterintelligence officer who conducted the first accusation against Dreyfus, and who remained convinced of Dreyfus's guilt long after the actual author of the document that began the case was revealed.

[8] **General Mercier**: Mercier was the war minister who originated the case against Dreyfus and continued it to avoid political embarrassment after making public pronouncements of his certainty of Dreyfus's guilt.

[9] **General Billot**: Jean-Baptiste Billot was a French general and war minister during the later stages of the Dreyfus affair, 1896–1898.

[10] **General de Boisdeffre and General Gonse**: General Gonse was the general to whom the counterintelligence division (called for secrecy purposes the Statistical Section) reported. Boisdeffre was the chief of staff of the French Army — its highest-ranking soldier — at the time of the initial accusation, and according to Zola, a strong supporter of the Catholic clergy in France.

I accuse General de Pellieux and Major Ravary[11] of conducting a disgraceful inquiry, by which I mean an inquiry characterized by the most monstrous partiality, of which we have, in the report of the latter of these two men, an imperishable monument of stupid audacity.

I accuse the three handwriting experts, MM. Belhomme, Varinard, and Couard, of drawing up misleading and lying reports, unless, indeed, a medical examination should reveal them to be suffering from some pathological abnormality of sight and judgment.

I accuse the War Office of conducting an abominable campaign in the Press, and particularly in the newspapers *l'Eclair* and *l'Echo de Paris*, in order to mislead public opinion and to conceal their own misdeeds.

I accuse the first Court-Martial of acting contrary to law by condemning an accused man on the strength of a secret document; and I accuse the second Court-Martial of having, in obedience to orders, concealed that illegality, and of committing in its turn the crime of knowingly acquitting a guilty man.

In bringing these charges, I am not unaware that I render myself liable to prosecution under Clauses 30 and 31 of the Act of the 29th of July, which deals with defamation of character in the public Press. But I do so of my own free will and with my eyes open.

As for those whom I accuse, I do not know them, I have never seen them. I entertain for them neither hatred nor ill-will. They are so far as I am concerned mere entities, spirits of social maleficence, and the action to which I have here committed myself is but a revolutionary means of hastening the explosion of Truth and Justice.

I have but one passion, and that is for light, and I plead in the name of that humanity which has so greatly suffered and has a right to happiness. My fiery protest is but the outcry of my soul. Let them drag me, then, into a Court of Justice and let the matter be thrashed out in broad daylight. I am ready.

---

[11] **General de Pellieux and Major Ravary**: Pellieux was the general who investigated the accusations against Esterhazy — the man later proved to have committed the crime of which Dreyfus was accused — and found him innocent. Ravary oversaw the handwriting analysts, and reported on their findings, which turned out to be inaccurate.

READING AND DISCUSSION QUESTIONS

1. Based on this document, what is the relationship between the needs of the accused and the needs of the state in nineteenth-century France? How does Zola oppose this conception of justice?

2. Although the actions of the court that convicted Dreyfus were popular, were they compatible with the idea of government by the consent of the governed, which the French Third Republic claimed?

3. What motivations might Zola have had for making specific allegations against specific people, instead of charging a grand but vague conspiracy?

4. What role does Dreyfus seem to play in "J'Accuse"? Does Zola seem to care about Dreyfus, or is he more a political symbol than an individual? What gives you that impression?

DOCUMENT 24-5

LEO PINSKER

Auto-Emancipation: A Russian Zionist Makes the Case for a Jewish Homeland

1882

Nationalists in the second half of the nineteenth century were unsure how to categorize Europe's Jewish population. Anti-Semitism had a long history in Europe, but in an era worried about national identity, fear of Jews was based more on fears of disloyalty than religious motives. Leo Pinsker (1821–1891), a Jewish doctor born in Russian-ruled Poland, argued that the way to end these worries was not European tolerance but the creation of a nation-state (referred to as Zion[12]) to which the Jews could emigrate. The Zionist movement led to the creation of the state of Israel in the mid-twentieth century.

From Leo Pinsker, "Auto-Emancipation: An Appeal to His People by a Russian Jew," in *Modern Jewish History: A Source Reader,* ed. Robert Chazan and Marc Lee Raphael (New York: Schocken Books, 1974), pp. 163, 165–166, 169–171, 173–174.

[12]**Zion:** Originally referred to Mount Zion, near Jerusalem; and the term came to mean the homeland of the ancient Hebrews to which their descendants wished to return.

A fear of the Jewish ghost has passed down the generations and the centuries. First a breeder of prejudice, later in the conjunction with other forces we are about to discuss, it culminated in Judeophobia.

Judeophobia, together with other symbols, superstitions, and idiosyncrasies, has acquired legitimacy among all the peoples of the earth with whom the Jews had intercourse. Judeophobia is a variety of demonopathy[13] with the distinction that it is not peculiar to particular races but is common to the whole of mankind, and that this ghost is not disembodied like other ghosts but partakes of flesh and blood, must endure pain inflicted by the fearful mob who imagines itself endangered.

Judeophobia is a psychic aberration. As a psychic aberration it is hereditary, and as a disease transmitted for two thousand years it is incurable. . . .

The Jews are aliens who can have no representatives, because they have no country. Because they have none, because their home has no boundaries within which they can be entrenched, their misery too is boundless. The *general law* does not apply to the Jews as true aliens, but there are everywhere *laws for the Jews*, and if the general law is to apply to them, a special and explicit bylaw is required to confirm it. Like the Negroes, like women, and unlike all free peoples, they must be *emancipated*. If, unlike the Negroes, they belong to an advanced race, and if, unlike women, they can produce not only women of distinction, but also distinguished men, even men of greatness, then it is very much the worse for them.

Since the Jew is nowhere at home, nowhere regarded as a native, he remains an alien everywhere. That he himself and his ancestors as well are born in the country does [not] alter this fact in the least.

When we are ill-used, robbed, plundered, and dishonored, we dare not defend ourselves, and, worse still, we take it almost as a matter of course. When our face is slapped, we soothe our burning cheek with cold water; and when a bloody wound has been inflicted, we apply a bandage. When we are turned out of the house which we ourselves built, we beg humbly for mercy, and when we fail to reach the heart of our oppressor we move on in search of another exile.

When an idle spectator on the road calls out to us: "You poor Jewish devils are certainly to be pitied," we are most deeply touched; and when a Jew is said to be an honor to his people, we are foolish enough to be proud of it. We have sunk so low that we become almost jubilant when, as in the

---

[13] **demonopathy**: A mental disorder in which the victim believes he or she is possessed by a demon. Pinsker is comparing Judeophobia to mental illness, not to the belief in possession.

West, a small fraction of our people is put on an equal footing with non-Jews. But he who must be *put* on a footing stands but weakly. If no notice is taken of our descent and we are treated like others born in the country, we express our gratitude by actually turning renegades. For the sake of the comfortable position we are granted, for the fleshpots which we may enjoy in peace, we persuade ourselves, and others, that we are no longer Jews, but full-blooded citizens. Idle delusion! Though you prove yourselves patriots a thousand times, you will still be reminded at every opportunity of your Semitic descent. This fateful *memento mori*[14] will not prevent you, however, from accepting the extended hospitality, until some fine morning you find yourself crossing the border and you are reminded by the mob that you are, after all, nothing but vagrants and parasites, without the protection of the law.

But even humane treatment does not prove that we are welcome. . . . Moreover, the belief in a Messiah, in the intervention of a higher power to bring about our political resurrection, and the religious assumption that we must bear patiently divine punishment, caused us to abandon every thought of our national liberation, unity, and independence. Consequently, we have renounced the idea of a nationhood and did so the more readily since we were preoccupied with our immediate needs. Thus we sank lower and lower. The people *without a country forgot their country*. Is it not high time to perceive the disgrace of it all?

Happily, matters stand somewhat differently now. The events of the last few years in *enlightened* Germany, in Romania, in Hungary, and especially in Russia, have effected what the far bloodiest persecutions of the Middle Ages could not. The national consciousness which until then had lain dormant in sterile martyrdom awoke the masses of the Russian and Romanian Jews and took form in an irresistible movement toward Palestine. Mistaken as this movement has proved to be by its results, it was, nevertheless, a right instinct to strike out for home. The severe trials which they have endured have now provoked a reaction quite different from the fatalistic submission to a divine condign punishment. Even the unenlightened masses of the Russian Jews have not entirely escaped the influences of the principles of modern culture. Without renouncing Judaism and their faith, they revolted against undeserved ill-treatment which could be inflicted with impunity only because the Russian Government regards the

---

[14] ***memento mori***: The Latin phrase supposedly spoken in the ear of someone granted a Roman triumph — a parade celebrating an accomplishment — that is usually translated as "remember, you are mortal."

Jews as aliens. And the other European governments — why should they concern themselves with the citizens of a state in whose internal affairs they have no right to interfere? . . .

If we would have a secure home, give up our endless life of wandering and rise to the dignity of a nation in our own eyes and in the eyes of the world, we must, above all, not dream of restoring ancient Judaea. We must not attach ourselves to the place where our political life was once violently interrupted and destroyed. The goal of our present endeavors must be not the "Holy Land," but a land of our own. We need nothing but a large tract of land for our poor brothers, which shall remain our property and from which no foreign power can expel us. There we shall take with us the most sacred possessions which we have saved from the shipwreck of our former country, the *God-idea* and the *Bible*. It is these alone which have made our old fatherland the Holy Land, and not Jerusalem or the Jordan. Perhaps the Holy Land will again become ours. If so, all the better, but *first of all*, we must determine — and this is the crucial point — what country is accessible to us, and at the same time adapted to offer the Jews of all lands who must leave their homes a secure and indisputed refuge, capable of productivization.

READING AND DISCUSSION QUESTIONS

1. What are the characteristics that Pinsker believes distinguish Jews from everyone else? What reaction would you expect his "Judeophobia" argument to draw today?

2. What does Pinsker's statement of the problem of anti-Semitism reveal about the nationalism of his era? In what ways might Europe's Jews be barred from the national community?

3. In what ways could the creation of a Jewish nation-state ease the discrimination Pinsker sees in Europe? What about those who may choose not to emigrate, but remain in their original countries?

4. What dangers does Pinsker see for his fellow Jews in the Zionist movement? What mistake does he see as having already been made?

COMPARATIVE QUESTIONS

1. How did the definition of freedom and citizenship differ in Lincoln's America and Bismarck's Germany?

2. What positive aspects did the process of national consolidation have in the second half of the nineteenth century?

3. Consulting Pinsker and Zola, what was the place in the new nation-state for those people whose identities were not based on membership in a national community?

4. What is the balance between concepts of individual and collective rights and responsibilities in these documents, particularly Bismarck, Lincoln, and Leighton?

5. Where might the Paris Commune agree with Bismarck's view of society? Where might they disagree with him?

CHAPTER 25

The West and the World

1815–1914

I n the nineteenth century, Europeans had powerful motives for expansion, including a self-appointed obligation to spread their "superior" Western culture and religion, as well as the industrialists' search for untapped markets and raw materials. Added to traditional motives was the unfortunate misinterpretation of Darwin's theories that suggested that societies as well as organisms had to compete for resources; white Europeans used this argument to justify oppressing people of other, "inferior" races. While they fell short in their hunt for new markets, investors made fortunes off the raw materials they acquired as a result of imperialism. The push to spread European culture proved less fruitful, particularly in China, with its long-established customs. Ultimately, industrial innovation catapulted Europe into a position of global power. With the invention of the Maxim machine gun in 1884, European technology counterbalanced Asian and African man power. In the imperial climate, native resistance never fully faded, and an undercurrent of fear persisted among the uninvited occupiers.

VIEWPOINTS
Economic Imperialism

DOCUMENT 25-1

COMMISSIONER LIN ZEXU
Letter to Queen Victoria
1839

China, the most populous country on earth in the nineteenth century, was the prize in the search for markets for Western products. The Chinese imperial government's reluctance to allow Western access, combined with poverty and general disinterest in Western goods, restricted trade until the British discovered they had a product that would sell in China — opium. Lin Zexu, the imperial commissioner for the southern province of Guangdong, attempted to suppress the opium trade, and published this open letter to the British queen in 1839. That same year, the British started the First Opium War (1839–1842) to ensure their continued right to sell opium in China.

We have heard that in your own country opium is prohibited with the utmost strictness and severity: this is a strong proof that you know full well how hurtful it is to mankind. Since then you do not permit it to injure your own country, you ought not to have the injurious drug transferred to another country, and above all others, how much less to the Inner Land! Of the products which China exports to your foreign countries, there is not one which is not beneficial to mankind in some shape or other. There are those which serve for food, those which are useful, and those which are calculated for re-sale; but all are beneficial. Has China (we should like to ask) ever yet sent forth a noxious article from its soil? Not to speak of our tea and rhubarb, things which your foreign countries could not exist a single day without, if we of the Central Land were to grudge you what is beneficial, and not to compassionate your wants, then wherewithal could you foreigners manage to exist? And further, as regards your woolens,

From William H. McNeil and Mitsuko Iriye, eds., *Readings in World History*, Vol. 9, *Modern Asia and Africa* (New York: Oxford University Press, 1971), pp. 111–118.

camlets [goat or camel hair cloth], and longells [cloth of a specific weave], were it not that you get supplied with our native raw silk, you could not get these manufactured! If China were to grudge you those things which yield a profit, how could you foreigners scheme after any profit at all? Our other articles of food, such as sugar, ginger, cinnamon, &c., and our other articles for use, such as silk piece-goods, chinaware, &c., are all so many necessaries of life to you; how can we reckon up their number! On the other hand, the things that come from your foreign countries are only calculated to make presents of, or serve for mere amusement. It is quite the same to us if we have them, or if we have them not. If then these are of no material consequence to us of the Inner Land, what difficulty would there be in prohibiting and shutting our market against them? It is only that our heavenly dynasty most freely permits you to take off her tea, silk, and other commodities, and convey them for consumption everywhere, without the slightest stint or grudge, for no other reason, but that where a profit exists, we wish that it be diffused abroad for the benefit of all the earth!

Your honorable nation takes away the products of our Central Land, and not only do you thereby obtain food and support for yourselves, but moreover, by re-selling these products to other countries you reap a three-fold profit. Now if you would only not sell opium, this threefold profit would be secured to you: how can you possibly consent to forgo it for a drug that is hurtful to men, and an unbridled craving after gain that seems to know no bounds! Let us suppose that foreigners came from another country, and brought opium into England, and seduced the people of your country to smoke it, would not you, the sovereign of the said country, look upon such a procedure with anger, and in your just indignation endeavor to get rid of it? . . .

We have heard that in London the metropolis where you dwell, as also in Scotland, Ireland, and other such places, no opium whatever is produced. It is only in sundry parts of your colonial kingdom of Hindostan,[1] such as Bengal, Madras, Bombay, Patna, Malwa, Benares, Malacca, and other places where the very hills are covered with the opium plant, where tanks are made for the preparing of the drug; month by month, and year by year, the volume of the poison increases, its unclean stench ascends upwards, until heaven itself grows angry, and the very gods thereat get indignant! You, the queen of the said honorable nation, ought immediately to have the plant in those parts plucked up by the very root! Cause

---

[1] **Hindostan**: British India, particularly the northwestern section, in today's India and Pakistan.

the land there to be hoed up afresh, sow in its stead the five grains, and if any man dare again to plant in these grounds a single poppy, visit his crime with the most severe punishment. . . .

Suppose the subject of another country were to come to England to trade, he would certainly be required to comply with the laws of England, then how much more does this apply to us of the celestial empire! Now it is a fixed statute of this empire, that any native Chinese who sells opium is punishable with death, and even he who merely smokes it, must not less die.

READING AND DISCUSSION QUESTIONS

1. What sort of tone does Lin assume in his letter to the English queen?
2. How does Lin classify China's policy on trade with Britain?
3. What benefits does Lin believe the British reap from their relationship with China, and how does he feel this should affect that relationship?
4. Based on what you have read here, what is the difference between the British relationship with China and with the Indian areas Lin mentions?

DOCUMENT 25-2

JULES FERRY
Speech Before the French Chamber of Deputies
1884

France and imperialism had a long and complex relationship. In 1792 the revolutionaries decided to spread the benefits of liberty to the rest of Europe, and French colonial ambitions followed in the same tradition. Believing

From Jules François Camille Ferry, "Speech Before the French Chamber of Deputies, March 28, 1884," *Discours et Opinions de Jules Ferry*, ed. Paul Robiquet (Paris: Armand Colin & Cie., 1897), 1. 5, pp. 199–201, 210–211, 215–218. Translated by Ruth Kleinman in *Brooklyn College Core Four Sourcebook*.

themselves the height of European development, the French carried out their "Civilizing Mission" (Mission Civilizatrice) in Asia and North Africa, becoming one of Britain's leading competitors by 1898. Here, Ferry — a liberal by the definitions of the day — speaks in his capacity as prime minister, exhorting the Third Republic to follow in the footsteps of Napoleon III.

The policy of colonial expansion is a political and economic system . . . that can be connected to three sets of ideas: economic ideas; the most far-reaching ideas of civilization; and ideas of a political and patriotic sort.

In the area of economics, I am placing before you, with the support of some statistics, the considerations that justify the policy of colonial expansion, as seen from the perspective of a need, felt more and more urgently by the industrialized population of Europe and especially the people of our rich and hardworking country of France: the need for outlets [that is, for exports]. Is this a fantasy? Is this a concern [that can wait] for the future? Or is this not a pressing need, one may say a crying need, of our industrial population? I merely express in a general way what each one of you can see for himself in the various parts of France. Yes, what our major industries [textiles, etc.], irrevocably steered by the treaties of 1860–1861[2] into exports, lack more and more are outlets. Why? Because next door Germany is setting up trade barriers; because across the ocean the United States of America have become protectionists, and extreme protectionists at that; because not only are these great markets . . . shrinking, becoming more and more difficult of access, but these great states are beginning to pour into our own markets products not seen there before. This is true not only for our agriculture, which has been so sorely tried . . . and for which competition is no longer limited to the circle of large European states. . . . Today, as you know, competition, the law of supply and demand, freedom of trade, the effects of speculation, all radiate in a circle that reaches to the ends of the earth. . . . That is a great complication, a great economic difficulty; . . . an extremely serious problem. It is so serious, gentlemen, so acute, that the least informed persons must already glimpse, foresee, and take precautions against the time when the great South American market that has, in a manner of speaking, belonged to us forever will be disputed and perhaps taken away from us by North American products. Nothing is

---

[2] **the treaties of 1860–1861**: Negotiations between the British and French governments that resulted in lower trade barriers, particularly in lower tariffs on French wines.

more serious; there can be no graver social problem; and these matters are linked intimately to colonial policy.

Gentlemen, we must speak more loudly and more honestly! We must say openly that indeed the higher races have a right over the lower races. . . .

I repeat, that the superior races have a right because they have a duty. They have the duty to civilize the inferior races. . . . In the history of earlier centuries these duties, gentlemen, have often been misunderstood; and certainly when the Spanish soldiers and explorers introduced slavery into Central America, they did not fulfill their duty as men of a higher race. . . . But, in our time, I maintain that European nations acquit themselves with generosity, with grandeur, and with sincerity of this superior civilizing duty.

I say that French colonial policy, the policy of colonial expansion, the policy that has taken us under the Empire [the Second Empire, of Napoleon III, 1852–1871], to Saigon, to Indochina [Vietnam], that has led us to Tunisia, to Madagascar — I say that this policy of colonial expansion was inspired by . . . the fact that a navy such as ours cannot do without safe harbors, defenses, supply centers on the high seas. . . . Are you unaware of this? Look at a map of the world.

Gentlemen, these are considerations that merit the full attention of patriots. The conditions of naval warfare have greatly changed. . . . At present, as you know, a warship, however perfect its design, cannot carry more than two weeks' supply of coal; and a vessel without coal is a wreck on the high seas, abandoned to the first occupier. Hence the need to have places of supply, shelters, ports for defense and provisioning. . . . And that is why we needed Tunisia; that is why we needed Saigon and Indochina; that is why we need Madagascar . . . and why we shall never leave them! . . . Gentlemen, in Europe such as it is today, in this competition of the many rivals we see rising up around us, some by military or naval improvements, others by the prodigious development of a constantly growing population; in a Europe, or rather in a universe thus constituted, a policy of withdrawal or abstention is simply the high road to decadence! In our time nations are great only through the activity they deploy; it is not by spreading the peaceable light of their institutions . . . that they are great, in the present day.

Spreading light without acting, without taking part in the affairs of the world, keeping out of all European alliances and seeing as a trap, an adventure, all expansion into Africa or the Orient — for a great nation to live this way, believe me, is to abdicate and, in less time than you may think, to sink from the first rank to the third and fourth.

READING AND DISCUSSION QUESTIONS

1. Why does Ferry argue that the French deserve to conquer and maintain an empire?

2. What might Ferry mean when he says that there is no more urgent social question than imperialism?

3. How does Ferry believe that France will benefit from possessing an empire? How does this balance the supposed burden of extending the benefits of civilization?

DOCUMENT 25-3

SIR HENRY MORTON STANLEY

Autobiography: *European Imperialism in Africa*

1909

Henry Morton Stanley (1841–1904) was born John Rowlands in Great Britain but rose to fame as an American citizen in the employ of the king of the Belgians, Leopold II. In 1871, while working as a journalist for the New York Herald, *Stanley led an expedition to locate Dr. David Livingstone, a popular explorer and missionary who had gone missing in central Africa. Upon reading about Stanley's exploration of the Congo basin, Leopold II became interested in acquiring an empire in Africa, which in turn sparked the interest of other European countries fearful of being left behind in the race to colonize Africa. Stanley's expeditions were brutal even by the standards of other explorers, though his assumption of European superiority was very common.*

Ngalyema, chief of Stanley Pool district, had demanded and received four thousand five hundred dollars' worth of cotton, silk, and velvet goods for granting me the privilege of establishing a station in a wilderness of a place at the commencement of up-river navigation. Owing to this, I had advanced

From Henry Morton Stanley, *Autobiography*, ed. Dorothy Stanley (New York: Houghton Mifflin, 1909), pp. 339–344, 384–385.

with my wagons to within ten miles of the Pool. I had toiled at this work the best part of two years, and whenever I cast a retrospective glance at what the task had cost me, I felt that it was no joke, and such that no money would bribe me to do over again. Such a long time had elapsed since Ngalyema had received his supplies, that he affected to forget that he had received any; and, as I still continued to advance towards him after the warnings of his messengers, he collected a band of doughty warriors, painted their bodies with diagonal stripes of ochre, soot, chalk, and yellow, and issued fiercely to meet me.

Meantime, the true owners of the soil had enlightened me respecting Ngalyema's antecedents. He was only an enterprising native trader in ivory and slaves, who had fled from the north bank; but, though he had obtained so much money from me by pretences, I was not so indignant at this as at the audacity with which he chose to forget the transaction, and the impudent demand for another supply which underlay this. Ngalyema, having failed to draw any promise by sending messengers, thought he could extort it by appearing with a warlike company. Meantime, duly warned, I had prepared a surprise for him.

I had hung a great Chinese Gong conspicuously near the principal tent. Ngalyema's curiosity would be roused. All my men were hidden, some in the steamboat on top of the wagon, and in its shadow was a cool place where the warriors would gladly rest after a ten-mile march; other of my men lay still as death under tarpaulins, under bundles of grass, and in the bush round about the camp. By the time the drum-taps and horns announced Ngalyema's arrival, the camp seemed abandoned except by myself and a few small boys. I was indolently seated in a chair, reading a book, and appeared too lazy to notice anyone; but suddenly looking up and seeing my 'brother Ngalyema' and his warriors scowlingly regarding me, I sprang up, and seized his hands, and affectionately bade him welcome, in the name of sacred fraternity, and offered him my own chair.

He was strangely cold, and apparently disgruntled, and said: —

"Has not my brother forgotten his road? What does he mean by coming to this country?"

"Nay, it is Ngalyema who has forgotten the blood-bond which exists between us. It is Ngalyema who has forgotten the mountains of goods which I paid him. What words are these of my brother?"

"Be warned, Rock-Breaker. Go back before it is too late. My elders and people all cry out against allowing the white man to come into our country. Therefore, go back before it be too late. Go back, I say, the way you came."

Speech and counter-speech followed. Ngalyema had exhausted his arguments; but it was not easy to break faith and be uncivil, without plausible excuse. His eyes were reaching round seeking to discover an excuse to fight, when they rested on the round, burnished face of the Chinese gong.

"What is that?" he said.

"Ah, that — that is a fetish."

"A fetish! A fetish for what?"

"It is a war-fetish, Ngalyema. The slightest sound of that would fill this empty camp with hundreds of angry warriors; they would drop from above, they would spring up from the ground, from the forest about, from everywhere."

"Sho! Tell that story to the old women, and not to a chief like Ngalyema. My boy tells me it is a kind of a bell. Strike it and let me hear it."

"Oh, Ngalyema, my brother, the consequences would be too dreadful! Do not think of such a thing!"

"Strike it, I say."

"Well, to oblige my dear brother Ngalyema, I will."

And I struck hard and fast, and the clangorous roll rang out like thunder in the stillness. Only for a few seconds, however, for a tempest of human voices was heard bursting into frightful discords, and from above, right upon the heads of the astonished warriors, leaped yelling men; and from the tents, the huts, the forest round about, they came by sixes, dozens, and scores, yelling like madmen, and seemingly animated with uncontrollable rage. The painted warriors became panic-stricken; they flung their guns and powder-kegs away, forgot their chief, and all thoughts of loyalty, and fled on the instant, fear lifting their heels high in the air; or, tugging at their eyeballs and kneading the senses confusedly, they saw, heard, and suspected nothing, save that the limbo of fetishes had broken loose!

But Ngalyema and his son did not fly. They caught the tails of my coat, and we began to dance from side to side, a loving triplet, myself being the foremost, to ward off the blow savagely aimed at my "brothers," and cheerfully crying out, "Hold fast to me, my brothers. I will defend you to the last drop of my blood. Come one, come all," etc.

Presently the order was given, "Fall in!" and quickly the leaping forms became rigid, and the men stood in two long lines in beautiful order, with eyes front, as though "at attention." Then Ngalyema relaxed his hold of my coat-tails, and crept from behind, breathing more freely; and, lifting his hand to his mouth, exclaimed, in genuine surprise "Eh, Mamma! Where did all these people come from?"

"Ah, Ngalyema, did I not tell you that thing was a powerful fetish? Let me strike it again, and show you what else it can do."

"No! No! No!" he shrieked. "I have seen enough!"

The day ended peacefully. I was invited to hasten on to Stanley Pool. The natives engaged themselves by the score to assist me in hauling the wagons. My progress was thenceforward steady and uninterrupted, and in due time the wagons and goods-columns arrived at their destination. . . .

Some of you may, perhaps, wonder at the quiet inoffensiveness of the natives, who, on a former expedition, had worried my soul by their ferocity and wanton attacks, night and day; but a very simple explanation of it may be found in Livingstone's Last Journals, dated 28th October, 1870. He says: "Muini Mukata, who has travelled further than most Arabs, said to me, 'If a man goes with a good-natured, civil tongue, he may pass through the worst people in Africa unharmed.' This is true, but time also is required; one must not run through a country, but give the people time to become acquainted with you, and let their worst fears subside."

Now on the expedition across Africa I had no time to give, either to myself or to them. The river bore my heavy canoes downward; my goods would never have endured the dawdling requirement by the system of teaching every tribe I met who I was. To save myself and my men from certain starvation, I had to rush on and on, right through. But on this expedition, the very necessity of making roads to haul my enormous six-ton wagons gave time for my reputation to travel ahead of me. My name, purpose, and liberal rewards for native help, naturally exaggerated, prepared a welcome for me, and transformed my enemies of the old time into workmen, friendly allies, strong porters, and firm friends. I was greatly forbearing also; but, when a fight was inevitable, through open violence, it was sharp and decisive. Consequently, the natives rapidly learned that though everything was to be gained by friendship with me, wars brought nothing but ruin. . . .

The dark faces light up with friendly gleams, and a budding of good will may perhaps date from this trivial scene. To such an impressionable being as an African native, the self-involved European, with his frigid, imperious manner, pallid white face, and dead, lustreless eyes, is a sealed book.

We had sown seeds of good-will at every place we had touched, and each tribe would spread diffusively the report of the value and beauty of our labors. Pure benevolence contains within itself grateful virtues. Over natural people nothing has greater charm or such expansible power; its influence grows without effort; its subtlety exercises itself on all who come within hearing of it. Coming in such innocent guise, it offends not; there is naught in it to provoke resentment. Provided patience and good temper guides the chief of Stanley Falls station, by the period of the return of the steamers, the influence of the seedling just planted there will have been extended from tribe to tribe far inland, and amid the persecuted fugitives from the slave-traders. . . .

When a young white officer quits England for the first time, to lead blacks, he has got to learn to unlearn a great deal. . . . We must have white men in Africa; but the raw white is a great nuisance there during the first year. In the second year, he begins to mend; during the third year, if his nature permits it, he has developed into a superior man, whose intelligence may be of transcendent utility for directing masses of inferior men.

My officers were possessed with the notion that my manner was "hard," because I had not many compliments for them. That is the kind of pap which we may offer women and boys. Besides, I thought they were superior natures, and required none of that encouragement, which the more childish blacks almost daily received.

READING AND DISCUSSION QUESTIONS

1. In what ways does Stanley seek to present himself as a "great" explorer? What factors does he see as decisive in his success?

2. What attitudes does Stanley display toward the natives he encounters? What are the benefits of "friendship" for his expedition?

3. How does Stanley seem to view the Europeans with whom he works? What does the final paragraph reveal about nineteenth-century attitudes toward masculinity?

DOCUMENT 25-4

MARK TWAIN

King Leopold's Soliloquy

1905

Belgium led the way in colonizing sub-Saharan Africa, under the flag of the Congo Free State, a benevolent organization that claimed to bring the

From Mark Twain, *King Leopold's Soliloquy: A Defense of His Congo Rule* (Boston: The P. R. Warren Co., 1905), pp. 38–40.

benefits of European civilization to Africa. In fact it made massive sums
of money for Leopold II, at tremendous human cost to the Congo natives.
Despite tight Belgian control over travel to the Congo, reports filtered out of
forced labor and amputation of a hand for failing to meet rubber production
quotas. In 1905 Mark Twain published a pamphlet written from Leopold's
perspective, in which the king's speech on civilization was interspersed with
images like the ones shown here.

It is all the same old thing — tedious repetitions and duplications of shop-worn episodes; mutilations, murders, massacres, and so on, and so on, till one gets drowsy over it. Mr. Morel[3] intrudes at this point, and contributes a comment which he could just as well have kept to himself — and throws in some italics, of course; these people can never get along without italics:

> "It is one heartrending story of human misery from beginning to end, and *it is all recent.*"

Meaning 1904 and 1905. I do not see how a person can act so. This Morel is a king's subject, and reverence for monarchy should have restrained him from reflecting upon me with that exposure. This Morel is a reformer; a Congo reformer. That sizes *him* up. He publishes a sheet in Liverpool called *The West African Mail*, which is supported by the voluntary contributions of the sap-headed and the soft-hearted; and every week it steams and reeks and festers with up-to-date "Congo atrocities" of the sort detailed in this pile of pamphlets here. I will suppress it. I suppressed a Congo atrocity book there, after it was actually in print; it should not be difficult for me to suppress a newspaper.

[*Studies some photographs of mutilated negroes — throws them down. Sighs*]

The kodak has been a sore calamity to us. The most powerful enemy that has confronted us, indeed. In the early years we had no trouble in getting the press to "expose" the tales of the mutilations as slanders, lies, inventions of busy-body American missionaries and exasperated foreigners who found the "open door" of the Berlin-Congo charter closed against them when they innocently went out there to trade; and by the press's help

---

[3] **Mr. Morel**: E. D. Morel (1873–1924); British author and socialist politician who wrote important exposés of Leopold's brutality in the Congo.

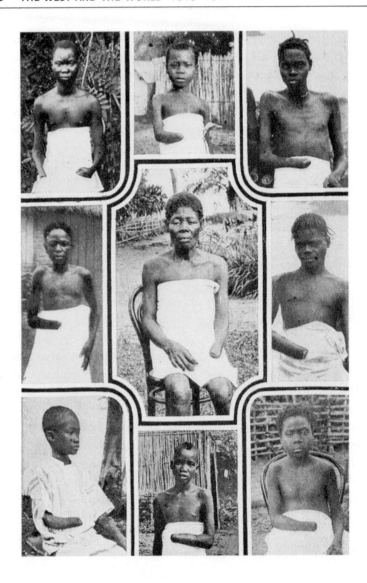

we got the Christian nations everywhere to turn an irritated and unbeliev-
ing ear to those tales and say hard things about the tellers of them. Yes, all
things went harmoniously and pleasantly in those good days, and I was
looked up to as the benefactor of a down-trodden and friendless people.
Then all of a sudden came the crash! That is to say, the incorruptible
kodak — and all the harmony went to hell! The only witness I have encountered in my long experience that I couldn't bribe. Every Yankee missionary
and every interrupted trader sent home and got one; and now — oh, well,
the pictures get sneaked around everywhere, in spite of all we can do to

ferret them out and suppress them. Ten thousand pulpits and ten thousand presses are saying the good word for me all the time and placidly and convincingly denying the mutilations. Then that trivial little kodak, that a child can carry in its pocket, gets up, uttering never a word, and knocks them dumb!

READING AND DISCUSSION QUESTIONS

1. Mark Twain had his satirical Leopold say that "the kodak has been a sore calamity to us." What point is he making with that assertion and these photographs?

2. What do these images say about the relationship between colonizer and colonized in the Belgian Congo?

3. Twain had a meaning in mind for these images. Are there any other possible interpretations?

DOCUMENT 25-5

The Boxers Declare Death to "Foreign Devils"

1900

Although China was never directly conquered or colonized by the West, the Chinese government was nearly powerless by the turn of the twentieth century. Various European states had extracted concessions and installed their own administrations within foreign territory, laying claim to land and stripping the Chinese government of control over foreigners in their territory. Disenchanted with their weakened government, some Chinese groups reacted independently. In 1900, followers of the Taoist religious secret society, the Society of Harmonious Fists (Boxers), became convinced they had discovered magical techniques to overcome Western technology and rose up against their Christian oppressors. The normally squabbling colonial powers, including the United States and Japan, united to suppress the Boxer Rebellion.

From Louis L. Snyder, ed., *The Imperialism Reader: Documents and Readings on Modern Expansionism* (Princeton, N.J.: Van Nostrand, 1962), pp. 322–323.

The gods assist the Boxers
The Patriotic Harmonious corps
It is because the "foreign Devils" disturb the " Middle Kingdom" [China]
Urging the people to join their religion,
To turn their backs on Heaven,
Venerate not the Gods and forget their ancestors.

Men violate the human obligations,
Women commit adultery,
"Foreign Devils" are not produced by mankind,
If you do not believe,
Look at them carefully.

The eyes of the "Foreign Devils" are bluish,
No rain falls,
The earth is getting dry,
This is because the churches stop Heaven,
The Gods are angry;
The Gods are vexed;
Both come down from the mountain to deliver the doctrine.

This is no hearsay,
The practices of boxing[4] will not be in vain;
Reciting incantations and pronouncing magic words,
Burn up yellow written prayers,
Light incense sticks
To invite the Gods and Genii [guardian spirits] of all the grottoes.

The Gods come out from grottoes,
The Genii come down from mountains,
Support the human bodies to practice the boxing.
When all the military accomplishments or tactics
Are fully learned,
It will not be difficult to exterminate the "Foreign Devils" then.

---

[4] **practices of boxing:** The society trained in Chinese martial arts techniques, which
included intense physical and mental discipline and meditation techniques. They
essentially believed that their physical prowess would allow them to deflect bullets
fired at them. When trying to describe society members, Westerners compared the
Taoists' techniques to the art of boxing, to which they actually bore little resemblance.

Push aside the railway tracks,
Pull out the telegraph poles,
Immediately after this destroy the steamers [steamboats].
The great France
Will grow cold and downhearted.
The English and Russians will certainly disperse.
Let the various "Foreign Devils" all be killed.
May the whole Elegant Empire of the Great Ching Dynasty[5] be ever
   prosperous.

READING AND DISCUSSION QUESTIONS

1.   What reasons do the Boxers cite for attacking foreigners?

2.   What are the Boxer's attitudes toward the culture of the West? What
     do their attitudes suggest about their vision of the ideal Chinese
     society?

3.   What reasons might the "Great Ching Dynasty" have for encouraging
     the Boxers in their rebellion? Why might the imperial government
     not be able to give its full support?

> DOCUMENT 25-6

J. A. HOBSON
Imperialism
1902

Not all Europeans were imperialists, although anti-imperialists were typi-
cally in the minority. One of the underlying assumptions of empire was that
colonies would trade exclusively with their mother countries, a theory at odds
with Adam Smith's eighteenth-century vision of free trade. In 1902, John

---

From Louis L. Snyder, ed., *The Imperialism Reader: Documents and Readings on*
Modern Expansionism (Princeton, N.J.: Van Nostrand, 1962), pp. 322–323.

[5] **Great Ching Dynasty**: Chinese imperial family between 1644 and 1912, who
encouraged the Boxer uprising; also rendered as Qing.

Atkinson Hobson, an English economist, published a critique of the prevailing link between colonies, economies, and national security, questioning the benefits of imperialism for the colonizing countries. His work influenced the communist leader Lenin's later critique of imperialism.

Although the new Imperialism has been bad business for the nation, it has been good business for certain classes and certain trades within the nation. The vast expenditure on armaments, the costly wars, the grave risks and embarrassments of foreign policy, the stoppage of political and social reforms within Great Britain, though fraught with great injury to the nation, have served well the present business interests of certain industries and professions.

It is idle to meddle with politics unless we clearly recognize this central fact and understand what these sectional interests are which are the enemies of national safety and the commonwealth. We must put aside the merely sentimental diagnosis which explains wars or other national blunders by outbursts of patriotic animosity or errors of statecraft. Doubtless at every outbreak of war not only the man in the street but the man at the helm is often duped by the cunning with which aggressive motives and greedy purposes dress themselves in defensive clothing. There is, it may be safely asserted, no war within memory, however nakedly aggressive it may seem to the dispassionate historian, which has not been presented to the people who were called upon to fight as a necessary defensive policy, in which the honor, perhaps the very existence, of the State was involved. . . .

What is the direct economic outcome of Imperialism? A great expenditure of public money upon ships, guns, military and naval equipment and stores, growing and productive of enormous profits when a war, or an alarm of war, occurs; new public loans and important fluctuations in the home and foreign Bourses [essentially a stock market]; more posts for soldiers and sailors and in the diplomatic and consular services; improvement of foreign investments by the substitution of the British flag for a foreign flag; acquisition of markets for certain classes of exports, and some protection and assistance for trades representing British houses in these manufactures; employment for engineers, missionaries, speculative miners, ranchers, and other emigrants.

Certain definite business and professional interests feeding upon imperialistic expenditure, or upon the results of that expenditure, are thus set up in opposition to the common good, and, instinctively feeling their way to one another, are found united in strong sympathy to support every new imperialist exploit. . . .

With them stand the great manufacturers for export trade, who gain a living by supplying the real or artificial wants of the new countries we annex or open up. . . . The proportion which such trade bears to the total industry of Great Britain is very small, but some of it is extremely influential and able to make a definite impression upon politics, through chambers of commerce, Parliamentary representatives, and semi-political, semi-commercial bodies like the Imperial South African Association or the China League.

The shipping trade has a very definite interest which makes for Imperialism. This is well illustrated by the policy of State subsidies now claimed by shipping firms as a retainer, and in order to encourage British shipping for purposes of imperial safety and defense.

The services are, of course, imperialist by conviction and by professional interest, and every increase of the army and navy enhances their numerical strength and the political power they exert. . . .

What is true of Great Britain is true likewise of France, Germany, the United States, and of all countries in which modern capitalism has placed large surplus savings in the hands of a plutocracy or of a thrifty middle class. A well-recognized distinction is drawn between creditor and debtor countries. Great Britain has been for some time by far the largest creditor country, and the policy by which the investing classes use the instrument of the State for private business purposes is most richly illustrated in the recent history of her wars and annexations.[6] But France, Germany, and the United States are advancing fast along the same path. . . .

Investors who have put their money in foreign lands, upon terms which take full account of risks connected with the political conditions of the country, desire to use the resources of their Government to minimize these risks, and so to enhance the capital value and the interest of their private investments. The investing and speculative classes in general also desire that Great Britain should take other foreign areas under her flag in order to secure new areas for profitable investment and speculation.

---

[6] **recent history of . . . wars and annexations**: One such example was the British government's decision to buy the khedive of Egypt's stock shares in the Suez Canal Company in 1875, about 40 percent of the company. This led to British control of the canal, and of Egypt when the khedive was unable to pay his debts. The most recent example would have been the expansion of the British Cape colony into the Boers' (European farmers of Dutch descent) Transvaal territories, resulting in the 1899–1902 Boer War. British companies gained access to gold and diamond mining as a result of the war.

READING AND DISCUSSION QUESTIONS

1. Based on this selection, what groups does Hobson see benefiting from imperialism? In what ways are the interests of these groups the same as or different from the interests of the nation as a whole?

2. What negative outcomes does Hobson believe result from imperial competition?

3. What is Hobson's attitude toward war, particularly regarding the relationship between the government and the citizens of the nation in wartime?

COMPARATIVE QUESTIONS

1. How did Chinese attitudes toward the West evolve between the time of Commissioner Lin's letter and the Boxer Rebellion? What continuities do you discern between the two documents? What might account for changes?

2. Compare the documents produced by the Westerners, Stanley, Twain, and Hobson. Where do they seem to differ, and what similarities can you see? What differences in perspective might account for their different ideas on colonization?

3. Based on their documents, would Commissioner Lin agree with Hobson's views on the dangers of imperial trade?

4. Compare Stanley's attitude toward Africans and the Boxer view of the "Foreign Devils." What conclusions can you draw from this?

5. How might Commissioner Lin respond to Jules Ferry's conception of economic empire? Does trade automatically mean empire?

CHAPTER 26

War and Revolution

1914–1919

The outbreak of World War I was greeted with widespread European enthusiasm. For decades, Europe's Great Powers had been divided into alliance blocs in anticipation of a conflict. The currents of extreme nationalism and Social Darwinism that characterized the prewar era convinced many that war was not only inevitable, but desirable — a brief, decisive test of "survival of the fittest." In reality, the conflict was a long, brutal, industrial war in which the combatants had to mobilize all of their resources — people, raw materials, transportation infrastructure, and factories — for the goal of victory. In the trenches on the western front, the war stagnated into a contest of attrition. In the east, the collapse of the Russian Empire paved the way for the eventual Soviet state. In the end, the human and economic costs of the war were catastrophic. During the subsequent peacemaking process, U.S. President Woodrow Wilson sought to ensure that no such bloodbath would ever happen again, but leaders of the other victorious powers, France and Great Britain, did not fully endorse his plans.

DOCUMENT 26-1

CHANCELLOR THEOBALD
VON BETHMANN-HOLLWEG
Telegram to the German Ambassador at Vienna
July 6, 1914

The assassination of Archduke Franz Ferdinand, heir to the Austro-Hungarian throne, in June 1914 tempted that power to launch a punitive war against Serbia, which was believed to be complicit in the plot. Doing so, however,

From Louis L. Snyder ed., *Documents of German History* (New Brunswick, N.J.: Rutgers University Press, 1958), pp. 310–311.

had the potential to provoke Russia, which regarded itself as the protector of the Serbs owing to their shared Slavic ethnicity. Worried about Russian intervention, the Austro-Hungarian government asked Germany, with which it had a defensive alliance, if it would stand with the dual monarchy. Germany's response, the telegram that follows, is known as the "blank check."

Confidential. For Your Excellency's personal information and guidance
The Austro-Hungarian Ambassador yesterday delivered to the Emperor[1] a confidential personal letter from the Emperor Francis Joseph,[2] which depicts the present situation from the Austro-Hungarian point of view, and describes the measures which Vienna has in view.[3] A copy is now being forwarded to Your Excellency.

I replied to Count Szagyeny[4] today on behalf of His Majesty that His Majesty sends his thanks to the Emperor Francis Joseph for his letter and would soon answer it personally. In the meantime His Majesty desires to say that he is not blind to the danger which threatens Austria-Hungary and thus the Triple Alliance[5] as a result of the Russian and Serbian Pan-Slavic[6] agitation. Even though His Majesty is known to feel no unqualified confidence in Bulgaria and her ruler, and naturally inclines more toward our old ally Rumania and her Hohenzollern prince,[7] yet he quite understands that the Emperor Francis Joseph, in view of the attitude of Rumania and of the danger of a new Balkan alliance aimed directly at the Danube Monarchy,[8] is anxious to bring about an understanding between Bulgaria and

---

[1] **Emperor**: German Emperor Wilhelm II (r. 1888–1918).

[2] **Emperor Francis Joseph**: Emperor of Austria-Hungary (r. 1848–1916).

[3] **the measures Vienna has in view**: That is, a war against Serbia.

[4] **Count Szagyeny**: László Szőgyény-Marich (1841–1916), Austro-Hungarian ambassador to Berlin.

[5] **Triple Alliance**: Germany and Austria-Hungary signed what was known as the Dual Alliance in 1879; three years later Italy joined the pact, and it was thenceforth called the Triple Alliance.

[6] **Pan-Slavic agitation**: Russians and Serbs both spoke Slavic languages; Bethmann-Hollweg was alleging that Serbia, egged on by Russia, was trying to provoke a confrontation with Austria-Hungary.

[7] **no unqualified confidence in Bulgaria . . . Rumania and her Hohenzollern prince**: Austria-Hungary was seeking Bulgarian support for its planned war against Serbia; Wilhelm II preferred an alliance with Romania, which was ruled by a member of the German royal family, the Hohenzollerns.

[8] **the attitude of Rumania and . . . a new Balkan alliance aimed . . . at the Danube Monarchy**: Wilhelm II appreciated Austria-Hungary's mistrust of Romania, and its fear of an alliance of Balkan states directed against the Dual Monarchy.

the Triple alliance. . . . His Majesty will, further more, make an effort at Bucharest, according to the wishes of the Emperor Francis Joseph, to influence King Carol[9] to the fulfillment of the duties of his alliance, to the renunciation of Serbia, and to the suppression of the Rumanian agitations directed against Austria-Hungary.

Finally, as far as concerns Serbia, His Majesty, of course, cannot interfere in the dispute now going on between Austria-Hungary and that country, as it is a matter not within his competence. The Emperor Francis Joseph may, however, rest assured that His Majesty will faithfully stand by Austria-Hungary, as is required by the obligations of his alliance and of his ancient friendship.

READING AND DISCUSSION QUESTIONS

1. What circumstances might have induced the German emperor to pledge to "faithfully stand by" Austria-Hungary and its emperor?

2. What about this message might have earned it the description "blank check," and why?

DOCUMENT 26-2

WILFRED OWEN

Poems: "Dulce Et Decorum Est" and "Disabled"

1917

Wilfred Owen (1893–1918) was only one of several outstanding poets who wrote of their experiences in World War I, but many critics regard him as the greatest of them, in part because of his vivid depictions of industrialized warfare: trenches, gas, disfigurement, and death. As he put it in a preface to a planned volume of his verse, his subject was "war, and the pity of war." Almost none of his war poems appeared during his lifetime, however. He was killed in battle only a week before the Armistice that stopped the fighting. His verse was collected and published after the war's end.

From Wilfred Owen, "Dulce et Decorum Est" and "Disabled," in *Poems of Wilfred Owen* (New York: Huebsch, 1921). Project Gutenberg. Web. February 23, 2010.

[9] **Bucharest . . . to influence King Carol**: Bucharest was Romania's capital and Carol its king.

Dulce et Decorum Est

Bent double, like old beggars under sacks,
Knock-kneed, coughing like hags, we cursed through sludge,
Till on the haunting flares we turned our backs
And towards our distant rest began to trudge.
Men marched asleep. Many had lost their boots
But limped on, blood-shod. All went lame; all blind;
Drunk with fatigue; deaf even to the hoots
Of disappointed shells that dropped behind.

GAS! Gas! Quick, boys! — An ecstasy of fumbling,
Fitting the clumsy helmets just in time;
But someone still was yelling out and stumbling
And floundering like a man in fire or lime. —
Dim, through the misty panes and thick green light
As under a green sea, I saw him drowning.

In all my dreams, before my helpless sight,
He plunges at me, guttering, choking, drowning.

If in some smothering dreams you too could pace
Behind the wagon that we flung him in,
And watch the white eyes writhing in his face,
His hanging face, like a devil's sick of sin;
If you could hear, at every jolt, the blood
Come gargling from the froth-corrupted lungs,
Obscene as cancer, bitter as the cud
Of vile, incurable sores on innocent tongues, —
My friend, you would not tell with such high zest
To children ardent for some desperate glory,
The old Lie: *Dulce et decorum est
Pro patria mori.*[10]

---

[10] *Dulce et decorum est / Pro patria mori*: "It is a noble and fitting thing to die for one's country." A quote from an ode by the Roman poet Horace (65 B.C.E.–8 B.C.E.). Owen sarcastically dedicated the original draft of this poem to Jessie Pope (1868–1941), an ardently patriotic poet whose wartime verse was intended to drum up support for Britain's war efforts.

DISABLED

He sat in a wheeled chair, waiting for dark,
And shivered in his ghastly suit of grey,
Legless, sewn short at elbow. Through the park
Voices of boys rang saddening like a hymn,
Voices of play and pleasure after day,
Till gathering sleep had mothered them from him.

About this time Town used to swing so gay
When glow-lamps budded in the light blue trees,
And girls glanced lovelier as the air grew dim, —
In the old times, before he threw away his knees.
Now he will never feel again how slim
Girls' waists are, or how warm their subtle hands;
All of them touch him like some queer disease.

There was an artist silly for his face,
For it was younger than his youth, last year.
Now, he is old; his back will never brace;
He's lost his colour very far from here,
Poured it down shell-holes till the veins ran dry,
And half his lifetime lapsed in the hot race
And leap of purple spurted from his thigh.

One time he liked a blood-smear down his leg,
After the matches, carried shoulder-high.
It was after football, when he'd drunk a peg,
He thought he'd better join. — He wonders why.
Someone had said he'd look a god in kilts,
That's why; and may be, too, to please his Meg;
Aye, that was it, to please the giddy jilts
He asked to join. He didn't have to beg;
Smiling they wrote his lie; aged nineteen years.
Germans he scarcely thought of; all their guilt,
And Austria's, did not move him. And no fears
Of Fear came yet. He thought of jewelled hilts
For daggers in plaid socks; of smart salutes;
And care of arms; and leave; and pay arrears;
Esprit de corps; and hints for young recruits.
And soon, he was drafted out with drums and cheers.

Some cheered him home, but not as crowds cheer Goal.
Only a solemn man who brought him fruits
Thanked him; and then inquired about his soul.
Now, he will spend a few sick years in institutes,
And do what things the rules consider wise,
And take whatever pity they may dole.
To-night he noticed how the women's eyes
Passed from him to the strong men that were whole.
How cold and late it is! Why don't they come
And put him into bed? Why don't they come?

READING AND DISCUSSION QUESTIONS

1. What might have prompted Owen to recount the experience of being gassed in such gruesome detail?

2. Drawing on "Disabled," what motives might have induced young men to volunteer for military service in World War I? What do you think of those motives? Why?

3. What is Owen's view of patriotism, and why do you think he held it?

DOCUMENT 26-3

VERA BRITTAIN
Testament of Youth
1933

Vera Brittain was raised in a prosperous middle-class environment. In 1914 she became a student at Somerville College, Oxford University, one of the very few British women prior to World War I to attend an institution of higher learning. Her desire to contribute to the British war effort led her to leave Oxford in 1915 and train as a nurse. She served in Britain, the Mediterranean theater, and eventually France. The war claimed her fiancé, her

From Vera Brittain, *Testament of Youth: An Autobiographical Study of the Years 1900–1925* (New York: Macmillan, 1933), pp. 164–166, 378–379.

brother, and her two closest male friends, leaving her, as she put it, "no longer capable of either enthusiasm or fear. Once an ecstatic idealist . . . I had now passed . . . into a state of numb disillusion." After the war she became an outspoken pacifist.

On Sunday morning, June 7th, 1915, I began my nursing at the Devonshire Hospital. . . .

My hours there ran from 7:45 a.m. until 1:00 p.m., and again from 5:00 p.m. until 9:15 p.m. — a longer day, as I afterwards discovered, than that normally required in many Army hospitals. No doubt the staff was not unwilling to make the utmost use of so enthusiastic and unsophisticated a probationer. Meals, for all of which I was expected to go home, were not included in these hours. As our house was nearly half a mile from the hospital on the slope of a steep hill, I never completely overcame the aching of my back and the soreness of my feet throughout the time that I worked there, and felt perpetually as if I had just returned from a series of long route marches.

I never minded these aches and pains, which appeared to me solely as satisfactory tributes to my love for Roland.[11] What did profoundly trouble and humiliate me was my colossal ignorance of the simplest domestic operations. Among other " facts of life," my expensive education had omitted to teach me the prosaic but important essentials of egg-boiling, and the Oxford cookery classes had triumphantly failed to repair the omission. I imagined that I had to bring the saucepan to the boil, then turn off the gas and allow the egg to lie for three minutes in the cooling water. The remarks of a lance-corporal to whom I presented an egg "boiled" in this fashion led me to make shamefaced inquiries of my superiors, from whom I learnt, in those first few days, how numerous and devastating were the errors that it was possible to commit in carrying out the most ordinary functions of everyday life. To me, for whom meals had hitherto appeared as though by clockwork and the routine of a house had seemed to be worked by some invisible mechanism, the complications of sheer existence were nothing short of a revelation.

Despite my culinary shortcomings, the men appeared to like me; none of them were very ill, and no doubt my youth, my naive eagerness and the clean freshness of my new uniform meant more to them than any amount of common sense and efficiency. Perhaps, too, the warm and

---

[11] **Roland:** Brittain's fiancé, Roland Leighton, who died in France in December 1915.

profoundly surprising comfort that I derived from their presence produced a tenderness which was able to communicate back to them, in turn, something of their own rich consolation.

Throughout my two decades of life, I had never looked upon the nude body of an adult male; I had never even seen a naked boy-child since the nursery days when, at the age of four or five, I used to share my evening baths with Edward.[12] I had therefore expected, when I first started nursing, to be overcome with nervousness and embarrassment, but, to my infinite relief, I was conscious of neither. Towards the men I came to feel an almost adoring gratitude for their simple and natural acceptance of my ministrations. Short of actually going to bed with them, there was hardly an intimate service that I did not perform for one or another in the course of four years, and I still have reason to be thankful for the knowledge of masculine functioning which the care of them gave me, and for my early release from the sex-inhibitions that even to-day — thanks to the Victorian tradition which up to 1914 dictated that a young woman should know nothing of men but their faces and their clothes until marriage pitchforked her into an incompletely visualized and highly disconcerting intimacy — beset many of my female contemporaries, both married and single.

In the early days of the War the majority of soldier-patients belonged to a first-rate physical type which neither wounds nor sickness, unless mortal, could permanently impair, and from the constant handling of their lean, muscular bodies, I came to understand the essential cleanliness, the innate nobility, of sexual love on its physical side. Although there was much to shock in Army hospital service, much to terrify, much, even, to disgust, this day-by-day contact with male anatomy was never part of the shame. Since it was always Roland whom I was nursing by proxy, my attitude towards him imperceptibly changed; it became less romantic and more realistic, and thus a new depth was added to my love.

In addition to the patients, I managed to extract approval from most of the nurses — no doubt because, my one desire being to emulate Roland's endurance, I seized with avidity upon all the unpleasant tasks of which they were only too glad to be relieved, and took a masochistic delight in emptying bed-pans, washing greasy cups and spoons, and disposing of odoriferous dressings in the sink-room. The Matron — described as "a slave-driver" by one of the elegant lady V.A.D.s[13] who intermittently trotted in to "help" in the evenings after the bulk of the work was done —

---

[12] **Edward**: Vera's brother, who was killed in Italy in 1918.

[13] **V.A.D.**: Voluntary Aid Detachment; Nursing organization that Brittain joined.

treated me with especial kindness, and often let me out through her private gate in order to save me a few yards of the interminable miles upon my feet. . . .

[*In the latter stages of the war Brittain served in a field hospital close behind the trench lines in France:*]

In the German ward we knew only too certainly when "the next show" [i.e., attack] began . . . and when we had no more beds available for prisoners, stretchers holding angry-eyed men in filthy brown blankets occupied an inconvenient proportion of the floor. Many of our patients arrived within twenty-four hours of being wounded; it seemed strange to be talking amicably to a German officer about the "Putsch" he had been in the previous morning on the opposite side to our own.

Nearly all the prisoners bore their dreadful dressings with stoical fortitude, and one or two waited phlegmatically for death. A doomed twenty-year-old boy, beautiful as the young Hyacinth in spite of the flush on his concave cheeks and the restless, agonized biting of his lips, asked me one evening in a courteous whisper how long he had to wait before he died. It was not very long; the screens were round his bed by the next afternoon.

Although this almost unbearable stoicism seemed to be an understood discipline which the men imposed upon themselves, the ward atmosphere was anything but peaceful. The cries of the many delirious patients combined with the ravings of the five or six that we always had coming round from an anesthetic to turn the hut into pandemonium; cries of "*Schwester!*" and "*Kamerad!*"[14] sounded all day. But only one prisoner — a nineteen-year-old Saxon boy with saucer-like blue eyes and a pink-and-white complexion, whose name I never knew because everybody called him "the Fish" — demanded constant attention. He was, he took care to tell us, "*ein einziger Knabe.*"[15] Being a case of acute empyema[16] as the result of a penetrating chest wound, he was only allowed a milk diet, but continually besieged the orderlies for "*Fleisch, viel Brot, Kartoffeln!*"[17] "*Nicht so viel schreien, Fisch!*" I scolded him. "*Die anderen sind auch krank, nicht Sie allein!*"[18] But I felt quite melancholy when I came on duty one morning to learn that he had died in the night.

---

[14] *Schwester* and *Kamerad*: "Sister" and "comrade"; the patients were calling for the nurses and orderlies.

[15] *ein einziger Knabe*: An only child.

[16] acute empyema: Accumulation of pus in the chest cavity.

[17] *Fleisch, viel Brot, Kartoffeln!*: "Meat, lots of bread, potatoes!"

[18] *Nicht so viel schreien, Fisch! . . . Die anderen sind auch krank, nicht Sie allein!*: "Do not scream so much, Fish! Others are sick too, not just you!"

There was no time, however, for regrets, since I had to spend half that day sitting beside a small, middle-aged Bavarian who was slowly bleeding to death from the subclavian artery. The hemorrhage was too deep-seated to be checked, and Hope Milroy [one of Brittain's colleagues] went vehemently through the dressings with her petrified cavalcade of orderlies while I gave the dying man water, and wiped the perspiration from his face. On the other side of the bed a German-speaking Nonconformist padre murmured the Lord's Prayer; the sombre resonance of its conclusion sounded like the rolling of some distant organ:

"Und vergieb uns unsere Schulden,[19] *wie wir unsern Schuldigern vergeben. Und fuhre uns nicht in Versuchung, sondern erlose uns von dem Ubel. Denn Dein ist das Reich und die Kraft und die Herrlichkeit in Ewikeit, Amen."*

But the dying patient was not much interested in the forgiveness of his sins; the evil from which neither friends nor enemies could deliver him prevailed all too obviously.

"Schwester, liebe Schwester!" he whispered, clutching at my hand. *"Ich bin schwach — so schwach!"*[20]

When I came back from luncheon he too had died, and Hope Milroy was sitting exhausted at the table.

"I've just laid that man out," she said; "and now I want some tea. I don't care about watching a man bleed to death under my very eyes, even if he is a Hun."

Before making the tea, I went behind the screens to take a last look at the wax doll on the bed. Now that the lids had closed over the anxious, pleading eyes, the small bearded face was devoid of expression. The window above the body happened to be closed, and Hope called to me to open it.

"I always open the windows when they die — so as to let their souls go out," she explained.

READING AND DISCUSSION QUESTIONS

1. What does Brittain's account of her ignorance about cooking suggest of her upbringing?

---

[19] *Und vergieb uns unsere Schulden . . .*: "And forgive us our trespasses. . . ."
[20] *Schwester, liebe Schwester! . . . Ich bin schwach — so schwach*: "Sister, loving Sister! I am weak, so weak."

2. What can be inferred about both Brittain's formative experiences and opinions from her observation that "Victorian tradition . . . dictated that a young woman should know nothing of men but their faces and their clothes"?

3. What can you tell of her attitude toward the Germans — the "Huns" — as her colleague called them?

DOCUMENT 26-4

HELENA SWANWICK

The War in Its Effect Upon Women

1916

The years immediately preceding World War I had witnessed a massive and sometimes violent campaign for women's suffrage in Britain. Helena Swanwick, a German-born academic and journalist, was one of the prominent participants in that campaign, editing the suffragist newspaper Common Cause *from 1909 to 1914. When war broke out, Swanwick split with much of the suffragist leadership which supported Britain's participation. Throughout the conflict, she advocated a negotiated peace and the establishment of an international organization to maintain it. As a feminist and a socialist, she regarded the war as an opportunity for women to improve their socioeconomic as well as their political status.*

How has the war affected women? How will it affect them? Women, as half the human race, are compelled to take their share of evil and good with men, the other half. The destruction of property, the increase of taxation, the rise of prices, the devastation of beautiful things in nature and art — these are felt by men as well as by women. Some losses doubtless appeal to one or the other sex with peculiar poignancy, but it would be difficult to say whose sufferings are the greater, though there can be no doubt at all

---

From Helena Swanwick, "The War in Its Effect Upon Women," in *World War I and European Society*, ed. Marilyn Shevin-Coetzee and Frans Coetzee (Lexington, Mass.: D. C. Heath, 1995), pp. 160–164, 166.

that men get an exhilaration out of war which is denied to most women. When they see pictures of soldiers encamped in the ruins of what was once a home, amidst the dead bodies of gentle milch [sic] cows, most women would be thinking too insistently of the babies who must die for need of milk to entertain the exhilaration which no doubt may be felt at "the good work of our guns." When they read of miles upon miles of kindly earth made barren, the hearts of men may be wrung to think of wasted toil, but to women the thought suggests a simile full of an even deeper pathos; they will think of the millions of young lives destroyed, each one having cost the travail and care of a mother, and of the millions of young bodies made barren by the premature death of those who should have been their mates. The millions of widowed maidens in the coming generation will have to turn their thoughts away from one particular joy and fulfillment of life. While men in war give what is, at the present stage of the world's development, the peculiar service of men, let them not forget that in rendering that very service they are depriving a corresponding number of women of the opportunity of rendering what must, at all stages of the world's development, be the peculiar service of women. After the war, men will go on doing what has been regarded as men's work; women, deprived of their own, will also have to do much of what has been regarded as men's work. These things are going to affect women profoundly, and one hopes that the reconstruction of society is going to be met by the whole people — men and women — with a sympathetic understanding of each other's circumstances. When what are known as men's questions are discussed, it is generally assumed that the settlement of them depends upon men only; when what are known as women's questions are discussed, there is never any suggestion that they can be settled by women independently of men. Of course they cannot. But, then, neither can "men's questions" be rightly settled so. In fact, life would be far more truly envisaged if we dropped the silly phrases "men's and women's questions"; for, indeed, there are no such matters, and all human questions affect all humanity.

Now, for the right consideration of human questions, it is necessary for humans to understand each other. This catastrophic war will do one good thing if it opens our eyes to real live women as they are, as we know them in workaday life, but as the politician and the journalist seem not to have known them. When war broke out, a Labour newspaper, in the midst of the news of men's activities, found space to say that women would feel the pinch, because their supply of attar of roses would be curtailed. It struck some women like a blow in the face. When a great naval engagement took place, the front page of a progressive daily was taken up with portraits of the officers and men who had won distinction, and the back page with portraits of simpering mannequins in extravagantly fashionable hats; not frank advertisement, mind you, but exploitation of women under the guise of news supposed to be peculiarly interesting to the feeble-minded creatures.

When a snapshot was published of the first women ticket collectors in England, the legend underneath the picture ran "Super-women"! It took the life and death of Edith Cavell[21] to open the eyes of the Prime Minister to the fact that there were thousands of women giving life and service to their country. "A year ago we did not know it," he said, in the House of Commons. Is that indeed so? Surely in our private capacities as ordinary citizens, we knew not only of the women whose portraits are in the picture papers (mostly pretty ladies of the music hall or of society), but also of the toiling millions upon whose courage and ability and endurance and good-ness of heart the great human family rests. Only the politicians did not know, because their thoughts were too much engrossed with faction fights to think humanly; only the journalists would not write of them, because there was more money in writing the columns which are demanded by the advertisers of feminine luxuries. Anyone who has conducted a woman's paper knows the steady commercial pressure for that sort of "copy." . . .

THE NEED FOR PRODUCTION

It is often forgotten that for full prosperity a country needs to be producing as much wealth as possible, consistently with the health, freedom, and happiness of its people. To arrive at this desired result, it is quite clear that as many people as possible should be employed productively, and it is one of the unhappy results of our economic anarchy that employers have found it profitable to have a large reserve class of unemployed and that wage-earners have been driven to try and diminish their own numbers and to restrict their own output. To keep women out of the "labor market" (by artificial restrictions, such as the refusal to work with them, or the refusal to allow them to be trained, or the refusal to adapt conditions to their health requirements) is in truth antisocial. But it is easy to see how such antisocial restrictions have been forced upon the workers, and it is futile to blame them. A way must be found out of industrial war before we can hope that industry will be carried on thriftily. Men and women must take counsel together and let the experience of the war teach them how to solve

---

[21] **Edith Cavell**: British nurse working in Belgium, who was executed by the Germans for providing aid to Belgian insurgents.

economic problems by co-operation rather than conflict. Women have been increasingly conscious of the satisfaction to be got from economic independence, of the sweetness of earned bread, of the dreary depression of subjection. They have felt the bitterness of being "kept out"; they are feeling the exhilaration of being "brought in." They are ripe for instruction and organization in working for the good of the whole. . . .

READJUSTMENT OF EMPLOYMENT

Most people were astonished in 1914 at the rapidity with which industry and social conditions adapted themselves to the state of war, and there are those who argue that, because the fears of very widespread and continued misery at the outbreak of the war were not justified, we need not have any anxiety about any widespread and continued misery at the establishment of peace. Certainly depression or panic are worse than useless, and a serene and cheerful heart will help to carry the nation beyond difficulties. But comfortable people must beware of seeming to bear the sorrows of others with cheerfulness, and a lack of preparation for easily foreseen contingencies will not be forgiven by those who suffer from carelessness or procrastination. We know quite well what some, at least, of our problems are going to be, and the fool's paradise would lead straight to revolution.

It would be wise to remember that the dislocation of industry at the outbreak of the war was easily met; first, because the people thrown out by the cessation of one sort of work were easily absorbed by the increase of another sort; second, because there was ample capital and credit in hand; third, because the State was prepared to shoulder many risks and to guarantee stability; fourth, because there was an untapped reservoir of women's labor to take the place of men's. The problems after the war will be different, greater, and more lasting. . . . Because it will obviously be impossible for all to find work quickly (not to speak of the right kind of work), there is almost certain to be an outcry for the restriction of work in various directions, and one of the first cries (if we may judge from the past) will be to women: "Back to the Home!" This cry will be raised whether the women have a home or not. . . . We must understand the unimpeachable right of the man who has lost his work and risked his life for his country, to find decent employment, decent wages and conditions, on his return to civil life. We must also understand the enlargement and enhancement of life which women feel when they are able to live by their own productive work, and we must realize that to deprive women of the right to live by their work is to send them back to a moral imprisonment (to say nothing of physical and intellectual starvation), of which they have become now for the first time fully conscious. And we must realize the exceeding danger that conscienceless employers may regard women's labor as preferable, owing to its cheapness and its docility, and that women, if unsympathetically treated by their male relatives and fellow workers, may be tempted to continue to be cheap and docile in the hands of those who have no desire except that of exploiting them and the community. The kind of man who likes "to keep women in their place" may find he has made slaves who will be used by his enemies against him. Men need have no fear of free women; it is the slaves and the parasites who are a deadly danger.

The demand for equal wage for equal work has been hotly pressed by men since the war began, and it is all to the good so far as it goes. But most men are still far from realizing the solidarity of their interests with those of women in all departments of life, and are still too placidly accepting the fact that women are sweated over work which is not the same as that of men. They don't realize yet that starved womanhood means starved manhood, and they don't enough appreciate the rousing and infectious character of a generous attitude on the part of men, who, in fighting the women's battles unselfishly and from a love of right, would stimulate the women to corresponding generosity. There are no comrades more staunch and loyal than women, where men have engaged their truth and courage. But men must treat them as comrades; they must no longer think only of how they can "eliminate female labor"; they must take the women into their trade unions and other organizations, and they must understand that the complexities of a woman's life are not of her invention or choosing, but are due to her function as mother of men. The sexual side of a woman's life gravely affects the economic side, and we can never afford to overlook this. As mothers and home-makers women are doing work of the highest national importance and economic value, but this value is one which returns to the nation as a whole and only in small and very uncertain part to the women themselves. . . . Unless men are prepared to socialize the responsibilities of parenthood, one does not see how women's labor is ever to be organized for the welfare of the whole, nor does one see how women are to perform their priceless functions of motherhood as well as possible if they are to be penalized for them in the future as they have been in the past. . . .

ENFRANCHISEMENT AND EMANCIPATION

The course and conduct of the war, throwing upon women greater and greater responsibilities, bringing home to them how intimately their own lives and all they hold dear and sacred are affected by the government of the country, will tend greatly to strengthen and enlarge their claim for a share in the government. The growth of what was known as "militancy," in the last few years of the British suffrage movement, was the disastrous result of the long denial of justice, the acrid fruit of government which had become coercion, because it was no longer by consent.[22] Now that, for two years past, the women of Great Britain have made common cause with their men in this time of stress, the heat of the internal conflict has died down, and one hears on all sides that prominent anti-suffragists have become ardent suffragists, while others have declared their resolve at any rate never again to *oppose* the enfranchisement of women. The battle of argument was won long ago, but we are not, as a people, much given to theory; custom has a very strong hold over us. The shock of war has loosened that hold, and now almost every one who used to oppose, when asked whether women should be given votes, would reply: "Why not? They have earned them!" I cannot admit that representation is a thing that people should be called upon to "earn," nor that, if essential contribution to the nation is to count as "earning," the women have not earned the vote for just as long as the men. . . .

What the war has put in a fresh light, so that even the dullest can see, is that if the State may claim women's lives and those of their sons and husbands and lovers, if it may absorb all private and individual life, as at present, then indeed the condition of those who have no voice in the State is a condition of slavery, and Englishmen don't feel quite happy at the thought that their women are still slaves, while their Government is saying they are waging a war of liberation. Many women had long ago become acutely aware of their ignominious position, but the jolt of the war has made many more aware of it.

READING AND DISCUSSION QUESTIONS

1. Having studied Swanwick's essay, how would you answer the two questions she poses at its beginning? "How has the war affected women? How will it affect them?"

2. Swanwick notes that the war brought about a major increase in the number of women in the workforce. What does she foresee happening to those women when the war ends?

---

[22] **"militancy," in the last few years . . . consent:** During the years preceding the war's outbreak, "militant" suffragists, led by Emmeline Pankhurst, had conducted a campaign of domestic terrorism to publicize their cause.

3. Why, according to Swanwick, do employers prefer to hire women?

4. Why does she charge, in the final paragraph, that "women are still slaves"?

DOCUMENT 26-5

VLADIMIR I. LENIN
What Is to Be Done?
1902

Whereas Britain, France, Germany, and Italy had evolved into constitutional regimes with mass electorates by the 1890s, Russia remained staunchly autocratic. The tsar's power was in theory as absolute as it had been in Peter the Great's time. There was no national legislature and citizens engaged in political activities, like the revolutionary socialist Vladimir Lenin (1870–1924), ran the risk of imprisonment or worse. Russia's economy posed an especially daunting problem for the revolutionaries. Marx had argued that industrial capitalism was a necessary prerequisite to communist revolution and, as of 1900, Russian industry was still in its infancy. Lenin's response to that conundrum is sketched out in the following document.

The history of all countries shows that the working class, exclusively by its own effort, is able to develop only trade union consciousness, *i.e.*, it may itself realize the necessity for combining in unions, for fighting against the employers and for striving to compel the government to pass necessary labor legislation, etc. The theory of socialism, however, grew out of the philosophic, historical, and economic theories that were elaborated by the educated representatives of the propertied classes, the intellectuals. According to their social status, the founders of modern scientific socialism, Marx and Engels, themselves belonged to the bourgeois intelligentsia. Similarly, in Russia, the theoretical doctrine of Social Democracy[23] arose quite

From *Collected Works of Vladimir Ilyich Lenin*, vol. 5 (Moscow: Foreign Languages Publishing House, 1961). Marxists Internet Archive. Web. February 23, 2010.

[23] **Social Democracy**: Lenin is referring to revolutionary communism, rather than moderate, democratic socialist parties.

independently of the spontaneous growth of the labor movement; it arose as a natural and inevitable outcome of the development of ideas among the revolutionary socialist intelligentsia. At the time of which we are speaking, *i.e.*, the middle of the nineties [1890s], this doctrine not only represented the completely formulated program of the Emancipation of Labor group,[24] but had already won the adherence of the majority of the revolutionary youth in Russia. . . .

It is only natural that a Social Democrat, who conceives the political struggle as being identical with the "economic struggle against the employers and the government," should conceive of an "organization of revolutionaries" as being more or less identical with an "organization of workers." And this, in fact, is what actually happens; so that when we talk about organization, we literally talk in different tongues. I recall a conversation I once had with a fairly consistent Economist, with whom I had not been previously acquainted. We were discussing the pamphlet *Who Will Make the Political Revolution?* and we were very soon agreed that the principal defect in that brochure was that it ignored the question of organization. We were beginning to think that we were in complete agreement with each other — but as the conversation proceeded, it became clear that we were talking of different things. My interlocutor accused the author of the brochure just mentioned of ignoring strike funds, mutual aid societies, etc.; whereas I had in mind an organization of revolutionaries as an essential factor in "making" the political revolution. After that became clear, I hardly remember a single question of importance upon which I was in agreement with that Economist!

What was the source of our disagreement? The fact that on questions of organization and politics the Economists are forever lapsing from Social Democracy into trade unionism. The political struggle carried on by the Social Democrats is far more extensive and complex than the economic struggle the workers carry on against the employers and the government. Similarly (and indeed for that reason), the organization of a revolutionary Social Democratic Party must inevitably *differ* from the organizations of the workers designed for the latter struggle. A workers' organization must in the first place be a trade organization; secondly, it must be as wide as possible; and thirdly, it must be as public as conditions will allow (here, and further on, of course, I have only autocratic Russia in mind). On the other hand, the organizations of revolutionaries must consist first and fore-

---

[24] **Emancipation of Labor group**: First Russian Marxist political organization, founded in 1883.

most of people whose profession is that of a revolutionary (that is why I speak of organizations of *revolutionaries*, meaning revolutionary Social Democrats). In view of this common feature of the members of such an organization, *all distinctions as between workers and intellectuals*, and certainly distinctions of trade and profession, must be obliterated. Such an organization must of necessity be not too extensive and as secret as possible. . . .

I assert:

1. that no movement can be durable without a stable organization of leaders to maintain continuity;
2. that the more widely the masses are spontaneously drawn into the struggle and form the basis of the movement and participate in it, the more necessary is it to have such an organization, and the more stable must it be (for it is much easier for demagogues to sidetrack the more backward sections of the masses);
3. that the organization must consist chiefly of persons engaged in revolutionary activities as a profession;
4. that in a country with an autocratic government, the more we *restrict* the membership of this organization to persons who are engaged in revolutionary activities as a profession and who have been professionally trained in the art of combating the political police, the more difficult will it be to catch the organization, and the *wider* will be the circle of men and women of the working class or of other classes of society able to join the movement and perform active work in it. . . .

The active and widespread participation of the masses will not suffer; on the contrary, it will benefit by the fact that a "dozen" experienced revolutionaries, no less professionally trained than the police, will centralize all the secret side of the work — prepare leaflets, work out approximate plans and appoint bodies of leaders for each urban district, for each factory district and to each educational institution, etc. (I know that exception will be taken to my "undemocratic" views, but I shall reply to this altogether unintelligent objection later on.) The centralization of the more secret functions in an organization of revolutionaries will not diminish, but rather increase the extent and the quality of the activity of a large number of other organizations intended for wide membership and which, therefore, can be as loose and as public as possible, for example, trade unions, workers' circles for self-education and the reading of illegal literature, and socialist and also democratic circles for *all other sections of the population*, etc., etc. We must have *as large a number as possible* of such organizations having the widest possible variety of functions, but it is absurd and dangerous to *confuse those with organizations of revolutionaries*, to erase the line of demarcation between them, to dim still more the masses already incredibly hazy appreciation of the fact that in order to "serve" the mass movement we must have people who will devote themselves exclusively to Social Democratic activities, and that such people must *train* themselves patiently and steadfastly to be professional revolutionaries.

Aye, this appreciation has become incredibly dim. The most grievous sin we have committed in regard to organization is that *by our primitiveness we have lowered the prestige of revolutionaries in Russia*. A man who is weak and vacillating on theoretical questions, who has a narrow outlook, who makes excuses for his own slackness on the ground that the masses are awakening spontaneously; who resembles a trade union secretary more than a people's tribune, who is unable to conceive of a broad and bold plan, who is incapable of inspiring even his opponents with respect for himself, and who is inexperienced and clumsy in his own professional art — the art of combating the political police — such a man is not a revolutionary but a wretched amateur!

Let no active worker take offense at these frank remarks, for as far as insufficient training is concerned, I apply them first and foremost to myself. I used to work in a circle that set itself great and all-embracing tasks; and every member of that circle suffered to the point of torture from the realization that we were proving ourselves to be amateurs at a moment in history when we might have been able to say, paraphrasing a well-known epigram: "Give us an organization of revolutionaries, and we shall overturn the whole of Russia!"

READING AND DISCUSSION QUESTIONS

1. Judging by his remarks, what sort of attitude did Lenin have toward the working class?

2. Why, if Lenin advocated establishing *"as large a number as possible"* of traditional trade unions and similar organizations, did he also maintain that there was urgent need for secret organization of "professional revolutionaries"?

VIEWPOINTS

The Conditions of Peace

DOCUMENT 26-6

WOODROW WILSON
The Fourteen Points
1918

From the war's outbreak through early 1917, the United States kept aloof from the fray, with President Woodrow Wilson (1856–1924) entreating the American people to be neutral "in spirit as well as in deed." In fact, the nation was heavily invested in the Allied (British, French, and Russian) war effort, and most Americans sympathized with the Allies. Wilson regarded himself and his country as arbiters in the bitter struggle. Even prior to the U.S. declaration of war against Germany in April, he outlined his vision of the postwar international order in "fourteen points" in a January 1918 speech to Congress.

1. Open covenants of peace, openly arrived at. Diplomacy shall proceed always frankly and in the public view.
2. Absolute freedom of navigation upon the seas, outside territorial waters.
3. The removal, so far as possible, of all economic barriers and the establishment of an equality of trade conditions.
4. Adequate guarantees given and taken that national armaments will be reduced.
5. A free, open-minded, and absolutely impartial adjustment of all colonial claims. In determining all such questions of sovereignty the interests of the populations concerned must have equal weight with the equitable claims of the Government whose title is to be determined.
6. The evacuation of all Russian territory.

Woodrow Wilson, "The Fourteen Points," in *The Great Events of the Great War*, ed. Charles F. Horne ([New York]: National Alumni, 1920), 6:3–6.

7. Belgium must be evacuated and restored. Without this healing act the whole structure and validity of international law is forever impaired.

8. All French territory should be freed and the invaded portions restored; and the wrong done to France by Prussia in 1871 in the matter of Alsace-Lorraine[25] should be righted.

9. A readjustment of the frontiers of Italy should be effected along clearly recognizable lines of nationality.

10. The peoples of Austria-Hungary, whose place among the nations we wish to see safeguarded and assured, should be accorded the freest opportunity of autonomous development.

11. Rumania, Serbia, and Montenegro should be evacuated; occupied territories restored; Serbia accorded free and secure access to the sea; and international guarantees of the political and economic independence and territorial integrity of the several Balkan states should be entered into.

12. Nationalities which are now under Turkish rule should be assured an unmolested opportunity of autonomous development, and the Dardanelles should be permanently opened as a free passage to the ships and commerce of all nations.

13. An independent Polish state should be erected which should be assured a free and secure access to the sea.

14. A general association of nations must be formed, for the purpose of affording mutual guarantees of political independence and territorial integrity to great and small states alike.

READING AND DISCUSSION QUESTIONS

1. How does Wilson want to treat Germany?

2. On what underlying principles did Wilson base points six through thirteen?

3. What do you think prompted Wilson's demand for "absolute freedom of the seas"?

---

[25] **the wrong done to . . . Alsace-Lorraine:** The German states, headed by Prussia, defeated France in the Franco-German War (1870–1871), and annexed all of Alsace and about two-thirds of Lorraine, both of them French provinces prior to the war.

DOCUMENT 26-7

A Defeated Germany Contemplates the Peace Treaty

1919

Unlike the Congress of Vienna (1814–1815), in which defeated France participated, the Treaty of Versailles was written without German input. Indeed, the German government was only presented with the completed treaty and told that it faced the choice of signing it or having the Allied armies resume their advance. By June 1919, the German army had been entirely demobilized. Moreover, the Allied naval blockade, which contributed to approximately 750,000 civilian deaths by starvation and disease during its duration, remained in place until Germany signed the treaty on June 28, 1919. The following document captures the reception of Germany's several political parties (the National Assembly of the Germany Republic) to the treaty.

Bauer,[26] [Social Democratic Party, acting chancellor]: Ladies and gentlemen!

The Reich president has entrusted me with the formation of a new cabinet, to replace the Scheidemann[27] government which has resigned. . . . The resignation of the cabinet resulted from its inability to reach an undivided position regarding the peace treaty that has been presented to us. . . . For each of us who were members of the former government it was a bitterly difficult matter to take a position between feelings of indignation and cold rage. And not less difficult was the decision to join this new government whose first and most pressing task it is to conclude this unjust peace. . . . We are here because of our sense of responsibility, aware that it is our damnable duty to try to salvage what can be salvaged. . . .

No matter how each one of us feels about the question of acceptance or rejection, we are all united about one thing: in strong criticism of this

---

From "Deutsche Parlamentsdebatten" in *The Making of Modern Germany*, eds. and trans. Benjamin Sax and Dieter Kuntz (Lexington, Mass.: D. C. Heath, 1992), pp. 45–47.

[26] **Bauer**: Gustav Adolf Bauer (1870–1944); German chancellor, August 1919–March 1920.

[27] **Scheidemann**: German journalist and politician Philipp Scheidemann (1865–1939), who led a short-lived government from February to June of 1919.

peace treaty (*"Very true!"*) to which we are being forced to affix our signatures! When this draft was first presented to us, it was greeted with a unanimous protest of indignation and rejection from our people. We defied disappointment and hoped for the indignation of the entire world. . . .

Rejection did not mean averting the treaty. (*"Very true!" from the Social Democrats.*) A no vote would only have meant a short delay of the yes vote. (*"Very true!"*) Our ability to resist has been broken; we do not have the capability to avert [signing]. . . . In the name of the national government, ladies and gentlemen, I ask you in view of the circumstances and pending ratification by the National Assembly,[28] to sign the peace treaty laid before you! . . .

The government of the German Republic pledges to fulfill the imposed conditions of the peace. The government, however, wishes during this solemn occasion to express its views quite clearly. . . . The imposed conditions exceed the limits of Germany's ability to comply. . . .

Moreover, we emphatically declare that we cannot accept Article 231 of the peace treaty, which demands that Germany accept responsibility for singly initiating the war. (*Applause.*)

Gröber,[29] *delegate of the Center Party:* Honored Assembly! The Center Party delegation of the National Assembly wishes to acknowledge the government's declaration. We accept this program and will support this government and accept [cabinet] participation. . . . We say we are prepared to accept the responsibility of fulfilling its terms as far as is humanly possible, but we do not recognize a responsibility for carrying out conditions that are impossible or intolerable. However, although these are oppressive and hardly fulfillable conditions and will have a detrimental effect on the German people, we must also take other facts into account.

First, the peace will shortly bring hundreds of thousands of prisoners back to German families. . . . Second, the peace will end starvation. . . . Third, only the peace will give us the possibility of economically rebuilding Germany. . . . Fourth, the peace also allows us to maintain our German unity. . . .

Schiffer,[30] *delegate of the DDP* [German Democratic Party]: Contrary to the first two speakers, I wish to declare to this esteemed assembly, that

---

[28] **pending ratification . . . Assembly**: It was a vote by individual delegates and, as the socialists were in a majority, the treaty was accepted even though, as Bauer states, they hated it too. The vote was 237 to 138 for *conditional* acceptance.

[29] *Gröber*: Conrad Gröber (1872–1948); Catholic archbishop and politician.

[30] *Schiffer*: Eugen Schiffer (1860–1954); German politician.

the great majority of my political friends have decided to withhold their approval of the peace treaty laid before us. . . .

Count von Posadowsky,[31] *delegate of the* DNVP [German National People's Party]: Our Fatherland finds itself in the most difficult hour of its history. The enemy stands before our gates, and in the country there are disconcerting signs of internal breakup. . . . We in our party are aware of the ramifications for our people which a rejection of the peace treaty will entail. (*"Very true!" from the right.*) The resultant harm, however, will only be temporary, but if we accept this treaty we will abandon countless generations of our people to misery. . . . For us, acceptance of the treaty is impossible for many reasons. . . . In addition to making Germany defenseless, there is also the matter of theft of our territory. . . .

Haase,[32] *delegate of the* USPD [Independent Social Democratic Party]: We know that the peace treaty will bring incredible burdens for our people. . . . Nonetheless, we have no choice but to accept the treaty. Not only will rejection increase the harm, it will moreover mean sure ruin. (*Agreement from the Independent Social Democrats.*) Our people are in this desperate situation only because of the wicked warmongers and war extenders. . . .

Kahl,[33] *delegate of the* DVP [German People's Party]: Gentlemen! The German People's Party unanimously rejects this peace. . . . We reject it because to accept it would mean the destruction of the German state. . . . We reject because we cannot justify the separation of precious segments of German earth, such as the eastern provinces, from the Motherland. . . . Yes, if only we had swords in our hands! (*Laughter from the Social Democrats.*) Then we would easily find a response! (*"Very true" from the right.*)

READING AND DISCUSSION QUESTIONS

1. Why were all of the speakers unhappy with the Treaty of Versailles?

2. Which spokesmen do you think represented left-leaning (socialist) parties and which represented right-leaning (conservative and nationalist) parties? Why?

---

[31] *Count von Posadowsky*: Arthur Adolf Graf von Posadowsky-Wehner (1845–1932); German politician.

[32] *Hasse*: Hugo Haase (1863–1919); German jurist, politician, and pacifist.

[33] *Kahl*: Wilhelm Kahl (1849–1932); German academic and politician.

3. On what grounds did Bauer, Gröber, and Haase advocate accepting the treaty?

4. On what grounds did Schiffer, Posadowsky, and Kahl advocate its rejection?

COMPARATIVE QUESTIONS

1. Contrast Wilhelm II's attitude toward war, as can be inferred from his willingness to support Austria-Hungary militarily in July 1914, with Owen's as expressed in "Dulce et Decorum Est."

2. Brittain's account of nursing wounded soldiers is written prosaically, with a matter-of-fact offhandedness, whereas Owen's poetry strives for artistry. Which approach do you find more compelling/moving? Why?

3. How did World War I open opportunities for women, as gleaned from Swanwick's and Brittain's accounts?

4. Compare and contrast Swanwick's views regarding women's place in the workforce during World War I with those of Clara Zetkin (Document 23-4) regarding prewar industrial society. What had changed? How?

5. What do Swanwick's and Lenin's differing views about the route to social and economic progress (women's emancipation in Swanwick's case, workers' emancipation in Lenin's) suggest about the political environments in which each lived?

6. What does the German legislature's universal condemnation of the Treaty of Versailles suggest about the degree to which Woodrow Wilson's views influenced its content? What might account for the inclusion of Article 231?

7. How do you think the German politicians quoted in document 7 regarded Wilhelm II's pledge to "faithfully stand by Austria-Hungary" in July 1914, a promise that helped create the situation in which they found themselves?

CHAPTER 27

The Age of Anxiety

ca. 1900–1940

A number of developments in the twentieth century began to suggest that reason and science had limits when it came to understanding and controlling the world. Even before the slaughter of the Great War demonstrated that advanced technological achievement did not translate into superior morality, philosophers like Nietzsche and Freud began to question the role of reason in morality and behavior. Their intellectual uncertainty was soon mirrored by economic troubles. The Treaty of Versailles, which essentially dictated the terms of peace and lay the moral and economic responsibilities of World War I at the feet of the Germans, left the future of western Europe under a cloud of uncertainty. When the Great Depression (1929–1939) hit the United States, the subsequent worldwide financial crisis forced many Europeans to reconsider their beliefs about economics, politics, and social relationships.

DOCUMENT 27-1

FRIEDRICH NIETZSCHE
The Gay Science: *God Is Dead,*
The Victim of Science
1882

Friedrich Wilhelm Nietzsche (1844–1900) was a tormented philosopher who deserted academic life in 1879 to wander Europe, writing books that criticized most aspects of European, particularly German, society. He rejected

From Friedrich Nietzsche, "The Madman," in *Movements, Currents, Trends: Aspects of European Thought in the Nineteenth and Twentieth Centuries,* ed. and trans. Eugen Weber (Lexington, Mass.: D. C. Heath, 1992), pp. 454–455.

nationalism, socialism, liberalism, and Christianity as promoting a weak herd morality and argued that the "overman" (ubermensch) should emerge to create his own morality, based on his will (choice) rather than external commandments. This excerpt from his 1882 work Die Fröliche Wissenschaft (The Gay Science) *is ironic given that Nietzsche collapsed seven years after its publication and spent the rest of his life in an insane asylum.*

Have you not heard of that madman who lit a lantern in the bright morning hours, ran to the market place, and cried incessantly, "I seek God! I seek God!" As many of those who do not believe in God were standing around just then, he provoked much laughter. Why, did he get lost? said one. Did he lose his way like a child? said another. Or is he hiding? Is he afraid of us? Has he gone on a voyage? or emigrated? Thus they yelled and laughed. The madman jumped into their midst and pierced them with his glances.

"Whither is God?" he cried. "I shall tell you. We *have killed him* — you and I. All of us are his murderers. But how have we done this? How were we able to drink up the sea? Who gave us the sponge to wipe away the entire horizon? What did we do when we unchained this earth from its sun? Whither is it moving now? Away from all suns? Are we not plunging continually? Backward, sideward, forward, in all directions? Is there any up or down left? Are we not straying as through an infinite nothing? Do we not feel the breath of empty space? Has it not become colder? Is not night and more night coming on all the while? Must not lanterns be lit in the morning? Do we not hear anything yet of the noise of the grave-diggers who are burying God? Do we not smell anything yet of God's decomposition? Gods too decompose. God is dead. God remains dead. And we have killed him. How shall we, the murderers of all murderers, comfort ourselves? What was holiest and most powerful of all that the world has yet owned has bled to death under our knives. Who will wipe this blood off us? What water is there for us to clean ourselves? What festivals of atonement, what sacred games shall we have to invent? Is not the greatness of this deed too great for us? Must not we ourselves become gods simply to seem worthy of it? There has never been a greater deed; and whoever will be born after us — for the sake of this deed he will be part of a higher history than all history hitherto."

Here the madman fell silent and looked again at his listeners; and they too were silent and stared at him in astonishment. At last he threw his lantern on the ground, and it broke and went out. "I come too early," he said then; "my time has not come yet. This tremendous event is still on its way, still wandering — it has not yet reached the ears of man. Lightning and thunder require time, the light of the stars requires time, deeds require time even after they are done, before they can be seen and heard. This deed is still more distant from them than the most distant stars — *and yet they have done it themselves.*"

It has been related further that on that same day the madman entered divers churches and there sang his *requiem aeternam deo*.[1] Led out and called to account, he is said to have replied each time, "What are the churches now if they are not the tombs and sepulchers of God?" . . .

READING AND DISCUSSION QUESTIONS

1. From Nietzsche's perspective of wanting others to abide by their own moralities, what benefits can you see to the death of God?

2. What in this passage indicates that the death of God may not be an entirely positive event in the author's mind?

3. What could Nietzsche's madman mean when he accuses his listeners — and himself — of murdering God?

4. What does the reaction of the crowd in the marketplace reveal about attitudes toward religion at the time, at least in some circles?

DOCUMENT 27-2

SIGMUND FREUD
The Interpretation of Dreams
1900

Sigmund Freud (1856–1939), a Viennese psychoanalyst, stunned the European intellectual world when he published The Interpretation of Dreams, *in which he argued that the body controls the mind. European scientific and moral thought at the time still reflected the Enlightenment belief in the*

From James Strachey, trans. and ed., *The Interpretation of Dreams* (New York: Basic Books, 1955), pp. 613–621.

[1] *requiem aeternam deo*: Funeral song for the "eternal god."

power of reason, and in the ability of humans to choose their own course. Freud later asserted that the mind was shaped more by events it did not remember (the unconscious) than by those it did, undermining European faith in the mind to actively and purposefully direct the world around them.

The unconscious is the true psychical reality; *in its innermost nature it is as much unknown to us as the reality of the external world, and it is as incompletely presented by the data of consciousness as is the external world by the communications of our sense organs.*

Now that the old antithesis between conscious life and dream-life has been reduced to its proper proportions by the establishment of unconscious psychical reality, a number of dream-problems with which earlier writers were deeply concerned have lost their significance. Thus some of the activities whose successful performance in dreams excited astonishment are no longer to be attributed to dreams but to unconscious thinking, which is active during the day no less than at night. If, as Scherner[2] has said, dreams appear to engage in making symbolic representations of the body, we now know that those representations are the product of certain unconscious fantasies (deriving, probably, from sexual impulses) which find expression not only in dreams but also in hysterical phobias and other symptoms. If a dream carries on the activities of the day and completes them and even brings valuable fresh ideas to light, all we need do is strip it of the dream disguise, which is the product of dream-work and the mark of assistance rendered by obscure forces from the depths of the mind . . . the intellectual achievement is due to the same mental forces which produce every similar result during the daytime. We are probably inclined greatly to over-estimate the conscious character of intellectual and artistic production as well. Accounts given us by some of the most highly productive men, such as Goethe[3] and Helmholtz,[4] show rather that what is essential and new in their creations came to them without premeditation and as an almost ready-made whole. There is nothing strange if in other cases,

---

[2] **Scherner**: Karl Albert Scherner; psychologist who published an 1861 work on dream theory, *The Life of Dreams*.

[3] **Goethe**: Johann Wolfgang von Goethe (1749–1832); German author of the classical and romantic schools, most famous for his dramatic retelling of Faust's deal with the devil.

[4] **Helmholtz**: Hermann Ludwig Ferdinand von Helmholtz (1821–1894); German doctor who wrote extensively on perception and theory of science.

where a concentration of every intellectual faculty was needed, conscious activity also contributed its share. But it is the much-abused privilege of conscious activity, wherever it plays a part, to conceal every other activity from our eyes.

It would scarcely repay the trouble if we were to treat the historical significance of dreams as a separate topic. A dream may have impelled some chieftain to embark upon a bold enterprise the success of which has changed history. But this only raises a fresh problem so long as a dream is regarded as an alien power in contrast to the other more familiar forces of the mind; no such problem remains if a dream is recognized as a *form of expression* of impulses which are under the pressure of resistance during the day but which have been able to find reinforcement during the night from deep-lying sources of excitation. The respect paid to dreams in antiquity is, however, based upon correct psychological insight and is the homage paid to the uncontrolled and indestructible forces in the human mind, to the "demonic" power which produces the dream-wish and which we find at work in our unconscious. . .

What role is now left, in our representation of things, to the phenomenon of consciousness, once so all-powerful and over-shadowing all else? None other than that of a sense-organ for the perception of psychic qualities. . . .

The whole multiplicity of the problems of consciousness can only be grasped by an analysis of the thought processes in hysteria. These give one the impression that the transition from a preconscious to a conscious cathexis[5] is marked by a censorship similar to that between the *Ucs.* [unconscious] and the *Pcs.* [preconscious]. This censorship, too, only comes into force above a certain quantitative limit, so that thought-structures of low intensity escape it. Examples of every possible variety of how a thought can be withheld from consciousness or can force its way into consciousness under certain limitations are to be found included within the framework of psychoneurotic phenomena; and they all point to the intimate and reciprocal relations between censorship and consciousness. I will bring these psychological reflections to an end with a report. . . .

I was called in to a consulation last year to examine an intelligent and unembarrassed-looking girl. She was most surprisingly dressed. For though as a rule a woman's clothes are carefully considered down to the last detail, she was wearing one of her stockings hanging down and two of the buttons

---

[5] **cathexis**: For Freud, this term represented the libido's energy, the driving force in most human behavior.

on her blouse were undone. She complained of having pains in her leg and, without being asked, exposed her calf. But what she principally complained of was, to use her own words, that she had a feeling in her body as though there was something "stuck into it" which was "moving backwards and forwards" and was "shaking" her through and through: sometimes it made her whole body feel "stiff". My medical colleague, who was present at the examination, looked at me; he found no difficulty in understanding the meaning of her complaint. But what struck both of us as extraordinary was the fact that it meant nothing to the patient's mother — though she must often have found herself in the situation which her child was describing. The girl herself had no notion of the bearing of her remarks; for if she had, she would never have given voice to them. In this case it had been possible to hoodwink the censorship into allowing a fantasy which would normally have been kept in the preconscious to emerge into consciousness under the innocent disguise of making a complaint. . . .

Thus I would look for the *theoretical* value of the study of dreams in the contributions it makes to psychological knowledge and in the preliminary light it throws on the problems of psychoneuroses. Who can guess the importance of the results which might be obtained from a thorough understanding of the structure and functions of the mental apparatus, since even the present state of our knowledge allows us to exert a favorable therapeutic influence on the curable forms of psychoneurosis? But what of the *practical* value of this study — I hear the question raised — as a means towards an understanding of the mind, towards a revelation of the hidden characteristics of individual men? Have not the unconscious impulses brought out by dreams the importance of real forces in mental life? Is the ethical significance of suppressed wishes to be made light of — wishes which, just as they lead to dreams, may some day lead to other things?

I do not feel justified in answering these questions. I have not considered this side of the problem of dreams further. I think, however, that the Roman emperor was in the wrong when he had one of his subjects executed because he had dreamt of murdering the emperor. He should have begun by trying to find out what the dream meant; most probably its meaning was not what it appeared to be. And even if a dream with another content had had this act of *lèse majesté*[6] as its meaning, would it not be right to bear in mind Plato's dictum that the virtuous man is content to *dream* what a wicked man really *does*? I think it is best, therefore, to acquit

---

[6] *lèse majesté*: Insulting the monarch; an act of treason.

dreams. Whether we are to attribute *reality* to unconscious wishes, I cannot say. It must be denied, of course, to any transitional or intermediate thoughts. If we look at unconscious wishes reduced to their most fundamental and truest shape, we shall have to conclude, no doubt, that *psychical* reality is a particular form of existence not to be confused with *material* reality. Thus there seems to be no justification for people's reluctance in accepting responsibility for the immortality of their dreams. When the mode of functioning of the mental apparatus is rightly appreciated and the relation between the conscious and the unconscious understood, the greater part of what is ethically objectionable in our dream and fantasy lives will be found to disappear. In the words of Hanns Sachs[7]: "If we look in our consciousness at something that has been told us by a dream about a contemporary (real) situation, we ought not to be surprised to find that the monster which we saw under the magnifying glass of analysis turns out to be a tiny infusorian."[8]

Actions and consciously expressed opinions are as a rule enough for practical purposes in judging men's characters. Actions deserve to be considered first and foremost; for many impulses which force their way through to consciousness are even then brought to nothing by the real forces of mental life before they can mature into deeds. In fact, some impulses often meet with no psychical obstacles to their progress, for the very reason that the unconscious is certain that they will be stopped at some other stage. It is in any case instructive to get to know the much trampled soil from which our virtues proudly spring. Very rarely does the complexity of a human character, driven hither and thither by dynamic forces, submit to a choice between simple alternatives, as our antiquated morality would have us believe.

And the value of dreams for giving us knowledge of the future? There is of course no question of that. It would be truer to say instead that they give us knowledge of the past. For dreams are derived from the past in every sense. Nevertheless the ancient belief that dreams foretell the future is not wholly devoid of truth. By picturing our wishes as fulfilled, dreams are after all leading us into the future. But this future, which the dreamer pictures as the present, has been molded by his indestructible wish into a perfect likeness of the past.

---

[7] **H. Sachs**: Hanns Sachs (1881–1947); Viennese psychologist and student of Freud's who later wrote an admiring biography of his teacher.
[8] **infusorian**: Single-celled organism.

READING AND DISCUSSION QUESTIONS

1. How might someone who believed in the absolute responsibility of individuals for their actions, particularly their moral actions, respond to Freud's theories?

2. What does Freud argue forms the basis of human behavior? What does he present as evidence of this pathway to expression?

3. Assume for a moment that Freud is correct, and that the unconscious influences behavior more than the conscious. What then does that say about how he proves his case?

4. How might Freud's theory be received by someone who believes in the power of science to reveal the nature of the world, and ultimately to control it? Knowing what we now know about the division of the brain by function (at least to a degree), how might you respond? Does our scientific understanding support or undermine Freud's argument?

DOCUMENT 27-3

JOHN MAYNARD KEYNES

The Economic Consequences of the Peace:
An Analysis of the Versailles Treaty

1920

Of the observers at Versailles, British economist John Maynard Keynes was one of the most prescient. Upset that the peace between Germany and the Allied powers had been decided on political rather than economic grounds, Keynes publicly criticized the leaders who had negotiated the treaty. He warned that it would destroy the European economy, a prediction that seemed to come true in 1923, with the German economic collapse, and again in 1929 with the U.S. stock market crash and ensuing Great Depression. Keynes's criticism of the treaty that ended World War I was unusual coming from an Allied nation; most of the Allies thought their economies would benefit from the agreement.

From John Maynard Keynes, *The Economic Consequences of the Peace* (New York: Harcourt, Brace and Howe, 1920), pp. 226–227, 296–297.

The Treaty includes no provisions for the economic rehabilitation of Europe, — nothing to make the defeated Central Empires[9] into good neighbors, nothing to stabilize the new States of Europe,[10] nothing to reclaim Russia; nor does it promote in any way a compact of economic solidarity amongst the Allies themselves; no agreement was reached at Paris for restoring the disordered finances of France and Italy, or to adjust the systems of the Old World and the New.

The Council of Four[11] paid no attention to these issues, being preoccupied with others, — Clemenceau to crush the economic life of his enemy, Lloyd George to do a deal and bring home something which would pass muster for a week, the President to do nothing that was not just and right. It is an extraordinary fact that the fundamental economic problems of a Europe starving and disintegrating before their eyes, was the one question in which it was impossible to arouse the interest of the Four. Reparation was their main excursion into the economic field, and they settled it as a problem of theology, of politics, of electoral chicane, from every point of view except that of the economic future of the States whose destiny they were handling. . . .

For the immediate future events are taking charge, and the near destiny of Europe is no longer in the hands of any man. The events of the coming year will not be shaped by the deliberate acts of statesmen, but by the hidden currents, flowing continually beneath the surface of political history, of which no one can predict the outcome. In one way only can we influence these hidden currents, — by setting in motion those forces of instruction and imagination which change opinion. The assertion of truth, the unveiling of illusion, the dissipation of hate, the enlargement and instruction of men's hearts and minds, must be the means.

In this autumn of 1919, in which I write, we are at the dead season of our fortunes. The reaction from the exertions, the fears, and the sufferings of the past five years is at its height. Our power of feeling or caring beyond the immediate questions of our own material well-being is temporarily eclipsed. The greatest events outside our own direct experience and the most dreadful anticipations cannot move us.

---

[9] **Central Empires**: Germany, Austria-Hungary, and the Ottoman Empire — the losing alliance in the Great War.

[10] **new States of Europe**: The Treaty of Versailles dismembered the Austro-Hungarian and German Empires in the process creating newly independent states, including Czechoslovakia, Hungary, Yugoslavia, Lithuania, Latvia, and Estonia.

[11] **Council of Four**: The leaders of the Allied nations at Versailles: Woodrow Wilson of the United States, Georges Clemenceau of France, David Lloyd George of Great Britain, and Vittorio Orlando of Italy.

We have been moved already beyond endurance, and need rest. Never in the lifetime of men now living has the universal element in the soul of man burnt so dimly.

READING AND DISCUSSION QUESTIONS

1. What motivations does Keynes believe shaped the treaty that emerged from the Versailles negotiations? Whose motivations were they? What does he think should have influenced the treaty instead?

2. In what ways does Keynes think Europeans have lost control of their lives? What, if any, ideas does he seem to offer to help them recover that control?

3. What about Keynes's document suggests that reason is not the driving force in international relations?

4. As Keynes portrays them, how have the citizens of the warring countries responded to the peace?

VIEWPOINTS

The Great Depression in Europe

DOCUMENT 27-4

SIR PERCY MALCOLM STEWART

First and Second Reports of the Commissioner for the Special Areas: *Parliament Addresses the Great Depression in Britain*

1934

Great Britain's response to the depression was dictated by classical economic theory: when tax revenues drop, government spending should drop as well.

From "First and Second Reports of the Commissioner for the Special Areas [England and Wales]," in *Documents and Readings in the History of Europe Since 1918*, rev. and enlarged ed., ed. W. C. Langsam (Philadelphia: Lippincott, 1951), pp. 303–304, 306.

Proponents of this view argued that in instances of financial instability, no government intervention was necessary, and that the economy would right itself after a time. When this righting took longer than expected, Parliament, under pressure, commissioned a study of which areas of the country were the hardest hit, and what steps could be taken to revitalize them. Despite the compelling findings, the government did little in response.

25. The Special Areas[12] are in their present unfortunate position owing to the decline of the main industries, coal mining, ship building and iron and steel, which attracted such large numbers of workers to them during the nineteenth century under more prosperous conditions. It seems unlikely that these industries will again employ the numbers engaged in them even up to ten years ago. During the period of prosperity large communities with full equipment of railways, roads, houses, schools, and other municipal and social services were created. Many millions of pounds were spent in building up these services. A large proportion of the inhabitants have been associated with the Areas for several generations; they are bound to the Areas by ties of home and family and religion, by local patriotism and, especially in Wales, by a fervent national spirit and, sometimes, a distinctive language. It is natural, therefore, that wherever one goes in these Areas one should be met by the demand that something should be done to attract fresh industries to the Area. This is the general request, and I regard it as at once the most important and the most difficult of my duties to try to satisfy it. I have given more time and personal attention to this side of my work than to any other, but it must be frankly admitted that up to the present the results have been negligible. Many of the negotiations I have initiated with this end in view were necessarily confidential, and it would only prejudice the present slender chances of success if I were to give a full account of them. The following paragraphs will, however, indicate the main lines on which I have been working.

26. In the first place I approached a number of the larger and more prosperous firms in the country in the hope that I might persuade them to open new branches of their industry in one or other of the

---

[12] **The Special Areas**: Specifically, the areas in South Wales supported by coal mining and areas such as Sheffield and Lancashire in northern England that were formerly centers of manufacturing and industry.

Special Areas. Without exception they were sympathetic to my representations, but except in one case they had good reasons which made it impossible for them to accede to my request. . . .

29. Some hundreds of new factories have been established in recent years in the Midlands and South, but very few in the Special Areas. Why is this so? The main reasons appear to fall in the following categories: —

(1) Inaccessibility to markets. This applies particularly to Cumberland.[13] . . .

(2) High rates.[14] These probably have a deterrent effect on employers out of proportion to their real significance. . . .

(3) Fear of industrial unrest. This fear is very general and is bred from past disputes mainly in the coal-mining industry. It prevails particularly with regard to South Wales, but the facts scarcely warrant the attitude adopted. Statistics apart from those of coal-mining do not justify the fear which undoubtedly exists in the minds of many employers. . . .

(4) The fact that the areas are, and for some years have been, suffering from industrial depression. This factor, coupled with the common application to them of the term "depressed" or "distressed" areas, has itself a deterrent effect. While it is true that "trade brings trade," the converse unfortunately is equally true. Unemployment undermines business confidence and reduces purchasing power. A vicious circle is thus set up. . . .

(5) Difficulty in obtaining finance to start new industries. . . .

255. . . . Probably the most serious human problem of the Special Areas is that presented by unemployment among young men between 18 and 21. . . .

256. Many of these young persons have done practically no work; they have been brought up in a home where the father has been continuously out of work, and they have little or no conception that a man's ordinary occupation should be such as will provide the means of subsistence for himself and for his family. They have seen their own families and their friends kept for years by the State, and they have come to accept this as a normal condition of life. It is hardly surpris-

---

[13] **Cumberland**: One of the two English counties that border Scotland — the other is Northumberland — and one of the industrial areas hardest hit by unemployment in Great Britain.

[14] **High rates**: Shipping rates, meaning that freight was more expensive to ship.

ing in the circumstances that young persons with this background and upbringing should be ready victims of all manner of demoralizing influences. In short, these young persons present in my view the most tragic aspect of the problem of the Special Areas and one fraught with great danger to the State.

READING AND DISCUSSION QUESTIONS

1. What factors make the Special Areas particularly unsuited for new business?

2. From the perspective of the workers mentioned in the report, what control do residents of the Special Areas seem to have over their lives in hard times? How do they react to this?

3. In what ways is the report concerned with workers, and in what ways with employers?

4. What reasons might members of Parliament who were generally opposed to taking action to relieve unemployment have had for commissioning this report?

DOCUMENT 27-5

HEINRICH HAUSER

With the Unemployed in Germany

1933

The Great Depression struck Germany with greater force than any other country. Unemployment neared 40 percent, and the German economy, which had been recovering from a previous disaster — largely created by the harsh terms of the Versailles treaty — collapsed again in 1923–1924. Facing the second economic catastrophe is less than ten years, the responses of the German people varied. Politically, the fortunes of extremist parties rose, but there were still masses of unemployed who sought some stability, from

From Heinrich Hauser, "With Germany's Unemployed," *The Living Age* 344 (Mar. 1933), pp. 27–38.

whatever source they could find it. Hauser, a journalist, travelled around
Germany writing a series of human-interest pieces for the nationalist maga-
zine Die Tat. Here he reflects on the despair of those seeking relief, a despair
the Nazis would soon exploit.

An almost unbroken chain of homeless men extends the whole length of
the great Hamburg-Berlin highway.

There are so many of them moving in both directions, impelled by the
wind or making their way against it, that they could shout a message from
Hamburg to Berlin by word of mouth.

It is the same scene for the entire two hundred miles, and the same
scene repeats itself. . . . All the highways in Germany over which I traveled
this year presented the same aspect. . . .

Most of the hikers paid no attention to me. They walked separately or
in small groups, with their eyes on the ground. And they had the queer,
stumbling gait of barefooted people, for their shoes were slung over their
shoulders. Some of them were guild members — carpenters with embroi-
dered wallets, knee breeches, and broad felt hats; milkmen with striped
red shirts, and bricklayers with tall black hats, — but they were in a minority. Far more numerous were those whom one could assign to no special
profession or craft — unskilled young people, for the most part, who had
been unable to find a place for themselves in any city or town in Germany,
and who had never had a job and never expected to have one. There was
something else that had never been seen before — whole families that had
piled all their goods into baby carriages and wheelbarrows that they were
pushing along as they plodded forward in dumb despair. It was a whole
nation on the march.

I saw them — and this was the strongest impression that the year 1932
left with me — I saw them, gathered into groups of fifty or a hundred men,
attacking fields of potatoes. I saw them digging up the potatoes and throwing them into sacks while the farmer who owned the field watched them
in despair and the local policeman looked on gloomily from the distance.
I saw them staggering toward the lights of the city as night fell, with their
sacks on their backs. What did it remind me of? Of the War, of the worst
periods of starvation in 1917 and 1918, but even then people paid for the
potatoes. . . .

I saw that the individual can know what is happening only by personal
experience. I know what it is to be a tramp. I know what cold and hunger
are. I know what it is to spend the night outdoors or behind the thin walls

of a shack through which the wind whistles. I have slept in holes such as hunters hide in, in hayricks, under bridges, against the warm walls of boiler houses, under cattle shelters in pastures, on a heap of fir-tree boughs in the forest. But there are two things that I have only recently experienced — begging and spending the night in a municipal lodging house.

I entered the huge Berlin municipal lodging house in a northern quarter of the city. . . .

There was an entrance arched by a brick vaulting, and a watchman sat in a little wooden sentry box. His white coat made him look like a doctor. We stood waiting in the corridor. Heavy steam rose from the men's clothes. Some of them sat down on the floor, pulled off their shoes, and unwound the rags that were bound around their feet. More people were constantly pouring in the door, and we stood closely packed together. Then another door opened. The crowd pushed forward, and people began forcing their way almost eagerly through this door, for it was warm in there. Without knowing it I had already caught the rhythm of the municipal lodging house. It means waiting, waiting, standing around, and then suddenly jumping up. . . .

We now stand in a long hall, down the length of which runs a bar dividing the hall into a narrow and a wide space. All the light is on the narrow side. There under yellow lamps that hang from the ceiling on long wires sit men in white smocks. We arrange ourselves in long lines, each leading up to one of these men, and the mill begins to grind. . . .

As the line passes in single file the official does not look up at each new person to appear. He only looks at the paper that is handed to him. These papers are for the most part invalid cards or unemployment certificates. The very fact that the official does not look up robs the homeless applicant of self-respect, although he may look too beaten down to feel any. . . .

Now it is my turn and the questions and answers flow as smoothly as if I were an old hand. But finally I am asked, "Have you ever been here before?"

"No."

"No?" The question reverberates through the whole room. The clerk refuses to believe me and looks through his card catalogue. But no, my name is not there. The clerk thinks this strange, for he cannot have made a mistake, and the terrible thing that one notices in all these clerks is that they expect you to lie. They do not believe what you say. They do not regard you as a human being but as an infection, something foul that one keeps at a distance. He goes on. "How did you come here from Hamburg?"

"By truck."

"Where have you spent the last three nights?"

I lie coolly.

"Have you begged?"

I feel a warm blush spreading over my face. It is welling up from the bourgeois world that I have come from. "No."

A coarse peal of laughter rises from the line, and a loud, piercing voice grips me as if someone had seized me by the throat: "Never mind. The day will come, comrade, when there's nothing else to do." And the line breaks into laughter again, the bitterest laughter I have ever heard, the laughter of damnation and despair. . . .

Again the crowd pushes back in the kind of rhythm that is so typical of a lodging house, and we are all herded into the undressing room. . . . I cling to the man who spoke to me. He is a Saxon with a friendly manner and he has noticed that I am a stranger here. A certain sensitiveness, an almost perverse, spiritual alertness makes me like him very much.

Out of a big iron chest each of us takes a coat hanger that would serve admirably to hit somebody over the head with. As we undress the room becomes filled with the heavy breath of poverty. We are so close together that we brush against each other every time we move. Anyone who has been a soldier, anyone who has been to a public bath is perfectly accustomed to the look of naked bodies. But I have never seen anything quite so repulsive as all these hundreds of withered human frames. For in the homeless army the majority are men who have already been defeated in the struggle of life, the crippled, old, and sick. There is no repulsive disease of which traces are not to be seen here. There is no form of mutilation or degeneracy that is not represented, and the naked bodies of the old men are in a disgusting state of decline. . . .

It is superfluous to describe what follows. Towels are handed out . . . then nightgowns — long, sacklike affairs made of plain unbleached cotton but freshly washed. Then slippers. . . .

Distribution of spoons, distribution of enameled-ware bowls with the words "Property of the City of Berlin" written on their sides. Then the meal itself. A big kettle is carried in. Men with yellow smocks have brought it and men with yellow smocks ladle out the food. These men, too, are homeless and they have been expressly picked by the establishment and given free food and lodging and a little pocket money in exchange for their work about the house.

Where have I seen this kind of food distribution before? In a prison that I once helped to guard in the winter of 1919 during the German civil war. There was the same hunger then, the same trembling, anxious expectation of rations. Now the men are standing in a long row, dressed in their plain nightshirts that reach to the ground, and the noise of their shuffling feet is like the noise of big wild animals walking up and down the stone floor of their cages before feeding time. . . .

My next recollection is sitting at table in another room on a crowded bench that is like a seat in a fourth-class railway carriage. Hundreds of hungry mouths make an enormous noise eating their food. The men sit bent over their food like animals who feel that someone is going to take it away from them. They hold their bowl with their left arm part way around it, so that nobody can take it away, and they also protect it with their other elbow and with their head and mouth, while they move the spoon as fast as they can between their mouth and the bowl. . . .

We shuffle into the sleeping room, where each bed has a number painted in big letters on the wall over it. You must find the number that you have around your neck, and there is your bed, your home for one night. It stands in a row with fifty others and across the room there are fifty more in a row. . . .

Only a few people, very few, move around at all. The others lie awake and still, staring at their blankets, wrapped up in themselves but not sleeping. Only an almost soldierly sense of comradeship, an inner self-control engendered by the presence of so many people, prevents the despair that is written on all these faces from expressing itself. The few who are moving about do so with the tormenting consciousness of men who merely want to kill time. They do not believe in what they are doing.

Going to sleep means passing into the unconscious, eliminating the intelligence. And one can read deeply into a man's life by watching the way he goes to sleep. For we have not always slept in municipal lodgings. There are men among us who still move as if they were in a bourgeois bedchamber. . . .

The air is poisoned with the breath of men who have stuffed too much food into empty stomachs. There is also a sickening smell of lysol. It seems completely terrible to me. . . . Animals die, plants wither, but men always go on living.

READING AND DISCUSSION QUESTIONS

1. To what other period in Germany's history does Hauser compare this depression? How might that have influenced his perception of the current situation?

2. In this account, what is the attitude of the people with power toward those without it, and how does that affect the job and relief seekers?

3. According to Hauser, what impact does the depression have on perceptions of social and economic class?

DOCUMENT 27-6

British Beauty

1926

Part of the uncertainty of the late nineteenth and early twentieth centuries stemmed from the transformation of traditional concepts of everything — from citizenship to beauty — by the emerging mass market. Representations of desirable mates began to focus on characteristics such as youth and vigor, while the depersonalized urban society required individuals to attract partners from among the other strangers around them. The urban world also sped up, leading to a new emphasis on first impressions rather than deeper personality. In this context, female (and male) beauty changed from a somewhat desirable characteristic to an essential one, a need that many products were designed to fill.

READING AND DISCUSSION QUESTIONS

1. What about this depiction suggests that this is a "modern" woman? How might her needs contrast with the women of previous generations?

2. Inferring from this advertisement, what features should women desire to have? Is the preservation the ad speaks of possible in the long term, and if not, what does this say about Western commercialized society?

3. What does this image suggest about the prosperity of the society that created it?

Mary Evans/ILN/The Image Works.

BRITISH BEAUTY

To-day, more than ever, Pond's two creams
are essential for the protection of Youth
and Beauty. Britain's Best for British Beauty.

In jars 1⁄3 and 2⁄6. In tubes 7½ᵈ and 1⁄-
Cold Cream only, extra large jars 5⁄ extra large tubes 2⁄6.

"To Soothe and Smooth your Skin"

Pond's Extract Co., 103 St John Street, London, E.C.1

Pond's
Vanishing & Cold
Creams

SAA

509

COMPARATIVE QUESTIONS

1. What similarities can you discern between Freud's and Nietzsche's understanding of human nature? How do their theories contrast with Hauser's observations?

2. In what ways do Keynes's forebodings about the Treaty of Versailles seem to have been borne out by the report on the Special Areas?

3. If the nineteenth century's science was defined by certainty, in what ways do these documents undermine that certainty? Do any of these authors see this loss of certainty as a good thing? Why or why not?

4. How might the Social Darwinists, particularly Herbert Spencer (Document 23-6) respond to the report of the commissioner for the Special Areas? In what ways might the depression support or undercut Spencer's ideology?

5. Compare the report on the Special Areas with Hauser's narrative. How do their perspectives differ? What differences might that lead to in their approach to the problems of the depression?

6. Compare the attitudes that the advertising image seems to convey to those found in Nietzsche and Hauser. How could these coexist?

CHAPTER 28

Dictatorships and the Second World War

1919–1945

The period of anxiety and depression that followed the Great War led many to question whether democracy and capitalism could meet the challenges of modern society. In this context, two radical totalitarian governments came to power. In the Soviet Union after 1928, Joseph Stalin led his nation through a brutal and repressive "second revolution." In 1933, Germany's new chancellor and Nazi Party leader Adolf Hitler began plans to create a German Nazi empire based on the ideology of Aryan supremacy. Hampered by their own worries, other nations, including Great Britain, seemed powerless to stop Stalin or Hitler. By 1939, Hitler had provoked World War II, and Great Britain, led by Winston Churchill, was forced to respond militarily. As the war intensified, the Nazis determined to exterminate all European Jews, a goal which they very nearly achieved.

DOCUMENT 28-1

JOSEPH STALIN

An Interview with H. G. Wells:
Marxism and Liberalism

July 23, 1934

While the liberal democracies of the West stumbled in the face of the Great Depression, the Soviet Union appeared to make tremendous strides forward, albeit at terrible human cost. An understandable fascination with Josef

---

From Josef Stalin, *Works*, vol. 14. (London: Red Star Press Ltd., 1978). Marxists Internet Archive, http://marxists.org/reference/archive/stalin/works/1934/07/23.htm, accessed February 3, 2010.

Stalin developed among those who wanted to help the disadvantaged in European society, and Stalinism spread as an ideology among the educated outside the Soviet Union. Stalin took full advantage of this fascination, offering tours and interviews to sympathetic reporters. Here he sits down with British historian and science-fiction writer H. G. Wells — author of The Time Machine, The War of the Worlds, *and* The Invisible Man — *to discuss the differences between the Soviet system and the reforms then underway in the capitalist world.*

WELLS: But there are very different kinds of capitalists. There are capitalists who only think about profit, about getting rich; but there are also those who are prepared to make sacrifices. Take old Morgan[1] for example. He only thought about profit; he was a parasite on society, simply, he merely accumulated wealth. But take Rockefeller.[2] He is a brilliant organizer; he has set an example of how to organize the delivery of oil that is worthy of emulation. Or take Ford.[3] Of course Ford is selfish. But is he not a passionate organizer of rationalized production from whom you take lessons? I would like to emphasize the fact that recently an important change in opinion towards the U.S.S.R. has taken place in English-speaking countries. The reason for this, first of all, is the position of Japan and the events in Germany. But there are other reasons besides those arising from international politics. There is a more profound reason namely, the recognition by many people of the fact that the system based on private profit is breaking down. Under these circumstances, it seems to me, we must not bring to the forefront the antagonism between the two worlds, but should strive to combine all the constructive movements, all the constructive forces in one line as much as possible. It seems to me that I am more to the Left than you, Mr. Stalin; I think the old system is nearer to its end than you think.

---

[1] **old Morgan**: J. P. Morgan (1837–1913); one of the most powerful investment bankers in the American industrialization process, who was able to loan gold to the U.S. government in the Panic of 1893.

[2] **Rockefeller**: John D. Rockefeller (1839–1937); founder of Standard Oil, which at one point controlled over 90 percent of American refining capacity, and the first American billionaire.

[3] **Ford**: Henry Ford (1863–1947); American who used the moving assembly line to create affordable automobiles, and an object of Bolshevik admiration — despite his sympathy for Hitler.

STALIN: In speaking of the capitalists who strive only for profit, only to get rich, I do not want to say that these are the most worthless people, capable of nothing else. Many of them undoubtedly possess great organizing talent, which I do not dream of denying. We Soviet people learn a great deal from the capitalists. And Morgan, whom you characterize so unfavorably, was undoubtedly a good, capable organizer. But if you mean people who are prepared to reconstruct the world, of course, you will not be able to find them in the ranks of those who faithfully serve the cause of profit. We and they stand at opposite poles. You mentioned Ford. Of course, he is a capable organizer of production. But don't you know his attitude to the working class?

Don't you know how many workers he throws on the street? The capitalist is riveted to profit; and no power on earth can tear him away from it. Capitalism will be abolished, not by "organizers" of production not by the technical intelligentsia, but by the working class, because the aforementioned strata do not play an independent role. The engineer, the organizer of production does not work as he would like to, but as he is ordered, in such a way as to serve the interests of his employers. There are exceptions of course; there are people in this stratum who have awakened from the intoxication of capitalism. The technical intelligentsia can, under certain conditions, perform miracles and greatly benefit mankind. But it can also cause great harm. We Soviet people have not a little experience of the technical intelligentsia.

After the October Revolution, a certain section of the technical intelligentsia refused to take part in the work of constructing the new society; they opposed this work of construction and sabotaged it.

We did all we possibly could to bring the technical intelligentsia into this work of construction; we tried this way and that. Not a little time passed before our technical intelligentsia agreed actively to assist the new system. Today the best section of this technical intelligentsia are in the front rank of the builders of socialist society. Having this experience we are far from underestimating the good and the bad sides of the technical intelligentsia and we know that on the one hand it can do harm, and on the other hand, it can perform "miracles." Of course, things would be different if it were possible, at one stroke, spiritually to tear the technical intelligentsia away from the capitalist world. But that is utopia.

Are there many of the technical intelligentsia who would dare break away from the bourgeois world and set to work reconstructing society? Do you think there are many people of this kind, say, in England or in France? No, there are few who would be willing to break away from their employers and begin reconstructing the world.

Besides, can we lose sight of the fact that in order to transform the world it is necessary to have political power? It seems to me, Mr. Wells, that you greatly underestimate the question of political power, that it entirely drops out of your conception.

What can those, even with the best intentions in the world, do if they are unable to raise the question of seizing power, and do not possess power? At best they can help the class which takes power, but they cannot change the world themselves. This can only be done by a great class which will take the place of the capitalist class and become the sovereign master as the latter was before. This class is the working class. Of course, the assistance of the technical intelligentsia must be accepted; and the latter in turn, must be assisted. But it must not be thought that the technical intelligentsia can play an independent historical role. The transformation of the world is a great, complicated and painful process. For this task a great class is required. Big ships go on long voyages. . . .

WELLS: I watch communist propaganda in the West and it seems to me that in modern conditions this propaganda sounds very old-fashioned, because it is insurrectionary propaganda. Propaganda in favor of the violent overthrow of the social system was all very well when it was directed against tyranny. But under modern conditions, when the system is collapsing anyhow, stress should be laid on efficiency, on competence, on productiveness, and not on insurrection.

It seems to me that the insurrectionary note is obsolete. The communist propaganda in the West is a nuisance to constructive-minded people.

STALIN: Of course the old system is breaking down and decaying. That is true. But it is also true that new efforts are being made by other methods, by every means, to protect, to save this dying system.

You draw a wrong conclusion from a correct postulate.

You rightly state that the old world is breaking down.

But you are wrong in thinking that it is breaking down of its own accord. No, the substitution of one social system for another is a complicated and long revolutionary process. It is not simply a spontaneous process, but a struggle, it is a process connected with the clash of classes. Capitalism is decaying, but it must not be compared simply with a tree which has decayed to such an extent that it must fall to the ground of its own accord. No, revolution, the substitution of one social system for another, has always been a struggle, a painful and a cruel struggle, a life and death struggle. And every time the people of the new world came into power they had to defend themselves against the attempts of the old world to restore the old power by force; these people of the new world always had to be on the alert, always had to be ready to repel the attacks of the old world upon the new system.

Yes, you are right when you say that the old social system is breaking down; but it is not breaking down of its own accord. Take Fascism for example.

Fascism is a reactionary force which is trying to preserve the old system by means of violence. What will you do with the fascists? Argue with them? Try to convince them? But this will have no effect upon them at all. Communists do not in the least idealize the methods of violence. But they, the Communists, do not want to be taken by surprise, they cannot count on the old world voluntarily departing from the stage, they see that the old system is violently defending itself, and that is why the Communists say to the working class: Answer violence with violence; do all you can to prevent the old dying order from crushing you, do not permit it to put manacles on your hands, on the hands with which you will overthrow the old system. As you see, the Communists regard the substitution of one social system for another, not simply as a spontaneous and peaceful process, but as a complicated, long, and violent process. Communists cannot ignore facts. . . .

STALIN: Do you deny the role of the intelligentsia in revolutionary movements? Was the Great French Revolution a lawyers' revolution and not a popular revolution, which achieved victory by rousing vast masses of the people against feudalism and championed the interests of the Third Estate? And did the lawyers among the leaders of the Great French Revolution act in accordance with the laws of the old order? Did they not introduce new, bourgeois revolutionary laws?

The rich experience of history teaches that up to now not a single class has voluntarily made way for another class. There is no such precedent in world history. The Communists have learned this lesson of history. Communists would welcome the voluntary departure of the bourgeoisie. But such a turn of affairs is improbable; that is what experience teaches. That is why the Communists want to be prepared for the worst and call upon the working class to be vigilant, to be prepared for battle. Who wants a captain who lulls the vigilance of his army, a captain who does not understand that the enemy will not surrender, that he must be crushed? To be such a captain means deceiving, betraying the working class. That is why I think that what seems to you to be old-fashioned is in fact a measure of revolutionary expediency for the working class.

WELLS: I do not deny that force has to be used, but I think the forms of the struggle should fit as closely as possible to the opportunities presented by the existing laws, which must be defended against reactionary attacks. There is no need to disorganize the old system because it is disorganizing itself enough as it is. That is why it seems to me insurrection against the old order, against the law, is obsolete; old-fashioned. Incidentally, I deliberately exaggerate in order to bring the truth out more clearly. I can formulate my point of view in the following way: first, I am for order; second, I attack the present system in so far as it cannot assure order; third, I think that class war propaganda may detach from socialism just those educated people whom socialism needs.

STALIN: In order to achieve a great object, an important social object, there must be a main force, a bulwark, a revolutionary class. Next it is necessary to organize the assistance of an auxiliary force for this main force; in this case this auxiliary force is the Party, to which the best forces of the intelligentsia belong. Just now you spoke about "educated people." But what educated people did you have in mind? Were there not plenty of educated people on the side of the old order in England in the seventeenth century, in France at the end of the eighteenth century, and in Russia in the epoch of the October Revolution? The old order had in its service many highly educated people who defended the old order, who opposed the new order. Education is a weapon the effect of which is determined by the hands which wield it, by who is to be struck down.

Of course, the proletariat, socialism, needs highly educated people. Clearly, simpletons cannot help the proletariat to fight for socialism, to build a new society. I do not underestimate the role of the intelligentsia; on the contrary, I emphasize it. The question is, however, which intelligentsia are we discussing?

Because there are different kinds of intelligentsia.

WELLS: There can be no revolution without a radical change in the educational system. It is sufficient to quote two examples: The example of the German Republic, which did not touch the old educational system, and therefore never became a republic; and the example of the

British Labour Party, which lacks the determination to insist on a radical change in the educational system.

STALIN: That is a correct observation.

Permit me now to reply to your three points.

First, the main thing for the revolution is the existence of a social bulwark. This bulwark of the revolution is the working class.

Second, an auxiliary force is required, that which the Communists call a Party. To the Party belong the intelligent workers and those elements of the technical intelligentsia which are closely connected with the working class. The intelligentsia can be strong only if it combines with the working class.

If it opposes the working class it becomes a cipher.

Third, political power is required as a lever for change. The new political power creates the new laws, the new order, which is revolutionary order.

I do not stand for any kind of order. I stand for order that corresponds to the interests of the working class. If, however, any of the laws of the old order can be utilized in the interests of the struggle for the new order, the old laws should be utilized.

I cannot object to your postulate that the present system should be attacked in so far as it does not ensure the necessary order for the people.

And, finally, you are wrong if you think that the Communists are enamored of violence. They would be very pleased to drop violent methods if the ruling class agreed to give way to the working class. But the experience of history speaks against such an assumption.

READING AND DISCUSSION QUESTIONS

1. Given this discussion, how did Stalin perceive the tension between the individual and the group, and what importance did he accord the individual in that process? How does he seem to differ from Wells on this score?

2. How does Stalin seem aware of his audience in this document? How could that influence his comments?

3. In what ways does Stalin add a political interpretation to areas that Wells might not consider political?

DOCUMENT 28-2

VLADIMIR TCHERNAVIN

I Speak for the Silent: *Stalinist Interrogation Techniques Revealed*

1930

To maintain his power and Communist rule in the Soviet Union, Joseph Stalin instituted a massive security apparatus that pervaded most aspects of Soviet life. Vladimir Tchernavin was a scientist in the northwestern port city of Murmansk, working to transform the Soviet Union from an agrarian to an industrial state. Such an ambitious project was bound to have its share of failures, but in the climate of paranoia that pervaded Stalinist society, such failures were attributed to sabotage, and sabotage was brutally punished.

It was my second day in prison — my second cross-examination. I was called before the tea ration was given out and had only time to eat an apple.

"How do you do?" the examining officer asked, scanning me attentively to see if I showed signs of a sleepless night.

"All right."

"It isn't so good in your cell. You are in 22?"

"A cell like any other."

"Well, did you do any thinking? Are you going to tell the truth today?"

"Yesterday I told only the truth."

He laughed. "What will it be today — not the truth?"

Then he returned to the subject of the cell.

"I tried to choose a better cell for you, but we are so crowded. I hope we will come to an understanding and that I will not be forced to change the regime I have ordered for you. The third category is the mildest: exercise in the yard, permission to receive food parcels from outside, a newspaper and books. The first two categories are much stricter. Remember, however, that it depends entirely on me; any minute you may be deprived of everything and transferred to solitary confinement. Or rather, this

---

From Vladimir Tchernavin, *I Speak for the Silent* (Newton Center, Mass.: Charles T. Branford, 1935), pp. 116–120.

depends not on me but on your own behavior, your sincerity. The more frank your testimony, the better will be the conditions of your imprisonment. . . ."

He spoke slowly, looking me straight in the eye, emphasizing his words with evident pleasure and relish, watching for their effect.

"Did you know Scherbakoff? He was a strong man, but I broke him and forced him to confess."

With great difficulty I controlled myself before replying.

"I don't doubt for a minute that you use torture, and if you believe that this assists in discovering the truth and speeding up the investigation, and since Soviet laws permit its use, I would suggest that you don't give up medieval methods: a little fire is a wonderful measure. Try it! I am not afraid of you. Even with that you can't get anything out of me."

"Well, we will see about that later. Now let's get down to business. Let's talk about your acquaintances. Did you know V. K. Tolstoy, the wrecker, executed in connection with the case of the '48'?"[4]

"Yes, I knew him. How could I not know him when he was the director of the fishing industry in the north?" I replied in frank astonishment. "We both worked in it for more than twenty years."

"And did you (know) him well?"

"Very well."

"How long did you know him?"

"From childhood."

His manner changed completely; he hurriedly picked up a statement sheet and placed it in front of me. "Write down your confession."

"What confession?"

"That you knew Tolstoy, that you were in friendly relation with him from such and such a time. I see that we will come to an understanding with you; your frankness will be appreciated. Write."

He evidently was in a hurry, did not quite know what he was saying, afraid that I might reverse my statements.

I took the sheet and wrote down what I had said.

"Excellent. Let's continue."

Then followed a barrage of questions about Tolstoy, about Scherbakoff and other people that I had known. He did not find me quite so tractable and we launched into a battle of wits that kept up hour after hour. He

---

[4] **the case of the '48'**: Tchernavin refers to the accusation and subsequent execution of forty-eight prominent Russian scientists accused of sabotaging the food supply in 1930.

questioned me with insistence and in great detail, trying without success to make me give dates.

"You'll not succeed in outwitting me," he snapped sharply. "I advise you not to try. I am going home to dinner now and you will stay here till evening. This examination will continue — not for a day or two, but for months and, if necessary, for years. Your strength is not equal to mine. I will force you to tell us what we need."

After threatening me still further he handed me some sheets of paper.

"You are going to state in writing your opinion regarding the building of a fertilization factory in Murmansk, its equipment and work in the future. I'll soon be back; when I return, your comments on these questions must be completed."

He put on his overcoat and left. His assistant took his place, and I busied myself with my writing. It was three or four hours before he returned, already evening.

Although I had eaten almost nothing for three days, I was still in good fighting form. He questioned me about the buying of a ship from abroad, trying to make me say that here was "wrecking," because the price had been exorbitant and the ship itself had proved unsatisfactory. It was most confusing and his questions far-fetched. We talked and we argued, but I would not give the answers he wanted.

He began on another tack. . . .

"All right," he said. "And what is your attitude regarding the subject of the fish supply in the Sea of Barents in connection with the construction of trawlers as provided for by the Five-Year Plan?"

Now he had broached a subject with which I could have a direct connection. The evening was already changing into night, but I was still sitting in the same chair. I was becoming unconscious of time: was it my second day in prison or my tenth? In spite of the depressing weariness, mental and physical, which was taking hold of me, I told him that I thought the fresh fish supply should be minutely and thoroughly investigated. I tried to make him see the hazards of the fishing industry in Murmansk and the enormous equipment that would be necessary to meet the proposals of the Five-Year Plan.

"And thus you confess that you doubted the practicability of the Five-Year Plan?" he said with a smile of smug satisfaction.

What could one say? I believed, as did everybody, that the plan was absurd, that it could not be fulfilled. For exactly such statements — no, for only a suspicion of having such thoughts — forty-eight men had been shot.

READING AND DISCUSSION QUESTIONS

1. From the perspective of the state, what purposes would be served by arresting and torturing Vladimir Tchernavin?

2. What incentives could Tchernavin have for resisting, and what might convince him to comply with the interrogator?

3. Based on your reading of this account, what relationship did truth and guilt have in the Stalinist justice system?

VIEWPOINTS

The Power of Propaganda

DOCUMENT 28-3

Soviet Propaganda Posters

1941 and 1945

Soviet propaganda efforts in the twenties and thirties attempted to break with history and create the "New Soviet Man." In the initial days of the German invasion of 1941, Soviet responses emphasized revolutionary and Leninist themes, with little success. Later efforts emphasized nationalism and the defense of the motherland, reviving Great Russian historical figures, even some from the tsarist era, as examples of heroic resistance to foreign invaders. The first poster exhorts the soldiers to go forward to victory under the banner of Lenin, and the second references Napoleon's 1812 defeat at Russian hands.

READING AND DISCUSSION QUESTIONS

1. What are the different ways in which Soviet soldiers are portrayed in the two images? How might this reflect a changing appreciation of the nature of the war?

2. How could the use of aristocratic generals from the nineteenth century be reconciled with the official Soviet emphasis on breaking with that tradition?

3. Which image might the intended audience find more persuasive or inspiring?

ПОД ЗНАМЕНЕМ ЛЕНИНА
— ВПЕРЕД К ПОБЕДЕ!

НАПОЛЕОН ПОТЕРПЕЛ ПОРАЖЕНИЕ.
ТО ЖЕ БУДЕТ И С ЗАЗНАВШИМСЯ
ГИТЛЕРОМ!

1812.

DOCUMENT 28-4

ADOLF HITLER

Mein Kampf: *The Art of Propaganda*

1924

While in prison for a failed 1923 coup attempt, Hitler dictated his autobiography, Mein Kampf (My Struggle), *detailing his views on politics and society. Based on his interpretation of the end of the Great War, Hitler argued that Germany had been defeated not by Allied armies, but by the failure of German propaganda to effectively counter Allied propaganda, something he proposed to change when he came to power. At the time,* Mein Kampf *was not popular, but it proved prophetic: one of Hitler's first acts as chancellor was to establish the Ministry for Enlightenment and Propaganda in March 1933.*

The psyche of the great masses is not receptive to anything that is half-hearted and weak. . . .

To whom should propaganda be addressed? To the scientifically trained intelligentsia or to the less educated masses?

It must be addressed always and exclusively to the masses. . . .

All propaganda must be popular and its intellectual level must be adjusted to the most limited intelligence among those it is addressed to. Consequently, the greater the mass it is intended to reach, the lower its purely intellectual level will have to be. . . .

The art of propaganda lies in understanding the emotional ideas of the great masses and finding, through a psychologically correct form, the way to the attention and thence to the heart of the broad masses. The fact that our bright boys do not understand this merely shows how mentally lazy and conceited they are.

Once we understand how necessary it is for propaganda to be adjusted to the broad mass, the following rule results:

It is a mistake to make propaganda many-sided, like scientific instruction, for instance. The receptivity of the great masses is very limited, their intelligence is small, but their power of forgetting is enormous. In consequence of these facts, all effective propaganda must be limited to a very

From Adolf Hitler, *Mein Kampf,* trans. Ralph Mannheim (Boston: Houghton-Mifflin, 1943), pp. 42, 179–185.

few points and must harp on these in slogans until the last member of the public understands what you want him to understand by your slogan. As soon as you sacrifice this slogan and try to be many-sided, the effect will piddle away, for the crowd can neither digest nor retain the material offered. In this way, the result is weakened and in the end entirely cancelled out. . . .

The broad mass of a nation does not consist of diplomats, or even professors of political law, or even individuals capable of forming a rational opinion; it consists of plain mortals, wavering and inclined to doubt and uncertainty. As soon as our own propaganda admits so much as a glimmer of right on the other side, the foundation for doubt in our own right has been laid. . . .

The people in their overwhelming majority are so feminine by nature and attitude that sober reasoning determines their thoughts and actions far less than emotion and feeling. . . . But the most brilliant propagandist technique will yield no success unless one fundamental principle is borne in mind constantly and with unflagging attention. It must confine itself to a few points and repeat them over and over. Here, as so often in this world, persistence is the first and most important requirement for success. . . .

The purpose of propaganda is not to provide interesting distraction for blasé young gentlemen, but to convince, and what I mean is to convince the masses. But the masses are slow-moving, and they always require a certain time before they are ready even to notice a thing, and only after the simplest ideas are repeated thousands of times will the masses finally remember them. . . .

[During World War I] at first the claims of the [enemy] propaganda were so impudent that people thought it insane; later, it got on people's nerves; and in the end, it was believed.

READING AND DISCUSSION QUESTIONS

1. What are Hitler's main suggestions for the propagandist who wants to be successful? How does it affect your evaluation of the passage to know that it took him almost ten more years to gain power?

2. What does Hitler's conception of who matters in society reveal about his attitudes toward both the powerful and the average members of society?

DOCUMENT 28-5

The Nuremberg Laws: The Centerpiece of Nazi Racial Legislation

1935

Part of Hitler's vision for Germany was based on a pseudoscientific racist division of the world that was not uncommon at the time. He believed that "Jewishness" was both biological and religious. Two years after the Nazi Party took power in Germany, the first legal restrictions on German Jews were announced at a Nazi rally in Nuremburg. Hitler presented the Nuremburg Laws as a means to curb popular violence against Jews, allowing him to present himself as a defender of law and order.

ARTICLE 5

1. A Jew is anyone who descended from at least three grandparents who were racially full Jews. Article 2, par. 2, second sentence will apply.
2. A Jew is also one who descended from two full Jewish parents, if: (a) he belonged to the Jewish religious community at the time this law was issued, or who joined the community later; (b) he was married to a Jewish person, at the time the law was issued, or married one subsequently; (c) he is the offspring from a marriage with a Jew, in the sense of Section 1, which was contracted after the Law for the Protection of German Blood and German Honor became effective. . . . (d) he is the offspring of an extramarital relationship, with a Jew, according to Section 1, and will be born out of wedlock after July 31, 1936. . . .

LAW FOR THE PROTECTION OF GERMAN BLOOD AND GERMAN HONOR OF 15 SEPTEMBER 1935

Thoroughly convinced by the knowledge that the purity of German blood is essential for the further existence of the German people and animated by the inflexible will to safe-guard the German nation for the entire future,

From U.S. Chief of Counsel for the Prosecution of Axis Criminality, *Nazi Conspiracy and Aggression* (Washington, D.C.: U.S. Government Printing Office, 1946), vol. 4, doc. no. 1417-PS, pp. 8–10; vol. 4, doc. no. 2000-PS, pp. 636–638.

the Reichstag[5] has resolved upon the following law unanimously, which is promulgated herewith:

Section 1

1. Marriages between Jews and nationals of German or kindred blood are forbidden. Marriages concluded in defiance of this law are void, even if, for the purpose of evading this law, they are concluded abroad. . . .

Section 2

Relation[s] outside marriage between Jews and nationals of German or kindred blood are forbidden.

Section 3

Jews will not be permitted to employ female nationals of German or kindred blood in their household.

Section 4

1. Jews are forbidden to hoist the Reich and national flag and to present the colors of the Reich. . . .

Section 5

1. A person who acts contrary to the prohibition of section 1 will be punished with hard labor.
2. A person who acts contrary to the prohibition of section 2 will be punished with imprisonment or with hard labor.
3. A person who acts contrary to the provisions of sections 3 or 4 will be punished with imprisonment up to a year and with a fine or with one of these penalties.

READING AND DISCUSSION QUESTIONS

1. From these laws, what can you conclude about Nazi attitudes toward women and marriage?
2. What do these laws suggest about the basis of personal and national identity in the Nazi mind-set?

---

[5] **Reichstag**: German legislative assembly; a holdover from Bismarck's Second Empire (1871–1919) that had little real power after it granted Hitler "temporary" dictatorial powers in March 1933.

3. Based on the document, what economic impact could these laws have had on the Jewish community in Germany? Why might the Nazis have wanted that impact?

DOCUMENT 28-6

WINSTON CHURCHILL

Speech Before the House of Commons

June 18, 1940

Once the World War II began in 1939, much of central and western Europe quickly fell to the German blitzkrieg strategy. After sending troops to aid the French against the Germans in 1940, the British army lost most of its tanks, trucks, and other heavy equipment while evacuating from Dunkirk following a decisive Nazi victory. Germany held the deep-water ports along the English Channel crucial for an invasion, and had the most feared air force in Europe. Facing these grim prospects, Churchill addressed the House of Commons to rally a nation unenthusiastic about another war.

The military events which have happened during the past fortnight have not come to me with any sense of surprise. Indeed, I indicated a fortnight ago as clearly as I could to the House that the worst possibilities were open, and I made it perfectly clear then that whatever happened in France would make no difference to the resolve of Britain and the British Empire to fight on, "if necessary for years, if necessary alone." During the last few days we have successfully brought off the great majority of the troops we had on the lines of communication in France — a very large number, scores of thousands — and seven-eighths of the troops we have sent to France since the beginning of the war, that is to say, about 350,000 out of 400,000 men, are safely back in this country. Others are still fighting with the French, and fighting with considerable success in their local encounters with the enemy. We have also brought back a great mass of stores, rifles, and munitions of

---

From Winston Churchill, "June 18, 1940, Speech Before House of Commons," in *The Past Speaks*, 2d ed., ed. Walter Arnstein (Lexington, Mass.: D. C. Heath, 1993), 2:376–378.

all kinds which had been accumulated in France during the last nine months.

We have, therefore, in this island to-day a very large and powerful military force. . . . This brings me, naturally, to the great question of invasion from the air and of the impending struggle between the British and German air forces. It seems quite clear that no invasion on a scale beyond the capacity of our land forces to crush speedily is likely to take place from the air until our air force has been definitely overpowered. In the meantime, there may be raids by parachute troops and attempted descents of airborne soldiers. We should be able to give those gentry a warm reception both in the air and if they reach the ground in any condition to continue the dispute. But the great question is, can we break Hitler's air weapon? Now, of course, it is a very great pity that we have not got an air force at least equal to that of the most powerful enemy within striking distance of these shores. But we have a very powerful air force which has proved itself far superior in quality, both in men and in many types of machine, to what we have met so far in the numerous fierce air battles which have been fought. In France, where we were at a considerable disadvantage and lost many machines on the ground, we were accustomed to inflict losses of as much as two to two and a half to one. In the fighting over Dunkirk, which was a sort of no man's land, we undoubtedly beat the German air force, and this gave us the mastery locally in the air, and we inflicted losses of three or four to one. . . .

There remains the danger of bombing attacks, which will certainly be made very soon upon us by the bomber forces of the enemy. It is true that the German bomber force is superior in numbers to ours, but we have a very large bomber force also which we shall use to strike at military targets in Germany without intermission. I do not at all underrate the severity of the ordeal which lies before us, but I believe our countrymen will show themselves capable of standing up to it. . . .

What General Weygand[6] called the "Battle of France" is over. I expect that the battle of Britain is about to begin. Upon this battle depends the survival of Christian civilization. Upon it depends our own British life and the long continuity of our institutions and our empire. The whole fury and might of the enemy must very soon be turned on us. Hitler knows that he will have to break us in this island or lose the war. If we can stand up to

---

[6] **General Weygand**: General Maxime Weygand took command of all French forces on May 17, 1940, and held that post until the French surrender, after which he collaborated with the German occupation.

him all Europe may be free, and the life of the world may move forward
into broad, sunlit uplands, but if we fail then the whole world, including
the United States, and all that we have known and cared for, will sink into
the abyss of a new dark age made more sinister, and perhaps more prolonged, by the lights of a perverted science. Let us therefore brace ourselves to our duty and so bear ourselves that if the British Commonwealth
and Empire lasts for a thousand years men will still say, "This was their
finest hour."

READING AND DISCUSSION QUESTIONS

1. What reasons would Churchill have for mentioning the United States
   specifically in the last paragraph? For what audiences might this
   speech be intended?

2. What could this speech reveal about Churchill's attitude toward the
   British citizenry, and the concept of democratic rule in general?

3. What are the advantages and disadvantages Churchill sees facing
   the British war effort? How convincing do you find his assessment of
   the situation, and why?

DOCUMENT 28-7

TRAIAN POPOVICI

Mein Bekenntnis: *The Ghettoization of the Jews*

1941

*Nazi policy toward Europe's Jews moved toward extermination after 1941,
though the shift in policy took some time to work out in practice. After forcing public identification of Jewish citizens, often by requiring them to wear
yellow stars, the next step was to segregate them, which made deportation to
the death camps easier. Romania was a German ally, and could be expected*

From Traian Popovici, "Mein Bekenntnis (My Declaration)," in *Antisemitism in the
Modern World*, ed. and trans. Richard Levy (Lexington, Mass.: D. C. Heath, 1991),
pp. 243–244.

to reap the same economic benefit Germany did from plundering those scheduled for death. Popovici, the mayor of the capital city of Czernowitz, nevertheless urged his government to resist Nazi pressure, eventually saving close to twenty thousand lives through his efforts.

On the morning of October 11 . . . I looked out the window. It was snowing and — I could not believe my eyes: on the street in front of my window long columns of people were hurrying by. Old people supported by children, women with infants in their arms, invalids dragging their maimed bodies along, all with their luggage in wagons or on their backs, with hastily packed suitcases, bedding, bundles, clothes; they all made silent pilgrimage into the city's valley of death, the ghetto. . . .

Great activity in the city hall. . . . The "abandoned" wealth of the Jews was to be inventoried and their dwellings sealed. Romanianization departments were to be formed and with police assistants to be distributed throughout the city neighborhoods.

It first dawned on me then that the procedure had been a long time in the planning. I hurried to military headquarters where General Jonescu informed me of events. He let me see the promulgated ordinances. . . . I paged through the instructions in haste and read the regulations for the functioning of the ghetto. The bakeries were to be under city hall control, as were the [food] markets. Then I hurried again to the city hall in order to see to the measures necessary for the uninterrupted provisioning of bread, food, and especially milk for the children. For the time being, this was the role that providence allotted to me, thanks to the military cabinet.

Only those who know the topography of the city can measure how slight was the space for the ghetto to which the Jewish population was confined and in which, under pain of death, they had to be by six o'clock.

In this part of the city, even with the greatest crowding, ten thousand people could be housed at most. Fifty thousand had to be brought in, not counting the Christian population already living there. Then, and even today, I compare the ghetto to a cattle pen.

The accommodation possibilities were minimal. Even if the available rooms were to receive thirty or more people, a great number would have to seek shelter from the snow and rain in corridors, attics, cellars, and similar sorts of places. I would rather not speak of the demands of hygiene. Pure drinking water was lacking; the available public fountains did not suffice. I noted that the city already suffered from a water shortage since two of the three pumping stations had been destroyed. The strong odors of sweat, urine, and human waste, of mold and mildew, distinguished the quarter from the rest of the city. . . . It was a miracle that epidemics that would endanger the whole city did not break out. With surprising speed the ghetto was nearly hermetically sealed with barbed wire. At the main exits, wooden gates were erected and military guards posted. I do not know whether it was intentional, but the effect was clear: the despised were being intimidated. . . .

Although . . . the regulation concerning the ghetto categorically stated that no one could enter without the authorization of the governor, no one observed this rule. As early as the second day after the erection of the ghetto, there began a pilgrimage consisting of ladies of all social strata and intellectual jobbers, well known to the Czernowitz public. Persons of "influence" from all strata and professions — hyenas all — caught the scent of cadaverous souls among the unfortunates. Under the pretext that they were in the good graces of the governor, the military cabinet, or the mayor, they began the high-level pillaging of all that was left to the unfortunates. Their gold coins, jewelry, precious stones, furs, and valuable foodstuffs (tea, coffee, chocolate, cocoa) were supposedly to be used to bribe others or to compensate [the interlopers] for putting in a good word to save someone from deportation. Trading in influence was in full bloom. Another category of hyena was the so-called friend who volunteered to protect all these goods from theft or to deliver them to family members and acquaintances elsewhere in the country. Individuals never previously seen in the city of Czernowitz streamed in from all corners of the country in order to draw profit from a human tragedy. If the deportation with all its premeditation was in itself monstrous, then the exploitation of despair surpassed even this.

READING AND DISCUSSION QUESTIONS

1. What issues did the ghettoization of Czernowitz's Jewish population raise, for Jews and non-Jews alike?

2. Traian Popovici obviously opposed the policies he carried out. What options did he have in the face of the Nazi orders?

3. Whom does Popovici see as the worst offenders during the ghettoization, and why?

4. What are some reasons why Popovici may not have heard of the segregation until it was well under way?

COMPARATIVE QUESTIONS

1. What similarities can you see between German and Soviet attitudes toward their citizens, and how might this contrast with the British attitude expressed by Churchill?

2. Apply Hitler's definition of effective propaganda to Churchill's speech. Where does it seem Churchill agrees with Hitler's principles, and where does it seem he departs from them?

3. Based on your reading of Tchernavin's and Popovici's documents, which dictatorship — Stalin's or Hitler's — took greater steps to transform their societies? On what do you base your evaluation?

4. Based on their documents, how do Stalin and Hitler agree on the conception of information and the role of politics in society? How do they appear to differ? According to the accounts of Tchernavin and Popovici, how much do those differences mean in practice?

CHAPTER 29

Cold War Conflict and Consensus

1945–1965

T he alliance that destroyed Nazi Germany crumbled shortly after its victory. Within five years, the Soviet Union and the United States had organized alliances aimed at thwarting the other's perceived attempts to dominate Europe. The development of nuclear weapons lent a new urgency to simultaneous desire for nuclear dominance and fear of nuclear destruction. The Soviets feared another attack from the West, and the West distrusted the Soviets, who had promised but never held free elections in Poland. Ironically, despite the ever-present threat of nuclear war between 1949 and 1991, these years were among the most peaceful Europe ever experienced. American aid gave the Western European economies the means to recover, and the means to develop a more consumer-oriented society, where the good life was measured in access to conveniences for everyday life. Meanwhile, the excluded in Western society, from women to the colonized, began to press, sometimes violently, for cultural and economic equality.

DOCUMENT 29-1

GEORGE C. MARSHALL
An American Plan to Rebuild a Shattered Europe
June 5, 1947

In 1945, American policymakers wanted to avoid repeating the mistake of withdrawing into neutrality as they had in 1919. George Marshall was the highest-ranking American officer in World War II and served as secretary of

"The Address of Secretary Marshall at Harvard," *The New York Times*, June 6, 1947.

state for the Truman administration. When communist parties began to win elections in France and Italy, Marshall used a speech to Harvard University's graduating class to propose spending billions to rebuild Europe and hopefully prevent another war, this time fought with atomic weapons. While Western nations embraced the Marshall Plan, the Stalin-headed Soviet Union rejected its terms, believing the Soviet Union would be stripped of its control of the Eastern bloc.

I need not tell you, gentlemen, that the world situation is very serious. That must be apparent to all intelligent people. I think one difficulty is that the problem is one of such enormous complexity that the very mass of facts presented to the public by press and radio make it exceedingly difficult for the man in the street to reach a clear appraisement of the situation. Furthermore, the people of this country are distant from the troubled areas of the earth and it is hard for them to comprehend the plight and consequent reactions of the long-suffering peoples, and the effect of those reactions on their governments in connection with our efforts to promote peace in the world.

In considering the requirements for the rehabilitation of Europe the physical loss of life, the visible destruction of cities, factories, mines, and railroads was correctly estimated, but it has become obvious during recent months that this visible destruction was probably less serious than the dislocation of the entire fabric of European economy. For the past ten years conditions have been highly abnormal.

The feverish preparation for war and the more feverish maintenance of the war effort engulfed all aspects of national economies. Machinery has fallen into disrepair or is entirely obsolete. Under the arbitrary and destructive Nazi rule, virtually every possible enterprise was geared into the German war machine. Long-standing commercial ties, private institutions, banks, insurance companies, and shipping companies disappeared, through loss of capital, absorption through nationalization, or by simple destruction.

In many countries, confidence in the local currency has been severely shaken. The breakdown of the business structure of Europe during the war was complete. Recovery has been seriously retarded by the fact that two years after the close of hostilities a peace settlement with Germany and Austria has not been agreed upon. But even given a more prompt solution of these difficult problems, the rehabilitation of the economic structure of Europe quite evidently will require a much longer time and greater effort than had been foreseen.

There is a phase of this matter which is both interesting and serious. The farmer has always produced the foodstuffs to exchange with the city dweller for the other necessities of life. This division of labor is the basis of modern civilization. At the present time it is threatened with breakdown. The town and city industries are not producing adequate goods to exchange with the food-producing farmer. Raw materials and fuel are in short supply. Machinery is lacking or worn out.

The farmer or the peasant cannot find the goods for sale which he desires to purchase. So the sale of his farm produce for money which he cannot use seems to him an unprofitable transaction. He, therefore, has withdrawn many fields from crop cultivation and is using them for grazing. He feeds more grain to stock and finds for himself and his family an ample supply of food, however short he may be on clothing and the other ordinary gadgets of civilization. Meanwhile, people in the cities are short of food and fuel. So the governments are forced to use their foreign money and credits to procure these necessities abroad. This process exhausts funds which are urgently needed for reconstruction. Thus a very serious situation is rapidly developing which bodes no good for the world. The modern system of the division of labor upon which the exchange of products is based is in danger of breaking down.

The truth of the matter is that Europe's requirements for the next three or four years of foreign food and other essential products — principally from America — are so much greater than her present ability to pay that she must have substantial additional help, or face economic, social, and political deterioration of a very grave character.

The remedy lies in breaking the vicious circle and restoring the confidence of the European people in the economic future of their own countries and of Europe as a whole. The manufacturer and the farmer throughout wide areas must be able and willing to exchange their products for currencies, the continuing value of which is not open to question.

Aside from the demoralizing effect on the world at large and the possibilities of disturbances arising as a result of the desperation of the people concerned, the consequences to the economy of the United States should be apparent to all. It is logical that the United States should do whatever it is able to do to assist in the return of normal economic health in the world, without which there can be no political stability and no assured peace.

Our policy is directed not against any country or doctrine but against hunger, poverty, desperation, and chaos. Its purpose should be the revival of a working economy in the world so as to permit the emergence of political and social conditions in which free institutions can exist. Such assistance, I am convinced, must not be on a piecemeal basis as various crises develop. Any assistance that this Government may render in the future should provide a cure rather than a mere palliative.

Any government that is willing to assist in the task of recovery will find full cooperation, I am sure, on the part of the United States Government. Any government which maneuvers to block the recovery of other countries cannot expect help from us. Furthermore, governments, political parties, or groups which seek to perpetuate human misery in order to profit therefrom politically or otherwise will encounter the opposition of the United States.

It is already evident that, before the United States Government can proceed much further in its efforts to alleviate the situation and help start the European world on its way to recovery, there must be some agreement among the countries of Europe as to the requirements of the situation and the part those countries themselves will take in order to give proper effect to whatever action might be undertaken by this Government. It would be neither fitting nor efficacious for this Government to undertake to draw up unilaterally a program designed to place Europe on its feet economically. This is the business of the Europeans. The initiative, I think, must come from Europe. The role of this country should consist of friendly aid in the drafting of a European program and of later support of such a program so far as it may be practical for us to do so. The program should be a joint one, agreed to by a number of, if not all, European nations.

An essential part of any successful action on the part of the United States is an understanding on the part of the people of America of the character of the problem and the remedies to be applied. Political passion and prejudice should have no part. With foresight, and a willingness on the part of our people to face up to the vast responsibility which history has clearly placed upon our country, the difficulties I have outlined can and will be overcome.

READING AND DISCUSSION QUESTIONS

1. According to Marshall, what problems did Europe face after World War II? What solutions does he propose?

2. In what ways might this document mean that Europe no longer dominated the world's economy? In what ways is it still critical?

3. In what ways does Marshall's plan incorporate the Soviets? What impact could their decision not to participate have had on the Eastern European economy?

4. How much American self-interest is involved in the program Marshall proposes? What concrete benefits, beyond not having another war, can you see in this plan?

DOCUMENT 29-2

ALEXANDER SOLZHENITSYN
One Day in the Life of Ivan Denisovich:
The Stalinist Gulag
1962

After Joseph Stalin died in 1953, the Soviet Union backed away from many of his policies. The next Soviet leader, Nikita Khrushchev (r. 1953–1964), denounced the gulag — the terror and labor camps Stalin had created — and considerably relaxed censorship. In this new period of increased critical freedom, Alexander Solzhenitsyn was permitted to publish an account of his life in the camps, to which he had been sentenced in 1945 for criticizing Stalin's conduct of the war. His continued criticism of the Soviet regime led to his deportation to the West in 1974. From his exile, Solzhenitsyn condemned both the repression of the Soviets and the materialism of the capitalist world.

At five o'clock that morning reveille was sounded, as usual, by the blows of a hammer on a length of rail hanging up near the staff quarters. The intermittent sounds barely penetrated the windowpanes on which the frost lay two fingers thick, and they ended almost as soon as they'd begun. It was cold outside, and campguard was reluctant to go on beating out the reveille for long.

The clanging ceased, but everything outside still looked like the middle of the night when Ivan Denisovich Shukhov got up to go the bucket. It was pitch dark except for the yellow light cast on the window by three lamps — two in the outer zone, one inside the camp itself.

And no one came to unbolt the barracks door; there was no sound of the barrack orderlies pushing a pole into place to lift the barrel of excrement and carry it out.

From Alexander Solzhenitsyn, *One Day in the Life of Ivan Denisovich*, trans. Ralph Parker (New York: E.P. Dutton & Co., 1963), pp. 17–25.

Shukhov never overslept reveille. He always got up at once, for the next ninety minutes, until they assembled for work, belonged to him, not to the authorities, and any old-timer could always earn a bit — by sewing a pair of mittens for someone out of his old sleeve lining; or bringing some rich loafer in the squad his dry valenki[1] — right up to his bunk, so that he wouldn't have to stumble barefoot round the heap of boots looking for his own pair; or going the rounds to the warehouses, offering to be of service, sweeping up this or fetching that; or going to the mess hall to collect bowls from the tables and bring them stacked to the dishwashers — you're sure to be given something to eat there, though there were plenty of others at that game, more than plenty — and, what's worse, if you found a bowl with something left in it you could hardly resist licking it out. But Shukhov had never forgotten the words of his first squad leader, Kuziomin — a hard-bitten prisoner who had already been in for twelve years by 1943 — who told the newcomers, just in from the front, as they sat beside a fire in a desolate cutting in the forest:

"Here, men, we live by the law of the taiga.[2] But even here people manage to live. The ones that don't make it are those who lick other men's leftovers, those who count on the doctors to pull the through, and those that squeal on their buddies."

As for squealers, he was wrong there. Those people were sure to get through the camp alright. Only, they were saving their own skin at the expense of other people's blood.

Shukhov always arose at reveille. But this day he didn't. He had felt strange the evening before, feverish, with pains all over his body. He hadn't been able to get warm all through the night. Even in his sleep he had felt at one moment that he was getting seriously ill, at another that he was getting better. He had wished morning would never come.

But morning came as usual.

Anyway, where would you get warm in a place like this, with the windows iced over and the white cobwebs of frost all along the huge barracks where the walls joined the ceiling!

He didn't get up. He lay there in his bunk on the top tier, his head buried in a blanket and a coat, both feet stuffed into one tucked-up sleeve of his wadded jacket.

---

[1] **valenki**: Knee-high felt boots worn in winter.
[2] **taiga**: Cold, coniferous forestland. The taiga comprises a large portion of Siberia, where the camps were located.

He couldn't see, but his ears told him everything going on in the barrack room and especially in the corner his squad occupied. He heard the heavy tread of the orderlies carrying one of the big barrels of excrement along the passage outside. A light job, that was considered, a job for the infirm, but just you try and carry out the muck without spilling any. He heard some of the 75th slamming bunches of boots onto the floor from the drying shed. Now their own men were doing it (it was their own squad's turn, too, to dry valenki). Tiurin, the squad leader, and his deputy Pavlo put on their valenki without a word but he heard their bunks creaking. Now Pavlo would be going off to the bread-storage and Tiurin to the staff quarters to see the P.P.D.[3]

Ah, but not simply to report as usual to the authorities for the daily assignment. Shukhov remembered that this morning his fate hung in the balance: they wanted to shift the 104th from the building shops to a new site, the "Socialist Way of Life" settlement. It lay in open country covered with snowdrifts, and before anything else could be done there they would have to dig holes and put up posts and attach barbed wire to them. Wire themselves in, so that they wouldn't run away. Only then would they start building.

There wouldn't be a warm corner for a whole month. Not even a doghouse. And fires were out of the question. There was nothing to build them with. Let your work warm you up, that was your only salvation.

No wonder the squad leader looked so worried, that was his job — to elbow some other squad, some bunch of suckers, into the assignment of the 104th. Of course with empty hands you got nowhere. He'd have to take a pound of salt pork to the senior official there, if not a couple of pounds.

There's never any harm in trying, so why not have a go at the dispensary and get a few days off if you can? After all, he did feel as though every limb was out of joint.

Then Shukhov wondered which of the campguards was on duty that morning. It was "One-and-a-half" Ivan's turn, he recalled. Ivan was a thin, weedy, dark-eyed sergeant. At first sight he looked like a real bastard, but when you got to know him he turned out to be the most good-natured of the guards on duty; he didn't put you in the guardhouse, he didn't haul you off before the authorities. So Shukhov decided he could lie in his bunk a little longer, at least while Barracks 9 was at the mess hall.

---

[3] **PPD**: Production Planning Department.

The whole four-bunk frame began to shake and sway. Two of its occupants were getting up at the same time: Shukhov's top-tier neighbor, Alyosha the Baptist, and Buinovsky, the ex-naval captain down below.

The orderlies, after removing both barrels of excrement, began to quarrel about which of them should go for hot water. They quarreled naggingly, like old women.

"Hey you, cackling like a couple of hens!" bellowed the electric welder in the 20th squad. "Get going." He flung a boot at them.

The boot thudded against a post. The squabbling stopped.

In the next squad the deputy squad leader growled quietly: "Vasily Fyodorovich, they've cheated us again at the supply depot, the dirty rats. They should have given us four twenty-five ounce loaves and I've only got three. Who's going to go short?"

He kept his voice down, but of course everyone in the squad heard him and waited fearfully to learn who would be losing a slice of bread that evening.

Shukhov went on lying on his sawdust mattress, as hard as a board from long wear. If only it could be one thing or the other — let him fall into a real fever or let his aching joints ease up.

Meanwhile Alyosha was murmuring his prayers and Buinovsky had returned from the latrines, announcing to no one in particular but with a sort of malicious glee: "Well, sailors, grit your teeth. It's twenty below, for sure."

Shukhov decided to report sick.

At that very moment his blanket and jacket were imperiously jerked off him. He flung his coat away from his face and sat up. Looking up at him, his head level with the top bunk, was the lean figure of The Tartar.

So the fellow was on duty out of turn and had stolen up.

"S 854," The Tartar read from the white strip that had been stitched to the back of his black jacket. "Three days' penalty with work."

The moment they heard that peculiar choking voice of his, everyone who wasn't up yet in the whole dimly lit barracks, where two hundred men slept in bug-ridden bunks, stirred to life and began dressing in a hurry.

"What for, citizen chief?" asked Shukhov with more chagrin than he felt in his voice.

With work — that wasn't half so bad. They gave you hot food and you had no time to start thinking. Real jail was when you were kept back from work.

"Failing to get up at reveille. Follow me to the camp commandant's office," said The Tartar lazily.

His crumpled, hairless face was imperturbable. He turned, looking around for another victim, but now everybody, in dim corners and under the lights, in upper bunks and in lower, had thrust their legs into their black wadded trousers or, already dressed, had wrapped their coats around themselves and hurried to the door to get out of the way until The Tartar had left.

Had Shukhov been punished for something he deserved he wouldn't have felt so resentful. What hurt him was that he was always one of the first to be up. But he knew he couldn't plead with The Tartar. And, protesting merely for the sake of form, he hitched up his trousers (a bedraggled scrap of cloth had been sewn on them, just above the left knee, with a faded black number), slipped on his jacket (here the same digits appeared twice — on the chest and on the back), fished his valenki from the heap on the floor, put his hat on (with his number on a patch of cloth at the front), and followed The Tartar out of the barrack room.

The whole 104th saw him go, but no one said a word — what was the use, and anyway what could they say? The squad leader might have tried to do something, but he wasn't there. And Shukhov said nothing to anyone. He didn't want to irritate The Tartar. Anyway he could rely on the others in his squad to keep his breakfast for him.

The two men left the barracks. The cold made Shukhov gasp.

Two powerful searchlights swept the camp from the farthest watchtowers. The border lights, as well as those inside the camp, were on. There were so many of them that they outshone the stars.

With the snow creaking under their boots, the prisoners hurried away, each on his own business, some to the parcels office, some to hand in cereals to be cooked in the "individual" kitchen. All kept their heads down, buried in their buttoned-up coats, and all were chilled to the bone, not so much from the actual cold as from the prospect of having to spend the whole day in it. But The Tartar in his old army coat with the greasy blue tabs walked at a steady pace, as though the cold meant nothing to him.

They walked past the high wooden fence around the guardhouse, the only brick building in the camp; past the barbed wire that protected the camp bakery from the prisoners; past the corner of the staff quarters where the length of frosted rail hung on thick strands of wire; past another pole with a thermometer hanging on it (in a sheltered spot, so that the registered temperature shouldn't drop too low). Shukhov looked hopefully out of the corner of an eye at the milk-white tube — if it had shown –41° they ought not to be sent out to work. But today it was nowhere near –41°.

They walked into the staff quarters and The Tartar led him straight to the guardroom; and Shukhov realized, as he had guessed on the way there, that he wasn't being sent to the guardhouse at all — it was simply that the guardroom floor needed scrubbing. The Tartar told him he was going to let him off, and ordered him to scrub the floor.

Scrubbing the guardroom floor had been the job of a special prisoner who wasn't sent to work outside the camp — a staff orderly. The fellow had long ago made himself at home in the staff quarters; he had access to the offices of the camp commandant, the man in charge of discipline, and the security officer (the Father Confessor, they called him). When working for them he sometimes heard things that even the guards didn't know, and after a time he got a big head and came to consider scrubbing the floor for rank-and-file campguards a bit beneath him. Having sent for him once or twice, the guards discovered what was in the wind and began to pick on other prisoners for floor-scrubbing.

In the guardroom the stove was throwing out a fierce heat. Two guards in grubby tunics were playing checkers, and a third, who had not bothered to remove his sheepskin and valenki, lay snoring on a narrow bench. In one corner of the room stood an empty pail with a rag inside.

Shukhov was delighted. He thanked The Tartar for letting him off and said: "From now on I'll never get up late again."

The rule in this place was a simple one: when you'd finished you left. And now that he'd been given work to do, Shukhov's aches and pains seemed to have gone. He picked up the pail and, bare-handed — in his hurry he'd forgotten to take his mittens from under his pillow — went to the well.

Several of the squad leaders who were on their way to the P.P.D. had gathered near the pole with the thermometer, and one of the younger ones, a former Hero of the Soviet Union, shinnied up it and wiped off the instrument.

The others shouted advice from below:

"See you don't breathe on it. It'll push up the temperature."

"Push it up? Not fucking likely. *My* breath won't have any effect."

Tiurin of the 104th — Shukhov's squad — was not among them. Shukhov put down the pail, tucked his hands into his sleeves, and watched with interest.

The man up the pole shouted hoarsely: "Seventeen and a half. Not a damn bit more."

And, taking another look for sure, slid down.

"Oh, it's cockeyed. It always lies," someone said. "Do you think they'd ever hang one up that gave the true temperature?"

The squad leaders scattered. Shukhov ran to the well. The frost was trying to nip his ears under his earflaps, which he had lowered but not tied.

The top of the well was so thickly coated with ice that he only just managed to slip the bucket into the hole. The rope hung stiff as a ramrod.

With numb hands he carried the dripping bucket back to the guard-room and plunged his hands into the water. It felt warm.

The Tartar was no longer there. The guards — there were four now — stood in a group. They'd given up their checkers and their nap and were arguing about how much cereal they were going to get in January (food was in short supply at the settlement, and although rationing had long since come to an end, certain articles were sold to them, at a discount, which were not available to the civilian inhabitants).

"Shut that door, you scum. There's a draft," said one of the guards.

No sense in getting your boots wet in the morning. Even if Shukhov had dashed back to his barracks he wouldn't have found another pair to change into. During eight years' imprisonment he had known various systems for allocating footwear: there'd been times when he'd gone through the winter without valenki at all, or leather boots either, and had had to make shift with rope sandals or a sort of galoshes made of scraps of motor tires — "Chetezes" they called them, after the Cheliabinsk tractor works. Now the footwear situation seemed better; in October Shukhov had received (thanks to Pavlo, whom he trailed to the warehouse) a pair of ordinary, hard-wearing leather boots, big enough for a double thickness of rags inside. For a week he went about as though he'd been given a birthday present, kicking his new heels. Then in December the valenki arrived, and, oh, wasn't life wonderful?

But some devil in the bookkeeper's office had whispered in the commandant's ear that valenki should be issued only to those who surrendered their boots. It was against the rules for a prisoner to possess two pairs of footwear at the same time. So Shukhov had to choose. Either he'd have to wear leather throughout the winter, or surrender the boots and wear valenki even in the thaw. He'd taken such good care of his new boots, softening the leather with grease! Ah, nothing had been so hard to part with in all his eight years in camps as that pair of boots! They were tossed into a common heap. Not a hope of finding your own pair in the spring.

READING AND DISCUSSION QUESTIONS

1. What motivations does Solzhenitsyn ascribe to the inhabitants of the gulags? Do they seem particularly criminal to you? Why or why not?

2. In what ways could this passage contradict the official Soviet image of the U.S.S.R. as a "worker's paradise"?

3. What motivations might the Soviet leadership have had for allowing this publication?

DOCUMENT 29-3

GENERALS LESLIE GROVES AND THOMAS F. FARRELL

Witnesses to the Birth of the Atomic Age

July 18, 1945

All major nations involved in World War II, including Japan, had active programs to develop an atomic bomb. Fears of apocalyptic destruction from the air dated from the early twentieth century, but by 1945 the United States had created the means to achieve and deploy it. On August 6 and 9, 1945, the Japanese cities of Hiroshima and Nagasaki witnessed the horrors of nuclear destruction in two U.S. strikes. In the aftermath, fears of nuclear obliteration intensified in both the West and the East, especially after Soviet detonation of its own atomic bomb in 1949.

TOP SECRET
MEMORANDUM FOR THE SECRETARY OF WAR.
SUBJECT: THE TEST.

1. This is not a concise, formal military report but an attempt to recite what I would have told you if you had been here on my return from New Mexico.

2. At 0530, 16 July 1945, in a remote section of the Alamogordo Air Base, New Mexico, the first full scale test was made of the implosion type

From Martin Sherwin, *A World Destroyed* (New York: Vintage Books, 1976), pp. 308–312.

atomic fission bomb. For the first time in history there was a nuclear explosion. And what an explosion! It resulted from the atomic fission of about 13½ pounds of plutonium which was compressed by the detonation of a surrounding sphere of some 5000 pounds of high explosives. The bomb was not dropped from an airplane but was exploded on a platform on top of a 100-foot high steel tower.

3. The test was successful beyond the most optimistic expectations of anyone. . . . There were tremendous blast effects. For a brief period there was a lighting effect within a radius of 20 miles equal to several suns in midday; a huge ball of fire was formed which lasted for several seconds. This ball mushroomed and rose to a height of over ten thousand feet before it dimmed. The light from the explosion was seen clearly at Albuquerque, Santa Fe, Silver City, El Paso and other points generally to about 180 miles away. The sound was heard to the same distance in a few instances but generally to about 100 miles. Only a few windows were broken although one was some 125 miles away. A massive cloud was formed which surged and billowed upward with tremendous power, reaching the substratosphere at an elevation of 41,000 feet, 36,000 feet above the ground, in about five minutes. . . . Huge concentrations of highly radioactive materials resulted from the fission and were contained in this cloud.

4. A crater from which all vegetation had vanished, with a diameter of 1200 feet and a slight slope toward the center, was formed. In the center was a shallow bowl 130 feet in diameter and 6 feet in depth. The material within the crater was deeply pulverized dirt. The material within the outer circle is greenish and can be distinctly seen from as much as 5 miles away. The steel from the tower was evaporated. 1500 feet away there was a four-inch iron pipe 16 feet high set in concrete and strongly guyed. It disappeared completely. . . .

11. Brigadier General Thomas F. Farrell was at the control shelter located 10,000 yards south of the point of explosion. His impressions are given below:

"The scene inside the shelter was dramatic beyond words. In and around the shelter were some twenty-odd people concerned with last minute arrangements prior to firing the shot. Included were: Dr. Oppenheimer,[4] the Director who had borne the great scientific burden of

---

[4] **Dr. Oppenheimer**: J. Robert Oppenheimer; civilian head of the project (Groves was the military head) who later came to oppose the development and deployment of nuclear weapons. He was stripped of his security clearance and blacklisted in 1954 for his loose communist affiliations in the 1930s.

developing the weapon from the raw materials made in Tennessee and Washington, and a dozen of his key scientists. . . .

"For some hectic two hours preceding the blast, General Groves stayed with the Director, walking with him and steadying his tense excitement. Every time the Director would be about to explode because of some untoward happening, General Groves would take him off and walk with him in the rain, counselling with him and reassuring him that everything would be all right. . . .

"Just after General Groves left, announcements began to be broadcast of the interval remaining before the blast. They were sent by radio to the other groups participating in and observing the test. As the time interval grew smaller and changed from minutes to seconds, the tension increased by leaps and bounds. Everyone in that room knew the awful potentialities of the thing that they thought was about to happen. The scientists felt that their figuring must be right and that the bomb had to go off but there was in everyone's mind a strong measure of doubt. The feeling of many could be expressed by 'Lord, I believe; help Thou mine unbelief.' We were reaching into the unknown and we did not know what might come of it. It can be safely said that most of those present — Christian, Jew, and Atheist — were praying and praying harder than they had ever prayed before. If the shot were successful, it was a justification of the several years of intensive effort of tens of thousands of people — statesmen, scientists, subatomic universe. . . .

"In that brief instant in the remote New Mexico desert the tremendous effort of the brains and brawn of all these people came suddenly and startlingly to the fullest fruition. Dr. Oppenheimer, on whom had rested a very heavy burden, grew tenser as the last seconds ticked off. He scarcely breathed. He held on to a post to steady himself. For the last few seconds, he stared directly ahead and then when the announcer shouted 'Now!' and there came this tremendous burst of light followed shortly thereafter by the deep growling roar of the explosion, his face relaxed into an expression of tremendous relief. Several of the observers standing back of the shelter to watch the lighting effects were knocked flat by the blast.

"The tension in the room let up and all started congratulating each other. Everyone sensed 'This is it!' No matter what might happen now all knew that the impossible scientific job had been done. Atomic fission would no longer be hidden in the cloisters of the theoretical physicists' dreams. It was almost full grown at birth. It was a great new force to be used for good or for evil. There was a feeling in that shelter that those concerned with its nativity should dedicate their lives to the mission that it would always be used for good and never for evil. . . .

"The effects could well be called unprecedented, magnificent, beautiful, stupendous and terrifying. No man-made phenomenon of such tremendous power had ever occurred before. The lighting effects beggared description. The whole country was lighted by a searing light with the intensity many times that of the midday sun. It was golden, purple, violet, gray, and blue. It lighted every peak, crevasse and ridge of the nearby mountain range with a clarity and beauty that cannot be described but must be seen to be imagined. It was that beauty the great poets dream about but describe most poorly and inadequately. Thirty seconds after the explosion came first, the air blast pressing hard against the people and things, to be followed almost immediately by the strong, sustained, awesome roar which warned of doomsday and made us feel that we puny things were blasphemous to dare tamper with the forces heretofore reserved to The Almighty. Words are inadequate tools for the job of acquainting those not present with the physical, mental and psychological effects. It had to be witnessed to be realized."

READING AND DISCUSSION QUESTIONS

1. Given the destructiveness of the atomic bomb, what motivations did the scientists and soldiers have for celebrating the successful test?

2. In what technical features of the bomb does General Groves seem interested?

3. What hints of unease over the power of atomic weapons can you find in the document? Does General Groves seem to share General Farrell's sentiment?

VIEWPOINTS

Criticisms of a "Civilized" Europe

DOCUMENT 29-4

FRANTZ FANON

The Wretched of the Earth

1961

World War II bankrupted the great European empires, and emerging science undermined the rhetoric of white supremacy that undergirded those empires. The Soviets also proclaimed their support for "Wars of National Liberation," since most of those movements were aimed at America's allies. Decoloniza-tion movements gathered force, and while the British retreated from empire mostly peacefully, the French fought bitterly in Vietnam (1945–1954) and Algeria (1954–1963). Key to the process of decolonization was the realiza-tion of the colonized that they possessed their own culture and worth. Here a European-trained Algerian psychiatrist, Frantz Fanon, denounces Europe as fundamentally uncivilized.

Come, then, comrades; it would be as well to decide at once to change our ways. We must shake off the heavy darkness in which we were plunged, and leave it behind. The new day which is already at hand must find us firm, prudent, and resolute.

We must leave our dreams and abandon our old beliefs and friend-ships of the time before life began. Let us waste no time in sterile litanies and nauseating mimicry. Leave this Europe where they are never done talking of Man, yet murder men everywhere they find them, at the corner of every one of their own streets, in all the corners of the globe. For centu-ries they have stifled almost the whole of humanity in the name of a so-called spiritual experience. Look at them today swaying between atomic and spiritual disintegration.

From Frantz Fanon, *The Wretched of the Earth*, trans. Constance Farrington (New York: Grove Press, 1963), pp. 311–316. Marxists Internet Archive, http://marxists.org/subject/africa/fanon/conclusion.htm, accessed March 1, 2010.

And yet it may be said that Europe has been successful in as much as everything that she has attempted has succeeded.

Europe undertook the leadership of the world with ardor, cynicism, and violence. Look at how the shadow of her palaces stretches out ever farther! Every one of her movements has burst the bounds of space and thought. Europe has declined all humility and all modesty; but she has also set her face against all solicitude and all tenderness.

She has only shown herself parsimonious and niggardly where men are concerned; it is only men that she has killed and devoured.

So, my brothers, how is it that we do not understand that we have better things to do than to follow that same Europe?

That same Europe where they were never done talking of Man, and where they never stopped proclaiming that they were only anxious for the welfare of Man: today we know with what sufferings humanity has paid for every one of their triumphs of the mind.

Come, then, comrades, the European game has finally ended; we must find something different. We today can do everything, so long as we do not imitate Europe, so long as we are not obsessed by the desire to catch up with Europe.

Europe now lives at such a mad, reckless pace that she has shaken off all guidance and all reason, and she is running headlong into the abyss; we would do well to avoid it with all possible speed.

Yet it is very true that we need a model, and that we want blueprints and examples. For many among us the European model is the most inspiring. We have therefore seen in the preceding pages to what mortifying setbacks such an imitation has led us. European achievements, European techniques, and the European style ought no longer to tempt us and to throw us off our balance.

When I search for Man in the technique and the style of Europe, I see only a succession of negations of man, and an avalanche of murders.

The human condition, plans for mankind, and collaboration between men in those tasks which increase the sum total of humanity are new problems, which demand true inventions.

Let us decide not to imitate Europe; let us combine our muscles and our brains in a new direction. Let us try to create the whole man, whom Europe has been incapable of bringing to triumphant birth.

Two centuries ago, a former European colony decided to catch up with Europe. It succeeded so well that the United States of America became a monster, in which the taints, the sickness, and the inhumanity of Europe have grown to appalling dimensions.

Comrades, have we not other work to do than to create a third Europe? The West saw itself as a spiritual adventure. It is in the name of the spirit, in the name of the spirit of Europe, that Europe has made her encroachments, that she has justified her crimes and legitimized the slavery in which she holds four-fifths of humanity.

Yes, the European spirit has strange roots. All European thought has unfolded in places which were increasingly more deserted and more encircled by precipices; and thus it was that the custom grew up in those places of very seldom meeting man.

A permanent dialogue with oneself and an increasingly obscene narcissism never ceased to prepare the way for a half delirious state, where intellectual work became suffering and the reality was not at all that of a living man, working and creating himself, but rather words, different combinations of words, and the tensions springing from the meanings contained in words. Yet some Europeans were found to urge the European workers to shatter this narcissism and to break with this unreality.

But in general the workers of Europe have not replied to these calls; for the workers believe, too, that they are part of the prodigious adventure of the European spirit.

All the elements of a solution to the great problems of humanity have, at different times, existed in European thought. But Europeans have not carried out in practice the mission which fell to them, which consisted of bringing their whole weight to bear violently upon these elements, of modifying their arrangement and their nature, of changing them and, finally, of bringing the problem of mankind to an infinitely higher plane.

Today, we are present at the stasis of Europe. Comrades, let us flee from this motionless movement where gradually dialectic is changing into the logic of equilibrium. Let us reconsider the question of mankind. Let us reconsider the question of cerebral reality and of the cerebral mass of all humanity, whose connections must be increased, whose channels must be diversified and whose messages must be re-humanized.

Come, brothers, we have far too much work to do for us to play the game of rearguard. Europe has done what she set out to do and on the whole she has done it well; let us stop blaming her, but let us say to her firmly that she should not make such a song and dance about it. We have no more to fear; so let us stop envying her.

The Third World today faces Europe like a colossal mass whose aim should be to try to resolve the problems to which Europe has not been able to find the answers.

But let us be clear: what matters is to stop talking about output, and intensification, and the rhythm of work.

No, there is no question of a return to Nature. It is simply a very concrete question of not dragging men towards mutilation, of not imposing upon the brain rhythms which very quickly obliterate it and wreck it. The pretext of catching up must not be used to push man around, to tear him away from himself or from his privacy, to break and kill him.

No, we do not want to catch up with anyone. What we want to do is to go forward all the time, night and day, in the company of Man, in the company of all men. The caravan should not be stretched out, for in that case each line will hardly see those who precede it; and men who no longer recognize each other meet less and less together, and talk to each other less and less.

It is a question of the Third World starting a new history of Man, a history which will have regard to the sometimes prodigious theses which Europe has put forward, but which will also not forget Europe's crimes, of which the most horrible was committed in the heart of man, and consisted of the pathological tearing apart of his functions and the crumbling away of his unity. And in the framework of the collectivity there were the differentiations, the stratification and the bloodthirsty tensions fed by classes; and finally, on the immense scale of humanity, there were racial hatreds, slavery, exploitation, and above all the bloodless genocide which consisted in the setting aside of fifteen thousand millions of men.

So, comrades, let us not pay tribute to Europe by creating states, institutions, and societies which draw their inspiration from her.

Humanity is waiting for something other from us than such an imitation, which would be almost an obscene caricature.

If we want to turn Africa into a new Europe, and America into a new Europe, then let us leave the destiny of our countries to Europeans. They will know how to do it better than the most gifted among us.

But if we want humanity to advance a step farther, if we want to bring it up to a different level than that which Europe has shown it, then we must invent and we must make discoveries.

If we wish to live up to our peoples' expectations, we must seek the response elsewhere than in Europe.

Moreover, if we wish to reply to the expectations of the people of Europe, it is no good sending them back a reflection, even an ideal reflection, of their society and their thought with which from time to time they feel immeasurably sickened.

For Europe, for ourselves and for humanity, comrades, we must turn over a new leaf, we must work out new concepts, and try to set afoot a new man.

READING AND DISCUSSION QUESTIONS

1. What is Fanon's fundamental critique of Western society? What evidence does he use to support these claims?

2. How does Fanon's training as a psychiatrist show through in his discussion of the flaws of the West?

3. Why might Fanon argue that a "return to nature" is neither possible nor desirable? Does this mean that he still accepts part of the European worldview?

DOCUMENT 29-5

SIMONE DE BEAUVOIR
The Second Sex: *Existential Feminism*
1949

In twentieth-century Europe, women achieved many goals of the nineteenth century's feminists, notably the rights to vote and to own property. Simone de Beauvoir (1908–1986) — a French writer and companion of the existentialist philosopher Jean-Paul Sartre — was part of the generation of women who wanted full inclusion in society, but realized that suffrage and proprietary equality did not always translate to social equality. De Beauvoir's writing took up the complex issues of attitudes and values, and was particularly concerned with the persistence of traditional attitudes long after the circumstances that had created them had evolved.

French law no longer includes obedience among a wife's duties, and every woman citizen has become a voter; these civic liberties remain abstract if

From Simone de Beauvoir, *The Second Sex*, trans. Constance Borde and Sheila Malovany-Chevallier (New York: Alfred A. Knopf, 2010), pp. 721–723, 735–736, 751.

there is no corresponding economic autonomy; the kept woman — wife or mistress — is not freed from the male just because she has a ballot paper in her hands; while today's customs impose fewer constraints on her than in the past, such negative licenses have not fundamentally changed her situation; she remains a vassal, imprisoned in her condition. It is through work that woman has been able, to a large extent, to close the gap separating her from the male; work alone can guarantee her concrete freedom. The system based on her dependence collapses as soon as she ceases to be a parasite; there is no longer need for a masculine mediator between her and the universe. The curse on the woman vassal is that she is not allowed to do anything; so she stubbornly pursues the impossible quest for being through narcissism, love, or religion. . . . It is also understandable that a shopgirl, an office worker, or a secretary should not want to give up the advantages of having a male to lean on. I have already said that it is an almost irresistible temptation for a young woman to be part of a privileged caste when she can do so simply by surrendering her body; she is doomed to have love affairs because her wages are minimal for the very high standard of living society demands of her; if she settles for what she earns, she will be no more than a pariah: without decent living accommodations or clothes, all amusement and even love will be refused her. Virtuous people preach asceticism to her; in fact, her diet is often as austere as a Carmelite's; but not everyone can have God as a lover: she needs to please men to succeed in her life as a woman. So she will accept help: her employer cynically counts on this when he pays her a pittance. Sometimes this help will enable her to improve her situation and achieve real independence; but sometimes she will give up her job to become a kept woman. She often does both: she frees herself from her lover through work, and she escapes work thanks to her lover; but then she experiences the double servitude of a job and masculine protection. For the married woman, her salary usually only means extra income; for the "woman who is helped," it is the man's protection that seems inessential; but neither woman buys total independence through her own efforts.

However, there are quite a lot of privileged women today who have gained economic and social autonomy in their professions. They are the ones who are at issue when the question of women's possibilities and their future is raised. While they are still only a minority, it is particularly interesting to study their situation closely; they are the subject of continuing debate between feminists and antifeminists. The latter maintain that today's emancipated women do not accomplish anything important, and that besides they have trouble finding their inner balance. The former exaggerate the emancipated women's achievements and are blind to their frustrations. . . .

There is one female function that is still almost impossible to undertake in complete freedom, and that is motherhood; in England and in America, the woman can at least refuse it at will, thanks to the practice of birth control; we have seen that in France she is often compelled to have painful and costly abortions;[5] she often finds herself burdened with a child she did not want, ruining her professional life. If this burden is a heavy one, it is because, inversely, social norms do not allow the woman to procreate as she pleases: the unwed mother causes scandal, and for the child an illegitimate birth is a stain; it is rare for a woman to become a mother without accepting the chains of marriage or lowering herself. If the idea of artificial insemination interests women so much, it is not because they wish to avoid male lovemaking: it is because they hope that voluntary motherhood will finally be accepted by society. It must be added that given the lack of well-organized day nurseries and kindergartens, even one child is enough to entirely paralyze a woman's activity; she can continue to work only by abandoning the child to her parents, friends, or servants. She has to choose between sterility, often experienced as a painful frustration, and burdens hardly compatible with a career.

Thus the independent woman today is divided between her professional interests and the concerns of her sexual vocation; she has trouble finding her balance; if she does, it is at the price of concessions, sacrifices, and juggling that keep her in constant tension. . . .

The free woman is just being born; when she conquers herself, she will perhaps justify Rimbaud's[6] prophecy: "Poets will be. When woman's infinite servitude is broken, when she lives for herself and by herself, man — abominable until now — giving her her freedom, she too will be a poet! Woman will find the unknown! Will her worlds of ideas differ from ours? She will find strange, unfathomable, repugnant, delicious things, we will take them, we will understand them." Her "worlds of ideas" are not necessarily different from men's, because she will free herself by assimilating them; to know how singular she will remain and how important these singularities will continue to be, one would have to make some foolhardy

---

[5] **birth control . . . costly abortions**: French women did not gain legal access to contraceptives until 1967, whereas Americans gained full access in 1936. Abortion was illegal in both countries in 1949, becoming legal in the United States in 1973 and in France in 1975.

[6] **Rimbaud**: Arthur Rimbaud (1854–1891); radical French poet.

predictions. What is beyond doubt is that until now women's possibilities have been stifled and lost to humanity, and in her and everyone's interest it is high time she be left to take her own chances.

READING AND DISCUSSION QUESTIONS

1. Based on this excerpt, what does "equality" mean to Simone de Beauvoir?

2. What problems does de Beauvoir see for women attempting to achieve her definition of equality?

3. What reasons could women have for not wanting to achieve the sort of liberation de Beauvoir promotes?

4. Based on your reading, what would de Beauvoir like to see change?

COMPARATIVE QUESTIONS

1. What similarities in outlook can you discern between George Marshall and Leslie Groves? How might the two differ in pursuit of their goals?

2. Based on *One Day in the Life of Ivan Denisovich*, would Frantz Fanon include the Soviet Union in his denunciation of the West? What would that suggest about the nature of the Cold War?

3. Based on her document, what critiques might Simone de Beauvoir make of Fanon's work? In what areas would they agree?

4. Compare Fanon's perspective to those of the documents of Chapter 25. How does his vision of the West compare to the ones found there?

5. How did ideas about feminism and women's rights change from the time that Mary Wollstonecraft wrote her *Vindication of the Rights of Woman* (Document 20-5) to when de Beauvoir wrote *The Second Sex*? What continuities in thinking can you discern?

CHAPTER 30

Challenging the Postwar Order

1960–1991

The West and the Soviets both faced identity crises in the 1970s and 1980s. Economic difficulties in the seventies, West and East, began to suggest that the promised lands of capitalism and communism were still incomplete. The workers for whom the Soviet bloc was ostensibly run began to grow restless, while the consumer society that the West created began to exhibit discontent as well. In the communist world the growing tide of protest proved difficult to stop, and by 1990 major demonstrations had either toppled or severely damaged the Soviet empire's members. The consumer society that seemed to beguile eastern Europe proved more able to win over its critics, but popular culture in the 1960s and 1970s began to reflect unease with the spread of cheap, mass-produced — and American — commodities.

VIEWPOINTS

Reforming Socialist Societies

DOCUMENT 30-1

SOLIDARITY UNION

Twenty-One Demands: A Call for Workers' Rights and Freedoms in a Socialist State

1980

Soviet control of eastern Europe did not go uncontested. Soviet troops intervened in Hungary in 1956 and crushed a 1968 reform movement in

"The Twenty-One Demands," in *The Passion of Poland*, by Lawrence Weschler (New York: Pantheon, 1984), pp. 206–208.

Czechoslovakia. Polish resistance in the 1980s emerged from the anti-communist shipbuilder's union Solidarność (Solidarity), in the port city of Gdansk. Shipyard workers looking for a better life hung the "Twenty-One Demands" at the entrance to a shipyard on a pair of wooden boards, since all media outlets were state-controlled. Labor unions and strikes were illegal in the Soviet empire, but Solidarity, headed by worker Lech Walesa, success-fully directed a group of ex-communist ally parties in broad resistance to the Soviets. In 1989, negotiations between Solidarity and the Community Party led to semi-free Polish elections.

1. Acceptance of Free Trade Unions independent of both the Party and employers, in accordance with the International Labor Organization's Convention number 87 on the freedom to form unions, which was ratified by the Polish government.
2. A guarantee of the right to strike and guarantees of security for strikers and their supporters.
3. Compliance with the freedoms of press and publishing guaranteed in the Polish constitution. A halt to repression of independent publica-tions and access to the mass media for representatives of all faiths.
4. (a) Reinstatement to their former positions for: people fired for defend-ing workers' rights, in particular those participating in the strikes of 1970 and 1976; students dismissed from school for their convictions.
   (b) The release of all political prisoners. . . .
   (c) A halt to repression for one's convictions.
5. The broadcasting on the mass media of information about the estab-lishment of the Interfactory Strike Committee (MKS) and publication of the list of demands.
6. The undertaking of real measures to get the country out of its present crisis by:
   (a) providing comprehensive, public information about the socioeco-nomic situation;
   (b) making it possible for people from every social class and stratum of society to participate in open discussions concerning the reform program.
7. Compensation of all workers taking part in the strike for its duration with holiday pay from the Central Council of Trade Unions.[1]

---

[1] **Central Council of Trade Unions**: Official Soviet union organization, state-run and officially responsible for preventing the sorts of situations about which the workers complained in Gdansk.

8. Raise the base pay of every worker 2,000 zlotys[2] per month to compensate for price rises to date.

9. Guaranteed automatic pay raises indexed to price inflation and to decline in real income.

10. Meeting the requirements of the domestic market for food products: only surplus goods to be exported.

11. The rationing of meat and meat products through food coupons (until the market is stabilized).

12. Abolition of "commercial prices" and hard currency sales in so-called "internal export" shops.[3]

13. A system of merit selection for management positions on the basis of qualifications rather than [Communist] Party membership. Abolition of the privileged status of MO[4] SB[5] and the party apparatus through: equalizing all family subsidies; eliminating special stores, etc.

14. Reduction of retirement age for women to 50 and for men to 55. Anyone who has worked in the PRL [Polish People's Republic] for 30 years, for women, or 35 years for men, without regard to age, should be entitled to retirement benefits.

15. Bringing pensions and retirement benefits of the "old portfolio" to the level of those paid currently.

16. Improvement in the working conditions of the Health Service, which would assure full medical care to working people.

17. Provision for sufficient openings in daycare nurseries and preschools for the children of working people.

18. Establishment of three-year paid maternity leaves for the raising of children.

19. Reduce the waiting time for apartments.

20. Raise per diem [allowance for work-related travel] from 40 zlotys to 100 zlotys and provide cost-of-living increases.

21. Saturdays to be days off from work. Those who work on round-the-clock jobs or three-shift systems should have the lack of free Saturdays

---

[2] **zloty**: Basic unit of Polish currency; not convertible into Western currency at the time. It was losing value due to rising inflation.

[3] **"internal export" shops**: State-run shops where people with Western currency could buy consumer goods not available to workers paid in zlotys (the government had introduced a special type of currency), as part of the communist government's efforts to keep its economy afloat.

[4] **MO**: *Milicja Obywatelska* ("People's Militia"); the main Polish police force.

[5] **SB**: *Służba Bezpieczeństwa*, literally "Security Service," the communist secret police; roughly analogous to the Russian KGB.

compensated by increased holiday leaves or through other paid holidays off from work.

READING AND DISCUSSION QUESTIONS

1. What sort of problems do Solidarity's leaders see with their workplace?

2. What does the document reveal about the relationship between the current Polish governance and the reality of everyday life in Soviet-occupied Europe? What do the workers consider the standard of care?

3. Although these demands were made against a communist state, in what ways do the authors accept the premise that the state has a responsibility to its citizens?

DOCUMENT 30-2

MIKHAIL GORBACHEV

Perestroika: New Thinking for Our Country and the World

1987

Soviet leadership in the late 1970s increasingly refused to adapt their ideology to real-world conditions, to disastrous effect. Years of focus on military production and heavy industry had created a shortage of consumer goods, a situation that led the West German chancellor to liken the Soviet Union to an abysmally poor African country, but with rockets. When Mikhail Gorbachev (GORE-beh-chof) rose to become head of the Communist Party in 1985, he worked to reform the Soviet economy and the apparatus by which the party controlled information. These changes were referred to, respectively, as perestroika — *"restructuring" — and* glasnost — *"openness."*

Perestroika is an urgent necessity arising from the profound processes of development in our socialist society. This society is ripe for change. It has

---

From Mikhail Gorbachev, *Perestroika: New Thinking for Our Country and the World* (New York: Harper & Row, 1987), pp. 3–5, 7–8, 10, 22–24.

long been yearning for it. Any delay in beginning perestroika could have led to an exacerbated internal situation in the near future, which, to put it bluntly, would have been fraught with serious social, economic and political crises. . . .

In the latter half of the seventies — something happened that was at first sight inexplicable. The country began to lose momentum. Economic failures became more frequent. Difficulties began to accumulate and deteriorate, and unresolved problems to multiply. Elements of what we call stagnation and other phenomena alien to socialism began to appear in the life of society. A kind of "braking mechanism" affecting social and economic development formed. And all this happened at a time when scientific and technological revolution opened up new prospects for economic and social progress. . . .

An absurd situation was developing. The Soviet Union, the world's biggest producer of steel, raw materials, fuel and energy, has shortfalls in them due to wasteful or inefficient use. One of the biggest producers of grain for food, it nevertheless has to buy millions of tons of grain a year for fodder. We have the largest number of doctors and hospital beds per thousand of the population and, at the same time, there are glaring shortcomings in our health services. Our rockets can find Halley's comet and fly to Venus with amazing accuracy, but side by side with these scientific and technological triumphs is an obvious lack of efficiency in using scientific achievements for economic needs, and many Soviet household appliances are of poor quality.

This, unfortunately, is not all. A gradual erosion of the ideological and moral values of our people began.

It was obvious to everyone that the growth rates were sharply dropping and that the entire mechanism of quality control was not working properly; there was a lack of receptivity to the advances in science and technology; the improvement in living standards was slowing down and there were difficulties in the supply of foodstuffs, housing, consumer goods and services.

On the ideological plane as well, the braking mechanism brought about ever greater resistance to the attempts to constructively scrutinize the problems that were emerging and to the new ideas. Propaganda of success — real or imagined — was gaining the upper hand. Eulogizing and servility were encouraged; the needs and opinions of ordinary working people, of the public at large, were ignored. . . .

The presentation of a "problem-free" reality backfired: a breach had formed between word and deed, which bred public passivity and disbelief in the slogans being proclaimed. It was only natural that this situation resulted in a credibility gap: everything that was proclaimed from the rostrums and printed in newspapers and textbooks was put in question. Decay began in public morals; the great feeling of solidarity with each other that was forged during the heroic times of the Revolution [1917], the first five-year plans,[6] the Great Patriotic War[7] and postwar rehabilitation was weakening; alcoholism, drug addiction and crime were growing; and the penetration of the stereotypes of mass culture alien to us, which bred vulgarity and low tastes and brought about ideological barrenness increased. . . .

An unbiased and honest approach led us to the only logical conclusion that the country was verging on crisis. . . .

I would like to emphasize here that this analysis began a long time before the April Plenary Meeting[8] and that therefore its conclusions were well thought out. It was not something out of the blue, but a balanced judgment. It would be a mistake to think that a month after the Central Committee Plenary Meeting in March 1985, which elected me General Secretary, there suddenly appeared a group of people who understood everything and knew everything, and that these people gave clear-cut answers to all questions. Such miracles do not exist.

The need for change was brewing not only in the material sphere of life but also in public consciousness. People who had practical experience, a sense of justice and commitment to the ideals of Bolshevism[9] criticized the established practice of doing things and noted with anxiety the symptoms of moral degradation and erosion of revolutionary ideals and socialist values. . . .

Perestroika is closely connected with socialism as a system. That side of the matter is being widely discussed, especially abroad, and our talk about perestroika won't be entirely clear if we don't touch upon that aspect.

Does perestroika mean that we are giving up socialism or at least some of its foundations? Some ask this question with hope, others with misgiving.

There are people in the West who would like to tell us that socialism is in a deep crisis and has brought our society to a dead end. That's how they interpret our critical analysis of the situation at the end of the seventies

---

[6] **five-year plans**: Stalin's attempts to transform the rural, agrarian Soviet Union into an industrial state. The first plan began in 1928, the second in 1932 (a year early), and succeeded but at tremendous human cost.
[7] **Great Patriotic War**: Soviet name for World War II, in which the Soviets lost at least twenty million people.
[8] **April Plenary Meeting**: Regular meeting of the Communist Party's officials.
[9] **Bolshevism**: Vladimir Lenin's — the first Soviet leader — interpretation of Marx's ideas; named after the Bolshevik faction of the prerevolutionary Social Democratic Party.

and beginning of the eighties. We have only one way out, they say: to adopt capitalist methods of economic management and social patterns, to drift toward capitalism.

They tell us that nothing will come of perestroika within the framework of our system. They say we should change this system and borrow from the experience of another socio-political system. To this they add that, if the Soviet Union takes this path and gives up its socialist choice, close links with the West will supposedly become possible. They go so far as to claim that the October 1917 Revolution was a mistake which almost completely cut off our country from world social progress.

To put an end to all the rumors and speculations that abound in the West about this, I would like to point out once again that we are conducting all our reforms in accordance with the socialist choice. We are looking within socialism, rather than outside it, for the answers to all the questions that arise. We assess our successes and errors alike by socialist standards. Those who hope that we shall move away from the socialist path will be greatly disappointed. Every part of our program of perestroika — and the program as a whole, for that matter — is fully based on the principle of more socialism and more democracy. . . .

We will proceed toward better socialism rather than away from it. We are saying this honestly, without trying to fool our own people or the world. Any hopes that we will begin to build a different, nonsocialist society and go over to the other camp are unrealistic and futile. Those in the West who expect us to give up socialism will be disappointed. It is high time they understood this, and, even more importantly, proceeded from that understanding in practical relations with the Soviet Union. . . .

We want more socialism and, therefore, more democracy.

READING AND DISCUSSION QUESTIONS

1. What attitudes does Gorbachev seem to hold toward the West, particularly Western culture, as gleaned from this document?

2. In what ways might this document be seen as a refutation of the policies of former Soviet leaders? In what ways does it seek to continue them?

3. Based on this document, what is Mikhail Gorbachev's relationship with Western free-market ideology?

4. To whom does Gorbachev ascribe the blame for the Soviet Union's recent economic failures? What solutions does he propose?

DOCUMENT 30-3

JEFF WIDENER

Tank Man, Tiananmen Square

1989

In 1989 prodemocracy demonstrations were not confined to Europe. Chinese students camped out in Tiananmen Square for weeks in the same sort of protests that seemed to have worked in Czechoslovakia and Poland. The Chinese government proved willing to use force to maintain itself, and the Chinese army proved willing to obey orders to suppress the demonstrations. As the tanks rolled toward the square, they were held up by a single man, apparently with his shopping purchases, who blocked their path. Photojournalist Jeff Widener snapped this picture of the scene, which came to symbolize resistance — albeit ultimately futile — to state power.

READING AND DISCUSSION QUESTIONS

1. To what use might this image be put by advocates of nonviolent revolution? How effective would those uses be given the ultimate fate of the Tiananmen Square demonstrators?

"The Unknown Rebel," June 5, 1989. AP Photo/Jeff Widener.

2. What sort of reaction might this image provoke in a supporter of strong state power?

3. What reasons does the tank commander have for not running down the man in his way? What could this suggest about the limits of military power?

DOCUMENT 30-4

ALEX HARVEY
"Give My Compliments to the Chef"
1975

While consumers behind the Iron Curtain were faced with few choices, those in the West found themselves with a different set of problems. The Marshall Plan succeeded in creating an Americanized consumer society in Europe, which was cause for both celebration and complaint. American commodities, including rock music, seemed to reach into all areas of culture and life, turning emotions and memories into things that could be bought and sold. Here, the moderately successful Scottish singer-songwriter Alex Harvey wrestles with the opportunities and problems of the consumer society, even as he tries to create an album, another item for sale.

GIVE MY COMPLIMENTS TO THE CHEF

Mother dear did you hear how they're teaching me to do the goose step
Father mine just in time you gave me a machine to wash my jeans in
the customer is always right the girl is much too young to know the
    difference
The guitar hanging in the hall is calling me in all its magnificence
Give my compliments to the chef
Give my compliments to the chef

Leo sits behind the desk he wanna see the woman cooking gravy
Nobody sent no argument and I gotta go and join the Royal Navy

---

The Sensational Alex Harvey Band, "Give My Compliments to the Chef," *Tomorrow Belongs to Me* (1975).

Mademoiselle you do so well you know the meaning of salvation
But the General wants me on the phone and he's alone and needs my
    consolation

Give my compliments to the chef
Give my compliments to the chef

He's crazy he got his head in a basket
She's lazy and you don't understand
You know I'm running and you don't wanna hide me
I know a woman who's a man is a man
One night I was dreaming as I lay on my pillow
The train I was riding was ten coaches long
And in the village they was looking at freedom
In the beginning when I knew it was any old time

Any old time
Any old time
Any old time

Bad boys don't get no toys and everybody wants to get to heaven
The Salvation Army's asking but nobody ever thinks of giving
You know I wish I could see yesterday
The way I can see tomorrow
Go and take a look in a history book
It's up to you to mix the stew
And when you do

Give my compliments to the chef
The chef any old time, any old time

READING AND DISCUSSION QUESTIONS

1. What seems to be worrying the speaker in this song? How might others
   see these worrisome things as positive?

2. What role does there seem to be for the individual in this song? What
   does this say about Western concepts of freedom in the context of a
   mass-produced society?

3. What does progress mean to Harvey, based on these lyrics? How might
   this contrast with the ways other generations defined it?

DOCUMENT 30-5

VACLAV HAVEL
New Year's Address to the Nation
1990

One of the last countries to fall under Soviet influence after the World War II was Czechoslovakia. In 1968 an attempt to escape that influence led to Soviet tanks on the streets of Prague. After Gorbachev announced in 1989 that he would no longer enforce membership in the Soviet bloc, the Czechs and Slovaks retreated from one-party rule in a revolution so bloodless it became known as the "Velvet Revolution." Simply escaping from communism did not solve all their problems, however, and here the newly elected president, playwright Vaclav Havel (VAH-slav HAH-vel), muses on the nature of the past and potential for the future.

My dear fellow citizens,

For forty years you heard from my predecessors on this day different variations on the same theme: how our country was flourishing, how many million tons of steel we produced, how happy we all were, how we trusted our government, and what bright perspectives were unfolding in front of us.

I assume you did not propose me for this office so that I, too, would lie to you.

Our country is not flourishing. The enormous creative and spiritual potential of our nation is not being used sensibly. Entire branches of industry are producing goods that are of no interest to anyone, while we are lacking the things we need. A state which calls itself a workers' state humiliates and exploits workers. Our obsolete economy is wasting the little energy we have available. A country that once could be proud of the educational level of its citizens spends so little on education that it ranks today as seventy-second in the world. We have polluted the soil, rivers, and forests bequeathed to us by our ancestors, and we have today the most contaminated environment in Europe. Adults in our country die earlier than in most other European countries.

Prague Castle Administration, archival webpage, http://old.hrad.cz/president/Havel/speeches/1990/0101_uk.html, accessed February 16, 2010.

Allow me a small personal observation. When I flew recently to Bratislava, I found some time during discussions to look out of the plane window. I saw the industrial complex of Slovnaft chemical factory and the giant Petr'alka housing estate right behind it. The view was enough for me to understand that for decades our statesmen and political leaders did not look or did not want to look out of the windows of their planes. No study of statistics available to me would enable me to understand faster and better the situation in which we find ourselves.

But all this is still not the main problem. The worst thing is that we live in a contaminated moral environment. We fell morally ill because we became used to saying something different from what we thought. We learned not to believe in anything, to ignore one another, to care only about ourselves. Concepts such as love, friendship, compassion, humility, or forgiveness lost their depth and dimension, and for many of us they represented only psychological peculiarities, or they resembled gone-astray greetings from ancient times, a little ridiculous in the era of computers and spaceships. Only a few of us were able to cry out loudly that the powers that be should not be all-powerful and that the special farms, which produced ecologically pure and top-quality food just for them, should send their produce to schools, children's homes, and hospitals if our agriculture was unable to offer them to all.

The previous regime — armed with its arrogant and intolerant ideology — reduced man to a force of production, and nature to a tool of production. In this it attacked both their very substance and their mutual relationship. It reduced gifted and autonomous people, skillfully working in their own country, to the nuts and bolts of some monstrously huge, noisy, and stinking machine, whose real meaning was not clear to anyone. It could not do more than slowly but inexorably wear out itself and all its nuts and bolts.

When I talk about the contaminated moral atmosphere, I am not talking just about the gentlemen who eat organic vegetables and do not look out of the plane windows. I am talking about all of us. We had all become used to the totalitarian system and accepted it as an unchangeable fact and thus helped to perpetuate it. In other words, we are all — though naturally to differing extents — responsible for the operation of the totalitarian machinery. None of us is just its victim. We are all also its co-creators.

Why do I say this? It would be very unreasonable to understand the sad legacy of the last forty years as something alien, which some distant relative bequeathed to us. On the contrary, we have to accept this legacy as a sin we committed against ourselves. If we accept it as such, we will understand that it is up to us all, and up to us alone to do something about it. We cannot blame the previous rulers for everything, not only because it would be untrue, but also because it would blunt the duty that each of us faces today: namely, the obligation to act independently, freely, reasonably, and quickly. Let us not be mistaken: the best government in the world, the best parliament and the best president, cannot achieve much on their own. And it would be wrong to expect a general remedy from them alone. Freedom and democracy include participation and therefore responsibility from us all.

If we realize this, then all the horrors that the new Czechoslovak democracy inherited will cease to appear so terrible. If we realize this, hope will return to our hearts.

In the effort to rectify matters of common concern, we have something to lean on. The recent period — and in particular the last six weeks of our peaceful revolution — has shown the enormous human, moral and spiritual potential, and the civic culture that slumbered in our society under the enforced mask of apathy. Whenever someone categorically claimed that we were this or that, I always objected that society is a very mysterious creature and that it is unwise to trust only the face it presents to you. I am happy that I was not mistaken. Everywhere in the world people wonder where those meek, humiliated, skeptical, and seemingly cynical citizens of Czechoslovakia found the marvelous strength to shake the totalitarian yoke from their shoulders in several weeks, and in a decent and peaceful way. And let us ask: Where did the young people who never knew another system get their desire for truth, their love of free thought, their political ideas, their civic courage and civic prudence? How did it happen that their parents — the very generation that had been considered lost — joined them? How is it that so many people immediately knew what to do and none needed any advice or instruction?

I think there are two main reasons for the hopeful face of our present situation. First of all, people are never just a product of the external world; they are also able to relate themselves to something superior, however systematically the external world tries to kill that ability in them. Secondly, the humanistic and democratic traditions, about which there had been so much idle talk, did after all slumber in the unconsciousness of our nations and ethnic minorities, and were inconspicuously passed from one generation to another, so that each of us could discover them at the right time and transform them into deeds.

We had to pay, however, for our present freedom. Many citizens perished in jails in the 1950s, many were executed, thousands of human lives were destroyed, hundreds of thousands of talented people were forced to leave the country. Those who defended the honor of our nations during the Second World War, those who rebelled against totalitarian rule and those who simply managed to remain themselves and think freely, were all persecuted. We should not forget any of those who paid for our present freedom in one way or another. Independent courts should impartially consider the possible guilt of those who were responsible for the persecutions, so that the truth about our recent past might be fully revealed.

We must also bear in mind that other nations have paid even more dearly for their present freedom, and that indirectly they have also paid for ours. The rivers of blood that have flowed in Hungary, Poland, Germany, and recently in such a horrific manner in Romania, as well as the sea of blood shed by the nations of the Soviet Union, must not be forgotten. First of all because all human suffering concerns every other human being. But more than this, they must also not be forgotten because it is these great sacrifices that form the tragic background of today's freedom or the gradual emancipation of the nations of the Soviet Bloc, and thus the background of our own newfound freedom. Without the changes in the Soviet Union, Poland, Hungary, and the German Democratic Republic, what has happened in our country would have scarcely happened. And if it did, it certainly would not have followed such a peaceful course.

The fact that we enjoyed optimal international conditions does not mean that anyone else has directly helped us during the recent weeks. In fact, after hundreds of years, both our nations have raised their heads high of their own initiative without relying on the help of stronger nations or powers. It seems to me that this constitutes the great moral asset of the present moment. This moment holds within itself the hope that in the future we will no longer suffer from the complex of those who must always express their gratitude to somebody. It now depends only on us whether this hope will be realized and whether our civic, national, and political self-confidence will be awakened in a historically new way.

Self-confidence is not pride. Just the contrary: only a person or a nation that is self-confident, in the best sense of the word, is capable of listening to others, accepting them as equals, forgiving its enemies and regretting its own guilt. Let us try to introduce this kind of self-confidence into the life of our community and, as nations, into our behavior on the international stage. Only thus can we restore our self-respect and our respect for one another as well as the respect of other nations.

Our state should never again be an appendage or a poor relative of anyone else. It is true that we must accept and learn many things from others, but we must do this in the future as their equal partners, who also have something to offer.

Our first president[10] wrote: "Jesus, not Caesar." In this he followed our philosophers Chelick[11] and Komensk.[12] I dare to say that we may even have an opportunity to spread this idea further and introduce a new element into European and global politics. Our country, if that is what we want, can now permanently radiate love, understanding, the power of the spirit and of ideas. It is precisely this glow that we can offer as our specific contribution to international politics.

Masaryk based his politics on morality. Let us try, in a new time and in a new way, to restore this concept of politics. Let us teach ourselves and others that politics should be an expression of a desire to contribute to the happiness of the community rather than of a need to cheat or rape the community. Let us teach ourselves and others that politics can be not simply the art of the possible, especially if this means the art of speculation, calculation, intrigue, secret deals, and pragmatic maneuvering, but that it can also be the art of the impossible, that is, the art of improving ourselves and the world.

We are a small country, yet at one time we were the spiritual crossroads of Europe. Is there a reason why we could not again become one? Would it not be another asset with which to repay the help of others that we are going to need?

Our homegrown Mafia, those who do not look out of the plane windows and who eat specially fed pigs, may still be around and at times may muddy the waters, but they are no longer our main enemy. Even less so is our main enemy any kind of international Mafia. Our main enemy today is our own bad traits: indifference to the common good, vanity, personal ambition, selfishness, and rivalry. The main struggle will have to be fought on this field.

There are free elections and an election campaign ahead of us. Let us not allow this struggle to dirty the so-far clean face of our gentle revolution. Let us not allow the sympathies of the world, which we have won so fast,

---

[10] **our first president**: Thomas Garrigue Masaryk, the first president of Czechoslovakia (1918–1935); a humanist and democrat.
[11] **Chelick**: Petr Chelčický; Bohemian author who lived roughly between 1390 and 1460, and who decried secular power and war as being in opposition to Christianity.
[12] **Komensk**: J. A. Komensky (1592–1670); Bohemian (Czech) religious reformer who valued education as a way to universal humanity, and who became a Czech national symbol in the nineteenth century.

to be equally rapidly lost through our becoming entangled in the jungle of skirmishes for power. Let us not allow the desire to serve oneself to bloom once again under the stately garb of the desire to serve the common good. It is not really important now which party, club or group prevails in the elections. The important thing is that the winners will be the best of us, in the moral, civic, political and professional sense, regardless of their political affiliations. The future policies and prestige of our state will depend on the personalities we select, and later, elect to our representative bodies.

My dear fellow citizens!

Three days ago I became the president of the republic as a consequence of your will, expressed through the deputies of the Federal Assembly. You have a right to expect me to mention the tasks I see before me as president.

The first of these is to use all my power and influence to ensure that we soon step up to the ballot boxes in a free election, and that our path toward this historic milestone will be dignified and peaceful.

My second task is to guarantee that we approach these elections as two self-governing nations who respect each other's interests, national identity, religious traditions, and symbols. As a Czech who has given his presidential oath to an important Slovak who is personally close to him, I feel a special obligation — after the bitter experiences that Slovaks had in the past — to see that all the interests of the Slovak nation are respected and that no state office, including the highest one, will ever be barred to it in the future.

My third task is to support everything that will lead to better circumstances for our children, the elderly, women, the sick, the hardworking laborers, the national minorities, and all citizens who are for any reason worse off than others. High-quality food or hospitals must no longer be a prerogative of the powerful; they must be available to those who need them the most.

As supreme commander of the armed forces I want to guarantee that the defensive capability of our country will no longer be used as a pretext for anyone to stand in the way of courageous peace initiatives, the reduction of military service, the establishment of alternative military service, and the overall humanization of military life.

In our country there are many prisoners who, though they may have committed serious crimes and have been punished for them, have had to submit — despite the goodwill of some investigators, judges, and above all defense lawyers — to a debased judiciary process that curtailed their rights. They now have to live in prisons that do not strive to awaken the better qualities contained in every person, but rather humiliate them and destroy them physically and mentally. In a view of this fact, I have decided to declare a relatively extensive amnesty. At the same time I call on the prisoners to understand that forty years of unjust investigations, trials, and imprisonments cannot be put right overnight, and to understand that the changes that are being speedily prepared still require time to implement. By rebelling, the prisoners would help neither society nor themselves. I also call on the public not to fear the prisoners once they are released, not to make their lives difficult, to help them, in the Christian spirit, after their return among us to find within themselves that which jails could not find in them: the capacity to repent and the desire to live a respectable life.

My honorable task is to strengthen the authority of our country in the world. I would be glad if other states respected us for showing understanding, tolerance, and love for peace. I would be happy if Pope John Paul II and the Dalai Lama of Tibet could visit our country before the elections, if only for a day. I would be happy if our friendly relations with all nations were strengthened. I would be happy if we succeeded before the elections in establishing diplomatic relations with the Vatican and Israel. I would also like to contribute to peace by briefly visiting our close neighbors, the German Democratic Republic and the Federal Republic of Germany. Neither shall I forget our other neighbors — fraternal Poland and the ever-closer countries of Hungary and Austria.

In conclusion, I would like to say that I want to be a president who will speak less and work more. To be a president who will not only look out of the windows of his airplane but who, first and foremost, will always be present among his fellow citizens and listen to them well.

You may ask what kind of republic I dream of. Let me reply: I dream of a republic independent, free, and democratic, of a republic economically prosperous and yet socially just; in short, of a humane republic that serves the individual and that therefore holds the hope that the individual will serve it in turn. Of a republic of well-rounded people, because without such people it is impossible to solve any of our problems — human, economic, ecological, social, or political.

The most distinguished of my predecessors opened his first speech with a quotation from the great Czech educator Komensk. Allow me to conclude my first speech with my own paraphrase of the same statement:

People, your government has returned to you!

READING AND DISCUSSION QUESTIONS

1. What were the successes and failures of the communist system as Havel describes them?

2. How does Havel appear to apportion responsibility for the system he has succeeded? Are the average citizens exempt from these criticisms?

3. What are the problems Havel sees for the future? How does he approach solving them?

COMPARATIVE QUESTIONS

1. On what priorities of society do the leaders of Solidarity and Mikhail Gorbachev seem to agree? About which priorities do they disagree?

2. What do Havel's critique of communism and Harvey's of commercialism have in common? About what do they differ?

3. How do Havel's thoughts on the nature of unfree society compare with the photograph from China of a single man holding up four tanks? Based on what happened to the Tiananmen demonstrators, are Havel's beliefs about the future justified?

4. How might the workers of the Solidarity union react to Alex Harvey's worries about the world?

CHAPTER 31

Europe in an Age of Globalization

1990 to the Present

Although global relationships have impacted the world's economy at least since the time of the Crusades, in the years after the collapse of the Soviet Union triumphal narratives of the expansion of Western ideals of democracy and capitalism began to speak of globalization. Europe's economy was unified as it had never been before, and the interchange of peoples, products, and ideas seemed to be proceeding on Western terms. In the late 1990s opposition emerged to the cultural and economic domination of the west, both among activists in the West and traditionalists in other parts of the world. The skeptical rationalist world that the Enlightenment had created was not welcoming for everyone, and some discontented groups began to return to and reinterpret their traditional identities in opposition to the West.

DOCUMENT 31-1

KOFI ANNAN

The Fall of Srebrenica: An Assessment

1999

The nation of Yugoslavia had been cobbled together out of several ethnic groups in 1919, and the 1980 death of Josip Tito, dictator since 1945, cata- lyzed the process of the country's disintegration. In the 1990s, ethnic Serbs attempted to create a greater Serbia, free of other ethnic groups, by driving

From UN General Assembly, *Report of the Secretary-General Pursuant to General Assembly Resolution 53/35: The Fall of Srebrenica*, 15 November 1999, pp. 105,108– 111. http://www.unhcr.org/refworld/docid/3ae6afb34.html, accessed June 3, 2010.

them out or through acts of genocide. Although the various civil and inter-national conflicts of the Bosnian War (1992–1995) were precisely the sorts of circumstances that the United Nations had been designed to mediate, the collective security body was unable to bring the war to a halt or protect the victims of Serbian attacks. UN Secretary-General Kofi Annan commissioned this report in an attempt to prevent future mistakes and thus avoid more bloody consequences.

XI. The Fall of Srebrenica: An Assessment

467. The tragedy that took place following the fall of Srebrenica is shocking for two reasons. It is shocking, first and foremost, for the magnitude of the crimes committed. Not since the horrors of World War II had Europe witnessed massacres on this scale. The mortal remains of close to 2,500 men and boys have been found on the surface, in mass grave sites and in secondary burial sites. Several thousand more men are still missing, and there is every reason to believe that additional burial sites, many of which have been probed but not exhumed, will reveal the bodies of thousands more men and boys. The great majority of those who were killed were not killed in combat: the exhumed bodies of the victims show large numbers had their hands bound, or were blindfolded, or were shot in the back or the back of the head. Numerous eyewitness accounts, now well corroborated by forensic evidence, attest to scenes of mass slaughter of unarmed victims.

468. The fall of Srebrenica is also shocking because the enclave's[1] inhabitants believed that the authority of the United Nations Security Council, the presence of UNPROFOR[2] peacekeepers, and the might of NATO air power, would ensure their safety. Instead, the Serb forces ignored the Security Council, pushed aside the UNPROFOR troops, and assessed correctly that air power would not be used to stop them. They overran the safe area of Srebrenica with ease, and then proceeded to depopulate the territory within 48 hours. Their leaders then engaged in high-level negotiations with representatives of the international community while their forces on the ground

---

[1] the enclaves: The United Nations set up six supposedly safe areas in which Bosnian Muslims and Croats could seek refuge from Serb attacks.
[2] UNPROFOR: United Nations Protection Force; multinational force sent by the United Nations to enforce the safe zones set up in 1993.

executed and buried thousands of men and boys within a matter
of days. . . .

E. The role of the security council and member states

488. With the benefit of hindsight, one can see that many of the errors
the United Nations made flowed from a single and no-doubt well-
intentioned effort: we tried to keep the peace and apply the rules of
peacekeeping when there was no peace to keep. Knowing that any
other course of action would jeopardize the lives of the troops, we
tried to create — or imagine — an environment in which the tenets
of peacekeeping — agreement between the parties, deployment by
consent, and impartiality — could be upheld. We tried to stabilize
the situation on the ground through ceasefire agreements, which
brought us close to the Serbs, who controlled the larger proportion
of the land. We tried to eschew the use of force except in self-defense,
which brought us into conflict with the defenders of the safe areas,
whose safety depended on our use of force.

489. In spite of the untenability of its position, UNPROFOR was able to
assist in the humanitarian process, and to mitigate some — but, as
Srebrenica tragically underscored, by no means all — the suffering
inflicted by the war. There are people alive in Bosnia today who
would not be alive had UNPROFOR not been deployed. To this
extent, it can be said that the 117 young men who lost their lives in
the service of UNPROFOR's mission in Bosnia and Herzegovina
did not die in vain. Their sacrifice and the good work of many others, however, cannot fully redeem a policy that was, at best, a half-
measure.

490. The community of nations decided to respond to the war in Bosnia
and Herzegovina with an arms embargo, with humanitarian aid,
and with the deployment of a peacekeeping force. It must be clearly
stated that these measures were poor substitutes for more decisive
and forceful action to prevent the unfolding horror. The arms
embargo did little more than freeze in place the military balance
within the former Yugoslavia. It left the Serbs in a position of overwhelming military dominance and effectively deprived the Republic of Bosnia and Herzegovina of its right, under the Charter of the
United Nations, to self-defense. It was not necessarily a mistake to
impose an arms embargo, which after all had been done when
Bosnia-Herzegovina was not yet a Member State of the United
Nations. But having done so, there must surely have been some

attendant duty to protect Bosnia and Herzegovina, after it became a Member State, from the tragedy that then befell it. Even as the Serb attacks on and strangulation of the "safe areas"[3] continued in 1993 and 1994, all widely covered by the media and, presumably, by diplomatic and intelligence reports to their respective governments, the approach of the Members of the Security Council remained largely constant. The international community still could not find the political will to confront the menace defying it.

491. Nor was the provision of humanitarian aid a sufficient response to "ethnic cleansing" and to an attempted genocide. The provision of food and shelter to people who have neither is wholly admirable, and we must all recognize the extraordinary work done by UNHCR [the United Nations High Commissioner for Refugees] and its partners in circumstances of extreme adversity. But the provision of humanitarian assistance could never have been a solution to the problem in that country. The problem, which cried out for a political/military solution, was that a Member State of the United Nations, left largely defenseless as a result of an arms embargo imposed upon it *by the United Nations*, was being dismembered by forces committed to its destruction. This was not a problem with a humanitarian solution.

492. Nor was the deployment of a peacekeeping force a coherent response to this problem. My predecessor openly told the Security Council that a United Nations peacekeeping force could not bring peace to Bosnia and Herzegovina. He said it often and he said it loudly, fearing that peacekeeping techniques inevitably would fail in a situation of war. None of the conditions for the deployment of peacekeepers had been met: there was no peace agreement — not even a functioning ceasefire — there was no clear will to peace and there was no clear consent by the belligerents. Nevertheless, *faute de mieux* ["for lack of anything better"], the Security Council decided that a United Nations peacekeeping force would be deployed. Lightly armed, highly visible in their white vehicles, scattered across the country in numerous indefensible observation posts, they were able to confirm the obvious: there was no peace to keep.

493. In so doing, the Council obviously expected that the "warring parties" on the ground would respect the authority of the United

---

[3] **safe areas**: UN Resolution 819 declared the areas around the cities of Sarajevo, Srebrenecia, Žepa, Goražde, Tuzla, and Bihać safe areas.

Nations and would not obstruct or attack its humanitarian operations. It soon became apparent that, with the end of the Cold
War and the ascendancy of irregular forces — controlled or uncontrolled — the old rules of the game no longer held. Nor was it sufficiently appreciated that a systematic and ruthless campaign such as
the one conducted by the Serbs would view a United Nations
humanitarian operation, not as an obstacle, but as an instrument of
its aims. In such an event, it is clear that the ability to adapt man-
dates to the reality on the ground is of critical importance to ensur-
ing that the appropriate force under the appropriate structure is
deployed. None of that flexibility was present in the management of
UNPROFOR.

F. The failure to fully comprehend the Serb war aims . . .

495. Nonetheless, the key issue — politically, strategically, and morally — underlying the security of the "safe areas" was the essential
nature of "ethnic cleansing." As part of the larger ambition for a
"Greater Serbia," the Serbs set out to occupy the territory of the
enclaves; they wanted the territory for themselves. The civilian
inhabitants of the enclaves were not the incidental victims of the
attackers; their death or removal was the very purpose of the attacks
upon them. The tactic of employing savage terror, primarily mass
killings, rapes, and brutalization of civilians, to expel populations
was used to the greatest extent in Bosnia and Herzegovina, where it
acquired the now-infamous euphemism of "ethnic cleansing." The
Bosnian Muslim civilian population thus became the principal victim of brutally aggressive military and para-military Serb operations
to depopulate coveted territories in order to allow them to be repop-
ulated by Serbs.

496. The failure to fully comprehend the extent of the Serb war aims
may explain in part why the Secretariat and the Peacekeeping
Mission did not react more quickly and decisively when the Serbs
initiated their attack on Srebrenica. In fact, rather than attempting
to mobilize the international community to support the enclave's
defense we gave the Security Council the impression that the situation was under control, and many of us believed that to be the case.
The day before Srebrenica fell we reported that the Serbs were not
attacking when they were. We reported that the Bosniacs had fired
on an UNPROFOR blocking position when it was the Serbs. We
failed to mention urgent requests for air power. In some instances

in which incomplete and inaccurate information was given to the Council, this can be attributed to problems with reporting from the field. In other instances, however, the reporting may have been illustrative of a more general tendency to assume that the parties were equally responsible for the transgressions that occurred. It is not clear in any event, that the provision of more fully accurate information to the Council — many of whose Members had independent sources of information on the ongoing events — would have led to appreciably different results.

497. In the end, these Bosnian Serb war aims were ultimately repulsed on the battlefield, and not at the negotiating table. Yet, the Secretariat had convinced itself early on that the broader use of force by the international community was beyond our mandate and anyway undesirable. A report of the Secretary-General to the Security Council spoke against a "culture of death," arguing that peace should be pursued only through non-military methods. And when, in June 1995, the international community provided UNPROFOR with a heavily armed Rapid Reaction Force, we argued against using it robustly to implement our mandate. When decisive action was finally taken by UNPROFOR in August and September 1995, it helped to bring the war to a conclusion.

G. Lessons for the future . . .

502. The cardinal lesson of Srebrenica is that a deliberate and systematic attempt to terrorize, expel, or murder an entire people must be met decisively with all necessary means, and with the political will to carry the policy through to its logical conclusion. In the Balkans, in this decade, this lesson has had to be learned not once, but twice. In both instances, in Bosnia and in Kosovo, the international community tried to reach a negotiated settlement with an unscrupulous and murderous regime. In both instances it required the use of force to bring a halt to the planned and systematic killing and expulsion of civilians.

503. The United Nations experience in Bosnia was one of the most difficult and painful in our history. It is with the deepest regret and remorse that we have reviewed our own actions and decisions in the face of the assault on Srebrenica. Through error, misjudgment, and an inability to recognize the scope of the evil confronting us, we failed to do our part to help save the people of Srebrenica from the Serb campaign of mass murder. No one regrets more than we the

opportunities for achieving peace and justice that were missed. No one laments more than we the failure of the international community to take decisive action to halt the suffering and end a war that had produced so many victims. Srebrenica crystallized a truth understood only too late by the United Nations and the world at large: that Bosnia was as much a moral cause as a military conflict. The tragedy of Srebrenica will haunt our history forever.

504. In the end, the only meaningful and lasting amends we can make to the citizens of Bosnia and Herzegovina who put their faith in the international community is to do our utmost not to allow such horrors to recur. When the international community makes a solemn promise to safeguard and protect innocent civilians from massacre, then it must be willing to back its promise with the necessary means. Otherwise, it is surely better not to raise hopes and expectations in the first place, and not to impede whatever capability they may be able to muster in their own defense.

505. To ensure that we have fully learned the lessons of the tragic history detailed in this report, I wish to encourage Member States to engage in a process of reflection and analysis, focused on the key challenges the narrative uncovers. The aim of this process would be to clarify and to improve the capacity of the United Nations to respond to various forms of conflict. I have in mind addressing such issues as the gulf between mandate and means; the inadequacy of symbolic deterrence in the face of a systematic campaign of violence; the pervasive ambivalence within the United Nations regarding the role of force in the pursuit of peace; an institutional ideology of impartiality even when confronted with attempted genocide; and a range of doctrinal and institutional issues that go to the heart of the United Nations' ability to keep the peace and help protect civilian populations from armed conflict. The Secretariat is ready to join in such a process.

506. The body of this report sets out in meticulous, systematic, exhaustive, and ultimately harrowing detail the descent of Srebrenica into a horror without parallel in the history of Europe since the Second World War. I urge all concerned to study this report carefully, and to let the facts speak for themselves. The men who have been charged with this crime against humanity reminded the world, and, in particular, the United Nations, that evil exists in the world. They taught us also that the United Nations' global commitment to ending conflict does not preclude moral judgments, but makes them necessary. It is in this spirit that I submit my report of the fall of Srebrenica to the General Assembly, and to the world.

READING AND DISCUSSION QUESTIONS

1. Based on this document, what were the negative consequences of the breakup of communist Yugoslavia for its citizens?

2. In what ways did Serbian goals conflict with the ideology that motivated the United Nations?

3. What problems prevented UN forces from responding effectively to Serbian attacks? Could these problems have been resolved without altering the nature of the United Nations?

4. For what does Annan accept responsibility on behalf of the United Nations?

DOCUMENT 31-2

AMARTYA SEN

A World Not Neatly Divided

November 23, 2001

The idea that the fall of the Soviet Union made the world a safer place died its final death on September 11, 2001. In the wake of the al-Qaeda terrorist attack on the Pentagon and World Trade Center towers, leaders and ordinary individuals alike cast about for an explanation of the horror they had witnessed. One argument hinged around the fact that all of the plane hijackers were Muslim, and many began to wonder if some fundamental trait of Islam could be blamed. Amartya Sen, an Indian academic then at Cambridge University, argued six weeks after the attacks that such categorizations were inherently flawed in dealing with a diverse world.

When people talk about clashing civilizations, as so many politicians and academics do now, they can sometimes miss the central issue. The inadequacy of this thesis begins well before we get to the question of whether civilizations must clash. The basic weakness of the theory lies in its program of categorizing people of the world according to a unique, allegedly commanding system of classification. This is problematic because civilizational

Amartya Sen, "A World Not Neatly Divided," *The New York Times*, November 23, 2001.

categories are crude and inconsistent and also because there are other ways of seeing people (linked to politics, language, literature, class, occupation, or other affiliations).

The befuddling influence of a singular classification also traps those who dispute the thesis of a clash: To talk about "the Islamic world" or "the Western world" is already to adopt an impoverished vision of humanity as unalterably divided. In fact, civilizations are hard to partition in this way, given the diversities within each society as well as the linkages among different countries and cultures. For example, describing India as a "Hindu civilization" misses the fact that India has more Muslims than any other country except Indonesia and possibly Pakistan. It is futile to try to understand Indian art, literature, music, food, or politics without seeing the extensive interactions across barriers of religious communities. These include Hindus and Muslims, Buddhists, Jains,[4] Sikhs,[5] Parsees,[6] Christians (who have been in India since at least the fourth century, well before England's conversion to Christianity [sixth century C.E.]), Jews (present since the fall of Jerusalem [70 C.E.]), and even atheists and agnostics. Sanskrit has a larger atheistic literature than exists in any other classical language. Speaking of India as a Hindu civilization may be comforting to the Hindu fundamentalist, but it is an odd reading of India.

A similar coarseness can be seen in the other categories invoked, like "the Islamic world." Consider Akbar and Aurangzeb, two Muslim emperors of the Mogul[7] dynasty in India. Aurangzeb tried hard to convert Hindus into Muslims and instituted various policies in that direction, of which taxing the non-Muslims was only one example. In contrast, Akbar reveled in his multiethnic court and pluralist laws, and issued official proclamations insisting that no one "should be interfered with on account of religion" and that "anyone is to be allowed to go over to a religion that pleases him."

---

[4] **Jains**: Followers of one of the oldest religions in India, which encompasses several ancient religions, who believe in the potential of each individual soul. Jains have many beliefs similar to Hindus.
[5] **Sikhs**: Followers of another Indian religion, founded in the fifteenth century but only becoming prominent in the seventeenth. Sikhs were once persecuted by both Hindus and Muslims.
[6] **Parsees**: Members of a branch of Zoroastrianism, the religion of the ancient Persians, believed to have been in India for at least a thousand years.
[7] **Mogul**: Descendants of the Mongols in central India who converted to Islam. Akbar ruled from 1556 to 1605, and Aurangzeb from 1658 to 1707.

If a homogeneous view of Islam were to be taken, then only one of these emperors could count as a true Muslim. The Islamic fundamentalist would have no time for Akbar; Prime Minister Tony Blair, given his insistence that tolerance is a defining characteristic of Islam, would have to consider excommunicating Aurangzeb. I expect both Akbar and Aurangzeb would protest, and so would I. A similar crudity is present in the characterization of what is called "Western civilization." Tolerance and individual freedom have certainly been present in European history. But there is no dearth of diversity here, either. When Akbar was making his pronouncements on religious tolerance in Agra [in northern India, near Nepal], in the 1590s, the Inquisitions were still going on; in 1600, Giordano Bruno[8] was burned at the stake, for heresy, in Campo dei Fiori in Rome.

Dividing the world into discrete civilizations is not just crude. It propels us into the absurd belief that this partitioning is natural and necessary and must overwhelm all other ways of identifying people. That imperious view goes not only against the sentiment that "we human beings are all much the same," but also against the more plausible understanding that we are diversely different. For example, Bangladesh's split from Pakistan was not connected with religion, but with language and politics.

Each of us has many features in our self-conception. Our religion, important as it may be, cannot be an all-engulfing identity. Even a shared poverty can be a source of solidarity across the borders. The kind of division highlighted by, say, the so-called "antiglobalization" protesters — whose movement is, incidentally, one of the most globalized in the world — tries to unite the underdogs of the world economy and goes firmly against religious, national or "civilizational" lines of division.

The main hope of harmony lies not in any imagined uniformity, but in the plurality of our identities, which cut across each other and work against sharp divisions into impenetrable civilizational camps. Political leaders who think and act in terms of sectioning off humanity into various "worlds" stand to make the world more flammable — even when their intentions are very different. They also end up, in the case of civilizations defined by religion, lending authority to religious leaders seen as spokesmen for their "worlds." In the process, other voices are muffled and other concerns silenced. The robbing of our plural identities not only reduces us; it impoverishes the world.

---

[8] **Giordano Bruno**: An Italian who argued that the earth went around the sun, though some of his unusual theological beliefs were the reason why he was burned in a Roman plaza.

READING AND DISCUSSION QUESTIONS

1. According to Sen, when are generalizations about the world possible? In what ways are they necessary in talking about a complex world?

2. Why might both the extremists behind the September 11 attacks and the leaders of the governments who oppose them find this article disturbing?

3. Sen cites the Mogul culture approximately four hundred years ago as an example of diversity. Does Sen's analogy underestimate the complexity of the Western societies to which he compares the Moguls, and why or why not?

VIEWPOINTS
Envisioning the World to Come

DOCUMENT 31-3

TARIQ RAMADAN
Western Muslims and the Future of Islam
2004

In the aftermath of World War II and the Algerian revolt of 1956–1963, large numbers of North African Muslims emigrated to France searching for economic opportunity (a process also at work for different reasons in Germany and Britain). Assimilation proved problematic for many of these immigrants, and many in their host countries were disinclined to accept them. Tariq Ramadan, a prominent Muslim scholar, has written several books that attempt to provide a way to reconcile the traditional, universalist claims of Islam with the skeptical, post-Enlightenment European society. Here, Ramadan sets out the basic issues his work attempts to address.

When I wrote *To Be a European Muslim: A Study of the Islamic Sources in Light of the European Context* in 1997, many readers were surprised and challenged by the approach to the Islamic textual sources (the Qur'an and the Sunna) that I was proposing, and by the propositions I was trying to articulate with regard to reading our sources. Their questions were usually aimed in the same direction: where would it lead *in practice?* For I had said that this was only a first step and that more work would have to follow to formulate the vision of the whole and to apply these reflections in practical terms on the ground. These past years have been fed by a constant threefold work of deepening my reflection on the sources, bringing them face to face with the realities on the ground, and analyzing the local dynamics in accordance with meetings and exchanges with Muslim association groups (and consequently a number of partners) in Europe and North America (not forgetting the very Western circumstances of Mauritius, Reunion, or Singapore). This has made it possible for me to take up the work begun five years ago and to synthesize it into a more global and coherent vision of Islamic principles, the available juridical instruments, and the means of employing them. This work makes up the whole of the first part of this present volume. I have not included all the elements of reflection contained in *To Be a European Muslim*, but I have restricted myself to those that had a direct link with my purpose here: to understand the universality of the message of Islam, and to highlight the means we are given to help us live in our own time, in the West, with respect for ourselves and for others. The approach I propose is anchored in the Islamic tradition and amplified from within it: in this sense it is both deeply classical and radically new. Beginning with the Qur'an and the Sunna and the methodologies set down by the ulama[9] throughout the history of the Islamic sciences, I have tried to immerse myself again in reading these sources in the light of our new Western context; even though the methodology adopted is classical, I have not hesitated sometimes to question certain definitions and categorizations and to suggest others. It is especially in my suggestions and my replies that one will doubtless find some new perspectives, which I hope may be useful. My conviction in elaborating on this work is that the movement toward reform, which was once intrinsic to the juridical compass of Islam, can take place effectively only from within, in, and through a rigorous faithfulness to the sources and the norms of reading them. This is the requirement I have laid upon myself.

---

[9] **ulama**: Sometimes spelled ulemma, the community of Muslim scholars who interpret Islamic law.

The second part of my study concentrates on the practical application of these reflections in Western society. Questions as essential as the spiritual life, or education in industrialized, more or less postmodern, more or less secularized societies, are studied with an attempt, wherever possible, to approach the subject from three perspectives: the principles to respect, the reality of the situation, and the reforms that seem to me necessary to face the challenges of life in Europe or North America. I have tried to follow the same stages in each chapter. Following on from spirituality and education, social engagement and political participation, economic resistance, interreligious dialogue, and the cultural equivalent are some of the subjects I have felt needed to be addressed at this precise juncture of our history in the West.

We are currently living through a veritable silent revolution in Muslim communities in the West: more and more young people and intellectuals are actively looking for a way to live in harmony with their faith while participating in the societies that are their societies, whether they like it or not. French, English, German, Canadian, and American Muslims, women as well as men, are constructing a "Muslim personality" that will soon surprise many of their fellow citizens. Far from media attention, going through the risks of a process of maturation that is necessarily slow, they are drawing the shape of European and American Islam: faithful to the principles of Islam, dressed in European and American cultures, and definitively rooted in Western societies. This grassroots movement will soon exert considerable influence over worldwide Islam: in view of globalization and the Westernization of the world, these are the same questions as those already being raised from Morocco to Indonesia.

Globalization contains the paradox that at the same time that it causes the old traditional points of reference to disappear, it reawakens passionate affirmations of identity that often verge on withdrawal and self-exclusion. The Muslim world is not exempt from such phenomena: from Africa to Asia, via America and Europe, this kind of discourse is multiplied. It is about self-protection, self-preservation, and sometimes even self-definition over and against the "Western megamachine," to use the formulation of Serge Latouche: "Whatever is Western is anti-Islamic" or "Islam has nothing in common with the West." This bipolar vision is widespread and gives some Muslims a sense of power, might, and legitimacy in Otherness. But not only is this bipolar and simplistic vision a decoy (and the claims that justify it are untruths) but the power that it bestows is a pure illusion: in practice, the Muslims who maintain these theses only isolate themselves, and sometimes, by their excessive emotional, intellectual, and social isolation, even strengthen the logic of the dominant system whose power, by contrast, lies in always appearing open, pluralistic, and rational.

The approach I propose here is the exact opposite of this attitude. Beginning with the message of Islam and its universal principles, I have investigated the tools that can give an impetus, from the inside, to a movement of reform and integration into the new environments. The power and effectiveness of the "principle of integration," which is the foundation upon which all the juridical instruments for adaptation must depend, lie in the fact that it comes with an entirely opposite perspective; instead of being sensitive, obsessed by self-protection and withdrawal and attempts to integrate *oneself* by "the little door," on the margin, or "as a minority" it is, on the contrary, a matter of *integrating*, making one's own all that people have produced that is good, just, humane — intellectually, scientifically, politically, economically, culturally, and so on. While our fellow-citizens speak of this "integration" of Muslims "among us," the question for the Muslims presents itself differently: their universal principles teach them that wherever the law respects their integrity and their freedom of conscience and worship, they are at home, and must consider the attainments of these societies as their own and must involve themselves, with their fellow-citizens, in making it good and better. No withdrawal, no obsession with identity — on the contrary, it is a question of entering into an authentic dialogue, as between equals, with all our fellow-citizens with respect foe the identical universality of our respective values, willingly open to mutual enrichment and eventually to becoming true partners in action.

I know these ideas are frightening and that they appear new and "offensive," to use the expression of a questioner who heard them at one of my lectures in the United Kingdom. Let me say that my reading of the scriptural sources and the study of our Western environment have led me to lay down two fundamental theses that involve the determined rejection of certain intellectual positions. First, for me it is not a question of relativizing the universal principles of Islam in order to give the impression that we are integrating ourselves into the rational order. In my view, the issue is to find out how the Islamic universal accepts and respects pluralism and the belief of the Other: it is one thing to relativize what I believe and another to respect fully the conventions of the Other. The postmodernist spirit would lead us unconsciously to confuse the second proposition with the first. I refuse: it is in the very name of the universality of my principle that my conscience is summoned to respect diversity and the relative, and that is why, even in the West (especially in the West), we have not to think of our presence in terms of "minority." What seems to be a given in our thinking: "the Muslim minority," "the law of minorities" (*fiqh al-aqalliyyat*), must, I believe, be rethought. We shall do a little of this in the following pages. Second, I defend fiercely the idea that Western Muslims must be intellectually, politically, and financially independent. Of course, this does not imply that exchanges and discussions with Muslim countries should cease — rather the contrary. We have more need than ever to maintain spaces for meeting and debate (especially since there are not yet any ulama we can refer to who were born and formed in the West). In this period of transition, links between Muslims of West and East are essential. What I mean exactly by the idea of "independence" is that Western citizens of the Muslim faith must think for themselves, develop theses appropriate to their situation, and put forward new and concrete ideas. They must refuse to remain dependent, either on the intellectual level, or more damagingly, on the political or financial levels. These types of dependences are the worst because they prevent the acquisition of responsibility and the liberation of heart and minds. In the same way, as a citizen, I refuse to support the colonialist reaction found among certain governments and commentators that consists of wanting to keep Muslims in these old (or other new) dependences and in wanting to "speak for them," as we reject the insidious new "paternalism" of some who "help" "young" Muslims eternally destined in their spirits never to become adults.

These two positions of principle are ultimately nothing but the reflection of the dynamics that are slowly coming into place in the West. I have consciously decided not to deal specifically with the problems of political security faced by European and American states, or with Islamophobia or social discrimination — not because I think these problems are secondary but because my thinking is based at a higher level. It is by acquiring the conviction that they can be faithful to their principles while being totally involved in the life of their society that Muslims will find the means to confront these difficulties and act to resolve them. It is an established and unacceptable fact that the governments of the United States (particularly after the outrages of 11 September 2001) and Europe maintain relations that are sometimes disrespectful of and even clearly discriminatory against citizens and residents of their countries who are of Muslim faith. It is no less true that they apply a security policy including constant surveillance: distrust is maintained, and the image of the "Muslim" often remains suspect. The general picture conceived by the Western population in general is so negative that one could call it Islamophobia, and this is a fact that many Muslims have lived with on a daily basis. One could extend the list of difficulties, complaints, and criticism at will. My response to all these phenomena is to insist to Muslims that they stay in the higher reaches, in awareness of their principles, values, and responsibilities. By developing a global vision of their points of reference and their objectives, by studying their situation and being reconciled with themselves, they have the responsibility to become engaged in all the areas we shall study in this book. Muslims will get what they deserve: if, as watchful and participating citizens, they study the machinery of their society, demand their rights to equality with others, struggle against all kinds of discrimination and injustice, establish real partnerships beyond their own community and what concerns themselves alone, it will be an achievement that will make political security measures, discrimination, Islamophobic behavior, and so on drift away downstream. In the end, the ball is in their court . . . unless they are determined to remain forever on the margins.

This book is only one step toward the building of the Muslim personality in the West and doubtless in the modern era, too. It will not be the last. Other works, *in sha Allah*,[10] must continue to trace the path back to the beginning. I have humbly tried to draw the theoretical and practical outlines of a vision for the future, full on. I want to engage with this in practice, and already, across all the countries of the West, this vision is being accomplished. The road is still long, but indwelt by this humble "need of Him," one must not be afraid or apologize for needing time.

READING AND DISCUSSION QUESTIONS

1. In what ways does Ramadan seem to reject Western thinking, and in what ways does he embrace it?

2. Ramadan seeks to solve the problem of retreating into isolation in the face of globalization. Is he convincing, or is his position a more sophisticated retreat into tradition?

---

[10] *in sha Allah*: "God willing."

DOCUMENT 31-4

FRANCIS FUKUYAMA

The End of History and the Last Man

1992

Francis Fukuyama, a student of the nineteenth-century German philoso-pher G. F. W. Hegel, argued in 1992 that the collapse of the Soviet system meant that the narrative of "history" that the West had constructed for itself was at an end, that the goals of liberal democratic capitalism had been ful-filled. Fukuyama's analysis was thoughtful and careful, but his work encour-aged simple — even simplistic — stories of the inevitable triumph of the West. The End of History *came to symbolize the optimism many felt at the end of the Cold War, though Fukuyama himself has renounced his more optimistic claims.*

At the end of history, there are no serious ideological competitors left to liberal democracy. In the past, people rejected liberal democracy because they believed it was inferior to monarchy, aristocracy, theocracy, fascism, communist totalitarianism, or whatever ideology they happened to believe in. But now, outside the Islamic world, there appears to be a general con-sensus that accepts liberal democracy's claims to be the most rational form of government, that is, the state that realizes most fully either rational desire or rational recognition. If this is so, why are all countries outside the Islamic world not democratic? Why does the transition to democracy remain so difficult for many nations whose people and leaderships have accepted democratic principles in the abstract? Why do we have the suspi-cion that certain regimes around the world currently proclaiming them-selves democratic are unlikely to remain that way, while others are scarcely conceivable as anything other than stable democracies? And why is the current trend toward liberalism likely to recede, even if it promises to be victorious in the long run?

The founding of a liberal democracy is meant to be a supremely ratio-nal political act, in which the community as a whole deliberates on the nature of the constitution and set of basic laws that will govern its public

From Francis Fukuyama, *The End of History and the Last Man* (New York: Free Press, 1992, 2006), pp. 211–212, 215–217.

life. But one is frequently struck by the weakness of both reason and politics to achieve their ends, and for human beings to "lose control" of their lives, not just on a personal but on a political level. For example, many countries in Latin America were established as liberal democracies shortly after winning independence from Spain or Portugal in the nineteenth century, with constitutions modeled on those of the United States or Republican France. And yet, not one of them has succeeded in maintaining an unbroken democratic tradition up to the present. Opposition to liberal democracy in Latin America on a theoretical level has never been strong, except for brief challenges from fascism and communism, and yet liberal democrats have faced an uphill battle winning and keeping power. There are a number of nations like Russia which have known a variety of authoritarian forms of government, but until recently never true democracy. Other nations like Germany have had terrible difficulties achieving stable democracy, despite their firm rooting in the Western European tradition, while France, the birthplace of liberty and equality, has seen five different democratic republics come and go since 1789. These cases stand in sharp contrast to the experience of most democracies of Anglo-Saxon origin, which have had a relatively easy time maintaining the stability of their institutions. . . .

Culture — in the form of resistance to the transformation of certain traditional values to those of democracy — thus can constitute an obstacle to democratization. What, then, are some of the cultural factors that inhibit the formation of stable liberal democracies? These fall into several categories.

The first has to do with the degree and character of a country's national, ethnic, and racial consciousness. There is nothing inherently incompatible between nationalism and liberalism; nationalism and liberalism were in fact closely allied in the national unity struggles of Germany and Italy in the nineteenth century. Nationalism and liberalism were also associated in Poland's drive for rebirth in the 1980s, and are today closely connected in the independence struggles of the Baltic states from the USSR. The desire for national independence and sovereignty can be seen as one possible manifestation of the desire for self-determination and freedom, provided that nationality, race, or ethnicity do not become the exclusive basis for citizenship and legal rights. An independent Lithuania can be a fully liberal state, provided it guarantees the rights of all its citizens, including any Russian minority that chooses to remain.

On the other hand, democracy is not likely to emerge in a country where the nationalism or ethnicity of its constituent groups is so highly developed that they do not share a sense of nation or accept one another's rights. A strong sense of national unity is therefore necessary prior to the emergence of stable democracy, just as it preceded the emergence of democracy in countries such as Britain, the United States, France, Italy, and Germany. The absence of such a sense of unity in the Soviet Union was one of the reasons why stable democracy could not emerge prior to that country's breakup into smaller national units. . . .

The second cultural obstacle to democracy has to do with religion. Like nationalism, there is no inherent conflict between religion and liberal democracy, except at the point where the religion ceases to be tolerant or egalitarian. We have already noted how Hegel believed that Christianity paved the way for the French Revolution by establishing the principle of the equality of all men based on their capacity for moral choice. A great majority of today's democracies have Christian religious heritages, and Samuel Huntington has pointed out that most of the new democracies since 1970 have been Catholic countries. In some ways, then religion would appear to be not an obstacle but a spur to democratization.

But religion *per se* did not create free societies; Christianity in a certain sense had to abolish itself through a secularization of its goals before liberalism could emerge. The generally accepted agent for this secularization in the West was Protestantism. By making religion a private matter between the Christian and his God, Protestantism eliminated the need for a separate class of priests, and religious intervention into politics more generally. Other religions around the world have lent themselves to a similar process of secularization: Buddhism and Shinto, for example, have confined themselves to a domain of private worship centered around the family. The legacy of Hinduism and Confucianism is mixed: while they are both relatively permissive doctrines that have proven to be compatible with a wide range of secular activities, the substance of their teachings is hierarchical and inegalitarian. Orthodox Judaism and fundamentalist Islam, by contrast, are totalistic religions which seek to regulate every aspect of human life, both public and private, including the realm of politics. These religions may be compatible with democracy — Islam, in particular, establishes no less than Christianity the principle of universal human equality — but they are very hard to reconcile with liberalism and the recognition of universal rights, particularly freedom of conscience or religion. It is perhaps not surprising that the only liberal democracy in the contemporary Muslim world is Turkey, which was the only country to have stuck with an explicit rejection of its Islamic heritage in favor of a secular society early in the twentieth century.

READING AND DISCUSSION QUESTIONS

1. What in Fukuyama's example and tone suggests that this was written as the Cold War was ending? How might that influence his argument?

2. How does Fukuyama seem to envision the relationship between the individual and the state, and how might this shape his view of the Islamic world?

DOCUMENT 31-5

Protesting Globalization

2001

The creation of the global economy sped up in the 1990s with the develop-ment of the Internet and the accompanying economic boom. As triumphal narratives of a global West emerged, a counternarrative of exploitation of the developing world for the comfort of the developed as well. Since 2001, every meeting of the G8 (the leaders of the eight largest economies in the world: France, Germany, Italy, Japan, the United Kingdom, the United States, Can-ada, and Russia) has met with organized, sometimes violent, protests. The marchers decry the consumerism and materialism of the West, and the use of poorly paid labor in Africa and Asia to sustain Western economies, as sug-gested by this Greenpeace protestor at the 2001 G8 summit in Genoa, Italy.

READING AND DISCUSSION QUESTIONS

1. What criticism is the protestor making of American policy? How might the people who benefit from those policies respond?

2. Is there any irony in the ability of the protestors to use the products of the globalized society to protest it? Does that compromise their mes-sage or strengthen it?

REUTERS/Stefano Rellandini, July 17, 2001. ©Reuters/CORBIS.

COMPARATIVE QUESTIONS

1. What are the important differences between the Serbian point of view Annan references in the UN report and Amartya Sen's vision of the world?

2. How might Amartya Sen and Tariq Ramadan disagree about the basis of personal identity in the globalized society? On what points might they agree?

3. What similarities are there between Francis Fukuyama's and Tariq Ramadan's visions of the world? About what do they appear to differ?

4. Does Tariq Ramadan support the process of globalization? What reaction do you think he would have to the protestors against the G8?

5. Compare Ramadan's writing to Leo Pinsker's (Document 24-5). What similarities do you see, and what differences, between the positions of Jewish and Muslim citizens in the West?

6. Based on the documents in this chapter, what are the bases for individual and group identity in the globalizing world?

7. How might Fukuyama's analysis contrast with Rousseau's (Document 17-5)?